The Construction and Fitting of the Sailing Man of War
1650–1850

The Construction and Fitting of the

SAILING MAN OF WAR

1650~1850

Peter Goodwin

CONWAY

MARITIME PRESS

Facing title:
Victory. *The 'closed' square stern, typical of the style of stern construction introduced at the end of the eighteenth century.*

© PETER GOODWIN 1987

First published in Great Britain 1987 by
Conway Maritime Press Ltd
24 Bride Lane, Fleet Street
London, EC4Y 8DR

ISBN 0 85177 326 5

Designed by John Mitchell
Typesetting and page make-up by C R Barber & Partners, Fort William
Printed and bound in Great Britain by
Butler and Tanner, Frome

Contents

Acknowledgements

I would like to thank the following: Mr David Lyon and the other staff of the National Maritime Museum, Greenwich; Mr Alec Barlow and Terry Wallbridge, and the shipwrights of Portsmouth Dockyard attached to HMS *Victory*; the Captain and naval staff of HMS *Victory*; Lt Cdr W Roderick Stewart, RNR of the Frigate *Unicorn* Preservation Society; Lt Cdr Peter Whitlock, RN (retd) MBE, Honorary Treasurer of the Society for Nautical Research; Captain Superintendant M A Hemmings and the staff of the frigate *Foudroyant*; Mr Robert Gardiner of Conway Maritime Press Ltd for his guidance and advice, without which this book would not have been possible; Mr Colin White of the Royal Naval Museum at Portsmouth Dockyard. I would like to thank Mr John Franklin for giving me permission to use photographs of his model of the 74-gun *Egmont* of 1768. The photographs of HMS *Victory* are reproduced courtesy of Portsmouth Dockyard and those of *Unicorn* courtesy of George Le Good. Those of *Foudroyant* belong to the author's collection.

Places of Research

The National Maritime Museum, Greenwich, including the Reading Room and Draught Room.
The Science Museum, South Kensington.
Southsea Castle Museum.
HMS *Victory* at Portsmouth Dockyard.
Royal Naval Museum, Portsmouth Dockyard.
Public Records Office at Kew, Surrey.
The frigate *Foudroyant* at Portsmouth Harbour.
The frigate *Unicorn* at Victoria Dock, Dundee.
The Transport Museum at Glasgow.
Edinburgh Castle.
The Maritime Museum at Great Yarmouth.
The City of Portsmouth Public Library.

Introduction

Most ship enthusiasts and modelmakers of today require an abundance of specific information that is explained in the minutest detail. It is not always enough to know what a particular feature looked like without knowing how it was manufactured, or how and why it was operated and employed. As a keen modeller myself I have learnt that there can be many pitfalls in the search for information on many aspects of ship construction. For example, most of the contemporary ship draughts that exist for the period covered by this book do not in themselves meet the needs of the modeller and student of naval architecture. They generally do not include the numerous deck fittings, have nothing on rigging, nor do they clarify details of the constructional techniques practised at the time.

To fill this void I began to quest for such knowledge, which was to be gleaned from innumerable sources. During this research I concluded that there is a wealth of information available but that it is very fragmentary, which to many people is far from practical. Therefore a single comprehensive source book seemed to be necessary, in which information on all the features of interest to the student of historic naval architecture would be summarised. This book is an attempt to do just that.

Much of the material included in this book has been accumulated from an in-depth examination of original contemporary models on public display in many museums, including the collection at the National Maritime Museum. From these sources it appears that there were many permutations of individual fittings and features, which suggests that most of the minor constructional details were left to the builder's discretion. However, this did not mean that they ignored the hard and fast rules specified by the Navy Board and the Admiralty, for the Navy Board laid down the basic measurements of vessels (and the exact sizing of their scantlings) in a series of orders generally known as the Establishments. These orders, however, did leave some room for inventiveness, particularly in

terms of design, but also produced guidelines compatible with the requirements of the Navy's ships. Lists of the dimensions of every rate of vessel are given in each Establishment (1706, 1719, 1733, 1741 and 1745) and these and later specifications are available in the National Maritime Museum. These figures are very useful to the ship modeller and enthusiast, but to overcome the problems of lengthy and repetitive lists of dimensions, the text includes calculations and tables of factors which I have formulated for the reader's convenience. Each specification is worked on a proportional basis using a common dimension as a foundation. The product of these equations are accurate to within half an inch generally speaking, which may not appear to be totally exact but when working to 1/48 scale the difference is virtually negligible. However, for the benefit of the historian the most detailed Establishment specifications (1719 and 1745) are given in Appendix 4a and 4c.

Of the many books on the subject written in the eighteenth and early nineteenth centuries a number tend to repeat some or all of earlier works, and it must be understood that quite a few were not written by practising shipwrights. Sutherland's *Shipbuilding Unveiled*, published in 1717, is perhaps the most original, and covers everything from construction to accounts for painting details, and costs. However, most of the various contemporary works have something to offer, and should not be dismissed entirely.

The Public Records Office retains many of the original contract specifications directed to builders from the Admiralty. These give not only the dimensions of the timbers, planking, knees and so forth, but some account of the methods of caulking, adornment and fitting out. In Appendix 1 I have included summaries of three such contracts drafted in the latter part of the seventeenth century.

Regardless of the multiplicity of data that is contained within books, lists, manuscripts and other archival sources, there is no better evidence than that of a real ship. To comprehend the subject fully I have found that there is no substitute for crawling about the confines of the surviving examples such as the *Victory, Foudroyant,* and *Unicorn.* This was not just a case of simple observation, sketching and measuring, but also of discussion. To know any subject to its utmost one has to start at the 'coal face', so to speak. Here I must add special thanks to Mr Terry Wallbridge and his colleagues with whom I have spent many hours conversing about the various aspects of the construction of the *Victory.* It was during these visits that the real implications of the practical construction of a 'wooden wall' dawned on me. It was all very well to know where a specific piece of timber was fitted but to comprehend the effort involved is quite another story. One must always remember that the men who originally built these vessels did not have the many labour-saving devices of today. A simple task such as fashioning a single tree into a sternpost of about 30ft in length and over 2ft width at its thickest point was achieved purely by muscle power. Then one has to consider how such baulks of timber were manhandled into position, bored with hand augers and retained in place with little more than oak trennals. The overall labour involved cannot really be appreciated by people of today's technical age, nor should the abilities, skills, and ingenuity of our forefathers be underestimated. It was also an advantage that during my youth I was fortunate to 'live' aboard the *Foudroyant.* This experience produced a personal affinity with the wooden man-of-war that has always remained, thanks to the opportunity to explore the confines of this vessel.

It may appear to some readers that throughout the period covered by this book the progress of constructional technology was relatively slow, specially when compared to today's standards. In many respects this is absolutely true, for the basic principles of ship construction remained virtually unchanged until the beginning of the nineteenth century. Here I may add that this fact also applied to the various other technical industries. The Industrial Revolution brought not only improved manufacturing techniques but also spurred new ideas about the materials employed and the manner of their application. The shipwright's trade had for centuries retained an isolated image governed by family concerns but was now to be infiltrated by a new breed of men of the technological era. Tradition stepped down to make way for reasoned thought verified by science.

Another major factor was the ever increasing shortage of suitable timber. Over the previous centuries the colossal demands of timber for both civil and naval construction had rapidly depleted the forests of the country. Even the vast woodlands of Sussex had been progressively consumed since Roman times, not only for building but for the production of charcoal for the iron industry. This problem necessitated the import of materials from the Baltic as early as the 1680s, pitch pine and Dantzig oak being the timbers generally involved.

One can see from the manner in which a ship's timber (or frame) was constructed that alterations had to be made. The frames of vessels built in the 1650s were designed with only a few individual pieces, specially selected for their natural curvature. By 1750 the manner in which a frame was fashioned entailed the employment of a number of shorter pieces, scarphed and bolted together to produce a complete timber. This was initially adopted to reduce both wastage and cost but it was soon realised that this manner of construction was also far stronger than the original method.

One way in which the problems associated with the use of timber were avoided was by building vessels from teak. This 'oily' wood was found to have the inherent property of withstanding long periods of immersion in salt water without undue decay. This can be verified by the fact that the frigate *Foudroyant* has been afloat almost continuously since her initial launching in 1817. This vessel, like many others, was built in Bombay, but in other cases teak was imported for use in British dockyards.

One final factor that affected construction was the employment of wrought iron. To conserve wood the general design of some major fittings was altered to accommodate iron. One such case is the hanging knee which supported the deck beams. At the end of the eighteenth century these knees were modified into a form of chock fitted directly below the beam which it supported and these chocks were further braced with flat, iron plate knees. The utility of this material was soon recognized and extended to other parts of the structure, which can clearly be seen in the ships designed by Seppings and Symonds.

Nevertheless, materials were not the only governing factor in the design. Much was dependent on the draughtsmen's skills, which were not always highly developed. During the seventeenth century most of the construction was determined by a shipwright's personal experience and acquired skills and by various rules of thumb. Many of the errors in design were due to incomplete and therefore inadequate draughts, so any miscalculations had to be rectified during or after construction. If a vessel was found to be too narrow in her beam she was therefore 'girdled', by fitting additional strakes of heavy planking along the waterline, which improved the stability. It was also at the time difficult for designers to formulate a predetermined waterline on which a vessel would 'swim', and problems arose with transferring the underwater shape of the hull from the plans to the building ship. Any improvements made to the lines had to be carried out when all the timbers (or frames) were erected, which would entail either 'trimming' the timbers or adding pieces of wood where necessary. All of this work relied entirely on the experienced eye of the shipwright, and did not always produce the most favourable of hull forms. It was only when Anthony Deane completed his *Doctrine of Naval Architecture* in 1670 that some predetermined calculations could be made. Other designers such as Edward Dummer followed this practice, thereby beginning the process of divorcing the builder from the designer, which was eventually to lead to the setting up of a School of Naval Architects a little over a century later. One could say that Deane was the man that changed shipbuilding from a medieval craft to a science in its own right.

In recent years the interest in our maritime heritage has increased enormously, and in Britain we are fortunate to have preserved examples of ships representing the whole history of the sailing man-of-war. The *Mary Rose*, now showing her ancient oak timbers to the modern world after lying in her murky grave for over four centuries, will in time give us a greater insight into the techniques and practices employed by the shipwrights of the Tudor period. The *Victory*, a First Rate of 104 guns at Portsmouth, presents us with an example of the classic capital ship and mainstay of the Georgian Navy. Likewise we have the frigates *Foudroyant* at Portsmouth and *Unicorn* at Dundee, each of which reveals the constructional changes introduced in the early nineteenth century. There is also at Portsmouth the screw sloop *Gannet* which is presently undergoing restoration. This vessel opens another chapter when the steam engine and screw propeller were adopted to supplement the proven power of sail. Lastly, the Royal Navy's first ironclad warship, HMS *Warrior* (1861) is currently undergoing full restoration and is due to be moved to Portsmouth in 1987. She represents the end of the 'wooden walls' and the final era of the sailing man-of-war.

PETER G GOODWIN, 1984

The Construction and Fitting of the
SAILING MAN OF WAR

CHAPTER 1

The Construction of a Ship of War in Frame

During the seventeenth, eighteenth, and early nineteenth centuries naval ships were built at yards that were not too distant from forests that supplied the timber. The Dockyard at Portsmouth and the private concerns found on the River Hamble, Southampton Water, and the River Beaulieu received most of their timber from the New Forest. Chatham Dockyard and the builders on the Thames obtained wood from the Wealden forests of Kent and Sussex. The Forest of Dean also contributed great quantities of timber to all the building areas.

The master shipwright of the dockyard would send a 'purveyor' to these forests with a body of men and it was his job to select and determine which trees would provide the most suitable timber. This can be divided into two groups, compass oak and straight oak. Compass oak was taken from the parts of a tree where the grain followed the curvature of a bough or where a branch grew out from the bole of the tree. This timber was used for the ship's frames and knees where the requirement of grain-following timber would give the required strength needed in the construction.

Apart from oak – elm, fir, beech and pitch pine were used, and throughout the book I will state where each was employed. Once the timber was felled and its branches removed, it was transported to the yards by various means. In some cases it was easy to transfer the timber by very stout inshore craft known as 'timber hoys' that could navigate the rivers and sheltered coastal waters. Generally the haulage was done by road as most of the forests were not situated near useful waterways. This road haulage was achieved by large waggons often known as 'buses' and they would require as many as ten pairs of oxen or horses to haul the loaded waggons. The poor quality of the roads during this era did nothing to facilitate the delivery of timber promptly and it was not unusual for a ship which was under construction to be left uncompleted during the winter months due to the weather turning the roads to a quagmire. The amount of timber carried on one waggon would be up to 50ft³

and was referred to as a load. To give some idea of how much timber was used in shipbuilding, a 74-gun ship would require approximately 3000 loads (which was roughly 150,000ft³ for the hull). The Royal Dockyards used about 50,000 loads between the years 1760 and 1786 (25,000,000ft³), but one must remember that timber was also used for warship construction in civilian yards and is not included in the figure given.

The Design Criteria

Many aspects had to be considered by the master shipwright before any draughts were started, including the ship's purpose and required speed, the underwater shape and the stability. The latter was the most important factor that governed a ship of war, for unlike the merchant vessels of the time which carried their principal weights (cargo) low in the hold, a fighting ship carried a lot of weight above the waterline in the form of her armament. To overcome this problem the ship would be designed with a considerable beam to obtain a steady gun-platform. The completed design was usually a compromise between the requirements of speed and stability.

First the ship's length had to be determined, which according to Abraham Rees was dependent on the number of guns to be mounted on the lowest gundeck and the amount of room required to work those guns. Before deciding on the number of guns to be mounted the actual size or poundage of the guns had to be considered. This indirectly determined the size of the gunports to be employed, which varied from 3ft 5in for a 32- or 42-pounder gun on a First Rate ship to a port 2ft in width for a 3- or 6-pounder on an armed cutter. (A comparative table of gun size and gunport width is

Table 1: Values of A (Gunport Width) and C (Working Room)

Guns (pounder)	A ft	A in	C ft	C in	Guns (pounder)	A ft	A in	C ft	C in
42	3	6	7	7	9	2	4	6	8
32	3	5	7	6				6	11
24	3	4	6	9	6	2	0	6	9
18	2	11	6	7				6	11
			6	10	3	2	0	6	9
12	2	6	6	9				6	10

Table 2: Values of Multiplication Factors D and E

Ship (no of guns)	D	E
110–100	One and three-fifths	One
90	One and three-fifths	One and one-tenth
84– 80	One and a half	One
74– 70	One and two-fifths	One
64– 60	One and three-fifths	One
50	One	Three-fifths
46– 44	Nine-tenths	Three-fifths
40– 38	Four-fifths	Three-quarters
36	One	Half
32– 30	One and one-tenth	Half
28	One and one-fifth	Nine-tenths
24– 20	One and four-fifths	One and a quarter
Sloop	One and three-fifths	One and two-fifths
Armed cutter	One	Four-fifths

given in Table 1 above; this also includes the estimated working room required to man and fire each gun with considerable ease.) Having obtained a figure for the width of the ports and the space between them it was a simple mathematical task to multiply the width of the gunports by the number required along the ship's length plus the spaces between.

How the early builders decided on the length between the fore edge of the foremost gunport and the length aft of the aftermost port I do not know, but having made my own calculations I have come up with the following method. First add the width of one single gunport to that of the working room for one gun (figures given in Table 1). The sum is then multiplied by factor D given in Table 2. The distance at the fore end of the ship was to allow sufficient room for the 'manger' and a satisfactory measurement for the curvature of the ship's side turning towards the centreline at the stempost. By a similar method we can determine the length aft of the aftermost gunport to the after perpendicular, the factors for this being given in the second column of Table 2. This distance aft was to accommodate the recoil length of the stern-chase guns and the steering arrangements. The sum of all four measurements obtained – the width of the gunport, the working room for one gun, the length forward, the length aft – will give the length of the gundeck between the fore and after perpendiculars. This measurement is also generally known as that between the fore edge of the rabbet of the stem and the after edge of the rabbet of the sternpost.

The formula below is a summary of the process outlined above.

$$L = A.B + C(B-1) + D(A+C) + E(A+C)$$

where
- $L =$ the length of the lowest gundeck between the rabbet of the stempost and the rabbet of the sternpost.
- $A =$ the fore and aft width of the gunport.
- $B =$ the number of guns to be mounted on the lowest gundeck.
- $C =$ the working room to operate a single gun.
- $D =$ the multiplication factor to determine the length between the fore edge of the foremost gunport and the fore perpendicular.
- $E =$ the multiplication factor to determine the length between the after edge of the aftermost gunport and the after perpendicular.

The values of A and C are given in Table 1; values of D and E in Table 2.

The above factors will have a maximum error of approximately 6in which is only apparent in the smaller classes of vessel. The factors in Table 2 only apply to vessels built after 1725 whereas the measurements given in Table 1 can be applied to all vessels built during the era covered by this book.

To calculate the overall length of the lowest gundeck of the vessels built during the latter half of the seventeenth century and early eighteenth century it is wise to study the works of Sir Anthony Deane (his manuscript *Doctrine of Naval Architecture*, written in 1670, was published in book form in 1981). It has been claimed that he was the first to be able to determine the actual waterline and the displacement of a vessel prior to her launch.

During this period it was the length of the ship's keel that was the primary dimension and the complete length of the vessel afore and abaft of the extremities of the keel was worked out from the moulded beam. The moulded beam was obtained by multiplying the length of the keel by three-tenths, so a ship with a keel length of 120ft had a moulded beam of 36ft. The ruling for the length between the fore end of the keel and the fore perpendicular was three-quarters of the moulded beam, so if the moulded beam was 36ft this length would be 27ft. This was generally referred to as the length of the rake for the stempost.

The distance between the after end of the keel and the after perpendicular was taken as eleven-twelfths of one-sixth of the moulded beam. Thus a vessel with a moulded beam of 36ft would have a length from the after end of the keel to the after perpendicular of 5ft 5in. Therefore the total equation required to determine the length of the ship along its lower gundeck is as follows:

$$L = K + (K \times 3)/10 \times \tfrac{3}{4} + (K \times 3)/10 \times \tfrac{11}{36}$$

where L = total length; K = keel length

Returning now to vessels built after about 1720–25, the moulded beam was taken as:

$$B^M = (G \times 3)/11$$

where B^M = moulded beam; G = length of lower gundeck

The position at which this greatest width was placed along the ship's length to give the required velocity through the water was set as follows from the fore perpendicular:

$$W = (G \times 5)/12$$

where W = position of main breadth; G = length of lower gundeck

All of the above apply to all vessels except armed cutters where the moulded beam is taken as three-eighths of the length of the gundeck.

The Keel Assembly

THE KEEL

The keel, which formed the 'backbone' of the ship, was first laid on to the tops of the blocks that were set at regular intervals along the length of the slipway. Elm was generally used for keel construction due to its property of durability when immersed in salt water for extensive periods. The only drawback was that English elm was not obtainable in the great lengths required for a keel, but this problem was overcome by building the keel in a number of pieces, each being scarphed and bolted together. The number of sections varied according to the size of the vessel: those of 38 guns and above would have six sections; those of between 24 and 36 had five; and those of the smaller classes four.

When considering the length of the keel some confusion could arise between the actual length and the 'length of the keel for tonnage'. The latter was always the shorter measurement and was more or less theoretical as will be explained separately.

The actual length is measured from the fore edge of the boxing to the aftermost face where the sternpost meets the keel. To determine this measurement does however cause a few problems, because for most ships built prior to 1700 a keel length is quoted, whereas those built later use the 'length of keel for tonnage' and the length of the gundeck (or lower deck on single-decked ship) between the fore edge of the rabbet of the stempost and the after edge of the rabbet of the sternpost.

In the works of Sir Anthony Deane the length of the keel only is given and from this he calculated all of the vessel's scantlings. It would at this point be well to digress from the subject, which may initially confuse matters but does throw light on the methods of defining the ship's overall length between the stem and sternposts.

It is important here to be able to calculate the moulded beam of the ship; the reason for doing so will become apparent later. Deane said that the moulded beam should be three-tenths of the keel's length and once this figure was obtained it was employed to make other important calculations. From this figure the overall length of the vessel could be derived, by finding the length of the rake of the sternpost and the arc rake of the stempost.

The arc of the stem was laid off as three-quarters of the moulded beam running from the fore edge of the keel. The rake of the sternpost was taken as approximately five thirty-seconds of the moulded beam abaft of the keel. The actual figures given by Deane for this were as follows:

$$R = (B^M/6) \times \tfrac{11}{12}$$

where R = length of rake of sternpost; B^M = moulded beam

The depth of the keel throughout the years 1670–1710 was expressed as half an inch for every foot of the moulded beam. This scantling also included the depth of the false keel which varied from one-fifth to one-sixth of that calculated for the depth of the keel. Therefore it can be said that the actual depth of the keel of a large man-of-war was one-sixth less and in some cases the width was one-twelfth greater.

Although the rules outlined in the above paragraphs are taken from Deane's *Doctrine* of 1670, there is no reason to believe that practice in the two decades preceding this period was very different.

Having discussed the rake of the stem and sternposts we may now return to the determination of the actual length of the keel of ships built after about 1700–1720. Here we have to work in the reverse from the given length of the gundeck (or lower deck of single-decked ships) to produce the actual length of the keel. (The length of the keel was also referred to as the tread of the keel.) There are two methods of calculating this. One can multiply the quoted length of keel for tonnage by ten-ninths but this does not give an exact length, or follow a method that I have devised which is more accurate and works as follows:

Actual length of the keel $= A - B + C + D$

where $A =$ the length of the gundeck (or lower deck of single-decked ships) from the fore edge of the rabbet at the stem to the after edge of the rabbet of the sternpost.

         $B =$ this is the radius or arc of the stempost which is calculated as: $M^B/2$.

         $C =$ this is the length abaft the after end of the keel which forms the aftermost boundary for the rake aft of the sternpost and is calculated as: $(M^B/8) \times \tfrac{1}{2}$

$D =$ this is for the length of the 'boxing' (the type of scarph employed for attaching the stempost to the keel). To calculate this the depth of the keel is required, which is then multiplied by a given constant. The constant for First, Second and Third Rate ships is four and for the remaining smaller classes it is three and one-fifth.

$M^B =$ moulded beam.

Example: to calculate the actual length of the keel of a 28-gun frigate of about 1775 with a length on the lower deck of 120ft 6in, a moulded beam of 33ft and a given keel depth of 13·5in.

$$\text{Actual keel length} = 120·5\text{ft} - (^{33}/_{2}) + (^{33}/_{8}) \times (^1/_2) + 1·125\text{ft} \times (^{16}/_5)$$
$$= 109\text{ft } 8\text{ in}$$

If we had employed the cruder method the result would have been 110ft 6in, based on ten-ninths of a keel for tonnage length of 99ft 5in.

During this period the depth of the keel was exactly the same as its width and unlike vessels of Deane's time the depth did not include the false keel, which was calculated separately. However, the proportional figures did not remain constant for all classes of ship as they apparently did during the second half of the seventeenth century. Proportions for depth of keel were as follows: Ship, number of guns (fraction of an inch per foot of moulded beam) – 110, 100, 50, 44, 28 and 24 ($^{13}/_{32}$in); 90, 38, 36 and 32 ($^{25}/_{64}$in); 84, 80, 74, 70, 64 and 60 ($^3/_8$in); 20 and sloops ($^{17}/_{32}$in); armed cutters ($^7/_8$in).

Throughout the period covered by this book, the fore and after ends of the keel diminished to two-thirds of its width amidships.

The Length of the Keel Scarphs

To ensure that the joints of each section of the keel overlapped sufficiently, the length of the scarph was made to between one-fifth and one-sixth of the length of the individual piece. To be more accurate the length can be calculated by using the depth of the keel and a given constant for the size of the vessel. For ships built between 1650 and 1690 the following formula applied to all vessels:

$$S = K^d \times (^{16}/_5) \times (^1/_{12})$$

where S = scarph length; K^d = keel depth

Example: a Third Rate ship of 1667 with a depth of the keel of 15in.

$$\text{Length of the keel scarph} = 15 \times (^{16}/_5) \times (^1/_{12})$$
$$= 15 \text{ in} \times 3·2 \times 0·08333$$
$$= 3·99\text{ft } (4\text{ft})$$

From about 1730 there seems to be more of a variation in scarph lengths throughout the different Rates. The formula given below applies to all vessels except those sloops and armed cutters where

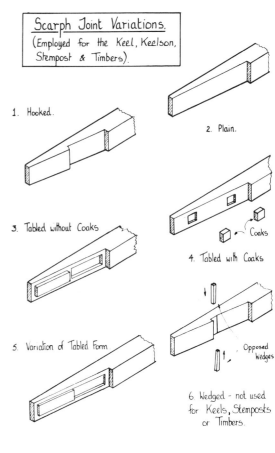

Scarph Joint Variations.
(Employed for the Keel, Keelson, Stempost & Timbers).

1. Hooked.
2. Plain.
3. Tabled without Coaks
4. Tabled with Coaks — Coaks
5. Variation of Tabled Form
6. Wedged – not used for Keels, Stemposts or Timbers. — Opposed Wedges.

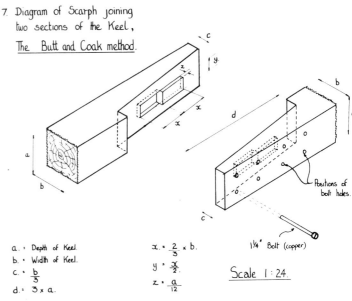

7. Diagram of Scarph joining two sections of the Keel,
The Butt and Coak method.

a. = Depth of Keel.
b. = Width of Keel.
c. = $\frac{b}{3}$
d. = 3 x a.

x. = $\frac{2}{3}$ x b.
y. = $\frac{x}{2}$.
z. = $\frac{a}{12}$

1¼" Bolt (copper)

Positions of bolt holes.

Scale 1 : 24.

Fig 1/1

6

due to the small size of the keel there is no need to divide by twelve.

$$S = (K^D \times \beta)/12$$

where S = scarph length; K^d = keel depth

Ship, number of guns (β) – 110, 100 (3·5); 98, 90 (3·4); 84–70 (3·6); 64–50 (3·9); 44–36 (3·8); 32–20 (4·0); sloops and armed cutters (4·0).

Having determined the length of the scarph the actual method of its construction must be discussed. Various styles were employed (see Fig 1/1). The most common was the butt and coak fashion shown in Fig 1/1(7) and like all the methods used the scarph was set in the vertical. (The scarph length of three times the moulded depth is typical, but varied as outlined above.)

The butt end of the joint was made to one-third of the siding of the keel and the coaks to a length of two-thirds of the siding and to a half of their own length for their width. The depth of the coaks was never any more than one-twelfth of the moulded depth of the keel. Before the joint was fastened together it would be lined with tarred flannel as a crude form of rot prevention. The number of bolts for securing the scarph increased from six to eight during the period covered in this book. A contract for the building of a Third Rate ship from about 1666 (most likely that of the *Warspite* or the *Defiance*) clearly states that six bolts should be fitted. Having said this I believe that at this period the number would depend on the length of the scarph and therefore I would guess that the larger ships most probably had eight bolts. After 1725 I think one can be safe in assuming that eight were used on all vessels of 30 guns or more and six on those below this figure. The bolts were made from copper* and varied in diameter according to the size of the ship. Each pair would be driven through horizontally from opposite sides of the keel.

Bolt diameter = keel depth/γ

Ship, number of guns (γ) – 100, 90 (16); 80 (15); 74, 64, 44 (14); 38 (13); 36 (15); 32 (14); 28, 24 (15); sloop (16); cutter (17).

The details and dimensions of the joints for both the stempost and the sternpost will be discussed later.

Once the keel was complete in its make-up a rabbet (angled rebate) was cut along both vertical faces throughout its length to receive the lower edge of the garboard strake, the lowest strake of the external planking. The practice in naval ships was to have this set a little (approximately 1–1½in at the most) distance from the upper edge of the keel. Some builders had it cut along the top of the side and built up the surface above with a 'hog' (see Fig 1/2). This

*The general belief is that copper bolts were used below the waterline after about 1783, a few years after the introduction of copper sheathing. However, I believe that copper was used below the waterline well before this date, as bolts of this material were withdrawn from *Victory*'s deadwood in the last decade.

practice was more common prior to about 1780 but it was not until Seppings became Surveyor of the Navy in 1813 that the rabbet was officially lowered to between 1½in and 3in below the upper edge. The reader should note that all the vertical measurements of the vessel were taken from the lower edge of the rabbet. Merchant vessels at this time, and even earlier, had the rabbet cut at a distance of half the depth of the keel. Now that the main keel was complete, the oak caps that sat on the blocks were removed and the false keel was fitted.

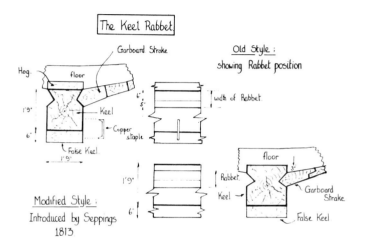

Fig 1/2

The False Keel

The false keel served two purposes: firstly, it acted as a protective cap for the main keel in the event of grounding; secondly, it was found that increasing the overall depth of the keel reduced the amount of 'leeway' (sideways movement as the ship surged forward) of the vessel. The false keel was fitted to all rates of ship except armed cutters. Generally it comprised the same number of lengths that made up the main keel, the joints giving a sufficient shift to those of the main keel. ('Shift' is the term used to describe the way the joints in adjacent strokes of planking are staggered so they do not fall alongside one another, rather like the way bricks are laid in a wall.) Although each section may have been scarphed together with a plain flat scarph set in the horizontal plane, I doubt whether this was practised, for the concept required that it could be removed easily for refitting or could be easily torn off in the event of grounding.

With this possibility of grounding in mind it was not secured to the main keel with bolts or nails but with a form of staple made from copper (see Fig 1/2). These staples were fitted either side of the keel, so if the ship hit, say, a sandbank the false keel was torn off without causing too much damage to the main keel.

Victory. A view of the port side of the sternpost, showing the inner post, the deadwood, the keel and false keel. The aftermost cant frames and the sternson knee with one remaining transom piece are also visible. Note the false keel staples, fish or dovetail plates and the rudder braces.

The siding of the false keel was the same as the main keel throughout its entire length and tapered in the same manner both fore and aft, but its depth was much less, and varied. Although I give some guiding figures in the text I believe that the depth was more of a personal choice governed by the builder's individual practice. The depth given for a Third Rate ship of about 1666 is 4in while the main keel has a depth of 15in, thus making the false keel approximately one-quarter of the main keel's depth. Ships designed by Deane only a few years later have their false keels made to about one-sixth. During the eighteenth century the proportional figures became more varied and can be estimated in the following way:

$$K^f = K^M \times \delta$$

where K^f = false keel depth; K^M = main keel moulded depth

Ship, number of guns (δ) – 110–100 (one-fifth); 90 (five-sixteenths); 84–80 (one-third); 74–70 (one-third); 64–50 (one-third); 44–40 (two-fifths); 38–36 (one-third); 32–sloop (seven-sixteenths).

The timber used varied from beech or elm to teak, the former because of its low cost, the latter two due to their ability to withstand long periods of immersion in salt water. One point of interest here is that the *Victory* was given two false keels, one 6in thick made from beech and a second below that 4in thick made from teak. Whether she was built with this I do not know but it is likely that it was fitted later, possibly to reduce leeway. From about 1800 it was quite a common practice to have two false keels fitted.

THE STERNPOST

The sternpost was the next item to be constructed and would be fitted to the after end of the keel. The purpose of this great vertical timber was to support the after body of the ship, the stern timbers and the rudder. Because of the immense size of this timber it would be fashioned from a very carefully selected oak. The height can be taken as the height of the wing transom's upper side from the top side of the keel, plus one-third the moulded depth of the keel for the tenon at the heel of the post. In some cases the sternpost extends above the top of wing transom, usually by about the depth of the keel, so it would be necessary to add this length to that given above. The height of the wing transom can be approximately determined as one-sixth of the overall length of the keel in the larger men-of-war and two-thirteenths of the keel for the smaller. The heel of the sternpost was made to an athwartships dimension equal to that at the keel and to a scantling of one-tenth of the overall height of the sternpost in the fore and aft plane. The head of the sternpost was one-fifteenth of its length in both the fore and aft and athwartships planes.

The heel of the sternpost was tenoned into the keel, the tenon being fashioned to one-third the moulding of the keel in depth, and one-third the siding of the keel in width. In some cases the sternpost was additionally fastened with copper fish-plates (see Chapter 10). The whole post was set with a rake aft at an angle, usually of about 5 degrees from the vertical in English ships.

A rabbet was cut on the fore part of each side, the angle varying from head to heel to accommodate the curvature of planking. The after edge of the sternpost was bearded or chamfered, to an angle of 60 degrees to allow the pivoting action of the rudder, which was fitted to the after side of the sternpost.

The Inner Post

The inner post was fitted to give additional support to the sternpost and was made from oak. Its length was the distance from the upper

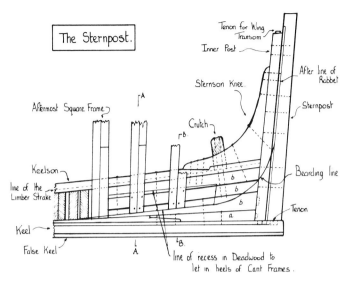

The Sternpost.

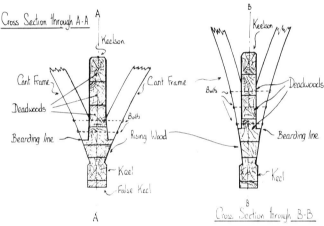

Cross Section through A·A

Cross Section through B·B

Fig 1/3

Victory. *The port side of the stem showing the lower part of the stempost with its scarph, the apron, and the hawse piece forming the heel of the knighthead. The 'bird's throat' rabbet for the hood ends of the planking, and the upper part of the gripe can also be seen.*

side of the keel to the bottom edge of the wing transom, plus one-third the moulding of the keel for the tenon at its heel and 1in at the head for the tenon into the wing transom. In the fore and aft direction it remained parallel from head to heel while its siding was made to that of the sternpost. The scantling in the fore and aft plane was of half the fore and aft length of the heel of the sternpost. Thus if the sternpost was 30ft in length, its heel being one-tenth of its length (*ie* 3ft), the inner post would be 18in.

The tenons at each end were reduced to a width and breadth of one-third, the heel being fastened in an identical manner to that of the sternpost, in some cases with fish-plates. The whole post was fayed and bolted with copper clench bolts to the fore face of the sternpost. The top end acted as a landing for the wing transom.

STEMPOST CONSTRUCTION
The Scarphing of the Stempost to the Keel

The joint that formed the union between the fore end of the keel and the heel of the stempost was generally referred to as the 'boxing'. This term originated from the word 'boxsum', an earlier shipbuilder's description of this particular item. The fashion of the scarphs used varied from a plain flat type to a more complex and intricate 'slotted' form. The plain type, and a coaked scarph similar to that employed for the joining of the keel section, were more widely used in vessels built in the second half of the seventeenth and first quarter of the eighteenth centuries. Prior to their fastening the mating surfaces would be lined with tarred flannel and then secured with six or eight copper clench bolts, of the same diameter as those used for the keel. (Fig 1/4(1 and 3)). The 'slotted' type is more complicated and the reader is referred to Fig 1/4(2).

One of the alternative methods was to have the fore end of the keel fashioned with a step on its upper edge, the after vertical face

9

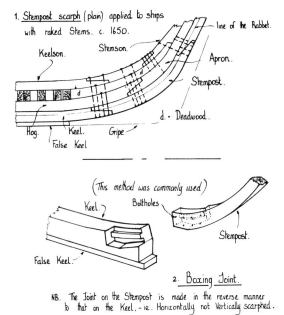

The Various Methods used for Joining the Stempost to the Keel

1. Stempost scarph (plan) applied to ships with raked Stems. c. 1650.

Keelson. Stemson. line of the Rabbet. Apron. Stempost. d. — Deadwood. Keel. Gripe. Hog. False Keel

(This method was commonly used)

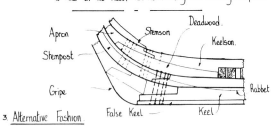

Keel. Boltholes. False Keel. Stempost.

2. Boxing Joint.

NB. The Joint on the Stempost is made in the reverse manner to that on the Keel. — ie. Horizontally not Vertically scarphed.

Deadwood. Apron. Stemson. Keelson. Stempost. Rabbet. Gripe. False Keel — Keel

3. Alternative Fashion

Fig 1/4

having a mortice cut horizontally into it to receive the tenon at the heel of the stempost. This technique would have been employed mostly on the smaller ships and cutters where its somewhat weaker construction was of less consequence. There does not seem to be any specific period for its use and therefore I assume that it was a practice throughout the period covered by this book. Having described the most common types one must understand that individual builders had their own eccentricities, possibly handed down from their forefathers. The variations most likely applied to those merchant builders who worked under contract to the Royal Dockyards.

One particular case of an unusually shaped joint was of that used on the 44-gun ship *Charon*, built by Barnard at Harwich in 1778 which burnt at her moorings in 1781 at Yorktown during the War of American Independence. A Combined Services Diving Team based at Southampton working on the wreck of the *Charon* found that they could not understand the manner in which the stem was fitted to the keel. From the description I was able to produce a

sketch which showed that a baulk of timber was fitted to the upper side of the keel, into which the tenon of the stem was received. In addition, a 'side fish' was set into the stem, apron and the timber baulk and bolted through in the horizontal, thus locking the whole together to prevent sideways distortion. There are two 'grey' areas here: firstly the timber baulk may have been part of the actual keel and was fashioned in this manner; secondly where I have assumed that side fish were applied this could have been the way in which the heel of the stem was made. I have included a drawing (Fig 1/5) of this type of scarph but it cannot be guaranteed as accurate because it is only based on secondhand description.

The following equation can be used to determine the length of the most common type of scarph used:

$$X = K^D \times Y$$

where X = length of boxing; K^D = keel depth; and the values for Y are:

Rate	1650–1719	1719–1810
First	4·125	4·333
Second	4·125	4·333
Third	4·00	4·00
Fourth	4·00	3·75
Fifth	3·75	3·50
Sixth	3·75	3·25

Fig 1/5

NB – This was drawn from a description given by a Diver working on the Wreck.

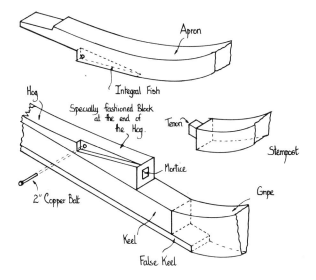

The Boxing of the 'Charon'

Apron. Integral Fish. Hog. Specially fashioned Block at the end of the Hog. Tenon. Stempost. Mortice. 2" Copper Bolt. Gripe. Keel. False Keel

Authors note :—
Alternatively the Fish may have been made separately with a recess cut into the Apron. Until more evidence is available the complete nature of this technique is a little uncertain.

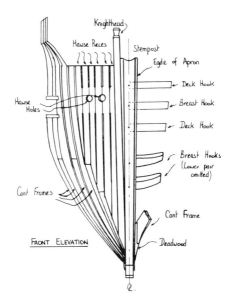

The Construction of the Stempost
and its associated timbers and
Strengthening Members
64 Gun ship - circa 1768

Fig 1/6

Victory. *Starboard side of stempost. This view shows a new section of the stem being fitted to the foreside of the apron. The hawse pieces, the rabbet, the hood ends of the planking and the upper part of the gripe are also discernible. Note the diminishing strakes at the top right corner of the photograph.*

Since ships of the Commonwealth and Restoration were constructed with the stempost set at a greater angle from the perpendicular, one would have thought that the scarph length should be longer to withstand the strain of the overhang produced, but on the contrary the scarph was shorter and was strengthened by the build up of deadwood and the apron (see Figs 1/4 and 1/6). One can only assume that the amount of deadwood employed was due to the greater rise of floors.

The Stempost

The stem (or stempost) formed the foremost edge of the ship, but unlike the sternpost its shape was more curved; therefore the construction was more complex and was thus made up of a series of suitably grained and fashioned timbers. The desired shape of the stem was derived by the arc formed between the upper edge of the keel and the height of the lowest gundeck (or lower deck of ships with their guns mounted on a single deck) at the foremost perpendicular. This arc was three-quarters of the moulded beam in radius on the ships built during the Restoration but by the year 1719 it was diminished to half of the moulded beam. From the height given it was then continued upward in a straight line, or with

a slight rake forward of approximately 5 degrees to the height of the toptimber line at the dead-flat.

For all periods the moulding remained the same throughout its entire length and was equal to that of the depth of the keel, but the siding did vary in the period covered by this book. At the time Deane was working, it remained parallel at a width of fifteen-sixteenths of its moulding, but during the eighteenth and early nineteenth centuries there were two schools of practice. Some builders produced ships with the stem increasing in width from heel to head, the heel being made the width of the keel at its fore end, increasing to twice that width at the head. The alternative practice was to have the width remaining the same to the height of the lowest gundeck, or equivalent deck and then broadening out to twice its width at its heel.

Either two or three individual pieces were used to create the complete stempost, three more generally being the number used on the larger ships, each being joined together by a scarph similar to those used on the keel sections. The only difference in this type of scarph was that its flats were set in the athwartships plane and the number of bolts employed was either six or five. Usually those at the centre of the joint were omitted until the apron was fitted, but were then driven through both timbers. Below is the data for finding the approximate length of the scarph, these figures being biased towards the latter half of the eighteenth and early nineteenth centuries, though I would imagine that there would be hardly any difference for vessels built before this time.

$$S = M \times \varepsilon$$

where S = stem scarph length; M = stem moulded depth

Ship, number of guns (ε) – 110–90 (two and two-thirds); 84–60 (two and three-quarters); 50–38 (two and five-sixteenths); 36–20 (two and two-thirds); sloops and armed cutters (two and two-thirds).

The lips of the scarph can be taken as one-third of the moulding of the stem, but this was not always so, for in part of a draught in John Fincham's book *An Introductory Outline of the Practice of Shipbuilding*, of 1821, the lips are one-quarter of the moulding. Like the scarphs of the keel and the boxing these scarphs were lined with tarred flannel prior to bolting, the bolts varying from $1\frac{1}{4}$in to $\frac{3}{4}$in diameter, according to the size of the ship. The head of the stem was cut at an angle to accommodate the steeve of the bowsprit and was lined with either thick leather or copper to prevent wear and keep out damp.

The Apron (or False Stem)

Because the 'boxing', or any other type of joint used where the stem was fastened to the keel, was comparatively weak, a false stem was constructed and fayed to the after side of the main stempost. Indirectly this false stem or apron was just a continuation of the 'hog' used to stiffen the whole structure. Like the stem it was made from oak in either one or two sections, the scarphs being given 'shift' to those of the stem.

The apron was made in the following manner: its moulding was two-thirds of that of the stem while its siding was made to conform with that of the stem throughout its length. This statement can be confirmed by Rees' *Naval Architecture* of 1819 and by works written by John Fincham. Although this seems the more accepted practice a discrepancy arises when one refers to the 'Principal Dimensions & Scantlings' taken from the 1789 edition of the *Shipbuilder's Repository*, of which an extract is given below.

Ship (no of guns)	100	90	64	38	24	Sloop
Apron to be thick (inches)	12	12	$11\frac{3}{4}$	$9\frac{1}{2}$	9	8
Apron to be in breadth (inches)	30	*	26	20	17	14
Length of the scarphs (inches)	16	15	14	11	10	9

* At this point in the tables it notes that the breadth is the same as that of the stem, whereas the remaining figures imply that the apron stays at a constant width throughout its length. I can only assume that if this is the case then a considerable amount of timber would be trimmed off towards the lower end to allow the correct shaping of the peak.

Unlike the scarphs of the stem, those employed on the apron were of the plain flat type, secured with copper bolts driven right through to the stem; bolts only passed to the stem at the intervals where the scarphs of the stem were sited. All the remaining bolting was completed when the stemson was fitted, the bolts passing through the stem, apron and stemson together.

It does appear that the dimensions of the false stem of vessels built during the second half of the seventeenth century and earlier part of the eighteenth century were made even greater in their breadth than those mentioned previously in this section, whereas they were smaller in their moulding.

The dimensions taken from a Third Rate ship of 1667 give the following proportional sizes. The moulding of the false stem was made to approximately nine-sixteenths of the moulded depth of the keel while its breadth was as much as twice the moulded depth of the keel. This seems sensible in respect of securing the fore ends of the external planking, for the fore edge of the timber was bearded off to a considerable landing for the planks. By this one can safely assume that at this period the rabbet was continued right up the height of the stempost.

THE DEADWOOD

The deadwood, or as it is often called, the rising wood, was fitted to the top edge of the keel to act as a seating for the floor timbers. Oak was used for the rising wood in lengths similar to those used on the keel except that the type of scarphs employed were of the plain flat fashion and were only made to a length of one-eighth of the length of timber, in one individual length. For convenience, it can be said that deadwood falls into three separate sections: that which was fitted aft, that fitted forward, and the timber fitted along the major length of the keel.

Taking first rising wood along the keel, the moulding of this did not remain constant throughout its length but tended to 'rise' towards the fore and aft extremities following the designed rise in the floors. This was important for without the floors rising the underwater shape would not diminish giving a clear run for the ship to 'slide' through the water. The moulded depth of the rising wood at the midships position was $0.5 \times$ the moulded depth of the keel. This is a fair approximation for most classes of ship, the maximum discrepancy being 0.05. There was a tendancy for ships of 38 guns and sloops to have a greater depth, this being $0.6 \times$ the moulded depth of keel, and those of 44 guns to be less with a factor of $0.4 \times$ the depth of keel. The siding of the rising wood was generally little greater than that of the keel, either 2in, 3in or 4in. Thus if it was 3in wider then this would give $1\frac{1}{2}$in on each side. The timber that overlapped would be trimmed away at the same angle as that of the approach of the garboard strake (see Fig 1/3). In some cases the rising wood was made to the same siding as that of the keel. The forward end of the rising wood increased in its moulded depth to fair in with the apron, joined to the same with a plain flat scarph. The after end also increased to fair in with the desired rise in the deadwood.

At the turn of the century Robert Seppings (later to become the Surveyor of the Navy) introduced a number of changes in constructional techniques, and one was to alter the height of the rabbet line in relation to the depth of the keel. Previously this had been set just below the upper edge but was now to be set at half the height of the keel. By this alteration the floor timbers were set directly upon the keel as the hog was eliminated. This practice had been applied to merchant vessels for some time previously. Because of this the rising wood that covered the main length of the keel was omitted and the floor timbers were bolted directly to the keel. The method of having the undersides of the floor timbers scored to fit was still retained (see Fig 1/3). The rising wood had also acted as a landing for the garboard strake to which the latter was secured as well as fitting into the rabbet.

Turning to what is more generally called the deadwood, this was fitted at the fore and after ends of the keel, its purpose to generate the correct underwater shape of the hull. The height at which these timbers were set depended on whether a relatively 'sharp' or 'full' hull form was required. It was not always the practice to have deadwood at the fore end and it was only fitted where a sharper entry was needed. If it was used then it was placed directly over the 'boxing' and the scarph of the 'hog' to the apron. This would raise the floors of the four foremost square frames. A second piece of deadwood was usually fitted over the top of this, its after end butting onto the fore face of the foremost frame. Its siding remained equal to that below while its moulding was the difference between the lower deadwood and the keelson. To all this were fastened the forward cant frames.

The after deadwood was affected by the rising line of the after floor timbers which rose steeply and therefore the deadwood had to be built up to a greater height. This line can be seen on a sheer plan and is called the stepping line or bearding line. All the deadwood that was set below this line was made with an increased scantling and trimmed to the shape of the body, while all that was above was made to a siding equal to that of the keelson. Thus a curved ledge was formed onto which the heels of the after cant frames were set (see Fig 1/3). These frames were bolted directly onto the deadwood that was of equal thickness to the keelson. Approximately eight pieces made up the deadwood at the stern, the lower three – which were set more or less horizontal – were tenoned into the inner post for a depth of one-third the fore and aft width of the post. The largest of the timbers used was fashioned in the form of a large inverted knee and sat on top of all the rest of the deadwood, this being known as the knee of the sternpost (see Fig 1/3). The whole assembly was fastened together with copper clench bolts of 2½in diameter (in the case of a First Rate) and as long as 6ft. The fore end of the after deadwood was cut vertical and fayed against the after face of the aftermost square frame. However, the number of individual pieces could vary, depending on the builder, for here was a good opportunity to use up large offcuts of timber to minimise wastage.

Framing the Ship

Once the initial 'backbone' of the ship was completed and the stem and sternposts were shored up in position, the timbers that formed the shape of the hull were assembled. These frames were divided into three types: square, cant, and filling frames. Compass (ie naturally curved) timber was preferred and it was usually oak.

Before explaining the actual method of construction it would be well to discuss how each shape was derived. When one looks at an official draught of a ship, to the left side of the sheer plan is the body plan. This plan is divided into two halves by a centreline. All those shapes to the right side are of the frames (or 'stations' if using the modern idiom) forward of the dead-flat, while those to the left are of those aft of the dead-flat. Those frames forward are denoted by letters and those aft by numbers. The dead-flat is the point of extreme beam and was usually fixed at a point a little forward of the mainmast and was marked on both the sheer and body plan by the symbol '⊕'.

The shape was transferred from the body plan to the mould loft where the frames were constructed. Here the full-size shape was either 'screived' on the mould loft floor or templates of plank were made. Using one of these methods the frames were shaped before being erected on the actual ship. The next thing to be considered was the position at which each frame would be set. This was determined by the number of gunports that were required since the fore and aft sides of each gunport were formed by the square frames. Thus a frame forming the after side of one gunport on the lower gundeck would form the fore side of the gunport on the deck above and, in the case of a three-decked ship, the same frame would then form the after side of the gunport on the upper gundeck.

It was also imperative that the spaces between each frame were given adequate ventilation to prevent damp and eventually rot. Therefore stringent rules established the distances between each 'main' frame so that this could be achieved. This was known as the 'room and space' provision, and measured the distance between the face edge of one complete (or main) frame and the equivalent face edge of the next main frame. This measurement can be roughly estimated as twice the fore and aft breadth of a single frame plus between 2in and 6in for the overall small spaces between the filling frames and main frames. The rule of 'room and space' – or 'timber and room' as it was earlier known – had been applied in naval construction well before 1650 (see Fig 1/7). The 'room and space' regulation did not vary much over the last hundred years of the sailing warship and there was only a matter of about a 3in increase over the same period. The *Victory* at Portsmouth has a 'room and space' of 2ft 9⅜in. Typical figures for ships of the 1780s are: 100 guns (33in), 90 guns (33.5in), 74 guns (33in), 64 guns (30in), 44 guns (28.5in), 38 guns (28.875in), 36 guns (30in), 32 guns (27.75in), 28 guns (27in), 24 guns (27in), sloop (24in). The space taken from a draught of a 74-gun ship in Rees' *Naval Architecture* of 1819 is given as 36in. The frames on this draught vary between 14½in and 15in, so the overall room for ventilation between each frame is 2in to 2¼in.

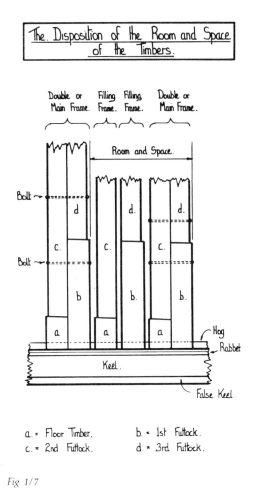

Fig 1/7

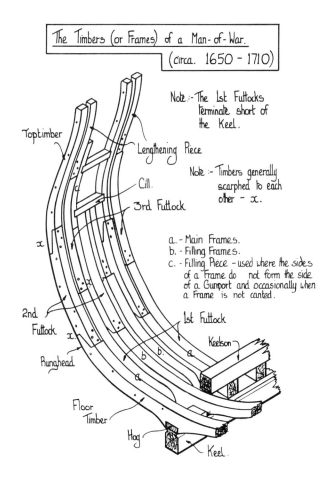

Fig 1/8

In general terms frame constructional techniques became progressively more complex during the period covered by this book. The evolution was due to a number of factors which can be listed as follows: a need for greater strength; improvements to minimise the problems of rot; and lastly, newer techniques in response to the ever increasing shortages of suitable timber while maintaining strength. To allow the reader to understand the methods more clearly and to appreciate the technical advances made throughout the period covered, the description has been divided into four basic periods.

FRAME CONSTRUCTION 1650–1710

First a floor timber was laid down at right angles across the keel, its underside scored at the centreline to enable it to be set down upon the 'hog' or 'rising wood'. Before this timber was finally secured with two copper bolts it was 'horned'. This term applies to the check made by the shipwright to ensure that the timber was exactly at 90 degrees to the keel and completely level. The length of the floor was made equal to two-thirds of the moulded beam at that point of the

vessel where it would be fitted (thus the floor at the dead-flat was of the greatest length). The extremities of the floor were generally referred to as the rungheads. The fore and aft width or siding was made to approximately 1in less than the depth of the keel. The depth of the floor at the centreline was made to 1in for every foot in length of the longest floor (that which lay at the dead-flat). This given depth applied to all of the floor timbers whereas their lengths did not. At this period the floor extended either side of the keel for equal lengths and the timbers fitted above were mirror images of each other on either side of the ship. All the sizes in the following tables are approximate, based on proportion of keel depth.

The Floor as a Proportion of Keel Depth

Ship	Fore and aft width	Ship	Depth at the centreline
First Rate	five-sevenths	First Rate	six-sevenths
Second Rate	five-sevenths	Second Rate	six-sevenths
Third Rate	thirteen-sixteenths	Third Rate	thirty-one thirty-seconds
Fourth Rate	thirteen-sixteenths	Fourth Rate	thirty-one thirty-seconds
Fifth Rate	six-sevenths	Fifth Rate	fifteen-sixteenths
Sixth Rate	three-quarters	Sixth Rate	three-quarters

Ship	Depth at the rungheads
First Rate	five-eighths
Second Rate	five-eighths
Third Rate	seven-tenths
Fourth Rate	twenty-one thirty-seconds
Fifth Rate	eleven-sixteenths
Sixth Rate	seven thirty-seconds

Next to be fitted was the lower or first futtock (the term 'futtock' derives from 'foot hook', where the foot of one timber was joined to the head of another, sometimes by a hook scarph). This timber was fayed and bolted to the adjacent side of the floor in such a way that its heel terminated at a position about 18in to 24in away from the keel. The bolts were made from copper and about three or four were employed, set in the fore and aft direction, and the whole assembly further secured with trennals. These were wooden dowels that were driven into a pre-bored hole in each timber. Their advantage was that when wet the wood would swell making them secure more tightly. The wood for their manufacture was selected from the topmost branches of oak trees where the grain run was straight and close. The frame timbers had to be carefully selected to correspond to the curvature of the hull at the 'turn of the bilge' up to the waterline. The moulding of this timber was made equal to that of the floor throughout the portion that was fayed to the floor and then diminished by a small amount towards its head. Its fore and aft siding was also a little less.

The Lower Futtock as Proportion of Keel Depth

Ship	Lower futtock sided fore and aft	Ship	Moulded (in and out) at its head
First Rate	eleven-sixteenths	First Rate	half
Second Rate	eleven-sixteenths	Second Rate	half
Third Rate	four-fifths	Third Rate	nine-sixteenths
Fourth Rate	twenty-five thirty-seconds	Fourth Rate	seventeen thirty-seconds
Fifth Rate	six-sevenths	Fifth Rate	fifteen thirty-seconds
Sixth Rate	five-eighths	Sixth Rate	three-eighths

The next timber was the second futtock, which was often referred to as the upper futtock, because a third futtock was not always necessary for smaller vessels. The second futtock was scarphed to the runghead of the floor timber, and fayed to the side of the first futtock, to which it was bolted with horizontally driven bolts.

Depending on the size of the vessel, the head of the second futtock often formed the landing for the sill of the lower deck gunports. The siding of this timber diminished slightly less than that of the floor timber below. This was both to allow ventilation of the timber, and reduce its overall weight without decreasing its strength. In its moulding it decreased towards its head, but it also remained equal to that of the adjacent first futtock. The general length of the overlap between the first and second futtocks was

approximately half of the given length. This of course varied a little, depending on the disposition of the timber itself and the size of the vessel.

The Second Futtock as a Proportion of Keel Depth

Ship	Upper futtock sided fore and aft	Ship	Moulded at its head
First Rate	thirteen-twentieths	First Rate	half
Second Rate	thirteen-twentieths	Second Rate	half
Third Rate	seven-tenths	Third Rate	nine-sixteenths
Fourth Rate	eleven-sixteenths	Fourth Rate	seventeen thirty-seconds
Fifth Rate	five-sevenths	Fifth Rate	fifteen thirty-seconds
Sixth Rate	seven-sixteenths	Sixth Rate	three-eighths

The Lengthening Pieces (Toptimbers) as a Proportion of Keel Depth

Ship	Sided fore and aft at its heel	Ship	Sided fore and aft at its head
First Rate	five-eighths	First Rate	seven-sixteenths
Second Rate	five-eighths	Second Rate	half
Third Rate	seven-tenths	Third Rate	half
Fourth Rate	five-eighths	Fourth Rate	seven-sixteenths
Fifth Rate	three-fifths	Fifth Rate	two-fifths
Sixth Rate	seven-sixteenths	Sixth Rate	one-third

Ship	Moulded at its head above the toptimber line
First Rate	seven thirty-seconds
Second Rate	one-fifth
Third Rate	one-fifth
Fourth Rate	five thirty-seconds
Fifth Rate	one-sixth
Sixth Rate	five thirty-seconds

Alongside the second futtock was the third futtock. This timber had its heel scarphed to the head of the first futtock and like the second futtock it was bolted horizontally to the adjacent timber. Each third futtock generally formed either the fore or after boundary of a lower deck gunport. Its siding and moulding were diminished to reduce weight and aid in ventilation. All of the bolting arrangements were carried out in the same manner as for the other timbers. The head of the third futtock often formed the landing for the sills of the upper gundeck ports, or in the case of a three-decker, the middle gundeck ports.

Scarphed to the head of the second futtock was the toptimber, so called because it extended up to the toptimber line, which corresponded with the line of the vessel's sheer. This timber formed the boundary of the uppermost ports. It was bolted in exactly the same way as the other timbers. In some cases a second toptimber, commonly termed a lengthening piece, was fitted adjacent to the toptimber. Its heel was scarphed to the head of the third futtock, and it was bolted to the toptimber horizontally. This practice was not always used in the early part of this period, and the lengthening piece was probably dispensed with to reduce topweight. However, by 1750 the use of lengthening pieces had become general practice.

Between the main frames were the filling frames which were identical to the main frames, except that they were not made in a 'double form'. During the earlier years of this period the frames were occasionally set so that they did not extend directly upwards from the keel. This meant that some of these frames must have been worked after completion of the main and channel wales. If this was the case their heads were tenoned into the gunport sills and those fitted higher up had their heels tenoned into the gunport lintels. If the heels of those fitted lower down in the hull terminated at a considerable distance from the keel, they were firmly bolted to the internal and external planking at that point. It is difficult to calculate the precise size of these timbers, but their moulding (in and out) would have been equal to that of the main frames. Likewise it is hard to estimate how many were employed between the frames as, especially between the years 1650 and 1660, their disposition varied from one builder to the next.

FRAME CONSTRUCTION 1710–1750

One of the major sources of rot in vessels of the seventeenth century was the area between the floor timbers, where bilge water drained to the lowest point. A number of unsuccessful attempts had been made to overcome this problem. It was finally solved by the introduction of a second floor timber, or cross chock as it became known. This timber 'tied' the heels of both the first futtocks together. The chock was also bolted to the adjacent floor timber with horizontally driven clenches or trennals.

Over the next forty years various innovations aimed at improving strength and economising on timber were made. By 1725 a fourth futtock had been introduced. The purpose of this was to allow the frame to be constructed with shorter lengths of timber, which also had less curvature. This practice was probably primarily intended to improve overall strength, and secondly to overcome the increasing shortage of compass oak. The fourth futtock had probably been used for a number of years before 1725, especially on the larger men-of-war where the height of the hull was considerably greater (see Fig 1/9).

During this period some builders also found that the plain flat scarph joint, employed to join the individual futtocks together, was relatively weak. A new method was introduced in which a timber chock or 'anchor piece' was firmly bolted or secured with trennals to the two futtocks it spanned. (The only remaining normal scarph type joint was where the toptimbers and lengthening pieces were fitted to the rest of the frame.) The first recorded use of this new method was in 1714. It helped to reduce timber wastage, as the

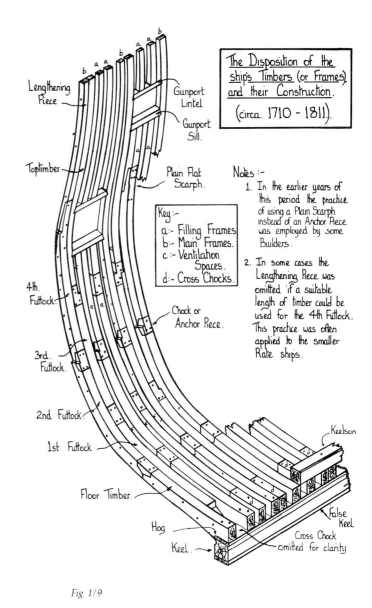

Fig 1/9

chocks could be manufactured from offcuts and the individual futtocks could be cut shorter, as no allowance needed to be made for the long scarphs previously used. This practical idea was probably inspired by the introduction of the cross chock.

FRAME CONSTRUCTION 1750–1811

By 1750 the arrangement of the floor timbers had changed, from one of long arms and one of short arms to a combination of both (see Fig 1/9). Thus there was one floor with a long and a short arm, the next one being made in reverse. Both were fayed together and bolted in position on the keel. A fourth futtock had been introduced and also a second toptimber. Now that there were first, second,

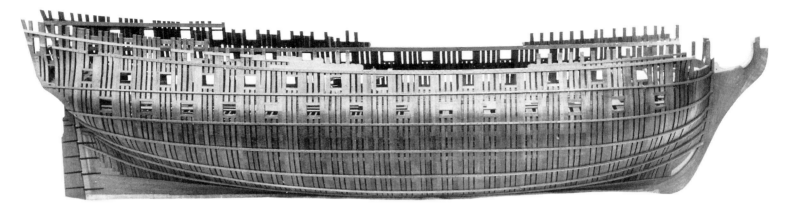

Egmont. Starboard side. A model illustrating the overall arrangement of the framing. The fore and aft lines of thin planking are the ribands and the harpins.

third and fourth futtocks, and two toptimbers, selection of timber was made somewhat easier, and wastage was minimised. (The abundance of oak was now beginning to dwindle and alternative wood was being considered.) Butt joints were replaced either by scarphs or by anchor pieces or cross chocks, fastened by trennals, although the joint between the third and fourth futtocks and their respective toptimbers was a plain flat scarph.

Now that these timbers were fastened by chock or scarphs, there was no need for them to be fayed and bolted to the adjacent timbers. Therefore a vertical ventilation space could be set between them. This was achieved by reducing the scantling of each futtock and toptimber in the fore and aft direction; this also reduced weight. To ensure that the structure remained rigid, filling pieces were worked in at intervals. The filling pieces were made to the same siding as the timbers in their vicinity, and bolted in place in the fore and aft direction. Then they were bored through vertically to allow ventilation, the holes being $1\frac{1}{2}$in diameter. The timber used for these pieces was generally beech, or offcuts of oak. The filling pieces were also used in way of the preventer plates to give a firmer footing for the preventer plate bolts. The additional toptimber or lengthening piece as it came to be known, gave extra strength to the upperworks, aided in the spacing of the gunports, and also gave more security to the ringbolts for the gun tackle.

After a while a change was made to the floor timbers. One floor was abandoned, and the other floor reverted to having both its arms made of equal length, to which the heel of the second futtock was butted. Instead of having a second floor, the first futtocks were extended to the line of the keel and secured together with a cross chock.

The floor was 'horned' and securely bolted to the keel with a scarph, of the plain flat type, at its outer extremities. To this was fitted the heel of the second futtock, which was fashioned with the same type of scarph, but not in the opposing direction. A cross chock or anchor piece was fitted across both, and fastened with either copper bolts or trennals. Before the use of cross chocks, normal scarphs were used, and each joint was secured with three copper bolts, the sizes being as follows: Ship, number of guns (diameter of bolt) – 100, 90($1\frac{1}{2}$in); 74, 64, 44, 38, 36 ($1\frac{1}{4}$in); 32

Egmont. Starboard side of a model showing the arrangement of the framing, the gunport sills and lintels. Note how some of the toptimbers are canted to form the sides of the gunports, and the standards fitted at the side of the ship's waist.

($1\frac{1}{8}$in); 28, 24 (1in); sloop ($\frac{7}{8}$in).

To the head of the second futtock the heel of the fourth futtock was fitted, secured in the manner described above. The heel of the lengthening piece was fitted to the head of the fourth futtock, but in this case the joint was always of the plain flat scarph type. This lengthening piece then continued up to the toptimber line, which corresponded to the sheer line, or, as is sometimes called, the planksheer.

Now we must look at the next 'slice' of the frame, which was designed to give the joints of the futtocks a shift, thus maintaining strength. As there were no actual floor timbers, the heels of the first futtocks were placed beside the floor, butting on to the hog, where both were secured by cross chocks bolted to the keel. Copper clench bolts and trennals were driven through the first futtock through to

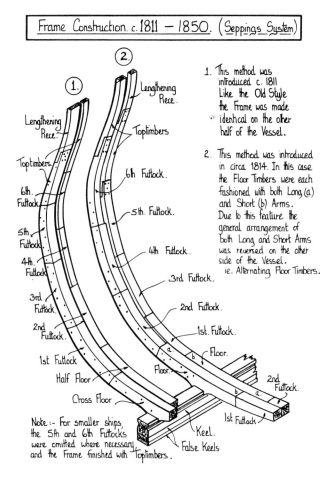

Frame Construction. c.1811 – 1850. (Seppings System)

1. This method was introduced c. 1811. Like the Old Style the Frame was made identical on the other half of the Vessel.

2. This method was introduced in circa 1814. In this case the Floor Timbers were each fashioned with both Long (a) and Short (b) Arms. Due to this feature the general arrangement of both Long and Short Arms was reversed on the other side of the Vessel. ie. Alternating Floor Timbers.

Lengthening Piece.
Toptimbers.
6th Futtock.
5th Futtock.
4th Futtock.
3rd Futtock.
2nd Futtock.
1st Futtock.
Floor.
Floor.
a. b.
2nd Futtock.
1st Futtock.
Keel.
False Keels.

Note :- For smaller ships the 5th and 6th Futtocks were omitted where necessary and the Frame finished with Toptimbers.

Fig 1/10

the adjacent floor in the fore and aft direction.

The heads of the first futtocks were joined to the heels of the third futtocks, in a similar manner to those of the other 'slice'. However, the moulding of this futtock was less than that below. Therefore filling pieces were fitted, then bolts were driven through to the second and fourth futtocks in the fore and aft direction.

Lastly came the toptimber, which was joined to the head of the third futtock by a plain flat scarph secured with trennals. This timber continued up to the toptimber line, and was secured fore and aft by copper clench bolts. Filling pieces were packed in between the toptimber and the lengthening piece.

The methods of bolting the floors to the keel also varied with the altering fashions of construction. In the case of the frames made with floor timbers, every other floor was bolted to the keel with two bolts, the sizes being as follows: Ship, number of guns (diameter of bolt) – 100 ($1\frac{7}{8}$in); 90 ($1\frac{5}{8}$in); 74 ($1\frac{1}{2}$in); 64 ($1\frac{3}{8}$in); 44, 38, 36 ($1\frac{3}{8}$in); 32, 28 ($1\frac{1}{4}$in); 24 ($1\frac{1}{8}$in); sloop (1in).

Between the main frames, filling frames were fitted. The simplest way of understanding their construction is to imagine each as a 'slice' of the main frame, but set apart. One frame was made up of a floor, second and fourth futtocks and a lengthening piece; the other of a floor, first and third futtocks and a toptimber. (The second frame

could also be made without an actual floor, but with a cross chock securing the first futtocks.) These frames would be continued upward until they met the sill of a gunport, either on the lower gundeck or on the next above. They would then be continued from above the lintel of that gunport, to the toptimber line (see Fig 1/9).

Where the line of the filling frames was interrupted by gunports, the heads of these timbers were tenoned into the underside of the sills of the gunports. In the same manner, they were extended above the gunport lintels up to the toptimber line.

THE SEPPINGS METHOD OF FRAME CONSTRUCTION 1811-1850

The system introduced by Sir Robert Seppings was to become the main style after 1820. The use of scarphs or anchor pieces was done away with, and the joints were made by means of dowels pinning both butts of the futtocks together. This was beneficial for two reasons: firstly, it was a quicker and easier method; secondly, timber could be more economically used. Because there were more futtocks the curvature of each piece was less, therefore each futtock was straighter, and shorter. In all, one side of a complete frame consisted of eleven individual pieces: a full floor, a half floor, six futtocks, two toptimbers and one lengthening piece. The system can best be explained by describing the frame in 'slices'. First there was a full floor, laid on the keel, horned, and bolted to the keel with copper bolts. The length of this timber was approximately twelve times the siding of the keel (this applies only at the midship section, for the heads of the floor were higher on the frames closer to the bow and stern). The heel of the first futtock butted to the head of the floor. It was secured by a large dowel set into the head of the floor and the heel of the first futtock. The futtock was relatively short, it only spanned the 'turn of the bilge'; in general it was half the length of the floor.

Following this were the third and fifth futtocks, and the toptimber. All were made to the same length, and were fastened as already described. Finally, a lengthening piece was added to fill the space between the head of the toptimber and the sheer line. (In some cases where the freeboard of the ship was relatively low, this lengthening piece was omitted.)

The second 'slice' was made in the following manner. Two half floors were dowelled together and laid upon the keel, and were then bolted in the fore and aft direction to the adjacent full floor timber. In midship, each half floor was nine times the siding of the keel in length. Thus the heads of these timbers extended one-third of the length of a half floor beyond the heads of the full floor. The two half floors met on the centreline of the ship.

Next came the second futtock, two-thirds of the half floor in length. It was followed by the fourth and sixth futtocks and finally by a toptimber. The heads and heels of all these timbers were fastened together by dowels. All were secured to the other 'slice' by copper bolts in the fore and aft plane, filling pieces being fitted at intervals as required. The use of anchor pieces or cross chocks was

Above: Foudroyant. *Port side, aft, showing the framing and gunport sill. The quarter gallery stool and lower finishing have been removed to allow restoration work to be carried out.*

Right: Foudroyant. *Port side, aft. The frames are made in short length futtocks with their heads and heels butted plainly together. The heads of the filling frames are tenoned into the sill of the gunport.*

abandoned, saving much labour and timber.

The filling frames between the main frames were made in an identical manner, except that the 'slices' were separate. They still had a full floor set next to a half floor, but a space of 1in to 2in was left between them (for a complete diagram see Fig 1/10).

During this period it was common to fill up the spaces between the floor timbers with wedges of timber, thus producing a completely solid structure from stem to stern. This was done by driving wedges in opposite each other, from inside and outside the hull.

It was quite common for the timbers to be pickled in salt prior to construction. Seppings believed this helped to prevent rot and its success is proved by the fact that this process was used on the

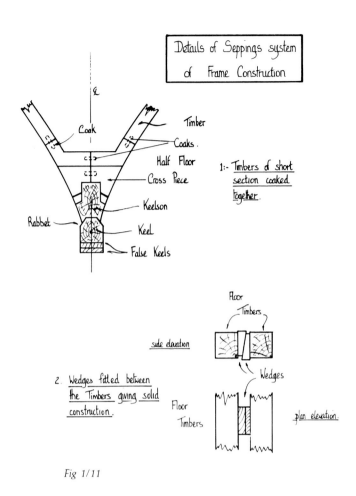

Details of Seppings system
of Frame Construction

1:- Timbers of short section coaked together.

2. Wedges fitted between the Timbers giving solid construction.

side elevation

plan elevation

Fig 1/11

timbers of the frigate *Unicorn* – she is still afloat at Dundee. Timbers subjected to this treatment can be distinguished by the word 'salt' engraved on them.

The exact dimensions of timbers are very complex, and from here on they are simplified to save space. The details given should be sufficient for modelmakers.

The moulding of the centre of a floor (excluding the wood removed for the score) was usually the same scantling as that of the keel at midships, and diminished to approximately 2in less at the heads of the timber. This applies only to a full floor; where two floors were used, it would be the floor that rose to the greatest height.

The head of the second futtock was approximately 1in smaller than its heel (which was the same as the head of the floor). The head of the fourth futtock was about 4½in less than its heel, and the toptimber and lengthening pieces were approximately 3½in less at their heads on those that extended to the toptimber line.

The head of the first futtock was the mean of the head and heel of the second futtock. Likewise the head of the third futtock was the mean of the head and heel of the fourth futtock, and so on for the other timbers. Normally the timbers mentioned in this paragraph 'faired' with the adjacent timbers.

On the whole, the head of the toptimber at its maximum height

was about one-third the thickness of the maximum moulding of the floor at the centreline, within ½in. The greatest change in the moulding was between the line of the third futtock head and the fourth futtock head. Below is a table to determine the moulding at the heads of all of the timbers. The multiplying factors are all calculated from the moulding of the floor at the centreline. For example, the moulded depth of the keel of a ship of 24 guns is 13in, giving the moulding of the floor as 13in. To determine the moulding of the head of the third futtock, the 13in would be multiplied by 0·558.

Timber, moulded at the head

Ship of 100 guns	Keel depth, multiplied by	Ship of 90 guns	Keel depth, multiplied by
Floor	0·725	Floor	0·72
First futtock	0·7	First futtock	0·71
Second futtock	0·675	Second futtock	0·685
Third futtock	0·65	Third futtock	0·666
Fourth futtock	0·45	Fourth futtock	0·45
Toptimber	0·275	Toptimber	0·27

Timber, moulded at the head

Ship of 74 guns	Keel depth, multiplied by	Ship of 64 guns	Keel depth, multiplied by
Floor	0·736	Floor	0·75
First futtock	0·7	First futtock	0·74
Second futtock	0·7	Second futtock	0·7
Third futtock	0·645	Third futtock	0·64
Fourth futtock	0·58	Fourth futtock	0·57
Toptimber	0·29	Toptimber	0·29

Timber, moulded at the head

Ship of 44 guns	Keel depth, multiplied by	Ship of 38 guns	Keel depth, multiplied by
Floor	0·77	Floor	0·78
First futtock	0·74	First futtock	0·68
Second futtock	0·68	Second futtock	0·65
Third futtock	0·645	Third futtock	0·61
Fourth futtock	0·56	Fourth futtock	0·53
Toptimber	0·27	Toptimber	0·33

Timber, moulded at the head

Ship of 32 guns	Keel depth, multiplied by	Ship of 28 guns	Keel depth, multiplied by
Floor	0·714	Floor	0·704
First futtock	0·68	First futtock	0·685
Second futtock	0·62	Second futtock	0·65
Third futtock	0·544	Third futtock	0·546
Fourth futtock	0·5	Fourth futtock	0·50
Toptimber	0·285	Toptimber	0·296

Timber, moulded at the head

Ship of 24 guns	Keel depth, multiplied by	Sloop	Keel depth, multiplied by
Floor	0·712	Floor	0·59
First futtock	0·673	First futtock	0·536
Second futtock	0·635	Second futtock	0·29
Third futtock	0·558	Toptimber	0·29
Fourth futtock	0·50		
Toptimber	0·31		

Timber, moulded at the head

Armed cutter	Keel depth, multiplied by		
Floor	0·66		
First futtock	0·625		
Second futtock	0·50		
Toptimber	0·44		

Only two futtocks, plus a toptimber and a lengthening piece were used in the construction of sloops and cutters.

Fig 1/12

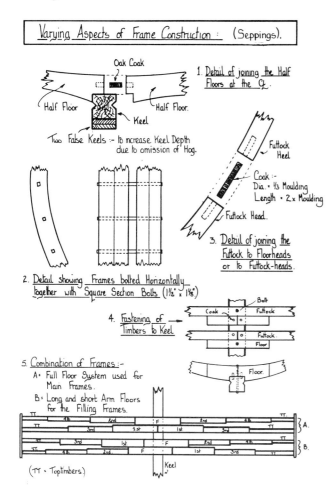

Varying Aspects of Frame Construction : (Seppings).

The adjacent tables can be applied to ships built up to about 1820, when the new method of constructing with six futtocks was introduced. Modelmakers wishing to determine the head of the topmost toptimber after this date should divide the depth of the keel by one-third, remembering that the moulding diminishes at a greater exponential rate above the waterline than it does below. For ships built between 1650 and 1710, the above tables would suffice, but it would be wise to make a template and fair the pieces of wood used in the model to conform with the shape.

The siding of the frames throughout this period, and well before 1650, did not always remain parallel throughout their entire height from heel to toptimber line. As previously mentioned, this reduction in scantling was intended to allow for air circulation to prevent rot, and to reduce the overall topweight of the vessel.

The tables below are applicable to any ship built to the four futtock method of construction between 1750 and 1820. The toptimbers are given as two scantlings, one for the heel and one for the head because there was a tendency to slightly taper the toptimber towards its head.

Timbers, sided

Ship of 100 guns	Keel depth, multiplied by	Ship of 90 guns	Keel depth, multiplied by
Floor	0·80	Floor	0·718
First futtock	0·788	First futtock	0·795
Second futtock	0·75	Second futtock	0·718
Third futtock	0·725	Third futtock	0·718
Fourth futtock	0·70	Fourth futtock	0·692
Toptimber, heel	0·694	Toptimber, heel	0·692
Toptimber, head	0·65	Toptimber, head	

Timbers, sided

Ship of 74 guns	Keel depth, multiplied by	Ship of 64 guns	Keel depth, multiplied by
Floor	0·888	Floor	0·882
First futtock	0·805	First futtock	0·882
Second futtock	0·75	Second futtock	0·824
Third futtock	0·743	Third futtock	0·794
Fourth futtock	0·72	Fourth futtock	0·794
Toptimber, heel	0·75	Toptimber, heel	0·76
Toptimber, head	0·72	Toptimber, head	0·76

Timbers, sided

Ship of 44 guns	Keel depth, multiplied by	Ship of 38 guns	Keel depth, multiplied by
Floor	0·903	Floor	0·933
First futtock	0·871	First futtock	0·90
Second futtock	0·791	Second futtock	0·819
Third futtock	0·71	Third futtock	0·766
Fourth futtock	0·677	Fourth futtock	0·733
Toptimber, heel	0·677	Toptimber, heel	0·70
Toptimber, head	0·645	Toptimber, head	0·666

Timbers, sided

Ship of 36 guns	Keel depth, multiplied by	Ship of 32 guns	Keel depth, multiplied by
Floor	0·993	Floor	0·929
First futtock	0·90	First futtock	0·929
Second futtock	0·817	Second futtock	0·821
Third futtock	0·766	Third futtock	0·786
Fouth futtock	0·733	Fourth futtock	0·768
Toptimber, heel	0·717	Toptimber, heel	0·75
Toptimber, head	0·70	Toptimber, head	0·714

Timbers, sided

Ship of 28 guns	Keel depth, multiplied by	Ship of 24 guns	Keel depth, multiplied by
Floor	0·910	Floor	0·923
First futtock	0·945	First futtock	0·923
Second futtock	0·80	Second futtock	0·827
Third futtock	0·764	Third futtock	0·769
Fourth futtock	0·745	Fourth futtock	0·769
Toptimber, heel	0·745	Toptimber, heel	0·769
Toptimber, head	0·727	Toptimber, head	0·769

Timbers, sided

Sloop	Keel depth, multiplied by	Armed Cutter	Keel depth, multiplied by
Floor	0·786	Floor	0·75
First futtock	0·714	First futtock	0·808
Second futtock	0·679	Second futtock	0·692
Toptimber	0·643	Toptimber	0·654

Boundaries of the Square Frames

Class of ship	Square frame continued from station	Terminated at station
100 guns	S	23
90 guns	S	23
74 guns	O	28
64 guns	O	21
44 guns	O	20
38 guns	Q	21
36 guns	P	21
32 guns	P	21
28 guns	N	21
24 guns	N	18
Sloop	L	23
Armed cutter	H	12

eighteenth century) the requirement for ships-of-war was quantity not quality.

The way in which the square frames were constructed suited the shape of the ship where the body was full, but because the shape diminished at the fore and after ends it proved impractical to fair off the outer edge of the frames for a good line of planking. The amount of timber that would have to be removed to give a fair run as the shape approached the centreline would render the frame weak.

To overcome this it was necessary to 'cant' the frames at varying angles so that a flatter area was created for fixing the planking. These frames were called the cant frames and were first introduced around 1715. Prior to this the construction of the fore and after frames must have caused a considerable waste of timber, due to the amount of trimming which was necessary.

All the frames forward of the dead-flat were set so that the floors formed the fore face of the complete or main frame, whereas those aft of the dead-flat had their floors aft. In ships where two floor timbers were used, the shortest was set forward in the fore body and aft in the after body. Frames aft of the dead-flat were denoted by numerals, and those forward by lettering. Through experience the builders knew how many square frames to have in the length of the ship, thus a set number and position of termination was developed.

All frames set forward and aft of these stations were cant frames. As rot was a major problem, especially between the frames, beech was often worked between the floors from the hog to the turn of the bilge. Many methods were used to prevent rot, for it was not unknown for ships to be condemned after only six years' service. A simple but effective method was to char the framing prior to laying on the planking. A fine example of this method of preservation is to be found in the working life of the *Royal William*. She was built in 1719 and remained on active service until she was finally broken up in 1813. However, in times of war (a considerable part of the

Unicorn. Close-up of timbers, starboard side, forward showing a square sectioned bolt driven horizontally between the frames holding them together and enhancing longitudinal strength. To the right is part of a diagonal iron rider plate.

THE CANT FRAMES

The basic construction of cant frames differed very little from that of the square frames, except in the manner in which the floors were fitted. The floors were bolted to the sides of the deadwood instead of passing across it as they did for the normal framing. The 'room and space' was reduced in the vicinity of the cants, so that the angle could be decreased in the run forward or aft. No cant frames were used after the angle became less than 45 degrees to the keel.

The angles at which these frames were set could be taken from the half breadth plan. The remaining space forward of these frames was completed with hawse pieces and at the after end by transoms and filling pieces. Because of the shape of the underwater body, the rise of the floors increased at each end of the ship, and more so in the fore part.

As the frames extended upwards towards the toptimber line, the spaces between them were increased, so that by the height of breadth line they ran parallel to each other. Filling pieces were used at various points between the frames, and were bolted in a similar fashion to those employed for the square frames. Likewise, they would be bored through vertically to aid ventilation of the timbers.

Prior to 1715 cant frames were not generally adopted on British warships. The English fashion before this date was to have the aftermost square frame set in the vertical with a fashion piece fayed and bolted to its after face. The heel of the fashion piece would be fayed and bolted to the rise of the deadwood and the remaining area aft fitted with transoms and filling pieces. At the desired height the topmost transom, known as the wing transom, was bolted to the after side of the fashion piece, this timber being the main cross member that supported the stern and its upperworks.

Egmont. *The port quarter of a model showing the overall disposition of the cant frames, fashion piece, transom pieces and stern timbers. Note the two doorways which gave access to the quarter gallery, typical of vessels built with a stern walk.*

Egmont. *The starboard side hawse pieces and fore cant frames. The model shows the relationship between the hawse pieces, stempost and apron. The various timbers forming the knee of the head are particularly well defined.*

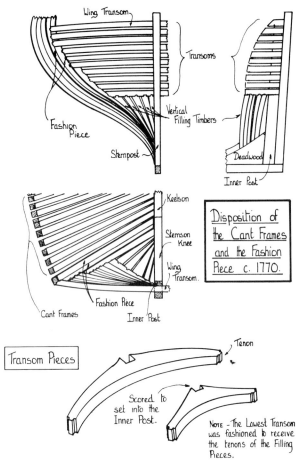

Fig 1/13

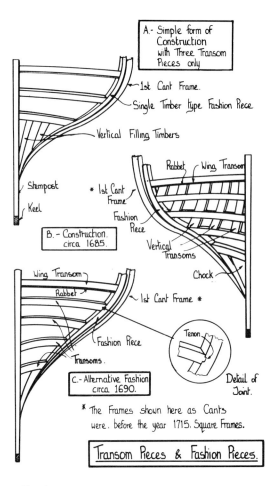

Fig 1/14

THE FASHION PIECES

These were merely the aftermost cant frames. Between 1720 and 1775 the fashion piece evolved from being a single timber structure to one of two or three timbers. Most ships only had two fashion pieces, though a few classes had three; sloops and armed cutters remained with a single timber.

When three pieces were employed they were called the foremost, middle and after fashion pieces. When only two were used, the timber known as the middle piece was omitted. The introduction of these additional timbers was due to the increase in the number of transom timbers being fitted aft to give greater strength to the hull.

The list below shows the approximate height at which the foremost fashion piece finished above the upper edge of the wing transom. It cannot be applied to all ships, for some builders continued the timber up to the toptimber line in the same manner as a normal single or filling frame. Ship, number of guns (height) – 110–100 (4ft); 90–74 (3ft 9in); 64–44 (3ft 6in); 38–32 (3ft); 28 (2ft 9in); 24–20 (2ft 6in); sloop etc (2ft).

A middle fashion piece was generally used only on ships of between 84 and 64 guns. The head of this timber terminated where

its tenon was set into the lower side of the lowest gundeck deck transom. The after fashion piece varied in length according to the vessel in which it was fitted. It had its head tenoned into one of the following timbers: the gundeck transom, the first or second transom, or the filling transom. The list that follows gives the various positions on different types of ship. 64-gun ships were often constructed with only a fore and after fashion piece. For ships of 100–90 guns the after fashion piece terminated at the lowest gundeck deck transom; for 84–70 guns, at the second transom; for 64–60 guns, at either the first or second transom; for 50–44 guns at the first transom; for 38–36 guns, at the gundeck transom; for 32–20 guns at the filling transoms; (sloops and armed cutters did not have an after fashion piece).

All fashion pieces were made to the same moulding as the cant frames; siding in the fore and aft plane differed. The foremost fashion piece was made to the following approximate scantlings (as fractions of the moulded depth of keel): Ships of 100–90 guns, eleven-sixteenths; 50–24 guns, three-quarters; sloops and armed cutters, five-eighths. The remaining middle and after fashion pieces were approximately fifteen-sixteenths of the siding of the foremost fashion piece.

Victory. *Starboard side aft, showing the transom pieces and the fashion piece (the after part is not shown). The after cant frames and the bottom planking are also shown. Note the tenons fashioned on the ends of the transom pieces.*

of the *Practice of Shipbuilding* of 1821, the holes are let through a separate timber and the parts of the hawse piece above and below are fayed to those on either side and bolted through in the horizontal plane. The alternative method, which involved cutting the hole into two hawse pieces, can be seen in many draughts and is clearly described in Rees' *Naval Architecture* of 1819, 'Let it be observed, that the hawse pieces should be so disposed as to be equally cut by the hawse holes.'

The timber that was set beside the stempost was made longer than the others, and extended above the toptimber line, so that it would give athwartship support for the bowsprit. The heads of these two timbers were usually fashioned into a knighthead, and in some cases a cross member was fastened between them as a brace to stop the bowsprit from riding upward. The actual position of the knighthead varied, the determinant being the line of the rabbet on the stempost. If the rabbet was set towards the after side of the stem, the hawse piece forming the knighthead was set and fayed to the apron. When the line of the rabbet was set halfway back on the stem, the knighthead was fayed to the after part of the stem.

The moulding of the hawse pieces and the siding was the same as that of the cant frames. The heads of the hawse pieces of ships with a beakhead bulkhead were sided to the same dimensions as the cant frames at the same height. Ships with a round bow had the head made equal to the other frames at the toptimber line. Each hawse piece had its heel made to the siding of the cant frame at the point at which it was joined.

THE HAWSE PIECES

As the bows of ships built between 1650 and 1750 were of a very bluff construction, it proved impractical to continue the cant frames right up to the stem. This problem was overcome by the use of frames called hawse pieces, so called because they were bored for the passage of the anchor cables through the hawse holes (see Fig 1/6).

Like the rest of the ship's frames, the hawse pieces were made from oak, sawn to the required siding and moulding. They were generally made in one continuous length up to the toptimber line. This of course would vary depending on whether the ship was constructed with the round bow or with a beakhead bulkhead.

The heels of the hawse pieces were cut to the angle of the face of the foremost cant frame, to which they were joined by means of tenons. These were cut square, to one-third the siding and moulding of the frame, and given a depth equal to one-third of the siding of the foremost cant frame. Each piece was set up vertically, with a space of approximately 2in between them. In the area of the hawse holes, the scantling was increased so that each timber was fayed to the next. The hawse holes were not cut into a single timber, for cutting the hawse holes would weaken the timber. Instead, half of the hawse hole was cut into one timber and the other half into the adjacent timber. Thus the complete hole was formed when both pieces were fayed together.

On some draughts, for example in Fincham's *Introductory Outline*

THE TRANSOM BEAMS

As in the fore end of the ship, the cant frames at the stern could only be set at a maximum of 45 degrees to the keel. The remaining space was filled with a series of horizontal beams called transom beams which ran between the fashion pieces either side of the ship and were secured to the inner sternpost at the centreline.

The most important was the wing transom. This formed the foundation for the upperworks of the stern and its various fitments. It was made from a single piece of oak cut to the required siding and depth, and given both a round up and round aft. Rounding is the term used when a timber is fashioned with a cambered surface. The round up would be equal to that of the deck at that point and the round aft would be determined by the distance between the fore edge of the sternpost and after edge of the fashion piece. The length of this timber can be found from the draught of the ship at a given height on the fashion piece. At this point one takes the moulded breadth of the fashion piece, this will give the overall length of the wing transom.

The height at which this measurement should be taken is given in the following list, from the 1789 edition of *Shipbuilder's Repository*. The height given is from the upper side of the keel to the upper edge of the wing transom. Ship, number of guns (height taken at the centreline) – 100 (29ft 9in); 90 (28ft 7in); 74 (26ft 6in); 64 (26ft); 44

(23ft 4in); 38 (22ft 1in); 36 (21ft 2in); 32(20ft 10in); 28 (19ft 4in); 24 (18ft 6in); sloop (14ft 4in); armed cutter (13ft).

The width of the wing transom was approximately 1in for every foot in length, and its depth was five-twelfths of its width. Thus a wing transom with a length of 36ft would be 3ft in width and 15in in depth.

A recess was cut vertically on the after face at the centreline, with a width equal to that of the sternpost, and a depth that would line up the after face with the rabbet on the sternpost. When the wing transom was put in position it had to be accurately set up, as any distortion would have put the whole of the stern's upperworks out of line. Therefore it would be very rigidly fastened with copper clench bolts, driven through the transom and the sternpost in a fore and aft direction. The lower edge of the transom sat on the head of the inner post. Two copper bolts were driven vertically downward through both the transom and the inner post. The outboard ends of the wing transom were fayed and clenched with copper bolts to the after face of the fashion pieces.

To strengthen the joint of the wing transom to the fashion piece, a knee set in the horizontal plane was fitted between the inner surfaces of the cant frames and the after edge of the wing transom. The fore arm of this knee extended forward to cover three complete cant frames. The after arm extended inboard for a distance of between one-third and one-quarter of the length of the wing transom. The thickness of this knee was the same depth as the wing transom, while its width at the throat was between 1ft 6in and 2ft, narrowing down to between 4in and 6in. The upper surface of the wing transom also served as the lower sill of the after stern-chase gunports.

The transom below the wing transom was generally known as the deck transom, as it was designed to have its fore edge lapped under the ends of the lower deck planking. Because of this the deck transom was wider than all the other transoms, apart from the wing transom. It was fastened in the same way as the wing transom, except that the outboard end was tenoned into the fashion piece, to a depth of approximately 1½in, and clenched with copper bolts worked from the fore face of the fashion piece.

The remaining transoms were worked in the same fashion, each being set approximately 3in to 6in apart, to about half way down the sternpost. They varied between 10in and 15in in depth, depending on the size of the ship and how the builder disposed them. As can be seen from Fig 1/13, the lower transoms were shorter in length, and the angle to which they were formed increased in relation to the ship's underwater lines. Where several fashion pieces were fitted, the middle piece usually terminated below the deck transom, and the after piece finished below the fourth transom. The lowest transom piece had three or four mortices set into its bottom face to accommodate the heads of the vertical filling pieces that were used to fill the remaining space between the lower transom and the deadwood.

The method of transom construction was much simpler in the seventeenth century when only three transom pieces were employed, excluding the wing transom. The spaces between were

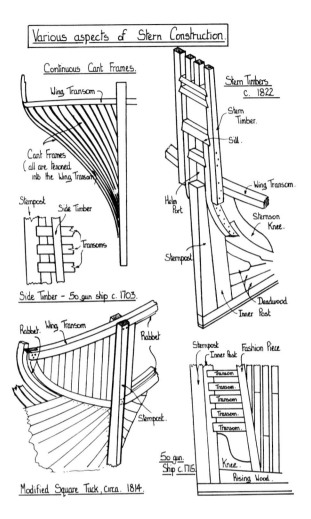

Fig 1/15

filled with a series of curved timbers, the heads of which were tenoned into the underside of the transoms and the heels into either the transom below or the after face of the fashion piece (see Fig 1/14). After 1810, only the wing transom was employed, the remaining space being covered by a number of vertical filling pieces extending from the deadwood to the underside of the wing transom (see Fig 1/15). This form of construction remained standard until Seppings introduced the circular stern in 1817. With this the whole concept of the after timbers changed, and the cant frames were carried aft to the sternpost and continued up to the toptimber line. The heels of these timbers were bolted to the deadwood and the inner post. Each frame was fashioned with floors, futtocks and toptimbers as required. Fastening was carried out in the normal manner, as on the older cant frames (Fig 1/16).

There were many exceptions to the rules. A model at the National Maritime Museum in Greenwich, of a 50-gun ship of about 1703, appears to be fitted with a vertical timber at a set distance on each side of the sternpost. The transoms still run their normal course between the sternpost and the fashion piece and are given a recess on their after face to fit into a corresponding recess on

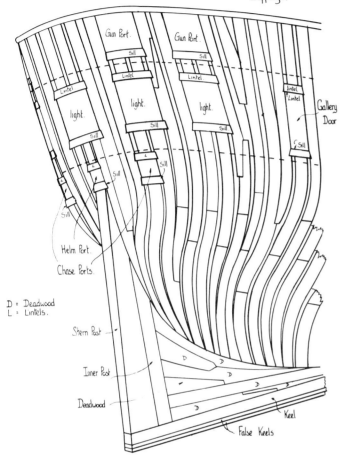

The Disposition of the Framing as applied to the Circular Stern designed by Seppings

The illustration has been adapted from the Draught of the 'Forth' built at Pembroke. The draught is dated 21st April 1830 at the Navy Office and has been signed by Seppings.

D = Deadwood
L = Lintels.

Fig 1/16

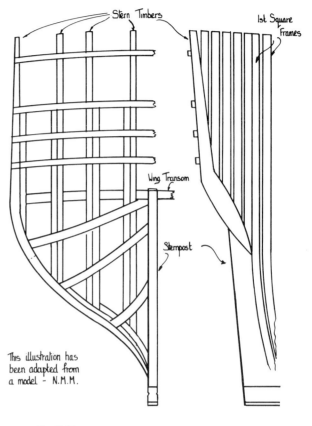

The Practice of Continued Timbers above and below the Wing Transom.

This illustration has been adapted from a model – N.M.M.

Fig 1/17

THE SETTING UP AND ALIGNMENT OF THE TIMBERS

the fore face of the vertical timber. It is not known whether this was a common fashion. It may be a modelmaker's error, but this seems unlikely, for these craftsmen were masters of their trade. If this model is correct there are a number of other points that do not adhere to the common practices of the period, for there are also gangways fitted either side of the waist between the quarterdeck and the forecastle, an innovation not in common use until the 1740s.

Another ship model at the National Maritime Museum has no transoms, but a series of vertical timbers set parallel to the sternpost. These timbers, are shaped to conform to the underwater lines, and run from the fashion piece to a form of wing transom. Some of the timbers terminate a short distance above the transom whereas the others, the stern counter timbers, are continued up to the toptimber line. The outboard counter timbers were made to a greater scantling and shaped at their heels to produce the 'knuckle' at the lower quarters (Fig 1/17). This was probably an alternative method that was employed just before Seppings introduced the circular stern.

As each frame was manufactured it was temporarily stiffened by diagonal pieces of timber known as 'spiles'. These were nailed across the extremities of the frame to prevent distortion during its conveyance to the slipway or when being fitted. The frames were then erected upon the keel and horned (set up at right angles athwart the keel) and it was checked that the centre of the floor was parallel to the upper edge of the keel. Finally the frame was plumbed to ensure that it was perpendicular when viewed from abeam. The whole assembly was then supported with shores until it was fastened permanently, and the necessary bolts were driven well into the keel itself.

The next step was to fasten long lengths of timber, approximately 6in square in cross-section, along the hull in various lines, which corresponded to lines marked on the draught. These were known as the rib-bands, or ribands. Similar pieces called harpins were fitted to the cant frames, but these had to be specially manufactured to conform to the shape of the ship. The harpins and ribands enabled the shipwrights to check that all the frames were set

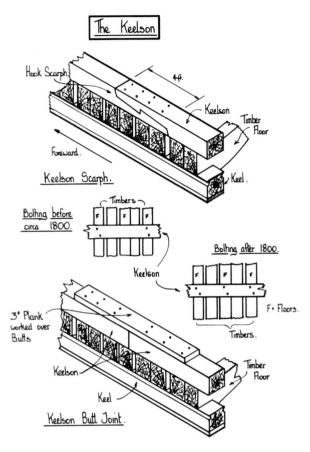

Fig 1/18

up true, and to make any adjustments necessary, so that the correct lines were achieved.

Once all the timbers were set in place, they were bolted to the keel; the manner in which this was done depended on the period in which the ship was built.

THE KEELSON ASSEMBLY

The Keelson

A longitudinal timber, called the keelson, was attached to the full length of the hull, on the centreline, across the floors of the timbers, directly above the keel. This internal keel gave additional strength to the vessel and ensured that all the timbers were fixed rigidly to the keel.

The keelson was made from straight oak of approximately the same breadth and depth as the keel. It was square in cross-section in all classes of ship. Similarly the number of lengths making up the keelson was identical to the number that made up the keel. For ships of 38 guns and over, 6 were used; 5 for ships of between 24 and 36 guns and 4 for sloops and armed cutters.

Each section was joined to the next by a flat hook and butt scarph

set in the horizontal plane. The length of each butt scarph was about one-fifth more than each keel scarph. The length of the keelson scarphs in relation to those of the keel can be calculated by multiplying the length of the keel scarph by a given multiplication factor. Ship, number of guns (multiplication factor) – 100 (1·13); 90 (1·14); 74 (1·2); 64 (1·3); 44 (1·2); 38 (1·14); 36 (1·12); 32 (1·23); 28 (1·3); 24 (1·3); sloop (1·2); armed cutter (1·3).

The timbers making up the keelson were arranged so that the centre of each scarph was set over the floors that would not be bolted through to the keel alone. Before 1800 the keelson was only bolted through to the keel at every other floor. After this the keelson was bolted through every floor. Two bolts were used, the sizes varying from 2in to 1in, though bolts of 2½in diameter were used on the *Victory*. The bolts used to join the scarph together were of smaller diameter, ranging from 1in to ½in. All the bolts were copper. Bolting was not the only method of fastening the scarph; between 1650 and 1760 trennals were used. Following this there was a period when both methods were used. The *Shipbuilder's Repository* of 1789 refers to the employment of copper clench bolts. Alternatively the lengths of timber were fastened by a simple butt joint, with a 3in thick plank the same width as the keelson worked over the butts and fastened with nails or dumps.

The Stemson

The keelson was worked forward to a position a little afore the 'boxing', then a separate piece of timber was worked up the after side of the apron. This timber is known as the stemson and it terminated just below the bowsprit, usually at the point where the upper deck breast hook was fitted. The width of the stemson diminished towards its head, to a scantling of seven-tenths of its siding at its heel. An illustration in Fincham's *Outline of Shipbuilding* of 1821 shows the stemson as finishing at a lower position, at the deck hook supporting the lowest gundeck. The stemson was fastened to the apron with copper clench bolts of the same diameter as those used for the keelson. They were driven through the apron into the stem between the bolts that secured the breast and deck hooks.

The Sternson

Before 1750 the keelson terminated where the after deadwood began, and the whole of the deadwood supported the sternpost and inner post. After that date the keelson was carried further aft, rising up over the deadwood to the head of the inner post. The section of the keelson that was set on top of the deadwood was known as the sternson. The after face of this timber was scored to receive the siding of the transom beams. It was fashioned to fair in with the inner post, and the deadwood below. Between 1750 and 1810 there were a number of changes in design. These can be divided into two categories: the continued keelson running into the sternson, as

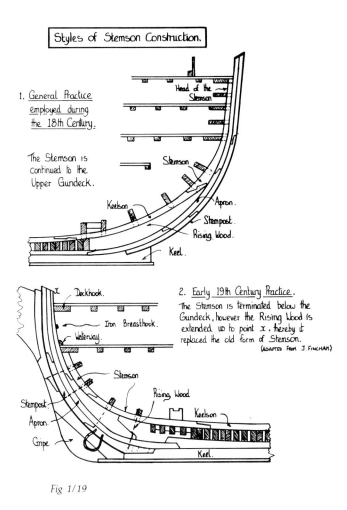

Styles of Stemson Construction.

1. General Practice employed during the 18th Century.

Head of the Stemson

The Stemson is continued to the Upper Gundeck.

Stemson
Keelson
Apron.
Stempost.
Rising Wood.
Keel.

2. Early 19th Century Practice.
The Stemson is terminated below the Gundeck, however the Rising Wood is extended up to point x, thereby it replaced the old form of Stemson.
(ADAPTED FROM J. FINCHAM)

Deckhook.
Iron Breasthook.
Waterway.
Stemson
Stempost.
Apron.
Gripe
Rising Wood
Keelson
Keel.

Fig 1/19

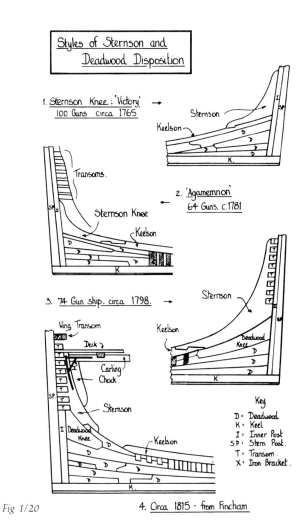

Styles of Sternson and Deadwood Disposition

1. Sternson Knee: 'Victory' 100 Guns circa 1765 →

Sternson
Keelson
K.

Transoms.
Sternson Knee
SP
K

2. 'Agamemnon' 64 Guns. c.1781 ←
Sternson
Keelson

3. 74 Gun ship. circa 1798. →

Wing Transom
Deck
Carling Chock
Sternson
Deadwood Knee
Keelson
SP

Sternson
Keelson
Deadwood Knee
K

Key
D · Deadwood
K · Keel
I · Inner Post
SP · Stern Post.
T · Transom.
X · Iron Bracket.

Fig 1/20

4. Circa 1815 - from Fincham

mentioned above, and the sternson knee, this being the later design. The change in the configuration of the deadwood construction over the years seems to be the main reason for the alteration in the sternson design. The older method had a large knee called the knee of the sternpost, integral to the deadwood (see Fig 1/20). The keelson continued to the head of the inner post and its moulding only increased when the angle of the deadwood changed from the horizontal to the near perpendicular – this was to become the sternson.

In later construction the knee of the sternpost was considerably shorter. Therefore the scantling of the sternson had to be increased to give the additional support to the inner post and sternpost. The sternson then became similar to a knee and was thus known as the sternson knee (see Fig 1/20/(2)). Alternatively the keelson was continued aft to the inner post, forming the top strake of the deadwood. The sternson knee was then fayed to the upper edge of the keelson and fore face of the inner post by a specially designed scarph set at the fore foot of the knee and let down into the keelson.

Fincham shows the keelson finishing abruptly a little aft of the last cant frame floor, followed by a space before the foot of the sternson knee. The knee is further supported by a chock and iron

Victory. *The sternson knee and transom pieces. On the left is the fashion piece with the tenons of the transoms. Note the two transom knees (or sleeper beams) on each side bracing the whole structure.*

29

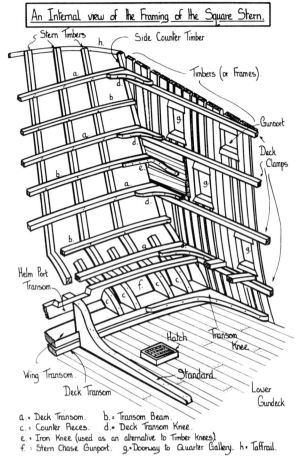

An Internal view of the Framing of the Square Stern.

Stern Timbers · h. · Side Counter Timber · Timbers (or Frames). · Gunport · Deck Clamps · Helm Port Transom · Wing Transom. · Deck Transom · Hatch · Standard. · Transom Knee · Lower Gundeck

a. = Deck Transom.   b. = Transom Beam.
c. = Counter Pieces.   d. = Deck Transom Knee.
e. = Iron Knee (used as an alternative to Timber knees).
f. = Stern Chase Gunport.   g. = Doorway to Quarter Gallery.   h. = Taffrail.

Fig 1/21

knees fitted either side (see Fig 1/20/(4)).

The whole structure was fastened with copper bolts of the same diameter as those that secured the rest of the keelson. They were driven through into the deadwood, their lengths depending on their position (one bolt withdrawn during restoration work on the *Victory* was 6ft long).

The Stern Timbers

The last major part of the ship's framing to be explained is that which formed the stern from above the wing transom to the taffrail. Three separate designs were introduced between 1650 and 1850: the square stern already the standard design in 1650, the circular stern introduced by Seppings in 1819–20 and the elliptical stern, an improved design by Symonds which became the norm after its introduction in 1827.

The weak construction of this type of stern proved a great disadvantage in action. This was due not only to the ornamentation but to the combination of too many lights (windows), galleries, relatively thin framing and light planking. As this part of the ship was known to be vulnerable it became the practice of commanders to lay their vessels broadside across the stern of an enemy ship. The other disadvantage of the square stern was that very few guns could be brought to bear to give protection aft. Usually only two or four stern-chase guns were mounted on the lower gundeck, protruding through ports cut in the lower counter. A temporary provision could be made by moving some of the after guns of each deck to bear aft and firing through ports normally concealed between the stern timbers. This would require the removal of various fittings, and is explained fully in Chapter 8.

The lack of armament aft was of great consequence as early as 1670 during actions against the Barbary Corsairs, who used swift galleys. These vessels were heavily armed both fore and aft and would attack a ship from her undefended sides. Deane introduced a type of vessel that evolved into the galley-frigate which by manoeuvring with its oars could protect its stern.

The stern was built up from a series of upright timbers – six, seven or eight in number, depending on the breadth of the vessel. The upper parts were made from straight oak and the counter timbers below were made from compass oak. Each stern timber can be thus divided into three sections, the lower counter, the upper counter and the stern timber. Each timber was placed equidistantly along the upper edge of the wing transom, those at the outsides being called the side counter timbers. All conformed to the round up and round aft of the wing transom but inclined towards an imaginary centre point above the centreline. The straight parts were also canted aft at an angle of between 70 to 85 degrees from the horizontal.

The lower counters formed the base of the whole of the stern structure, and were made from well seasoned compass oak. They were curved to conform to the round up of the wing transom, and the angle to which they were set inclined towards the centreline. The heel of each lower counter was firmly bolted to the upper edge of the wing transom. The athwartships dimension remained the same throughout its length, while its depth diminished by half towards its head. The heel was the same width as the upper edge of the wing transom.

Before about 1700, the angle to which the lower counter was set was over 60 degrees, and the head of the rudder did not penetrate the ship. Therefore the touch (outer extremity) of the lower counter was nearer to the after perpendicular than on vessels built after that date. In ships built before 1700 the touch was set a distance of approximately one-ninth of the ship's moulded beam aft of the after perpendicular. The height of the touch was one-eighth of the moulded beam above the upper edge of the wing transom, and the radius forming the concave lower surface was approximately one-fifth of the moulded beam.

Generally a lower counter was made in one piece, and was fashioned with a scarph at its head to which the heel of the upper counter was fitted. The length of this flat plain scarph was half the width of the wing transom, and the lips were one-third of the depth of the timber at the head.

The upper counter was set aft of the lower counter, with its touch at a distance of one-quarter of the distance that the lower counter was set aft of the perpendicular. The height at which the touch was set was three-quarters of the height of the lower counter above the lower counter. To ease work and attain greater strength a builder may in some cases have made both counters out of a single timber. This of course would only be done if suitably grained compass oak was available. Regardless of whether the upper counter had been made as a separate item, or combined with the lower counter, a scarph was fashioned at its head to enable the vertical stern timber to be attached.

After 1700 the angle of the counters was reduced so that the rudder head would pass into the ship where it was protected from the weather and enemy shot. The lower counter was set at about 30 degrees to the horizontal, the upper counter at about 60 degrees and the stern timber altered from 70–75 degrees to between 80–85 degrees from the horizontal.

Each scarph was fastened with copper (later iron) bolts, the roves being set into the timber. The heel of the lower counter had to be made specially secure so was also fastened by bolts. Later, towards the end of the eighteenth century, wrought iron straps, or plates and brackets, were used to give additional strength at this point. They were made to a width approximately three-quarters of the width of the lower counter and to a thickness of between 3/4–1 in, and inserted into the timber for half of their thickness. Iron clench bolts were driven through both the wing transom and the counter timber. This is a fine example of the improvements made to strength by the production of iron during the Industrial Revolution.

The sides of the counter timbers usually formed the sides of the stern-chase ports, if fitted. In some cases an additional counter was employed to form one side of a port. This was more common in vessels built with seven stern timbers. It became customary to fit extra counter timbers between the outboard side counter timber and the next timber. This practice seems to have been introduced around 1780. I can only assume that this was intended to give additional strength, and to produce an extra landing for the planking of the counter.

The ships that were built with seven stern timbers, obviously had one set directly on the centreline. This created a problem, for it would obstruct the rudder head and tiller. To overcome this the lower counter timber was omitted. The timber was therefore secured to the helm port transom and additional counter pieces fitted on either side to give strength. These were disposed so that they did not interfere with the motion of the tiller and rudder head. The centreline stern timber was not fitted until helm port transom and other athwartships timbers were fitted. An example of this can be seen on the draught of a 74-gun ship illustrated in Rees' *Naval Architecture*. Fincham shows alternative methods in which counters

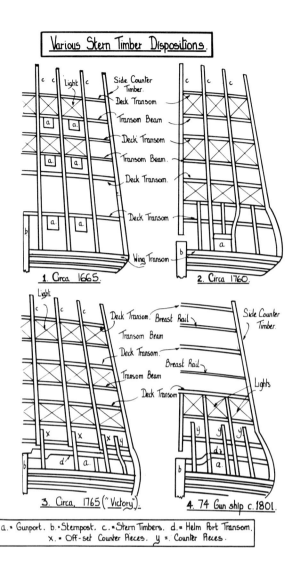

Fig 1/22

are worked from the top edges of the chase port lintels. In all of the above cases, the extra counters were only carried up to where the vertical stern timbers commenced.

The timbers that rose upward from the heads of the upper counters formed the sides of the lights (windows). They were scarphed and bolted to the heads of the upper counters. The siding and width of these timbers were related to the dimensions of the upper counters: their heels were identical to the scantlings of the heads of the upper counters (disregarding the scarph), they then diminished to half of the upper counters' fore and aft dimensions, and at their heads they were two-thirds of the upper counters' athwartships dimensions. The size of the heads of these timbers for vessels built after 1760, can be calculated by multiplying the heel athwartships by the fraction given in brackets. Ship, number of guns (fraction of the heel athwartships) – 110–90 (three-quarters); 84–80 (seven-tenths); 74–60 (six-tenths); 50–44, 38–24, sloops (one half).

Foudroyant. *Captain's day cabin. This view clearly shows the stern counter timbers which are furnished with eyebolts for securing guns. The heavy carlings set in the deckhead are fitted in way of bollards fitted on the deck above. The doorway gives access to the starboard quarter gallery.*

THE HELM PORT TRANSOM

The whole of the stern assembly was braced together by a series of transverse beams known as tie beams, deck hooks and a single stout transom piece called a helm port transom. The latter was so called because it formed the upper boundary of the port through which the rudder head passed. This transverse timber was wrought across the inboard sides of the counter timbers, scores being made at each point of contact so that it could be set in for half of its thickness. Sometimes it was only let in about 1½in to 2in. It was set at a suitable height to form the lintels of the stern-chase gunports.

It would appear that up to 1700 this timber was given a round up and round aft conforming to the lines of the vessel. Prior to 1700, when the angle of the lower counter was larger, the height at which the tiller passed into the ship was greater, and in some cases it may have been necessary to increase the scantling to attain this level, for the distance between the gunports and the helm port was considerable. The height of the helm port transom is well illustrated in Van de Velde's drawing of the *Superbe* and Van de Velde the Elder's sketch of 1648 of the 32-gun *Constant Reformation*.

When the angle of the lower counter changed in 1700, the position of the helm port dropped so much that some vessels had a flattened U-shaped helm port transom. The depth of this timber varied from 12in to 9in, while its fore and aft siding at its upper edge was approximately one and a half times its depth. The after face was bearded away to give a fore and aft width of about three-quarters of its upper width. The helm port transom that is at present fitted on the *Victory* at Portsmouth is completely square in section. Whether the original was similar, I do not know, but it seems likely that it was made square to facilitate restoration. It was apparently more common for seventeenth-century ships to be fitted with the square section type of port helm transom, due to the steeper angle of the

lower counter. Those that were fitted with the U-shaped transom were designed so that the faces of the U were angled to allow free movement of the tiller from side to side. The complex form of the U-shaped transom is shown in Fig 1/23, which is based on the draught of a 74-gun ship as given in Rees' *Naval Architecture*.

The helm port transom was bolted firmly to the counter timbers with iron clench bolts, and later it was reinforced by the wrought iron strapping that also passed over the wing transom.

Throughout the period, the length of the helm port transom was equal to the distance between the frames at that position. Vessels built before 1790 had the timber made to a fore and aft siding of either one and one-fifth or one and two-fifths the distance between the frames at that position, the latter being for the larger ships. In all types of vessel, the depth of the timber was generally half its width. They were usually fashioned with a square cross-section. The size of the helm port transom on ships built after 1700 can be calculated as follows: The proportional size of the timber in the fore and aft plane was as follows:

$$Depth\ of\ the\ keel \times A$$

Ship, number of guns (A) – 110–90 (three-quarters); 84–50 (seven-tenths).

The depth of the timber was proportional to its greatest width. Therefore it can be calculated as:

$$Fore\ and\ aft\ siding \times B$$

Ship, number of guns (B) – 110–90 (two-thirds); 84–50 (four-fifths).

Fig 1/23

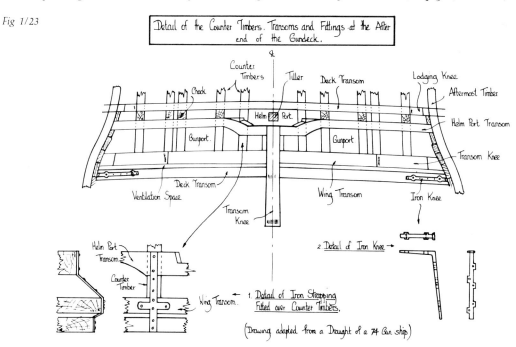

Detail of the Counter Timbers. Transoms and Fittings at the After end of the Gundeck.

(Drawing adapted from a Draught of a 74 Gun ship)

The siding of the lower edge was narrower than that of the upper, so it is proportional to the fore and aft siding of the upper edge:

Siding of the upper face × C

Ship, number of guns (C) – 110–90 (three-quarters); 84–50 (seven-tenths).

The transom was generally supported by a horizontal knee, set with its toe forward. This knee had a depth of approximately seven-eighths of the depth of the helm port transom, and the fore arm had a length of seven thirty-seconds of the ship's moulded beam. The athwartships arm was usually about five-ninths of the length of the fore arm. Bolts were driven through to the cant frames and into the transom, and firmly clenched with roves. To prevent springing, a few bolts were driven vertically through the transom into the wing transom.

THE DECK HOOKS

Above and aft of the helm port transom, a deck hook was fitted which corresponded to the deck above. It was positioned either a little below the 'knuckle' or 'touch' of the upper counter or a little above that of the lower counter. It was set athwartships across the inner faces of the stern timbers. Its width was the same as the deck beams of that deck, but its depth was generally half its width.

The after edge was scored to fit into the stern timbers and therefore was shaped to the same angle as that at the stern. The deck hook was given the appropriate round up for that deck, and the desired round aft to conform to the shape of the stern.

The remaining deck hooks were fitted in a similar manner, one for each deck. The outboard extremities were secured to the ship's side by lodging knees made from oak, and at the turn of the nineteenth century by wrought iron brackets. Iron clench bolts were used to fasten the deck hooks to stern timbers, as well as knees.

When the quarter galleries were set back flush with the stern, at the end of the seventeenth century, the deck hooks were extended through the hull beyond the side counter timbers, to support the galleries. The construction of these galleries will be explained fully in a later chapter. Deck hooks are sometimes referred to as deck transoms, like the one fitted at the after end of the lowest gundeck.

TIE BEAMS

These beams were used, in addition to deck hooks, to stiffen the structure of the stern. Unlike the deck hooks they were fitted directly onto the fore face of the stern timbers, and fayed instead of being scored like the deck hooks. They generally followed the lines

of the sills for the lights or the breast rails of the balconies (if these were fitted). They were fastened with trennals, and later by iron bolts or spikes. The outboard ends were secured to the ship's side by lodging knees, the after faces of which were bearded to correspond to the angle of the stern. At the turn of the nineteenth century these knees were replaced by iron brackets. Like the deck hooks, these timbers did not extend beyond the limits of the hull until the quarter galleries were positioned flush with the stern. The dimensions of these timbers were approximately two-thirds of the width of their appropriate deck, and they were square in section.

The heads of the stern timbers were capped with the taffrail. This capping was made to a width equal to that of the heads of the stern timbers, plus the thickness of the lining planks on either side. Additional support was given to the stern timbers by transom knees fitted to the fore side of the inboard planking, their fore arms extending along the quarterdeck or poop. These knees or 'standards' were firmly bolted to the beam. The standards which braced the fore side of stern timbers are discussed fully in Chapter 2.

PROGRESS TOWARDS THE CIRCULAR STERN 1810–17

Between the years of square stern construction and the introduction of the circular stern, there appears to have been a transitional design, which was the precursor of the Seppings circular stern of 1817. This transitional design eliminated the transom pieces below the waterline and continued the cant frames aft, around to the inner post. The heads of these timbers terminated with a tenon which fitted into mortices cut in the lower edge of the wing transom. The wing transom was also modified, being now fashioned with a greater round aft. This produced a stern with a greater convexity, similar to that of the round bow which had been recently introduced. The advantage of this design was that it greatly reduced the effect of the impact of shot, thus making the lower part of the stern less vulnerable to 'raking fire'.

Set above the wing transom were the counter timbers, which remained similar to those previously used for the old square stern. The only difference was that the lower counter was omitted. Each timber was inclined aft and upward at an angle of approximately 10 degrees and braced in the old manner, with deck transoms and transom beams (see Fig 1/17).

It soon became clear to Seppings that by removing the wing transom completely, and lengthening the cant frames up to the toptimber line, an even stronger stern could be constructed. This meant that the whole stern would be built in the same manner as the ship's broadside.

Unicorn. *The port quarter showing the circular stern introduced by Seppings in 1817 which replaced the old square stern. It was far stronger and more guns could be mounted aft to give a greater arc of fire power.*

THE SEPPINGS CIRCULAR STERN

Before and during his term of office as Surveyor of the Navy (1813–32) Sir Robert Seppings introduced a number of revolutionary techniques in both construction and design. One of his major innovations was the circular stern, first constructed in 1817. The advantages of the circular stern were twofold. Firstly, a complete arc of fire could be achieved, especially at the quarters. Secondly, the overall strength of the structure was far superior to any other stern previously built. By abolishing the long-standing practice of fitting a wing transom, the cant frames could be continued up to the toptimber line. There was generally an even number of full frames within the structure to allow for various features of the overall design. The centre space was solely used for the rudder head and the central light, if fitted. The remaining spaces were used for gunports and doorways to the galleries. This design also made it possible for gunports to be pierced on the quarters of the lower gundeck.

Each of the gunports and doorways (or lights) were constructed in the same manner as those along the broadside. This was achieved by fitting sills and lintels, the ends of which were placed into scores at the side of the full frames. Filling frames were fitted in the normal manner, tenoned into the sills and lintels as required. The whole structure was braced internally by the deck transoms and the waterways, the latter being made of increased scantling. Transom beams were omitted for they would interfere with the entry to the galleries. The senior officers still had well illuminated cabins, even though they had to share them with a number of guns. For the sake of vanity, some captains had chintz covers placed over the guns.

The galleries were constructed by the same basic technique used for the quarter galleries of the old square stern. This involved an upper and lower stool, each of which was built up from a series of baulks of timber, bolted together and fastened to the frames. Between these stools were box-like structures that formed the mullions of the lights. These were constructed from vertical timbers about 4in thick and 10in wide. These 'boxes' were furnished with the appropriate ledges and window frames. The outboard side was planked up as required. In plan view these box-like projections varied. In some cases they were semi-circular and in others three-sided. Each gallery served a specific function. Most were used as the captain's or officers' heads and were fitted with water closets, which had been introduced in about 1780.

The gunports on each deck were directly above those of the deck below. The gallery projection generally terminated at the level of the quarterdeck or poop deck. Above this point the deck and the stern were plainly planked, with gunports cut for the stern-chase guns, which were generally carronades.

The whole of the stern structure was thus now made in the same manner as the remainder of the ship's frames. The aftermost frames either side of the centreline were fayed and bolted to the side of the sternport and the inner post. The remaining timbers were bolted and fayed to the deadwood and to the heels of each other. The size of the timbers that formed the frames of Seppings' round-sterned

ships varied very little from those that formed the main part of the hull. The sills and lintels were made to the same thickness as the rest of the frames, and to a depth of between 6in and 12in. Vertical filling frames were set above as in the after parts of the frame. The only part of the construction that proved awkward was at the transition between the aftermost cant frame and the first of the stern timbers. At this point the stern timber had to have its heel set into the lintel of the gunport at the quarter, and its toptimber was tenoned into the after face of the cant frame in question. This produced the desired rake aft for the stern timbers.

The design was unpopular with naval officers, who preferred to have an open gallery to stroll along. Moreover, its overall appearance was not very pleasing to the eye. Because of this it was replaced by the elliptical stern. The 46-gun frigate *Unicorn*, launched in 1824 has a circular stern and is typical of Seppings' designs. She is at present undergoing restoration at Dundee and is open to the public.

THE SYMONDS ELLIPTICAL STERN

This was a modified version of the circular stern, first introduced in 1827 by Captain William Symonds. It gave the stern more graceful lines, and made possible the return of the stern walks and galleries that were popular with the officers. This style of stern was not, however, fully recognised until Symonds became Surveyor of the Navy in 1832.

If a stern walk was fitted, it was generally of very light construction, supported with iron brackets bolted to the timbers. The balustrading was made from wrought iron work, some of the pillars being extended to support a light canopy over the gallery which was generally concave. Like the circular stern, the appropriate deck hooks and tie beams (if fitted) were wrought across the inboard faces of the stern timbers to stiffen the whole structure. This was all secured with iron bolts, which were probably of the new type, covered in tin.

The Bow Timbers

THE KNEE OF THE HEAD

The knee of the head was a large bracket protruding from the stem of the ship. It had several functions. Firstly, it gave the bowsprit lashings, known as the gammoning, a rigid foundation. Secondly, it supported the figurehead and its surrounding decoration, and thirdly, the lower ends of the bobstays, which prevented the extremities of the bowsprit from riding up, could be fastened to it. Because of the many changes in fashion that the head was subjected to, I will describe only the construction which was used around 1760.

The knee of the head was derived from the beakhead. This was

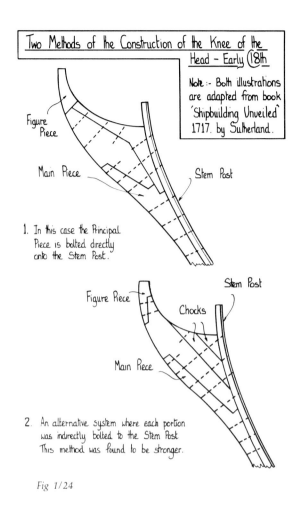

Two Methods of the Construction of the Knee of the Head – Early 18th

Note:- Both illustrations are adapted from book 'Shipbuilding Unveiled' 1717. by Sutherland.

Figure Piece

Main Piece

Stem Post

1. In this case the Principal Piece is bolted directly onto the Stem Post.

Figure Piece

Stem Post

Chocks

Main Piece

2. An alternative system where each portion was indirectly bolted to the Stem Post. This method was found to be stronger.

Fig 1/24

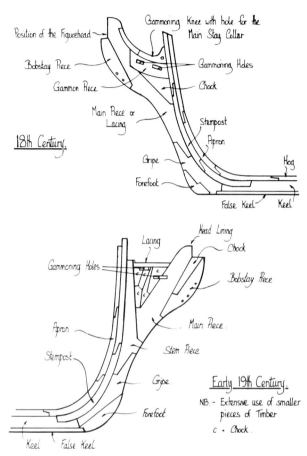

The Knee of the Head

Position of the Figurehead

Gammoning Knee with hole for the Main Stay Collar

Bobstay Piece

Gammoning Holes

Gammon Piece

Chock

Main Piece or Lacing

Stempost

Apron

18th Century.

Gripe

Hog

Forefoot

False Keel

Keel

Head Lining

Lacing

Chock

Gammoning Holes

Bobstay Piece

Apron

Main Piece

Stempost

Stem Piece

Gripe

Early 19th Century.

Forefoot

NB.- Extensive use of smaller pieces of Timber

c - Chock.

Keel

False Keel

Fig 1/25

introduced during the Tudor period when it was very long, low and narrow. By 1750 it had become very much shorter in width, with its height increased so that the top of the head was more or less equal to that of the deck of the forecastle. After this the head itself changed little, except in relation to the surrounding ornamentation, such as head rails. Many of these changes were caused by the introduction of the round bow, the evolution of which started in 1732, but did not become general in all men-of-war until the second decade of the nineteenth century.

The dimensions of the knee of the head were quite considerable, and it was therefore made from a number of sections. It comprised six separate timbers: the lacing; chock piece; gammon piece; gammoning knee; its extension piece, the main (or bobstay) piece; and the gripe. Each piece was oak, cut out in the dead-flat and sawn to its required siding. All the components were fayed and bolted together with copper clenches or secured by trennals.

The lacing was the largest component. It extended from just below the waterline to the after edge of the bobstay piece, where the figurehead was situated. Its after face was fayed and bolted to the stempost, while its top surface supported the chock, gammon piece and gammoning knee. The heel of this timber was fashioned with a scarph to which the gripe was fastened. The chock acted as both a filling piece and as a support to the gammon piece. It was triangular with the hypotenuse edge set forward, fayed and bolted to the lacing, and its after edge was secured to the stem.

The gammon piece was set with its after edge fayed to the stem and its bottom edge to the top surface of the chock. It was rectangular, and pierced with either one or two slots set slightly off the horizontal in the athwartships direction, through which the gammoning passed. The gammoning knee was set with its throat aft, one face being fayed to the stem and the other bolted to the gammon piece. Apart from serving as an anchoring piece for the timbers below, it acted as a brace to ensure that any movement aft was prevented. A hole of approximately 8in diameter was bored through the throat, through which the main forestay collar passed.

The main or bobstay piece was fitted to the fore side of the lacing. It served two functions, acting as a landing for the foot of the figurehead and as a plate to which the bobstays were fastened. The number of holes cut for the bobstays depended on how many were fitted. The gripe was the section that extended from the heel of the

37

Unicorn. *Close-up of the spacing between the timbers, starboard side, forward, showing the 'race' mark 'SALT', which indicated that this timber had been pickled in brine prior to its use. This practice was introduced by Seppings to prevent the premature rotting of frames.*

lacing to the fore lower edge of the keel, where it faired in with the joint of the stem and the keel. The siding of the gripe was increased to that of the keel at its heel, and diminished towards its head. The after edge was fayed and bolted to the stem with copper bolts, the fore face being fashioned with a graceful serpentine curve which was continued to the top of the head. The extent to which the head of the ship projected forward of the stem was between one-tenth and one-twelfth of the length of the ship's gundeck.

After the Framing

Once the ship was completed 'in frame' it was the normal practice to leave the hull to season and settle. During this period the shipwrights would keep a constant check on the hull form and make good any distortion caused by the drying out of the timbers. Until 1771, there were no regulations governing the length of time the hull had to remain unplanked. Thus ships were often planked on 'green' timber, with the result that rot set in. In 1771 First Lord of the Admiralty, the Earl of Sandwich, visited Chatham Dockyard where he 'went on board the *Ardent*, found here in a total decay, her timber and planks rotted almost universally; this ship built at Hull in the year 1764 and never was at sea, her prime cost was £23,000, and her repairs are now estimated at £17,000'.

It is significant that on 4 February 1771 the Naval Board issued an order that all hull frames were to be left unplanked for a year, so that the timbers should settle down without distortion.

CHAPTER 2

The Planking of a Ship of War

Before discussing in detail the various types and methods of planking a brief account of the order in which it was fitted to the ship's frame is necessary. In order to follow this account, refer to Figs 2/1 and 2/2.

The internal planking was fitted first, starting from the lowest part of the ship and working upwards. As the planking reached deck level, the beams of that deck and its associated knees were fitted before continuing. The main wale and its counterparts were fitted at the same time. The limber strake was wrought first. It was set a small distance out from the keelson. Next the footwaling was fitted, followed by a fore and aft stringer, made in the same manner as the footwaling, and set over the heads of the floor timbers. At the level of the lowest deck (generally the orlop), timber of greater scantling was worked fore and aft, onto which the ends of the beams were set. This structure was referred to as the beam shelf, or the deck clamp. The beams for the orlop were laid next, and secured to the ship's timbers, or frames. Beam shelves were then wrought as necessary at deck levels throughout the ship, and the beams fitted. Over the beams a waterway was fastened, followed by the spirketting which consisted of a number of heavier timbers laid parallel to the wales. Again this was continued throughout the ship. Finally, the spaces left by this internal longitudinal framework were filled in with planking of smaller dimensions, thus completing the 'internal skin'. All the required standards and knees (both hanging and lodging) were then inserted, giving rigidity to the beams.

The external planking from the keel upward consisted of the following: the garboard strake, the bottom planking, the diminishing strake (or thick stuff as it is sometimes called), the main wale, and similar strakes at each deck level with thinner ship's side planking between them.

Internal Planking after 1700

THE LIMBER STRAKE

The limber strake was the lowest internal planking in the ship. It was set at a given distance abeam of the keelson between the fore magazine and the fish room. From this position it was brought in towards the keelson until the space separating them was half that in amidships. The distance between the limber strake and the keelson in midships was 12in on a First Rate, and 9in on a Fifth Rate. In most cases two strakes were laid, but this was reduced to one during the first 30 years of the nineteenth century.

The first strake fitted on a 100-gun ship was approximately 1ft 3in wide and 8in thick, each plank being about 25ft long. Plain flat scarphs, secured with oak trennals joined the planks. The second strake was smaller: about 1ft 2in wide and 6in thick and the planks were the same length as those of the first strake, although the scarphs were given shift of half their length in that strake.

From the table overleaf the approximate width and thickness of both strakes of planking can be calculated by taking the moulding of the keel as the constant figure and multiplying that by the given figures.

Each strake was reduced to a third of its width at the fore and after ends. The first strake had a groove cut in its top surface, about 2in deep and wide, into which the limber board was fitted. This board was set across the channel between the keelson and the first strake of the limber strake. Its purpose was to prevent rubbish entering the channel, which acted as a fore and aft drainage gully, and was generally known as the limber passage. The limber boards were made in short lengths, to allow for easy removal.

The outboard edge of the second strake was chamfered to fair in with the footwaling, the next layer of planking. The *Foudroyant* at

The Limber Strake Planking

No of guns	First strake		Second strake	
	Width	Depth	Width	Depth
100	0·75	0·40	0·70	0·30
90	0·82	0·41	0·72	0·30
84–80	0·80	0·41	0·72	0·34
74–70	0·80	0·41	0·60	0·36
64–60	0·82	0·41	0·70	0·35
50–44	0·86	0·40	0·80	0·36
38	0·86	0·43	0·80	0·36
36	0·86	0·40	0·80	0·30
32	0·92	0·35	0·86	0·285
28	0·88	0·33	0·88	0·26
24	0·92	0·31	0·85	0·27
Sloop	0·92	0·27	0·83	0·25
Armed cutter	0·95	0·39	0·95	0·32

Portsmouth has only one limber strake. This is probably because she was built outside England at a time of great change in shipbuilding methods. (See the bottom drawing in Fig 2/1). *Victory's* limber strake appears to be made up of two pieces, each 8in wide. This may be another method of construction but it is more likely that it was related to the size of timber available for her restoration.

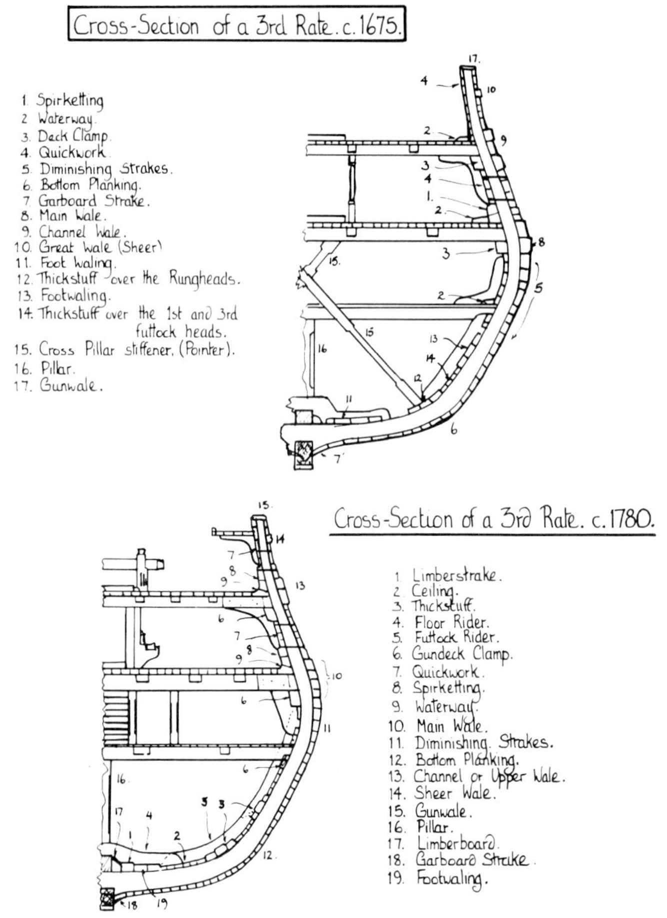

THE FORE AND AFT LONGITUDINALS (OR STRINGERS)

According to the *Shipbuilder's Repository* of 1789, these longitudinals were called 'the thick stuff at the floorheads' (or at the first futtock heads). This band of planking of gradually increased scantling was worked fore and aft over the heads of the timbers, or frames, in order to give additional strength to the joints. Most ships had five strakes, except in sloops and armed cutters, which had three.

The centre plank was of the greatest width and depth, and was laid directly over the floorhead joints. The planks above and below were of progressively reduced scantling. For example, a 36-gun ship had the following dimensions: the centre strake was 15in wide and 6in thick, the strake above and below that was 12in wide and 5½in thick and the outer strakes above and below were 11in wide and 4½in thick.

The tables that follow give the keel moulding as the known dimension. To calculate the strake dimensions multiply the moulding of the keel, taken from the sheer draught, by the figures given, then round off to the nearest half inch.

The Strake Laid Over the Joints of the Floorheads

No of guns	100–80	74–50	44–36	32–24	Sloop and armed cutter
Width	0·88	0·86	0·97	1·00	1·00
Depth	0·48	0·47	0·41	0·38	0·35

Cross-Section of a 3rd Rate. c.1675.

1. Spirketting
2. Waterway.
3. Deck Clamp.
4. Quickwork.
5. Diminishing Strakes.
6. Bottom Planking.
7. Garboard Strake.
8. Main Wale.
9. Channel Wale.
10. Great Wale. (Sheer)
11. Foot Waling.
12. Thickstuff over the Rungheads.
13. Footwaling.
14. Thickstuff over the 1st and 3rd futtock heads.
15. Cross Pillar stiffener. (Pointer).
16. Pillar.
17. Gunwale.

Cross-Section of a 3rd Rate. c.1780.

1. Limberstrake.
2. Ceiling.
3. Thickstuff.
4. Floor Rider.
5. Futtock Rider.
6. Gundeck Clamp.
7. Quickwork.
8. Spirketting.
9. Waterway.
10. Main Wale.
11. Diminishing Strakes.
12. Bottom Planking.
13. Channel or Upper Wale.
14. Sheer Wale.
15. Gunwale.
16. Pillar.
17. Limberboard.
18. Garboard Strake.
19. Footwaling.

Fig 2/1

The Strakes Laid Above and Below the Floorhead Joints

No of guns	100–80	74–50	44–36	32–24	Sloop and armed cutter
Width	0·65	0·74	0·80	1·00	1·00
Depth	0·47	0·46	0·37	0·38	0·30

The Outer Strakes Above and Below

No of guns	100–80	74–50	44–36	32–24
Width	0·65	0·68	0·74	0·90
Depth	0·42	0·38	0·30	0·30

By 1820 the number of strakes had been reduced from five to four, with a space for ventilation running down the centre. This is shown in Fig 2/4. This also applied to the thick stuff that was wrought over the first futtock heads.

In a similar way, strakes of heavier planking were wrought across the joints of the first futtock heads. Here only three strakes were used, the centre one being set directly over the joints of the timbers

The Middle Strake Fitted Over the First Futtock Head Joints

No of guns	100–80	74–50	44–36	32–34	Armed cutter
Plank width as a proportion of keel depth	seventeen-twentieths	five-sixths	equal	equal	equal
Plank thickness as a proportion of plank width	half	two-fifths	one-third	one-third	one-third

The Strakes Above and Below the Middle Strake

No of guns	100–80	74–50	44–36	32–34	Armed cutter
Plank width as proportion of keel depth	three-quarters	thirteen-seventeenths	four-fifths	eleven-twelfths	eleven-twelfths
Plank thickness as a proportion of plank width	five-tenths	two-fifths	one-third	one-third	one-third

(except in sloops). A 28-gun ship of around 1780 had the centre strake made to the following scantling: 14in wide and 4½in thick, while the strakes above and below were 12in wide and 3½in thick.

The thickness of the strakes that were worked over the floorheads and first futtock heads was diminished towards the fore and after ends, to approximately half. All the planking was secured to the timbers with oak trennals, the manner depending on the builder and current practice. The butts of the planks were usually fastened together by plain flat scarphs. It was quite normal for the thick stuff laid over the floorheads to be worked in the anchor stock, or top and butt style, because there were two strakes either side of the middle strake. Provision was made for the extra width of the planks, the overall width of both strakes being equal to that used in the normal planking method.

With the introduction of the trussed frame in the second quarter of the nineteenth century, these methods of stiffening the hull were superseded, although longitudinals were still laid in the same areas. This will be explained in more detail later in the text.

THE DECK CLAMPS (OR BEAM SHELVES)

A deck clamp was a thick band of planking that was wrought fore and aft with the sheer of its appropriate deck. It was made in two strakes, its upper edge bevelled to the round up of the deck beams it supported, while its lower edge was square to the planking below. The top edge had to be carefully positioned and was set down the thickness of the deck planking and the depth of the beam that supported that deck, indicated by the lines that were 'screeved' on the inside faces of the timbers. Where the clamps fitted over the gunports, the inboard face was given a chamfer for half its depth and about 1in proud of the plank below, except directly over the ports, where the gun muzzles were housed when not in use. The butts of the planks were fastened to the timbers with trennals and iron dumps. The planks were secured along their lengths with trennals to every other timber. With the introduction of iron knees, the make-up of the deck clamp altered. There were three methods: the upper strake was laid at right angles to the lower strake, or the whole timber was fashioned with a curved inner face, or a combination of both the former was used. Firstly I will explain the type of deck clamps used on ships before the advent of iron knees.

The Orlop Deck Clamps

Not all ships were constructed with an orlop deck. This deck was built between the bottom of the hold and the lower gundeck on the larger ships, and below the berthing deck on the larger frigates. Ships of 28 guns and less, however, did not have sufficient room to have an orlop and therefore were constructed with a series of platforms, the deck levels of which varied according to the amount of space available within the hull.

Unlike the other decks, on the orlop deck the thickness of the deck planking did not have to be taken into consideration when laying off the position of the clamp, for the orlop planking was set down flush with the top edge of the beams. The other difference was that the orlop did not usually extend the full length of the ship. Thus the clamps on each side of the ship were wrought between the apron and the fashion piece, which was usually the position of the fore bulkhead of the bread room. The following table gives the approximate proportion of the upper strake in relation to the moulding of the keel. The lower strake was by 'rule of thumb' 2in narrower and 1in thinner than its counterpart above.

The Width of the Upper Strake Plank

No of guns	Fraction of keel depth	No of guns	Fraction of keel depth
120–90	four-fifths	44–36	five-sixths
84, 74, 70	five-sixths	32	equal
64–60	four-fifths		

The Thickness of the Upper Strake Plank

No of guns	Fraction of plank width	No of guns	Fraction of plank width
120–44	half	32	three-tenths
38–36	two-fifths		

As the orlop deck clamp reached the apron forward, and the fashion piece aft, the scantling of the planks was reduced to fair in with the rest of the planking. The width of each strake was decreased by 5in and the thickness by 3in in the First, Second and Third Rates. The width of Fourth and Fifth Rates was reduced by 3in and the thickness by half.

The Gundeck Clamps

The gundeck clamps were wrought in the same manner as those of the orlop, except that the beams they supported were of greater scantling, and because the weight of the heaviest armament had to be taken into account there were more strakes. First, Second, Third and Fourth Rate ships had three strakes and the Fifth and Sixth Rates, two.

Each plank was between 25ft and 30ft long, scarphed together by a hook and butt, the length of which varied between 3ft 8in on the First Rates and 2ft 6in on a 24-gun ship. Each was secured to the ship's timbers with iron dumps and trennals. Small bolts were used for securing the lips of the scarphs. The number of strakes was reduced to two or one at the fore and after ends at the fashion piece stations and at the apron, where the thickness was also reduced. The planks' full thickness began at a specific distance from the extremities, the following list giving these points from the fore and after ends. Ship, number of guns (distance as a fraction of gundeck length) – 100 (one-fifteenth); 90 and 84 (one-sixteenth); 74 (one-seventeenth); 64 (one-sixteenth); 44 (one-fifteenth); 38 and 38 (one-sixteenth); 32, 28 and 24 (one-fifteenth).

The width of the upper strake of planking was seven-eighths of the moulding of the keel for First Rate ships, fifteen-sixteenths for Second and Third Rates, and the same as the depth of the keel for the remaining classes. The thickness of the plank was approximately half of its width in the First, Second and Third Rates, and three-eighths for the remaining Rates.

The second strake was secured in the same manner as the upper strake, except that the butts were given a shift of one-third of the length of the plank when three strakes were used, and half the length of the plank when two strakes were employed.

The second strakes were about 2½in narrower and 1in thinner than the upper strakes, on First, Second, Third and larger Fourth Rates. The strakes of 38-, 36- and 32-gun ships were 1in narrower and thinner and on 28- and 24-gun ships they were 2in narrow and thinner. The third strake on ships of two decks or more was 1in less wide and thick than the corresponding second strakes.

The Middle Gundeck Clamps

The only ships with a middle gundeck were those that carried 90 guns or more, with the exception of ships with 80 guns on three decks built between 1694 and 1758. Each clamp was generally made from two strakes of oak planking and wrought fore and aft, each plank between 24 and 28ft long. It was usually worked in top and butt fashion. The width of the complete strake was the distance between the top of the gunports and the position of the lower edge of the beams that the clamp supported. The strake was approximately 2in thinner than the upper strake of the lower deck clamp. The bottom edge was bearded to the width of the plank below or to 1in less. Sometimes it was only wrought in one strake, the width and thickness being the same as if wrought in two strakes. The planks were joined together with a plain flat scarph about 3ft 6in long. Each scarph was fastened with two iron bolts driven vertically.

The Upper Deck Clamps

Like the middle deck clamps, each was made from either one or two strakes of oak. If just on a single strake, the planks were joined together by either a plain flat, or hook and butt scarph. The scarph was fastened together with two bolts driven vertically through the lips of the joint. The bolts varied between ½ and 1in diameter. If the clamp was made from two strakes, it was planked in the top and butt fashion. In both cases the planking was fastened to the ship's timbers with iron dumps and trennals. The lower half was bearded (or chamfered) reducing the thickness by 1in.

The following list gives the width of the clamp in relation to the moulding of the keel. Their thickness was in all cases half the width of the plank. Ship, number of guns (proportion of the keel depth) – 100 (five-eighths); 90, 84, 74 (nine-sixteenths); 64, 46 (five-eighths); 38, 36 (eleven-sixteenths); 32, 28 (nine-sixteenths); 24, sloop, cutter (seventeen thirty-seconds).

The Quarterdeck and Forecastle Clamps

Like the others, this type of clamp was made from either one or two strakes of oak planking. Due to the relatively small width of clamp necessary at this deck level, the builder probably made the clamp in a single strake. This economized on both timber and man-hours. As with all the other deck clamps, the planks would be scarphed together and fastened with two bolts driven vertically. If the clamp was made from two strakes it may have been constructed in the top and butt method in which the lower edge was bearded, diminishing the thickness of the strake by 1in on the First and Second Rates, ¾in on the Third and larger Fourth rates and ½in on the smaller vessels. The overall thickness of the plank was one-third of the width. The width was generally the distance between the top of the gunports of the deck below and the bottom edge of where the beams met the

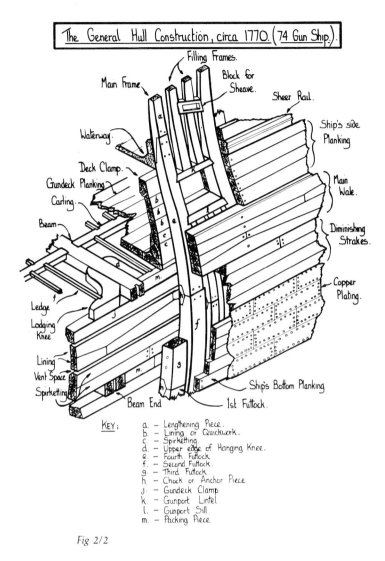

The General Hull Construction, circa 1770. (74 Gun Ship).

KEY;

a. – Lengthening Piece.
b. – Lining or Quickwork.
c. – Spirketting.
d. – Upper edge of Hanging Knee.
e. – Fourth Futlock.
f. – Second Futlock.
g. – Third Futlock.
h. – Chock or Anchor Piece.
J. – Gundeck Clamp.
k. – Gunport Lintel.
l. – Gunport Sill.
m. – Packing Piece.

Fig 2/2

ship's side. The figures in the following list illustrate the relationship between the width of the plank and the depth of the keel. Ship, number of guns (proportion of the keel depth) – 100–74 (eleven-sixteenths); 64 (three-quarters); 44–24 (thirteen-sixteenths); sloop (three-quarters).

The Roundhouse Clamps

These clamps were only employed on ships that were constructed with a roundhouse (also known as the poop deck or coach). Sometimes a deck was built above the poop, a fashion that only existed for a short time during the second quarter of the eighteenth century on First Rates. A fine example can be seen on the model of the *Victory* of 1737 (often called 'Balchen's *Victory*', after the Admiral on board when the ship foundered in the English Channel in 1744, with the loss of all hands). This deck was very short compared to the quarterdeck. It was known as the topgallant roundhouse or poop royal.

Each roundhouse clamp was usually wrought in a single strake and mostly in one length. The width of the plank was five-eighths of the depth of the keel on First Rate ships, and three-quarters on all other types. The thickness was one-third of the width of the plank, which was bearded on its lower edge, which decreased the thickness by 1in. It was fastened to the ship's timbers with bolts of ¾in diameter, one driven in below each beam and one between them.

THE STRINGER AT THE WAIST

Where the forecastle and quarterdeck clamps terminated at the ends of their respective decks it was found necessary to continue a fore and aft timber to stiffen the frames of the ship. Thus a strake of planking known as a stringer was worked between the clamps. Its width was identical to that of the clamps, but it was not the same thickness. Generally it was 1in or ½in thinner than the adjacent clamp. Likewise it would be made in either one or two strakes, being wrought top and butt, or from normal straight planking. It was locked to the clamps at either end by a hook and butt scarph. The side of the plank that was fayed to the timbers was scored so that it could be placed between them and secured with iron bolts of between ⅞ and ⅝in diameter. In earlier ships oak trennals were used for fastening stringers to the timbers.

The reason that the stringer was thinner than the other clamps was that it did not have to be load-bearing, as no beams were fitted across the waist. With the introduction of skid beams on which the ships boats were stowed, and the gradual closing of the waist, it became necessary to dispense with the stringer and merge the forecastle clamps with those of the quarterdeck, thus forming a continuous deck clamp.

Once all the supporting arrangements for the beams had been fitted into the ship, the beams themselves were laid at the desired positions and secured. The lodging and hanging knees were fitted after the remaining inner planking had been placed.

THE WATERWAYS

The waterway was a strake of specially fashioned plank worked fore and aft along each side of the ship across the ends of the deck beams. It is debatable whether the waterways should be categorised as part of the deck planking or as a part of the ship's side planking. I would tend to opt for the latter. The function of the waterway was to form a watertight seal between the side of the ship and the deck. If water was able to enter at this vulnerable area of the ship's structure both the ends of the beams and the ship's timbers to which they were joined would become rotten.

The waterway's cross-section changed over the years, from a concave form to a larger convex edged plank. The depth of the plank was usually the same as the thickness of the 'spirketting' fitted above it, while its width was about one-third greater than the spirketting. The only deck that the waterway was not fitted to was the orlop, because this deck was below the waterline. The following figures give a fair estimate of the size of waterways of ships that were built around 1770.

Approximate Size of Waterways on Vessels Built in about 1770

No of guns	Lower gundeck	Middle gundeck	Upper gundeck	Quarter-deck	Forecastle	Round-house
			(all dimensions in inches)			
100	5	4½	5½	4	4	4½
90	5½	4	5½	4	4	4
84	5½	–	5	4½	4½	4
74	5½	–	5	4½	4½	4
64	5	–	4½	4½	4½	4
44	5	–	4½	4	4	–
38	4*	–	4½	4	4	–
36	4*	–	4½	4	4	–
32	4*	–	4½	4	4	–
28	3¾*	–	4	3¾	3¾	–
24	3½*	–	4	3¾	3¾	–
Sloop	–	–	3¾	3	3	–
Cutter	–	–	3¾	–	–	–

*The figures given above do not apply to the lower gundeck, but to the berthing deck, which was below the gundeck where the crew were accommodated on such vessels.

THE SPIRKETTING

Like the deck clamps and the external wales, the spirketting served to stiffen the ship longitudinally, and to brace the timbers. Generally it was wrought fore and aft, with two strakes of planking worked between the waterways and the sills of the gunports. The sheer of this strake normally conformed to that of the wale at that deck. Because of this, the gunports at the fore and after ends cut into the upper edge of the top strake of planking.

Extreme care was taken when laying each plank, so that the butt of each was given a good shift away from the gunport, and the butts in each strake gave a good shift towards each other. Each plank was scarphed to the next by a hook and butt joint, with a bolt driven vertically through the lips of the scarph. Each plank was made as long as possible, the length of the scarph being about 2ft, with 4in lips and 6in shoulders. The seam between the lower strake and the waterway was caulked with oakum and payed with tar.

By about 1820, when the waterway below had increased in its scantling, it was only necessary to have one strake of spirketting. I have not given any widths for the planks, as this depended on the height to be built up. However, the data below will give a reasonable idea of the thickness of the planks at each deck. On most ships the thickness was diminished by between ½in and 1in at the top plank's upper edge, or the inboard edge was bearded. (See Fig 2/3.)

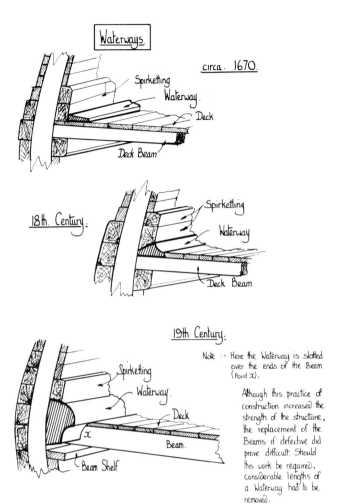

Fig 2/3

The Spirketting of the Lower Gundeck   Ship, number of guns (fraction of the keel depth) – 100–84 (five-sixteenths); 74–64 eleven thirty-seconds); 44 (three-eighths); 38 (one-third); 36 (five-sixteenths) 32–34 (nine thirty-seconds). The spirketting of the middle gundeck was five-sixteenths of the depth of the keel, in all ships fitted with a middle deck.

The Spirketting of the Upper Gundeck   Ship, number of guns (fraction of the keel depth) – 100–90 (seven thirty-seconds); 84 (one-quarter); 74 (nine thirty-seconds); 64 (one-quarter); 44–24, sloop and armed cutter (nine thirty-seconds).

The Spirketting of the Quarterdeck and the Forecastle   Ship, number of guns (fraction of the keel depth) – 100–90 (seven thirty-seconds); 84 (one-quarter); 74 (nine thirty-seconds); 64 (one-quarter); 44–24, sloop and armed cutter (nine thirty-seconds).

Some builders did employ the top and butt and occasionally the anchor stock, methods of planking when two strakes were used.

Egmont. *The after body showing the keelson, sternson limberstrakes, thick stuff and deck clamps. The heavy internal frames are the floor and futtock riders. Also visible are the mainmast step and the crutches, one of which is adapted to form the mizzen step. The wing transom, the helm port transom and their associated transom knees can also be seen.*

COMPLETING THE INTERNAL PLANKING

With the completion of the limber strakes, the thick stuff, deck clamps, waterways and the spirketting, there were just two types of planking to be fitted to finish the internal planking. These were the footwaling in the hold and the quickwork that lined the bulwarks of the gundecks.

The Footwaling

Unlike the rest of the planking that formed the 'inner skin' of the ship, the footwaling was often made from pitch pine. The first band was laid between the limber strakes and the thick stuff over the floor heads; the next was between the thick stuff at the floor heads and the thick stuff at the first futtock heads, and so on up to the orlop (or berthing deck) clamps. The number and width of the boards used varied from builder to builder, but it seems that a width of 9in was the average, some of the planks being thinner due to the lack of space. All were fastened with trennals, the butts being given as good a shift as possible. The thickness of the boards can be roughly estimated as half the thickness of the limber strakes for most ships, and about five-eighths on the smaller vessels. Towards the forward and after ends of the hold the lay of the planks was made to diminish in width so that they could be worked to the curvature formed by the rise of the floors. It can be seen in Fig 2/4 of the *Foudroyant* that in places small gaps were left between strakes to allow for the ventilation of the timbers. A small air flow between the timbers helped to prevent rot.

The Quickwork (or Lining)

The quickwork was the planking that formed the internal skin of the ship throughout the gundecks, and orlop and berthing deck, if fitted. Like the footwaling it was normally made from pitch pine, its lightness being ideal for the upperworks of the ship. This planking was often referred to as the lining. (See Figs 2/1 and 2/2.)

The Lining of the Orlop and the Berthing Deck The quickwork of the orlop was usually only a few strakes wide, as the height of this deck did not leave room for a wide band. I have come across three methods of planking: top and butt, anchor stock, and the normal straight butt fashion. The strakes varied between 10in and 15in in width and between 6in and 8in in thickness. Each plank was secured by bolts at the ends and by trennals between. The top and bottom edges did not always fay to the deck clamps or the spirketting, for a ventilation space of about 1½in to 3in was generally left.

The Lining of the Lower Gundeck Usually four and in some cases five strakes of planking were used here. They were normally wrought and fastened with bolts and trennals as on the orlop or berthing deck. The width of the planks varied with the number of the strakes, and the space between the spirketting and the deck clamp. The thickness of the planks in relation to the thickness of the spirketting was as follows: Ship, number of guns (fraction of thickness of spirketting) – 100 (nine-sixteenths); 90 (five-eighths); 84 and 74 (nine-sixteenths); 64 (seventeen thirty-seconds); 38 and 36 (five-eighths); 32 (three-quarters); 28 (five-eighths); 24 (three-quarters).

The Lining of the Middle Gundeck The quickwork on this deck was wrought in the same manner as that of the lower gundeck, the thickness of the planks being nine-sixteenths of the thickness of the spirketting.

The Lining of the Upper Gundeck This deck was lined in a similar manner to the other decks. The thickness of the strakes varied, and it can be seen how they compared with their respective spirketting in the following list: Ship, number of guns (fraction of thickness of spirketting) – 100–90 (five-eighths); 84–74 (seventeen thirty-seconds); 64 (nine-sixteenths); 44–36 (seven-sixteenths); 32–28 (half); 24 (nine-sixteenths); sloop (half); cutter (two-thirds).

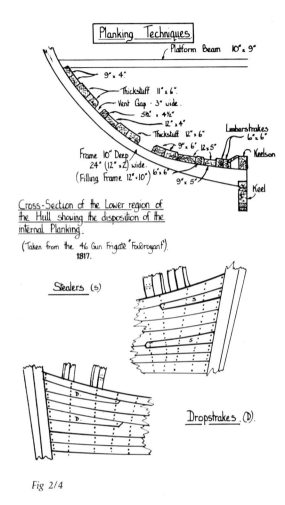

Cross-Section of the Lower region of the Hull showing the disposition of the internal Planking.
(Taken from the 46 Gun Frigate 'Foudroyant')
1817.

Fig 2/4

Unicorn. Starboard side of the fore platform outboard of the main magazine showing the diagonal iron rider plates, the beam shelf and the deck clamp of the berthing deck above. The two bands of thick stuff are wrought in top and butt fashion. This 'wing' served as the boatswain's store.

INTERNAL PLANKING 1650–1700

The manner in which these planks were laid and secured is covered in the section on internal planking after 1700. This section is thus in list form, giving the proportional sizes of planks in comparison to the depth of the keel, or to the given width of the plank in question. Any unusual features in the method of fastening are described.

The estimated proportions are calculated from figures in Deane's *Doctrine of Naval Architecture, 1670,* edited by Brian Lavery. Lavery's work also includes a contract written by Christopher Pett in 1664, giving details for the building of a number of Third Rate ships. Since this gives specific dimensions, I include some of these details, calculated proportionally, in a list in each section.

The Thick Stuff at the Floorheads

This was laid in three strakes, including the strake nearest to the keelson later known as the limber strake. No details are given in Deane's *Doctrine* for the width of these planks, therefore the following list gives thickness only. Ship, rate (proportion of keel depth) – First and Second (half); Third (seventeen thirty-seconds); Fourth (half); Fifth (fifteen thirty-seconds); Sixth (three-tenths). The Christopher Pett contract states that on Third Rates of 1666 the plank width was approximately seventeen thirty-seconds of the keel depth, but unless the planking was of square section I can only assume that this really applies to the plank's thickness, and corresponds to the list above.

The Footwaling

Four strakes were laid above the first band of thick stuff. No detail on the width is given in Deane's *Doctrine*, but this can be estimated from the distance between the strakes of thick stuff over the floorheads and over the first futtock heads. The thickness of the footwaling was as follows: Ship, rate (proportion of keel depth) – First (eleven thirty-seconds); Second (seven-twentieths); Third (three-eighths); Fourth (eleven thirty-seconds); Fifth (seven-twentieths); Sixth (three-tenths).

The thickness of the plank in the Third Rate of 1666 is not given. Therefore it can be assumed it was identical to that given above. The width of the plank was one and one-fifth of the depth of the keel. The number of strakes laid was six. Thus one can either assume that these planks were narrower, or that the distance between the strakes of thick stuff was greater – this would have been governed by the 'turn of the bilge'.

The Thick Stuff over the Futtock Heads

This was laid in either two or three strakes. Ship, rate (proportion of keel depth) – First (seven-sixteenths); Second (two-fifths); Third (thirteen thirty-seconds); Fourth (three-eighths); Fifth (two-sevenths).

This strake was not used on Sixth Rates, due to the position of the futtock heads at the line of the main wale. The width of plank for a Third Rate ship of 1666 was approximately fifteen thirty-seconds of the depth of the keel, while its thickness was the same as that given in the list above.

The Footwaling (Second Band)

This was laid in two strakes above the thick stuff, over the futtock heads. According to Deane the thickness of this planking was identical to the thick stuff (see the previous list). This layer of footwaling was wrought in Sixth Rate ships, and was made to a thickness of seven thirty-seconds of the depth of the keel (as no thick stuff was laid this proportion was not given in the above list). The figures given for a Third Rate ship of 1666 are: width, seventeen thirty-seconds of the depth of the keel; thickness, three-quarters of its width.

The Opening Strake

I believe this entry in Deane's *Doctrine* refers to the deck clamp for the orlop deck, for the measurements of this strake conform to those of a clamp. Although Deane does not state whether the measurement he gives is for the width or thickness of the strake I am certain that he is referring to its width. The depth of the opening strake was as follows: Ship, rate (proportion of keel depth) – First (half); Second (nine-twentieths); Third (fifteen thirty-seconds); Fourth (seven-sixteenths); Fifth (three-sevenths); Sixth (not applicable).

On the Third Rate of 1666 the width of the opening strake was about seventeen thirty-seconds of the depth of the keel, while the thickness was approximately half its width.

The Gundeck Clamp

This was laid in one strake, the width being two-thirds of the depth of the keel for the First, Second and Third Rates, and half of the depth of the keel for the remaining vessels. The figures for a Third Rate of 1666 correspond exactly with Deane's, and therefore need no further mention. The thickness of the plank was as follows: Ship, rate (proportion of the keel depth) – First and Second (half); Third (seventeen thirty-seconds); Fourth (half); Fifth (three-sevenths); Sixth (three-tenths).

The Spirketting

Deane only gives an entry about the gundeck spirketting but we can assume that this also applies to the decks above. During this period spirketting was generally called the 'spirkett rising'. The present name was adopted just before the turn of the eighteenth century. This band of planking was wrought in two strakes, the planks being joined by a Flemish scarph (an early name for a hook and butt scarph) and tabled into each other. The width was made as desired, to be worked up to the sills of the gunports. The thickness of these timbers was as follows: Ship, rate (proportion of the keel depth) – First (one-third); Second (three-tenths); Third (three-tenths); Fourth (one-quarter); Fifth (nine thirty-seconds); Sixth (seven thirty-seconds).

The proportional figures for a Third Rate of 1666 are: width, about fifteen-sixteenths of the depth of the keel; thickness of the plank, approximately nine thirty-seconds of its own width. This refers to the spirketting of the upper deck, and states that the width of each strake is one and one-eighth of the depth of keel, and the thickness is about three-sixteenths of its own width. Generally only one strake was wrought, the joints being the same as those employed for the spirketting of the gundeck.

The Lining

Deane gives no figures for the width of this planking. Therefore it can be assumed that four strakes were laid, the width of each being approximately one-quarter of the distance between the upper edge of the spirketting and the lower edge of the deck clamp. This planking was relatively thin. The lining of the middle and lower gundeck was the following width: Ship, rate (proportion of keel depth) – First (one-fifth); Second (Three-twentieths); Third (three-sixteenths); Fourth (five thirty-seconds); Fifth and Sixth (three-sixteenths).

The thickness of the upper gundeck planking was as follows, in relation to the depth of the keel: Ship, rate (proportion of keel depth) – First (one-seventh); Second (three-twentieths); Third (one-eighth).

The only reference to the thickness of the lining for a Third Rate

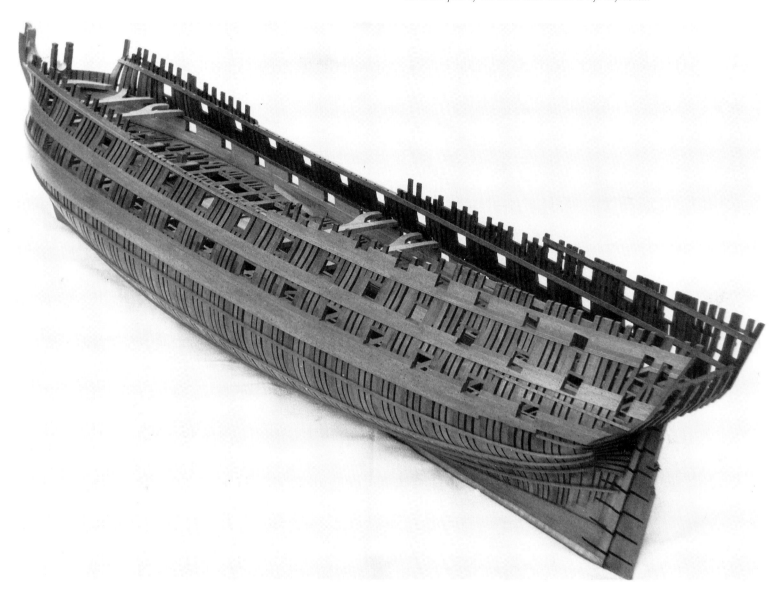

Egmont. *A general view of the model's framing. The main and channel wales are wrought fore and aft, binding the structure longitudinally. Note the hook scarph on the lower part of the main wale which is left unfinished.*

vessel of 1666 is that it was one-fifth of the depth of the keel.

The Deck Clamps

According to Deane, those of the middle gundeck of a First and Second Rate were nine thirty-seconds of the depth of the keel in thickness. Those of the upper gundeck of a Third, Fourth or Fifth Rate were a quarter of the depth of the keel. Upper gundeck clamps of First and Second Rates had a thickness of seven thirty-seconds of the depth of the keel.

Width and Thickness of the Forecastle and Quarterdeck Clamps as a Proportion of the Depth of the Keel

Ship, rate	Width	Thickness
First	one-fifth	half
Second	one-sixth	four-sevenths
Third	three-eighths	four-sevenths
Fourth	three-sixteenths	two-thirds
Fifth	one-seventh	three-quarters

Width and Thickness of the Coach or Roundhouse Clamps as a Proportion of the Depth of the Keel

Ship, rate	Width	Thickness
First	three-eighths	three-quarters
Second	eleven thirty-seconds	three-quarters
Third	three-eighths	five sixths
Fourth	eleven thirty-seconds	thirteen-sixteenths
Fifth	eleven thirty-seconds	four-fifths
Sixth	one-third	eight-ninths

The only reference made to deck clamps for a Third Rate of 1666, other than those of the gundeck, is of the forecastle and quarterdeck deck clamps, which were square in cross-section, and thirteen thirty-seconds of the depth of the keel.

The Waterways

Those of the lower gundeck were generally three-quarters of the depth of the keel in width and two-fifths of their own width thick, while those of the upper gundecks were two-thirds of the depth of the keel wide.

External Hull Planking after 1700

THE GARBOARD STRAKE

The garboard strake was the lowest line of external planking. It was always made from English straight oak, in lengths of approximately 25ft. Its width was two-thirds of the moulded depth of the keel, while its thickness was three-quarters of its width at the lower edge, and half of that at its top edge. It was not rectangular in cross-section but more of an irregular trapezium. The lower edge was bearded in two planes so that it would fit into the rabbet of the keel. Once this plank was fitted, caulked and payed, the joint was very watertight along the keel (see Fig 2/1).

Normally the garboard was wrought in the straight fashion but a few variations can be found. In Rees' *Naval Architecture* there is a draught showing the disposition of the planking. Here the lower strakes are of the top and butt method. The overall width of the garboard is about 2ft, each strake being 16in wide and butts half of that. The peaks of each were situated at a certain distance from the end of the plank, this being one-quarter of the total length of the plank.

THE BOTTOM PLANKING

There appears to have been some variation in both the method and the type of material used for planking a ship's bottom. The alternative practices, however, do not seem to have been introduced until very late in the eighteenth century.

Between 1650 and 1780, a very straightforward system was employed. Parallel strakes of plank, usually of English straight oak were worked in the normal square butt mode from the garboard strake to the line of the diminishing strakes. Each plank was approximately 25ft long, the butts were set at the frames and secured with clench bolts and trennals. There were several fastening styles, which I will discuss separately. Due to the very bluff shape of the bows, and the expanding area of planking surface at the stern, provision had to be made to prevent the planks from snying*. To achieve this, a drop strake or a series of stealers was worked in with the existing strakes. A stealer was a short length of plank that was wrought between two strakes, allowing those strakes to be bent around the bow to the rabbet in the stem. This was also done at the after end of the ship at the rabbet on the sternpost (see Fig 2/4). A drop strake was used for the same purpose, but was fitted at the top of a particular band of planking. In some cases it would consist of a specially fashioned plank that was of greater width and cut so that it could receive a butt at one side (see Fig 2/4).

The bottom planking was not always oak. There are instances where elm was used. This was probably due to its durability when immersed in salt water for long periods (keels were made from elm). Mr Terry Wallbridge, one of the shipwrights helping with the restoration of the *Victory* points out that the first 12 strakes worked from the garboard were made of elm. This elm was taken to the low waterline, a point that seems to have been significant to the builders. I have also come across other references stating that the first four to six strakes were elm. The width of these planks was between 10in and 12in; the thickness was identical to the top edge of the garboard strake, and remained so until the lower strake of the diminishing strakes.

*The term snying is defined as follows:

W Sutherland, *Shipbuilder's Assistant*, 1711: p 47 'In working up a round buttock of a ship, the lower edge of the planks will have a sudden sny aft.'; p 47 'As much as possible keep your work from extreme snying or cambering.'; p 164 'Snying – an arching upwards where the middle of the plank appears higher than the ends.'

Burney, *Falconers Marine Dictionary*, 1815: 'Snying – among shipwrights, a term used for a circular plank, edgeways, to work into the bow of a ship.'

A Young, *Nautical Dictionary*, 1845: p 288 'In shipbuilding a plank is said to have sny when its upward edge has an upward curve.'

Weale, *The Rudiments of Naval Architecture*, 1850: p 149 'The great sny occasioned in full bows is to be prevented by introducing stealers.'; p 149 'Snying – a term applied to planks when their edges round or curve upward.'; p 152 'Its use is to take out the snying edge.' (This passage refers to the employment of stealers.)

Knight, *Dictionary Mechanical*, 1875: 'The trend of the lines of a ship upwards towards the bow and the stern.' (This dictionary defines snying as similar to what is generally termed 'sheer'.)

An alternative and later method of planking the ship's bottom was as follows: between the garboard strake and the light (or low) waterline the planks of what was sometimes known as east country plank,* were wrought in parallel strakes of between 10in and 11in in width. They were the same thickness as the top edge of the garboard strake. The length of these planks was quite considerable, each being between 30ft and 50ft. The shift of the butts was set at 6ft. This was very important, because of the shift of the butts in conjunction with the lower strake of English oak above.

The planks at the fore and after ends were made from English straight oak because more strength was required for the 'hoods'† to go into the rabbets. Stealers and drop strakes were used at the fore and after ends to prevent snying.

According to Rees it was best to work a double shift for the first strake nearest to the English oak, or to set up the shifts of the topmost strake at a distance of 48ft. Special attention was also given to the position of the butts in the area of the pump inlets (elm tree pumps – see Chapter 5).

The planking between the low waterline and the diminishing strakes was of English straight oak. This would sometimes be wrought in the top and butt method. Each plank was cut to a length of 24ft, or to as near as a frame's centre lay. The overall width of a complete strake (of two planks) of top and butt was in this case 2ft. However, a plank used in the top and butt style was not made to the overall width of the two strakes, but to a width of approximately two-thirds of them (see Fig 2/5).

If the top and butt method was not used, the normal square butt ended boards were employed. This was the general practice until the end of the eighteenth century, although some builders did lay the strakes in top and butt. The only drawback of this method was the wastage of timbers, due to the shape of the planks. Fastening was done in the same manner, with clench bolts and trennals.

THE DIMINISHING STRAKES

These strakes were thus named because the thickness of the complete band tapered, from the main wale to the bottom planking. Two methods were used, depending on the builder and the period. Either top and butt or straight parallel planking was employed, the former from 1780–90, though some builders may have used it earlier. The planks were generally made from English oak. If parallel, they were cut to a length of between 25ft and 30ft and a width of 10in to 12in. When the strakes were wrought in top and butt they were approximately 24ft long, or long enough to ensure the butt was at the centre of the frames, to ensure a firm landing for the butts. In this case the overall width of the strake would be between 20in and 24in (this will be explained later).

*Planking made from timber imported from the Baltic countries and North Eastern Europe.

†The ends of the planks which were received into the rabbet.

A number of calculations were required to determine how much the band of planking diminished, and how each individual plank tapered. The simple formulae that follow will be of particular use to the modelmaker.

To determine the thickness of the bottom edge of the lower strake (this applies to both methods of planking) use Equation 1.

Equation 1 $$P = W/2$$

where P = thickness of lower plank; W = thickness of main wale.

When the diminishing strakes are wrought in parallel lengths, the amount to be tapered on each individual plank can be estimated by Equation 2.

Equation 2 $$P^R = P^*/S$$ *from equation above

where P^R = amount of reduction on the lower edge of the plank; S = number of diminishing strakes.

Example: The given thickness of the main wale = 9in. Therefore, using Equation 1:

$$S^T = 9/2 = 4\tfrac{1}{2}\text{in}$$

where S^T is the thickness of the lowest edge of the diminishing strakes

The number of diminishing strakes = 8. Thus by Equation 2:

$$P^R = 4\tfrac{1}{2}/8 = \tfrac{9}{16}\text{in}$$

Therefore if the top edge of the uppermost strake is 9in thick, the bottom edge of that plank will be 8$\tfrac{7}{16}$in thick. This applies to each plank in every strake, thus giving the correct dimension where the diminishing strakes meet with the bottom planking.

The above calculations do not apply to diminishing strakes wrought top and butt. This is because the strakes consist of two tiers of planks, therefore what appears to be ten strakes is called five strakes. To understand this fully, refer to the section on top and butt which follows. For the following equations take the strake as the overall width of two planks.

Equation 3 $$S^R = P/S$$

The amount of reduction on the lower edge of a strake = thickness of the lower plank (taken from Equation 1) ÷ the number of top and butt strakes.

where S^R = the reduction on the lower edge of a strake; P = thickness of lower plank (from Equation 1); S = number of top and butt strakes

Example: The overall width of one strake of 'top and butt' = 20in; thus

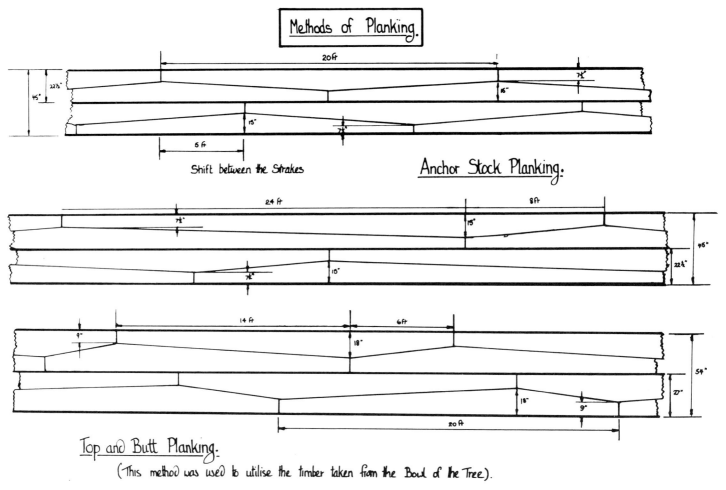

Fig 2/5

the width of six strakes in width = 10ft; the thickness of the main wale = 9in.

Therefore, from Equation 1

The thickness at the lower strake − $^9/_2$ = 4½in

Thus by Equation 2

The amount to be reduced on the lower edge of each strake − 4½/6 = ¾in.

Therefore each strake is reduced by ¾in from its top to bottom edges. In both methods the planking was fastened to the timbers with roves (clench bolts) and trennals. The way in which they were disposed will be explained further in the section on plank fastenings.

METHODS OF PLANKING

Top and Butt

This style of planking was used in various parts of the ship, for example, for the main wales, diminishing strakes, the upper strakes of the bottom planking, the spirketting, and sometimes in areas on the deck planking of the gundecks. The advantages of this method of laying planks were that it gave increased strength, and was more adaptable to the stresses produced by a ship working in heavy seas − as most of the timbers mentioned above were the principal longitudinal stiffeners.

Each plank was made with one straight edge, while its opposite side had two inclined surfaces, tapering down to half the width of the plank at the butts. The overall width of the plank was two-thirds of the total width of the strake, (ie two rows of interlocking planks). The peak, or touch as it was commonly called was where the two inclined edges met. It was not placed at the centre of the plank, but at a given distance, one-quarter of the plank's length, from one end. Thus the angles of the sloping sides differed. The plank that was laid adjacent (either forward or aft) was set in the same direction with the butts set close, ie the end with the short slope would have its butt end fayed to the butt of the long sloped side of the other plank.

The planking that was laid above completed one strake. It was inverted so that its long and short opposing edges fayed to the corresponding edges on the lower planks (see Fig 2/5). The lower planks of the next strake were laid in the opposite direction, with the butts set at a shift of half the length of a plank from the butts of the top planks of the strake below.

The position at the touch	= one-quarter of the length of the plank from one end.
The width of the plank at the touch	= two-thirds of the width of the strake desired.
The butts of the planks in width	= half the width of the touch.

Anchor Stock

This method was sometimes used for the main wale as an alternative to the top and butt style. Like the latter, it was used because of its strength and stress-resistant qualities. One edge of the plank was made straight while the other side had two inclined surfaces tapering the plank to half its maximum width at the butts. Both of the sloping sides were the same angle for in this case the touch was set in the middle of the plank. The width of the plank at the touch was two-thirds of the overall width of the strake, the butts being half the width of the touch. The second layer of planking that completed the strake was inverted. The corresponding inclined edges were fayed to each other, thus making the top and bottom edges of the strake parallel. If a second strake was to be wrought it was essential to have the shift of the butts at one-quarter of the length of the plank to the top butts of the strake below. The disadvantage of these two methods was that in making each plank a considerable amount of timber was wasted, due to the inclined edges.

THE MAIN WALES

The main wales were bands of heavy planking on each side of the ship between the waterline and the lower gundeck ports. The purpose of these strakes was to stiffen the hull fore and aft, in an attempt to overcome the problem of hogging. Hogging was the drop of the keel at the fore and after ends, which occurred due to the weight of both the head and stern of the ship. This was a considerable problem in the ships in the times of Pepys and during the first decade of the eighteenth century, when the elaborate carving and ornamentation that adorned the stern added excess weight. Hogging was also caused when a ship was riding heavy seas and was momentarily supported on the crest of a wave, leaving the stem and stern to droop until supported again by a wave.

The wales were not laid parallel to the gundeck, but to the designed sheer of the ship. Therefore the gunports at the fore and after ends had to be cut into the upper edge of the wale. From about 1650 until the second decade of the eighteenth century, the main wale consisted of two separate strakes of planking. The space between was wrought in plank of the same thickness as the remaining boards. At this time normal straight butt planking methods were employed. From 1715 it became the general practice to close the space between the two strakes of the main wale with a strake of planking of equal thickness, thus forming a wide band of heavy strakes. The first example of this was on the 80-gun ship Newark in 1717, and the 80-gun ship Humber in 1723. During the eighteenth century the ends of the main wale tended to taper, and conformed to the planksheer. This was only done on the lower edge of the wale. With this modification, a strake of planking that tapered in its cross-section was laid above the wale. This took the form of an inverted diminishing strake. This strake was often referred to as the black strake and was retained until vessels became smooth sided in the early 1820s.

It may be that the two strakes were first closed in Stuart times due to the practice of 'girdling' ships, when timber was added to the ship at its waterline to give a wider beam and reduce the effect of topweight.

Oak of the best quality was used for the wales, in lengths of approximately 25ft and about 12in in width. The thickness was approximately half the moulded depth of the keel. The alternative methods of planking were top and butt and anchor stock, these being preferred because of their strength and resistance to stress. The use of these two styles explains why the width of the main wale increased in the latter half of the eighteenth century.

If the wale was wrought anchor stock, the length of each plank was 20ft, the width of the touch 16in and the butts 8in. Thus a complete strake's width would be 24in. As two strakes were generally laid, the overall width of the main wale would be about 4ft. The main wale of a 38-gun frigate was 3ft 6in wide, the touch was 14in wide and the butts 7in. When the wales were wrought top and butt, the planks were approximately 25ft long on First Rate ships and 24ft on the Third Rates. Using these figures it is possible to determine the position and width of the touch by referring to the section on top and butt planking.

The planks were fastened temporarily with iron dumps, then the planking was bored for the trennals and clench bolts. Once bolted, the holes that received the trennals were left for a period to allow for ventilation, before the trennals were finally driven in.

THE CHANNEL WALES

Confusion as to which wale was the channel wale is understandable, due to the alteration of the level at which the channels were fitted. The simplest way of preventing confusion is to remember that the channel wale was the wale to which the chains of the shrouds were secured. This did not really concern ships with a single gundeck. On vessels with two complete gundecks built or altered according to the 1745 order to raise the channels, the channel wale was between the lower and upper gundecks, whereas on three-decked ships it was between the middle and upper gundecks. However, care must be taken when considering ships dating from a little before or after this date, as further alterations were made particularly to First Rates.

The channel wale on a three-decker was made up of three strakes of straight planking, each 10in wide. The length of the planks was 25ft, care being taken to ensure that the butts did not lie under any of the upper deck ports. Some builders preferred the lower strakes wrought in either top and butt or anchor stock. In this case the width of the plank at the touch would be 13in, making the butts 7in wide. No matter which method was employed, the thickness of the planks was approximately three-quarters of the thickness of the main wale.

The channel wale on two-deckers was generally wider than that of a First Rate ship. Usually it was 3ft wide, made up of three strakes of parallel planking in lengths of 28ft and 30ft. If the lower two strakes were wrought in top and butt or anchor stock, the overall width of the strake would be 2ft, thus making the width of the touch 16in, and the butts 8in. The plank thickness was as already described. The planking was secured to the timbers by exactly the same method that was used for the main wales. The upper strake of straight plank was given a shift of one-quarter of the length of the plank. If laid in parallel strakes, the shift of the butts was one-third of the length of the plank.

THE MIDDLE WALES

The middle wale was only used on three deckers, and was wrought between the lower and middle gundecks. The overall width of the wale was about 3ft and it was laid in parallel plank, top and butt, or anchor stock, in a similar manner to the channel wales. The planks were 25ft long and 12in wide. If the lower part was wrought in top and butt or anchor stock, the width at the touch was 16in and at the butts, 8in. When laid in this way, the top strake of parallel plank was given a shift of the butts one-quarter of the length of a plank from the butts of the lower strake. If all the planks were straight the shift was approximately one-third the length of the plank.

THE SHIP'S SIDE PLANKING BETWEEN THE WALES

Throughout most of the period covered by this book, a band of oak planking known as the black strake or the thick stuff was wrought above the wales. It was laid along the top of both the main and channel wales. The term black strake originated when the main wale was the only part of the ship's side that was painted black, this strake being the upper boundary of that paintwork.

Above the main wale, two complete strakes were laid on the First, Second and Third Rate ships, while one was used on the smaller vessels. The width of these planks varied between 16in and

11in, depending on the ship's size. The lower strake was approximately 2in thinner than the main wale on First to Third Rates, 1½in less on 64- and 44-gun ships and 1in less on ships of 38–28 guns, and on the remaining ships, ½in less. The second strake, when used, was 4in less thick than that of the main wale on First Rates and 3in less than on the Second and Third Rates.

Special care was taken to ensure that the butts of the planks were given a good shift to the gunports, and main wale where applicable. The continuity of the strakes was interrupted at the forward and after ends due to the rise of the sheer. By 1820, these planks were fashioned to fair in with the wales, thus producing a smooth-sided ship. Only two- or three-decked ships had strakes above the channel wale; both strakes were 12in wide. The lower strake was about 1in thinner than the channel wale, whereas the upper strake would be between 2½in less than it. This layer of planking was also faired off with the channel wale.

The remaining planking was also oak, sawn to its required width and siding. It was usually between 12in and 9in wide. Its thickness was half that of the wale below it. Thus the planks became thinner towards the toptimber line. Special care was taken with the shift of the butts in relation to the gunports. The written rule was that no butt was to be laid in the way of a gunport unless there were two strakes of planking between them. Planks that were wrought in way of the mainmast were given a three port shift, and the remaining planks in that strake a two port shift. It was considered good practice to shift the butts between the ports by 5ft 6in if one plank came between them and 5ft if two planks came between them. All the planking was fastened by oak trennals, iron clenches, and in places iron dumps.

THE PLANKING OF THE STERN AND THE BEAKHEAD BULKHEAD

The counter planks were not as thick as the ship's side planks, being 8in wide and only 2½ to 3½in thick. The only interruptions in the strakes were those of the stern-chase ports, and the elliptical hole through which the rudder passed. The stern was made from 2½in thick planking the same width as the counter planking. Similar boarding was used for the beakhead bulkhead. Both these areas were very vulnerable to raking fire. With the introduction of the round bow and the circular stern (and eventually the elliptical stern) the planking of the ship's side was continued round these extremities.

THE EXTERNAL PLANKING OF VESSELS 1650–1700

Detail on the manner in which the boards were laid and fastened is supplied on pages 50–54. Anchor stock and top and butt methods were not employed until the latter half of the eighteenth century. All planking during this period was laid in normal parallel strakes.

Egmont. *This is a fine example of a completed frame model built to illustrate the overall techniques and practices of ship construction of the latter half of the eighteenth century.*

As in the section, Internal Planking 1650–1700, the proportions are taken from the works of Deane's *Doctrine* and those of the Third Rate from Christopher Pett's contract of 1664.

Bottom Planking

This was generally wrought in oak, to a width of between 9in and 12in. The thickness was as follows: Ship, rate (proportion of the depth of the keel) – First and Second (one-fifth); Third (one-quarter); Fourth (three-sixteenths;) Fifth (two-sevenths); Sixth (three-tenths); Third of 1666 (nine thirty-seconds).

There does not appear to be any reference to the garboard strake. Therefore, to calculate the scantlings of this strake, use the data for the eighteenth century.

The Main Wale

During this period the main wale was not constructed as a wide band of heavy planking as on eighteenth-century vessels, but was wrought in two strakes with a line of planking of lesser dimensions set between. The wale was thus divided into two distinct strakes, which differed in dimensions, called the upper and lower wales.

55

The Lower Wale

This was the greater of the two wales, wrought in good straight oak of considerable length. The depth (or width) of this plank was identical or only a fraction less than the depth of the keel. Its thickness was generally about half of its width, the lists below giving the precise dimensions: Ship, rate (width in proportion to the depth of keel) – First, Second and Third (the same); Fourth (thirty-one thirty-seconds); Fifth (fifteen-sixteenths); Sixth (three-quarters). Ship, rate (thickness in proportion to depth) – First and Second (half); Third and Fourth (seven-sixteenths); Fifth and Sixth (three-sevenths).

The Upper Wale

This was wrought in oak, parallel to the lower wale, and set at a specific height above it. According to Deane, to calculate the distance between the upper edge of the lower wale and the lower edge of the upper wale, take 1in for every foot of the ship's moulded beam and multiply this figure by two-thirds.

Example: to find the height between the wales of a 40-gun ship of 1685, with a moulded beam of 34ft:

$$34 \times \tfrac{2}{3} = 22 \cdot 666\text{in } (22\tfrac{2}{3}\text{in})$$

The width of the upper wale was generally about five-sixths that of the lower wale. More exact dimensions are: Ship, rate (width in proportion to depth of keel) – First (thirteen-sixteenths); Second (four-fifths); Third (seven-eighths). Only a single wale was employed on Fourth, Fifth and Sixth Rates.

The thickness of the upper wale was equal to that of the lower wale in all vessels. For a Third Rate of 1666, the width of each wale is seven-eighths of the depth of the keel, and the thickness is five-eighths of the width.

The Diminishing Strakes

During this period only three strakes of this type of planking were wrought beneath the lower wale, and it is very unlikely that they were tapered in their cross-section, as they did in the eighteenth century. The width of this planking varied between 9in and 12in and each strake was of different thickness. The breadths were as follows:

First, Second and Third Rates: the first strake below the lower wale was three-fifths of the thickness of the lower wale. The second strake was 1in less than the first, and the third strake was 1in less than the second. Thus for a vessel with a 10in broad lower wale, the first strake would be 6in thick. The second strake would be 5in and the third 4in.

Fourth Rates: the first strake had a thickness of four-sevenths of the lower wale. The remaining two strakes were 1in thinner than the first and of equal thickness.

Fifth and Sixth Rates: the first strake had a thickness of two-thirds of the wale. The remaining two strakes were 1in thinner than the first strake. For example, in a 30-gun Fifth Rate with a wale of 6in breadth, the first line of the diminishing strakes would be 4in thick. The other two strakes would of course be 3in broad.

The Planking Between the Two Main Wale Strakes

This only applies to the First, Second and Third Rates, other vessels had only one main wale strake. The number of strakes depended on the width between the upper and lower strakes. This can be calculated from the formula in the upper wale section. There was very little difference in breadth between this planking and that above the upper wale. The following list gives the approximate thickness of the planking; it also applies to all rates built between 1650 and 1666. Ship, rate (thickness in proportion to the depth of the keel) – First (five-sixteenths); Second and Third (three-tenths); Fourth (one-quarter); Fifth (two-sevenths); Sixth (three-tenths).

This planking was laid to give a good shift of the butt to the upper and lower wales.

The Topside Planking Between the Main and Channel Wales

Here the number of strakes varied according to the distance between the main and channel wales. Generally, either four or five strakes were used. The breadth of this planking remained uniform throughout, and was of the following dimensions: Ship, rate (thickness in proportion to the depth of the keel) – First (three-sixteenths); Second (one-fifth); Third, Fourth and Fifth (three-sixteenths); Sixth (five-thirty-seconds).

The Channel Wales

Though the dimensions of these strakes are a little difficult to ascertain, their breadth in comparison to that of the main wale can be calculated. The thickness of both the upper and lower channel wale was half the depth of the lower channel wale.

The width of the lower channel wale, according to Deane, was two-thirds the width of the lower main wale, and the upper channel wale was five-sixths of the lower channel wale. The estimated size for the channel wale of a Third Rate of 1666 is as follows: the width was about two-fifths of the depth of the keel, and the thickness was approximately three-fifths of its width.

The Topside Planking above the Channel Wale

It appears that two methods were employed during the seventeenth century. Between 1650 and 1670, the first two strakes were of equal thickness and worked up to the level of the sill of the upper gundeck ports. The breadth was approximately 3 to 4in, or between 1 and 1½in less than that of the upper channel wale. It was wrought to give good shift to the butts of the channel wale, and between the gunports.

The manner in which these planks were cut after 1670 can be seen in the works of Deane. According to these, the first strake was made to the following proportions: Ship, rate (thickness in proportion to the depth of keel) – First (one-seventh); Second (five thirty-seconds); Third (three-sixteenths); Fourth (five thirty-seconds); Fifth (one-seventh); Sixth (one-eighth). The second strake was generally about ½in less than the first strake in thickness.

The Topside Planking

The planking used for the upperworks was comparatively thin. It seems that in the 1650s it was laid in two bands, the first worked up from the sills to the lintels of the upper gundeck ports. Here the thickness was approximately one-fifth of the depth of the keel. Above this it decreased in breadth, by 1in on the larger vessels and about ¾in on the smaller classes.

From Deane it can be seen that in 1670 the breadth of the planking remained constant up to the capping. The First, Second and Third Rates had planks of a thickness one-eighth of the depth of the keel, the other vessels about one-ninth.

THE RAILS

A number of strakes, loosely termed rails, were fitted along the length of the ship's upperworks. They conformed to the sheer of the ship and most were moulded along the outboard faces with different designs (see Fig 2/6). The names of the rails are: waist rail, sheer rail, drift rail, planksheer, and fife rail.

The Waist Rail

This, the lowest of all, was fitted a specific distance below the toptimber line. It can be seen from draughts and models that it was continuous in the after half of the ship but was interrupted by the gunports of the upper gundeck (or gundeck on single-decked ships). The rail was set to a depth of 2ft below the toptimber line on the larger vessels, and 1ft 3in on the smallest. Its width was approximately 8in for First Rates, 7½in for Second and Third Rates, 6in for Fourth and Fifth Rates, and 5½in for sloops and armed cutters.

The Sheer Rail

The sheer rail was wrought fore and aft along the toptimber line. Prior to the raising of the channels it was continuous. Once the channels had been raised it was interrupted. When the upperworks were decorated with friezes, the sheer rail usually divided this work into its two designs, the lower having a foliage pattern, and the

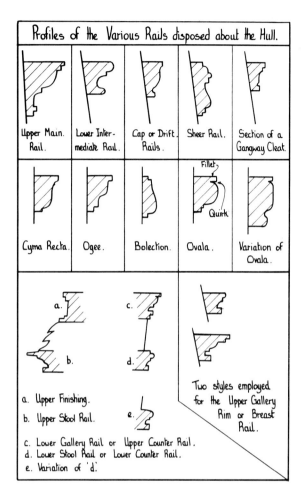

Fig 2/6

upper, arms and trophies. The width of the rail was usually the same as that of the waist rail, or ½in greater.

The Drift Rail

This rail conformed to the sheer of the forecastle, quarterdeck and poop. It generally terminated at the breaks of the forecastle and quarterdeck. Because of this division, each part was given its own name: the fore drift and the main drift. The fore drift was set at a given height above the sheer rail, and was wrought parallel to it. Its after end terminated with a scroll turning down to the sheer rail. In most ships the space below was planked in although the *Mordaunt* of 1681 appears to have this area open.

The main drift, although stepped at the levels of the decks, was usually given an additional hance at about a third of the length of the quarterdeck from the fore end. Each rise was fashioned with a scroll, or a small carved figure on some of the earlier ships. Like the fore drift it was laid parallel to the sheer rail. Some draughts differ in that the rail does not rise at the break of the poop, but continues aft to the quarter galleries. In such cases the planksheer acted as the after part of the drift. Until about 1785 the ship's side above remained open, with a rail laid across the timber heads. Thereafter the drift rails, both forward and aft, formed what was later called the planksheer. The drift rails had a width equal to that of the sheer rail.

Fife Rail

This rail can be easily confused with the planksheer, and in a sense it was the same thing. The only difference was that when the area above the drift rails was open, the rail above that was known as the fife rail. With the closing of this space, it became the planksheer. This rail was set between 12 and 9in above the drift, depending on the size of the ship. It was parallel to, and followed the steps of, the drifts. It was between 2 and 3in thick, fashioned with tenons to sit over the timberheads, and constructed so the timberheads passed through, to act as belaying points.

The planksheer was similar to the fife rail. By 1800 the bulwarks were built up square ended, and their top edges were parallel to the deck, thus sharpening the lines of the ships. This was designed to give the men more protection during action. However, it did take away the graceful sheer, but for a number of years these lines were maintained by having the drift and planksheer rails fitted, by the way of mouldings both inboard and outboard (this can be seen on the *Victory* at Portsmouth). By 1813 these mouldings had disappeared.

The Deck Planking

Either oak, elm or Prussian deal was used for the deck planking. Oak was used where strength was a priority, usually on the lower gundecks where the heaviest armament was borne. Elm was used for the gundecks for two reasons. Firstly, it was relatively strong. Secondly, it had a tough irregular grain. The latter quality was advantageous during action, for elm when smashed by enemy shot did not break into fine splinters, but into quite large chunks. The theory was that it was better to be killed outright by a large splinter than suffer under the surgeon's knife, or be maimed for life by small pieces. Prussian deal was used on decks that did not have excessive loading. It seems that deal and elm were introduced due to the dwindling supplies of oak, around the 1740s. Oak was generally only used in areas near the ship's side and in wake of hatchways and capstans.

Planking was laid in a specific pattern, in either a three- or four-butt shift (see Fig 2/7). This ensured that the planking did not all start and finish on the same beams, which would make the system weak. The other advantage was that the shipwright would be able to lay a deck without too much wastage and with the minimum of short lengths.

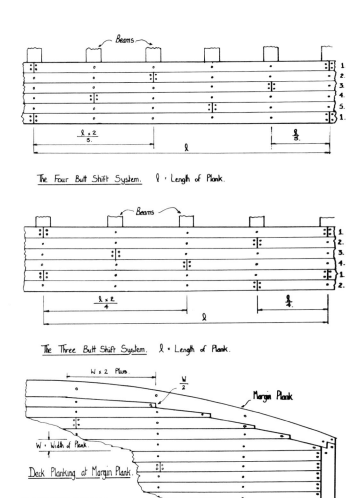

Fig 2/7

DETAILS OF INDIVIDUAL DECKS
The Orlop Deck

The planking of this deck was relatively thin, for it did not have to take any great weight. Also, for a number of reasons it was not completely planked over. In most ships the planks were only made in short lengths of approximately the same length as the distance between the beams.

Two methods of supporting these planks were used. By the first, battens about 2in square in section, were fitted to the fore and after faces of the beam, set down at a distance equal to the thickness of the planking. This formed a ledge on which the butts of the planks rested; but they were not secured, for reasons which will be explained later. By the second method the orlop beams were fashioned with ledges in the fore and after faces, for the same purpose. The dimensions were the same as given above. This portable decking gave access to the stores in the hold without having to shift everything below to get at what was required.

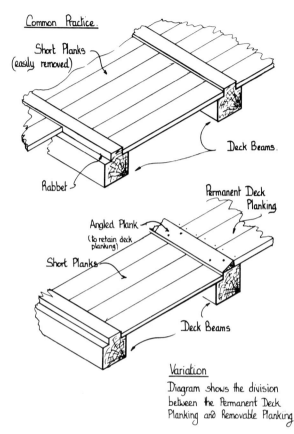

The Orlop Deck Planking.

Common Practice.

Short Planks (easily removed)

Deck Beams.

Rabbet

Permanent Deck Planking

Angled Plank (to retain deck planking)

Short Planks

Deck Beams

Variation
Diagram shows the division between the Permanent Deck Planking and Removable Planking.

Fig 2/8

The planks were generally made from deal, secured into sections or pallets by battens nailed to their undersides, thus allowing portions of deck to be lifted. The planks were about 9in wide and between 1½ and 2in thick. This overlapping of the beams gave this deck its name, orlop being the slang abbreviation for overlap.

Gratings were used extensively throughout this deck. Their purpose was twofold: they gave ventilation to the hold, and allowed light into areas such as the forepeak. These gratings were generally fitted along the outboard side of bulkheads, and at the waist. This area was referred to as the 'carpenter's walk', where the carpenter and his crew spent their time during action, checking for any shot damage that occurred below the waterline. They filled any shot holes with wooden plugs – an early form of the damage control team found on all warships today. This space was often very cramped; the carpenter's walk on the *Foudroyant* is only 4ft 4in high.

The Gundeck

What is referred to here as the gundeck is the lowest gundeck on two- and three-decked ships, and the only deck completely mounted with guns on single-decked ships. The planking of this deck had to be very sound to stand the weight of the heavier armament. A large ship had 28 or 30 guns, generally 32-pounders, each of which weighed approximately 2¾ tons. The total weight on this deck would be up to 82 tons. Although the beams, carlings and ledges that supported this deck were of considerable size, the planking was also fairly thick, varying between 4 and 6in. The width of the boards was generally 9 to 12in, with stealers worked in fore and aft where necessary. All the planks would be laid 'heart down' to prevent them warping upwards at their ends.

In most vessels all the planking was of parallel strakes, with the butts square. Some builders fitted two strakes of either top and butt or anchor stock 4ft from each side of the ship. This practice was probably adopted towards the end of the eighteenth century. The function of this was to resist any athwartships compression that occurred when the vessel was in heavy seas. This was important, for the deck not only supported the guns, but also acted as a rigid structure integral to the construction of the ship. All the planks were fastened to the beams and carlings with iron spikes, dumps or trennals. When trennals were used they would be driven in from underneath, through both beams and carlings. Running the full length of the deck either side of the numerous fittings on the centreline was a strake of planking known as the binding strake. The width of this was the same as the other planking, but it was about 1 or 1½in thicker. This did not mean that the plank protruded above the others, for it was scored on its bottom edge and let down on to the beams.

In 1790, a First, Second and Third Rate had planking 4in thick, Fourth Rates 3in, and the other rates 2½in thick. Armed cutters had planking 3in thick on their upper decks, which in this case can be classified as gundecks. When top and butt was employed, the strake was about 2ft in width and the planks 25ft in length. Unlike the normal style, the touch was set at two-fifths of the length of the plank from one end instead of one-quarter. When wrought parallel, the lengths varied between 30 and 36ft.

The Middle Gundeck

The planks on this deck were only 3in thick, as the loading was not so great. The guns were usually 24-pounders, giving a total weight of about 70 tons. The laying out and fastening arrangements were identical to those on the lower gundeck. This deck was only fitted on three-deckers.

The Upper Gundeck

This deck was also planked with 3in boards, secured in a similar manner to those described above.

The Quarterdeck

Most of the decks that were open to the elements were laid out in the four butt shift system. In most ships 3in plank was used, while in ships of 32 guns or less the plank was only 2½in thick. Unlike the gundecks, a plank of greater width known as the king plank was set along the centreline, and the planking was worked outward from this until it reached the margin plank (which is discussed later).

The Forecastle

This was planked in the same manner as the quarterdeck, but there seems to have been a variation in the thickness of the planks. Some vessels had planks identical to those of the quarterdeck, whereas others had planks ½in thinner. This depended on the armament carried, for before the introduction of the carronade in 1779, small 9-pounders were often fitted as bow-chasers. With the introduction of the carronade, and later the closing of the waist, the continuous 'upper deck' had to have the same planking throughout.

The Roundhouse

This deck was of lighter construction, and therefore made from planks only 2½in thick, and 9in wide. Special care was taken with regard to the margin plank.

The Gangways

The gangways (or gang boards), that passed between the quarterdeck and the forecastle on either side of the waist, were originally made from thin planks, about 2in thick, secured to iron brackets. Later when they became a more permanent structure, the planks were secured to the skid beams.

The Platforms

Ships that did not have orlop decks were fitted with platforms in the hold. These were supported by beams, and laid with planking 2 to 2½in thick and about 9in wide. These planks were fastened with iron spikes or trennals.

THE MARGIN PLANK

Parallel to the ship's side and fayed to the waterway was a strake of planking known as the margin plank. The function of this was to prevent the normal straight deck planking from being tapered to a fine angle where it met the curvature of the ship's side at the fore and after ends. The margin plank was thus fashioned to receive the butts of those planks (see Fig 2/7). It was stipulated that no plank was to be 'joggled' into the margin plank unless the length of its tapered edge was more than twice the width of the plank, and that the plank was only to be tapered or 'snaped' to half its width at the butt end. The margin plank was the same thickness as the deck plank, but one and a half times as wide.

The Fastenings

Many types of fastenings were employed for securing both the timbers and planking. Their use and their method of fitting was governed by the material from which they were made. Wood, iron, copper, bronze and muntz were the most common materials, although more complex ones such as tinned iron were introduced during the nineteenth century. Each type of fastening will be described before explaining the various techniques used throughout the vessel (see Fig 2/9).

TRENNALS

This name was derived from the words 'tree nail'. They were wood, usually oak, dowels mainly employed for securing planking. The wood from which they were made was selected from the top-most branches of the tree, where the grain was fine and supple. They were made by hand, and were up to 3ft long and ¾ to 2in diameter.

One rule stipulated that any timber that was to be secured had to be no more than three times the diameter of the trennal, but it seems that the actual application of the rule was more flexible. In one instance two trennals were used to fasten the ship's side planking, where the total sum of the diameters of the trennals was only a quarter of the width of a 12in plank.

The advantage of wooden dowels was that when they got wet the wood expanded, thus tightening the fastening. The disadvantages were, firstly, that the dowels could easily shrink, and could work loose in heavy seas. Secondly, although the sheer strength of a trennal of 2in in diameter was 4000lb per square inch, it was still relatively weak and was also prone to rot.

The method of fitting was simple. The flat faces of the two components to be joined were placed together or 'fayed'. They were then bored through with an auger of the same diameter as the dowel. The trennal was then driven in, and made flush. Some shipwrights cut a V-shaped slot along the axis of the dowel at its head. Once it was fitted a small wedge of pitch pine was driven into the slot and this tended to open up the head, tightening the fitting.

BOLTS

The bolts were different from those used today, which have a thread and are held by a nut. They were more like a rivet, especially those made from copper. Copper was used extensively throughout the ship, and always below the waterline where its properties made it free from the corrosive effects of sea water. The bolt consisted of a long parallel shaft of any diameter up to 2½in, with a head at one end. A rove, or what the layman would call a washer, was used in conjunction with the bolt. The method of fastening was relatively simple. The two timbers to be fitted together were fayed. A hole was then bored through both with an auger of the same diameter as the bolt. The bolt was driven through and the rove was fitted over

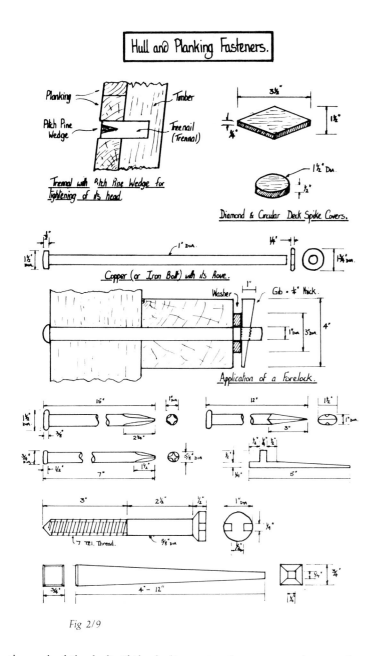

Fig 2/9

copper. Thus on close inspection one can see that these bolts were stamped with an official mark, commonly known as the 'pusser's arrow'. It was placed at intervals of approximately ¾in, spiralling around the periphery making it impossible to steal even a 1in length.

Bolts were also made from wrought iron, but they were more similar to a 'nail' because they were driven in without the use of the roves. In some cases roves were used, but this depended on how tight the joint had to be. It was probably very difficult to cold work wrought iron thus the 'forelock bolt' was used where tightening was possible. (This is explained in the next section.) I possess a wrought iron bolt that was used aboard the *Foudroyant*. Although it is badly corroded, it is possible to see the 'grain' of the iron, which gives a fair indication how it was made.

Copper and iron bolts had their advantages and disadvantages. Copper was good in that it did not corrode, but it was not particularly strong and did not always remain a tight fit. However, the opposite problem was found when shipwrights wanted to withdraw a bolt 6ft long from the deadwood aft on the *Victory*, during restoration work. Iron was far stronger, but it was very prone to corrosion. Once this had started, the timber surrounding it also began to rot, first indicated by its change to a black colour. Then the whole fitting became slack. Although wrought iron was reasonably strong and fairly ductile it could easily be shattered by shot.

FORELOCKS

Made from wrought iron, these bolts were fashioned in a manner that allowed them to be pulled up tight by the use of an iron wedge known as a gib. Initially this type of bolt was made the same way as a normal bolt, with its respective rove. The end of the bolt had a slot one-quarter of its diameter, cut radially through its axis. This slot tapered from one side to the other and the gib was made to the same angle (see Fig 2/9). The bolt was passed through the timbers, fastened, and the rove was fitted over the end. The gib was then placed into the slot and hammered in as far as it could go, thus tightening the rove hard up against the timbers. Any slackness that occurred later, due to the working of the ship, could be rectified by driving the gib further in, and if this was not satisfactory a second rove could be fitted. A similar device can be seen on the panel that forms the casing of ships' boilers today. This allows for simple and quick removal for maintenance. The only disadvantage is that the bolt has to be the correct length. Adjustment can only be made by the addition of roves at either end.

IRON SPIKES

These were generally used for securing the deck planks. They were made from wrought iron, square in section, tapering from ¾ to ¼in. Some were made with a flat head and others with a head in the form of an inverted truncated cone. Before being driven into the plank, a

the end of the bolt. If the bolt was too long it was shortened so about 1in protruded beyond the rove, which was now hard up against the timber. The excess part of the bolt was then hammered over the rove.

It was considered good practice to bore out the timber on either side, to a depth and diameter of the head and the rove. Once the bolt was fastened the remaining space was filled with some form of caulking, and faired off with the faces of the timbers. This explains why the bolts were often referred to as clench bolts. This is still done today when timber is fitted to ships as 'rubbing strakes', where the timber is bolted to studs welded to the structure and the recesses where the nuts fit into wood are filled with some form of epoxy putty.

The dockyards had to prevent the workforce from pilfering the recess of either a diamond or circular shape was cut into the plank. The spike was then hammered in with a pin maul. Once the spike was in, its head was covered with a dowel or diamond shaped sliver of timber, the former being about ½in thick. The latter was only ¼in thick as it was used more in the areas of the ship that accommodated the officers. The lengths of the spikes varied according to where they were used.

DUMPS

These, too, were made from wrought iron but were of round section with a slight taper. Their use was similar to that of iron spikes. The heads were either flat or slightly rounded.

BRONZE AND MUNTZ SPIKES

Bronze was used more widely during the first half of the period covered. Spikes varied in length and were made between ½ and 1in in diameter. They were extensively used, due to their ability to withstand corrosion. Bronze is an alloy made from approximately 90 to 95 per cent copper and 4 to 5 per cent tin. Its strength was about equal to that of copper, and, like the copper bolts it did not always maintain a tight fit. Its resistance to corrosion by sea water can be determined by inspecting the bronze gudgeon pin taken from the wreck site of Captain Bligh's ship *Bounty* that sank off Pitcairn Island. This can still be seen today at Southsea Castle Museum near Portsmouth.

Muntz was used as an alternative to bronze. It is a form of brass, made from 60 per cent copper and 40 per cent zinc. The percentage of zinc made the metal stronger than normal brass, which was usually categorised as alpha and beta brass. Alpha brass consisted of copper and between 30 and 38 per cent zinc (only 5 to 20 per cent zinc if to be cold worked). Beta brass was made with the zinc content as high as 46 to 49 per cent. Muntz was a combination of both alpha and beta brass. These Muntz spikes were first used below the waterline, but it was found that the zinc reacted with chlorides, and the fitting became devoid of zinc and honeycombed, rendering it weak and useless.

COAKS

These were not strictly fastenings, but were employed primarily for locating and keeping specific timbers in place. Their application was not dissimilar to the modern use of dowels in furniture manufacture, except that no adhesive was used.

Two types of coak were used; the block coak, and the cylindrical coak. Generally they were made from well seasoned straight oak, or lignum vitae. The latter had a number of advantages. Firstly, it was very hard, thus less prone to rot. Secondly, it was less likely to split under the strains caused by a ship working in a heavy sea. When comparing some coaks that had been removed during

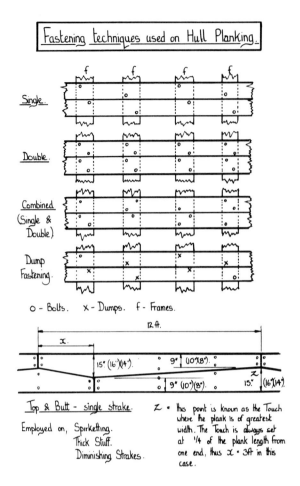

Fig 2/10

reconstruction work on the *Victory* I noticed that those made from oak had been eaten through with sea-worm, whereas those made from lignum vitae were intact.

The Block Coak

This type of coak was commonly oak, fashioned in the form of either a flat square or rectangular block. These blocks were set into mortices cut into the mating surfaces of flat scarphs, such as those employed for joining sections of the keel together (see Fig 1/1). They were also used occasionally for the scarphs of the keelson, stempost or apron. The dimensions of these coaks varied according to both the form of scarph and the width of the timber to which they were applied. Their width was approximately one-third of that of the parent timber, their length between one- and two-thirds of it, depending on whether the coak was square or rectangular. The depth varied betweed 2 and 6in depending on the depth of the joint, each mortice being cut to a depth of half that of the coak.

The Cylindrical Coak

This form was more common from the end of the eighteenth

century, and was used extensively with the construction techniques introduced by Seppings. When first introduced, they were generally confined to locating heads of the hanging knees to the beams. When Seppings brought in a form of framing where the heads and heels of the futtocks and floors remained butt ended, the two timbers concerned were joined by large coaks. This can be seen in Fig 1/12(1). With the introduction of heavy-built waterways and beam shelves, also by Seppings, each beam was positioned and located with coaks set both above and below. Once everything was bolted in place, the whole structure was locked rigid both vertically and horizontally by the coaks. Although this was a great advantage to the ship structurally, if repairs had to be carried out on one beam, extensive lengths of the waterways had to be removed. The water-ways were scored on their underside to set down upon each beam.

In order to be fitted, this form of coak had to have a hole bored in each respective timber, each bore being made to a depth of half the length of the coak. The coak was then fitted into one of the timbers, after being given a liberal coating of tar or pitch. Next, the second piece of timber was put in position, bored as required, and bolted firmly.

The dimensions of these coaks varied. Those in the framing of the vessel were made to a diameter of one-third of the moulding of the frame, and to a length twice that of the moulding. In other cases, the overall length was approximately one-third greater than the desired diameter. The diameter was either one-third or one-quarter of the width of the timber into which it was set.

Victory. *The orlop deck with its gundeck beams, beam arm and associated carlings and ledges, and chock knees braced with Roberts iron plate knees. The deck clamp at this point is exceptionally deep in order to support the weight of the gundeck. The spaces between the strakes of planking are to give ventilation to the timbers (or frames) visible in places. The two vertical timbers are the heads of the riders. Note that the orlop planking is made in short lengths set between and level with the upper edges of the orlop deck beams.*

CHAPTER 3

Beams, Knees and Internal Stiffening

The Beams

Beams were transverse timbers placed at deck level. They supported the decks, and gave lateral rigidity to the vessel, to prevent racking which occurs when a ship's hull shifts out of the square in the athwartships direction. This straining takes place when the vessel is beam-on to a heavy sea. The effect can be likened to collapsing a matchbox (without its tray) by exerting a force on one of its top edges in the direction of the opposite corner. Between 1650 and 1725 each beam was made in a single unit of straight oak. With the ever decreasing supplies of timber, new techniques had to be found. Thus beams made up in either two, three or four portions were developed. Not only did this increase the strength at its centre, but it helped to reduce the wastage of timber, by using shorter lengths.

Later it was found that greater strength could also be achieved with other types of timber, so pitch pine was used. This made the repair of beams easier, for it was generally the outer ends that tended to rot first. It was easier to remove the defective section and replace it with new and readily available timber. The joint between the sections was an elongated form of hooked scarph, but experience proved that a tabled and lipped scarph was stronger. This was a series of 'hooks' that were recessed into each timber alternately, and between the lips. The whole was bolted through in the horizontal with trennals, and coaks. Coaks were short dowels set between each timber, made from oak and later from lignum vitae. These prevented the sections moving apart yet allowed the beams to work with the ship to a small extent (see Fig 3/1).

The length of each section of the beam depended on the overall length. A beam of two sections would have the joint at one-third of the total length; thus each portion would have a length of two-thirds of the total. For example, a beam with an overall length of 36ft was made from two parts, each being 24ft long. Each timber of

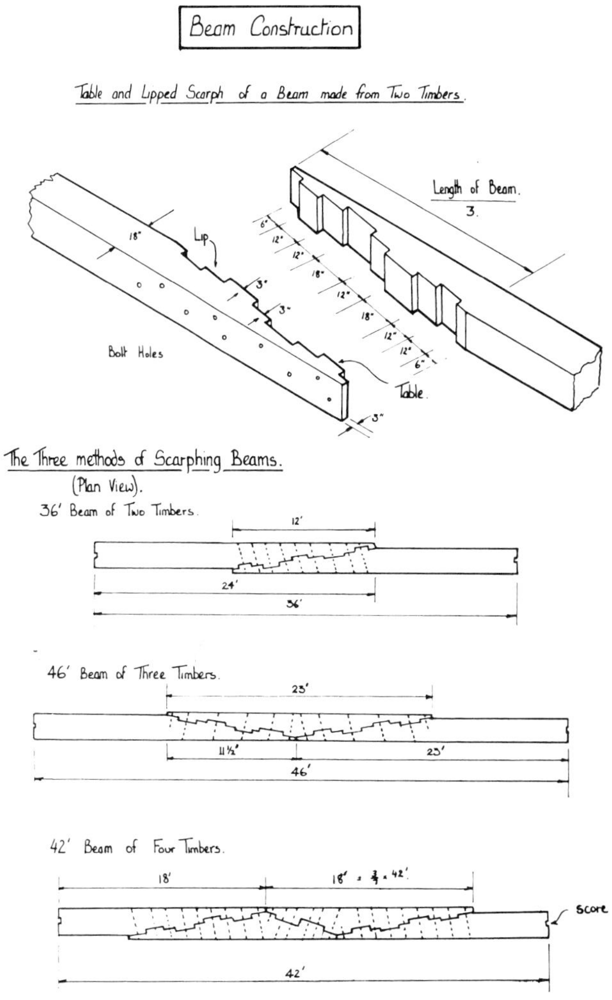

Beam Construction

Table and Lipped Scarph of a Beam made from Two Timbers.

The Three methods of Scarphing Beams. (Plan View).

36' Beam of Two Timbers.

46' Beam of Three Timbers.

42' Beam of Four Timbers.

Fig 3/1

65

a beam was in three pieces and half the total length of the beam. The centre portion thus overlapped each of the other two by half of its length. If the beam was fitted forward of the dead-flat, the centre part was set to the after side of the beam, while those fitted aft of the dead-flat were scarphed to the fore side of the beam. For example, if the beam was 48ft long, each section was 24ft long and the overlap would be 12ft.

Each part of a beam was made up of four pieces three-sevenths of the overall length of the beam. The two centre sections were scarphed on their adjoining faces, while their opposite sides were joined to the outer timbers. The length of the scarph between the centre sections was usually half that of the others. Each section of a beam with an overall length of 44ft 4in was 19ft long (see Fig 3/1).

Each beam was fashioned with a round up or camber on its upper surface, the lower surface was parallel to it. This allowed water to run off the decks to the scuppers at the ship's side. From the lowest to the highest deck the rise of the round up was increased. The table below gives an indication of the height at midships of the beams at each deck level.

Camber of Deck

No of guns	Orlop or platform	Lower gundeck	Middle gundeck	Upper gundeck	Quarter-deck	Forecastle	Poop
				(dimensions in inches)			
100	2	5½	7½	8½	9	7½	10
90	2	5	7	7	8	7	12
80	2	5	–	8½	8½	7½	11
74	2½	5	–	8½	8	7	10
64	2	4½	–	7½	7	7	9
44	1½	4	–	7½	8	6½	9*
38	1	4½	–	8	7	6	8*
36	1	4½	–	8	7	7	–
32	1	4	–	7½	6½	6	–
28	1	4	–	7	6	5½	–
24	1	4	–	6½	6	5½	–
Sloop	1	–	–	7	6½	6	–
Cutter	–	–	–	6½	–	–	–

*These figures are for ships of the class fitted with a poop deck.

The ends of the beams were bedded down upon the deck clamps, which were sometimes scored to a depth of 1in. The beam was then fastened to this clamp with either iron or copper bolts (bronze or Muntz was used in earlier ships).

The area where the beam end was adjacent to the timbers was very vulnerable to rot. This was due to the movement of these parts against each other when the ship rolled. The measures taken to prevent this were simple but effective. The ends of the beams were covered, and packed with either tarred flannel or brown paper treated with resin or tar. Another way of preventing decay was to have the beam end scored to a depth and width of about 2in. This allowed air to circulate around the area, thus keeping it relatively dry. The slot was cut in the vertical (see the bottom illustration in Fig 3/1).

THE LOWER GUNDECK (OR GUNDECK OF SINGLE-DECKERS)

Unlike the rest of the book where I have usually started at the lowest part of the ship, in this case I will start with the gundeck which had the beams of the heaviest construction. This deck was also the deck with the greatest breadth and was only a little above the waterline. The length of each beam can be determined from the deck plan. However, this was drawn to the moulded breadth, therefore, when considering the length of a beam, the thickness of the timbers (frames) in and out must be considered in the calculation, thus.

$$B^{L} = M - T \times 2$$

where B^{L} = beam length at each position; M = moulded breadth at the given station; T = thickness of timbers in and out.

Due to the number of permutations, the width and depth of the beams are not so easily calculated, but the following method of working seems to be fairly accurate.

$$(M/3) \times \beta = B^{W}$$

where M = moulded breadth at given deck height; B^{W} = beam width.

Here the moulded breadth is taken as the maximum moulded breadth of the ship on the deck in question; this measurement can be taken from the body plan. Ship, rate or number of guns (β) – First Rates (one and one-sixteenth); Second Rates (one); Third Rates (one); 64 guns (one and one-sixteenth); 44 guns (one); 38–36 guns (seven-eighths); Fifth Rates (three-quarters); Sixth Rates (three-quarters).

In all ships, the depth of the beam was less than the width and was determined as follows. Multiply the width of the beam by the factor given in brackets: 100–36-gun ships (fifteen-sixteenths); 32–20-gun ships (seven-eighths). The beam dimensions of some are different because certain sizes of beam were required, depending on the weight of the armament. On checking one of *Victory*'s draughts I discovered the size of her beams do not conform to figures given for other vessels of her period. Originally the *Victory* was armed with 42-pounder guns on her lower gundeck, these of course were heavier than her later 32-pounders. Some two-decked 64-gun ships were built with heavier beams on the upper deck to accommodate the change from 12- to 18-pounders after 1762. This is illustrated by the table on page 71.

The beams of the lower deck were disposed so that one was fitted under each gunport, and one in between. Consideration was given to the position of the masts, hatchways and other major constructions and fittings. Beam arms were placed at the position of the mainmast and the main hatch, and on some ships at the foremast. These specially fashioned timbers served to distribute stress, and will be discussed separately.

After some time the number of beams laid down was as follows: Ship, number of guns (number of beams) – 100 (27); 90 (28); 80 (28); 74 (27); 64 (27); 44 (24); 38 (27); 36 (26); 32 (26); 28 (24); 24 (24).

The depth of the first four beams forward, and last four aft, was less than the others. No guns were mounted at these points and there was no real need to fit in large timbers. If guns were mounted at the after end as stern-chasers, they were normally lighter and smaller than the main armament of that deck. Each of the beams was diminished by about ½in as they ran fore or aft, until the depth was approximately 2 to 3in less than the others on that deck.

The beams that were made up of several sections were bolted with the following number of bolts at their scarphs: 100-gun ships had nine 1⅛in diameter bolts; 90-, 80-, and 74-gun ships had eight 1⅛in diameter bolts, 64-gun ships had seven 1in diameter bolts; 44-, 38-, 36-, 32-, 28-, and 24-gun ships had six 1in diameter bolts.

THE MIDDLE GUNDECK

The number of beams fitted on three-deckers was as follows: ship of 100 guns, 31; 90 guns, 30, and three-deck ships with 80 guns, 28. The width of the beams was seven-eighths of the width of the lower gundeck beams. The depth was seven-eighths of its width. Like the gundeck, the beams were laid out with one under each gunport and

one between, the position of the masts and hatchways being taken into consideration. All the beams were the same scantling throughout this deck, except those in the way of the bowsprit step. Here the width was increased by 2 to 3in and the depth by 1 to 1½in. Beam arms were also used on this deck.

THE UPPER GUNDECK

The number of beams fitted on this deck was as follows: Ship, number of guns (number of beams) – 100 (32); 90 (32); 80 (28); 74 (28); 64 (27); 44 (26); 38 (28); 36 (26); 32 (27); 28 (24); 24 (22); sloop (19); cutter (16).

As most vessels had one or two decks, I have calculated the dimensions from those of the lower gundeck:

Width = seven-eighths of the width of the lower gundeck beam

Depth = 2in less than the width.

The above formulae apply to vessels with between 90 and 44 guns. First Rate ships of 100 guns had a factor of three-quarters for

Egmont. The general layout of the Egmont's lower gundeck beams, carlings, and ledges with the respective lodging knees. Along the centreline are the riding bitts, hatchways, capstan partners and the vertical casings of the chain pump (the cisterns are omitted from this model).

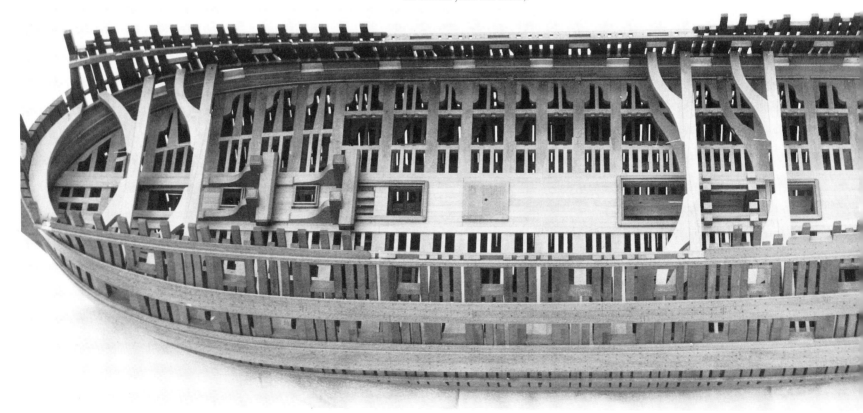

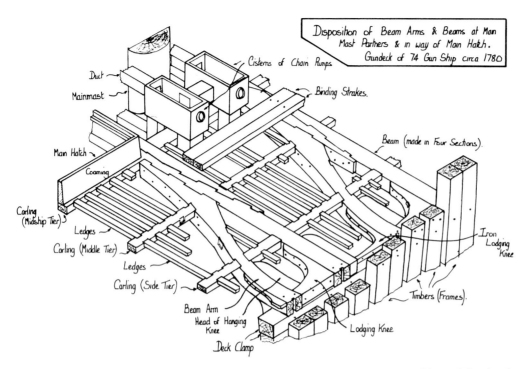

Disposition of Beam Arms & Beams at Main Mast Partners & in way of Main Hatch. Gundeck of 74 Gun Ship circa 1780

Fig 3/2

Egmont. The fore part of the upper gundeck. Here the disposition of the beams, beam arms, carlings and ledges is clear. The construction of the beakhead bulkhead with its catbeam and collar beam is of particular interest. The latter was made from a specially selected piece of compass oak in order to create the rise over the bowsprit.

width, and the depth was the same – 2in less than its width. Frigates had upper deck beams of greater scantling. Therefore for ships of 38 guns and less, add 2in to the width of the lower deck beam. Their depth was 1½in less than their width. The beams were disposed in the same manner as those of the other decks, but it was very rare to find beam arms along this deck.

THE QUARTERDECK

The number of beams on the quarterdeck increased over the years. Originally they ended aft of the mainmast, then a short distance afore it and finally merged with the forecastle. The list below applies to ships built with a quarterdeck which was at its maximum length while still an individual deck. Ship, number of guns (number of beams) – 100 (28); 90 (24); 80 (24); 74 (25); 64 (21); 44 (24); 38 (19); 36 (21); 32 (22); 28 (20); 24 (19); sloop (18).

$$B^{W} = G^{B} \times \alpha$$

where B^{W} = beam width; G^{B} = width of lower gundeck beams. Ship, number of guns (α): 100–90 (seventeen thirty-seconds); 84–64 (nineteen thirty-seconds); 44 (seventeen thirty-seconds); 38–28 (three-quarters); 24, sloop, cutter (seven-eighths).

The depth of the beams can be determined by subtracting 1½in from the width. Most were made in single pieces, for the loading was relatively little. The maximum size of guns mounted on this deck was 12 pounds. More often, only 6- or 9-pounders were placed this high in the ship to keep down topweight. No beam arms were employed at this level.

THE FORECASTLE

The dimensions of these beams were identical to those of the quarterdeck, except for the foremost beam on a ship with a beakhead bulkhead. This was called the catbeam and will be examined later. Ship, number of guns (number of beams) – 100 (12); 90 (11); 80 (13); 74 (13); 64 (9); 44 (10); 38 (10); 36 (10); 32 (11); 28 (10); 24 (9); sloop (6).

THE ROUNDHOUSE (OR POOP)

The number of beams was as follows: Ship, number of guns (number of beams) – 100 (19); 90 (13); 80 (18); 74 (22); 64 (17); 44 (13*); 38 (14*). *These figures apply only to those fitted with a roundhouse.

$$B^W = G^B \times \zeta$$

where B^W = beam width; G^B = width of lower gundeck beam. Ship, number of guns (ζ) – 100 (thirteen thirty-seconds); 90 (thirteen thirty-seconds); 80–64 (seven-sixteenths); 44 (half); 38 (half).

The depth of the beams was 1½in to 2in less than the width.

THE ORLOP DECK

Although the list below shows the number of beams on the orlop, these figures should not be relied on for all ships, because the orlop was not always the same length in proportion to the vessel. For instance *Foudroyant*'s orlop does not continue as far forward as those on other ships. Ship, number of guns (number of beams) – 100 (19); 90 (20); 80 (21); 74 (22); 64 (21); 44 (1); 38 (6); 36 (6); 32 (6). (These figures are taken from the *Shipbuilder's Repository*, 1789.) I cannot understand why the ships of 44 guns should only have one beam fitted. I presume this must be a printing error and that it should read 10. The following figures are from the same source.

The Position of the Fore and After Beams from the Fore and After Perpendiculars

No of guns	Aftermost beam ft in		Foremost beam ft in	
100	25	0	9	7
90	23	0	9	9
84	23	6	10	0
74	24	3	10	4
64	22	8	8	0

These figures again cannot be taken as universal. On a draught of a 74-gun ship of about 1796, the measurements differ. The

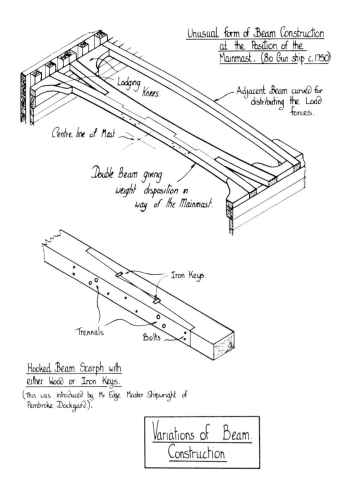

Unusual form of Beam Construction at the Position of the Mainmast. (80 Gun ship c.1750)

Lodging Knees.

Adjacent Beam curved for distributing the Load forces.

Centre line of Mast

Double Beam giving weight disposition in way of the Mainmast.

Iron Keys.

Trennals   Bolts

Hooked Beam Scarph with either Wood or Iron Keys.
(This was introduced by Mr Edge. Master Shipwright of Pembroke Dockyard).

Variations of Beam Construction

Fig 3/3

aftermost beam in this case was 21ft from the after perpendicular, and the foremost beam set 12ft 4in from the fore perpendicular. The *Victory* also has an extra three beams fitted aft, of smaller scantlings than the main beams of the orlop. This I assume was an addition made during her refit in 1812, for it seems the orlop was continued right aft during the early nineteenth century. The *Foudroyant*'s orlop is continued aft, it was constructed like this when she was built in 1817.

It is interesting to note when the orlop was extended to the full length of the ship, it was also altered so that it became a removable rather than a permanently planked deck. The following formulae give the distance that the foremost and aftermost beams were set from their respective perpendiculars:

$$B^A = (G \times 5)/37.5$$

$$B^F = (G \times 5)/\beta$$

where B^A = aftermost beam; B^F = foremost beam; G = length of lower gundeck. Ship, number of guns (β) – 100(19); 90 (18); 84(17); 74(17); 64(20).

The width of these beams was approximately 1 to 1½in less than those of the lower gundeck, and the depth was either the same as their width or 1in less. In some cases the foremost beam was smaller, and may have been added to give further support to the deck at the fore end. Some draughts have a note stating that no stores were to be placed in this deck area. The beams were fashioned with a ledge on each side of their upper faces. This was to receive the ends of the short lengths of planking that made up this deck (see Chapter 2). The beams were disposed as necessary, taking into account positions of the masts, and especially the hanging magazines, if fitted.

THE PLATFORMS

These beams were identical to those of the orlop in both width and depth, and were disposed as required, and worked into the hold to best advantage. All the beams were given the same round up as those of the orlop. The platforms were placed a suitable distance below the bottom face of the gundeck planking. The thickness of the planks of the platform must be added to the given height to give the correct position of the beams.

The following list gives the distances at which the platforms were set below the gundeck. 32-gun frigate, 6ft 6½in; 28-gun frigate, 6ft 2½in; 24-gun frigate, 6ft 2½in; sloop, 5ft 8½in; cutter, 5ft 9in.

THE HALF-DECK

The beams of this deck, if fitted, were similar dimensions to those of the quarterdeck. If guns were mounted, the beams would be set under each gunport, and one between. The round up was between the round up of the quarterdeck and poop deck. Thus, if the quarterdeck had a round up of 8in and the poop had a rise of 10in, that of the half-deck would be 9in. Other beams that were fitted were those of the coach, the skid beams, and the catbeam. Those of the coach were the same as those of the poop. There were two kinds of deck beam: temporary and permanent. When they were fitted permanently they had the same dimensions as those of the quarterdeck and forecastle. The temporary skid beams were common by 1768, and were fitted across the waist for the stowage of the boats. They were the same depth as width, and of slightly smaller dimensions than those of the decks both forward and aft. They were secured by being set into an iron housing bracket, and held with an iron pin or cotter. These beams became permanent around 1782, when the gangways were broadened. They influenced the reduction of the tumblehome and the closing of the waist (see Chapter 2).

The catbeam was the largest beam in the ship. Its length was equal to the width of the fore part of the forecastle. Its width and depth were considerable, for two reasons. Firstly, it had to take the weight of the anchors that were suspended from the catheads, which were bolted to the outer ends of this beam. Secondly, all the vertical stanchions that formed the beakhead bulkhead were set into

the fore face of the beam. The width and depth of this timber can be calculated from the equations given below.

Equation 1 is for ships of 100 to 74 guns, while Equation 2 is for those of 64 and 44 guns and all other smaller vessels that had a beakhead bulkhead. Ships that had a round bow had a beam of similar proportions, but as there were no stanchions for the bulkhead its width would be less, by approximately one-third. For example, a 32-gun frigate had a catbeam about 18in wide and a depth approximately 2in greater than that of the beams that supported the forecastle.

Equation 1 $\quad W = (B^M \times 1.6875)/3; \; D = (B^W \times 3)/8$

Equation 2 $\quad W = (B^M \times 1.875)/3; \; D = (B^W \times 5)/16$

where W = width; B^M = moulded beam; B^W = beam width.

There were other beams in the beakhead bulkhead, such as the chock, and the cat-tail. These are discussed later.

ALTERNATIVE BEAM DIMENSIONS

On some draughts the size of the beams vary according to the type and weight of the armament on each deck. The *Victory*, for example, carried 32-pounders on her lowest gundeck at the time of Trafalgar. The beams that supported that deck should have been about 18in wide, whereas in fact they were approximately 20–21in because this ship was originally fitted out with 42-pounders. Likewise the armament varied on other vessels. Some 74s had 24-pounders instead of the normal 18-pounders on their upper gundeck, while a few 64-gun ships had 18-pounders as an alternative to 12-pounders. There must have been some stipulation governing the actual width and depth a beam should have in order to bear a certain load. I have therefore worked out some calculations that will compensate for any variations of armament borne.

Beams carrying 42-pounder guns:

$$B^W = (B^M \times 13)/32$$

where B^M = moulded beam; B^W = beam width.

The beam width of a 32-pounder was 18in; 24-pounder 15½in; 18-pounder 14in and 12-pounder 12in. The depth of all the above are the same as given earlier for respective gundecks.

Armament Borne by Most Classes of Eighteenth-Century Vessels

1719

No of guns	Lower gundeck		Middle gundeck		Upper gundeck		Quarter-deck		Forecastle	
	No	Pdr	No	Pdr	No	Pdr	No	Pdr	No	Pdr
100	28	42	28	24	28	12	12	6	4	6
90	26	32	26	18	26	9	10	6	2	6
80	26	32	26	12	24	6	4	6	—	
70	26	24	—		26	12	14	6	4	6
60	24	24	—		26	9	8	6	2	6
50	22	18	—		22	9	4	6	2	6
40	20	12	—		20	6	—		—	
30	8	9	—		20	6	2	4	—	
20	—		—		20	6	—		—	

1743

No of guns	Lower gundeck		Middle gundeck		Upper gundeck		Quarter-deck		Forecastle	
	No	Pdr	No	Pdr	No	Pdr	No	Pdr	No	Pdr
100	28	42	28	24	28	12	12	6	4	6
90	26	32	26	18	26	12	10	6	2	6
80	26	32	26	18	24	9	4	6	—	
64	26	32	—		26	18	10	9	2	9
60	24	24	—		24	12	10	6	2	6
50	22	24	—		22	12	4	6	2	6
44	20	18	—		20	9	4	6	—	
20	—		—		20	9	—		—	

1757

Size	No of guns	Lower gundeck		Middle gundeck		Upper gundeck		Quarter-deck		Forecastle	
		No	Pdr	No	Pdr	No	Pdr	No	Pdr	No	Pdr
	100	28	42	28	24	28	12	12	6	4	6
Large	90	28	32	30	18	30	12	—		2	9
Small	90	26	32	26	18	26	12	10	6	2	6
Large	80	26	32	26	18	24	9	4	6	—	
Small	80	26	32	26	12	24	6	4	6	—	
Large	74	28	32	—		30	24	12	9	4	9
Small	74	28	32	—		28	18	14	9	4	9
	70	28	32	—		28	18	12	9	2	9
Large	64	26	24	—		26	18	10	9	2	9
Small	64 (58)	24	24	—		26	12	8	6	2	6
Large	60	26	24	—		26	12	6	6	2	6
Small	60	24	24	—		26	9	8	6	2	6
Large	50	22	24	—		22	12	4	6	2	6
Small	50	22	18	—		22	9	4	6	2	6
Large	44	20	18	—		22	9	—		2	6
Small	44	20	18	—		20	9	—		4	6
	36	—		—		26	12	8	6	2	6
	32	—		—		26	12	4	6	2	6
	28	—		—		24	9	4	3	—	
	24			2	9	20	9	2	3	—	
	20	—		—		20	9	—		—	
Sloops	(ship rigged)	—		—		14	6	—		—	
Sloops		—		—		12	4	—		—	
Sloops		—		—		10	4	—		—	
Sloops		—		—		8	3	—		—	

1762

Size	No of guns	Lower gundeck		Middle gundeck		Upper gundeck		Quarter-deck		Forecastle	
		No	Pdr	No	Pdr	No	Pdr	No	Pdr	No	Pdr
Large	100	30	42	28	24	30	12	10	6	2	6
Small	100	28	42	28	24	28	12	12	6	4	6
Large	90	28	32	30	18	30	12	—		2	9
Small	90	26	32	26	18	26	12	10	6	2	6
	80	26	32	26	18	24	9	4	6	—	
Large	74	28	32	—		30	24	12	9	4	9
Small	74	28	32	—		28	18	14	9	4	9
	70	26	32	—		28	18	12	9	2	9
Large	64	26	24	—		26	18	10	9	2	9
Small	64	26	24	—		26	12	8	6	2	6
	60	26	24	—		26	12	6	6	2	6
	50	22	24	—		22	12	4	6	2	6
	44	20	18	—		22	9	—		2	6
	36	—		—		26	12	8	6	2	6
	32	—		—		26	12	4	6	2	6
	28	—		—		24	9	4	3	—	
	24	2	9	—		20	9	2	3	—	
	20	—		—		20	9	—		—	
Sloops	(ship rigged)	—		—		14	6	—		—	
Sloops		—		—		12	4	—		—	
Sloops		—		—		10	4	—		—	
Sloops		—		—		8	3	—		—	

1792

Size	No of guns	Lower gundeck		Middle gundeck		Upper gundeck		Quarter-deck		Forecastle	
		No	Pdr	No	Pdr	No	Pdr	No	Pdr	No	Pdr
	110	30	32	30	24	32	18	14	12	4	9
Large	100	30	32	28	24	30	18	10	12	2	9
Medium	100	28	32	28	24	30	12	10	12	4	9
Small	100	28	32	28	24	28	12	12	12	4	9
Large	98	28	32	30	18	30	18	8	12	2	9
Small	98	28	32	30	18	30	12	8	12	2	9
	90	26	32	26	18	26	12	10	12	2	9
Large	80	30	32	—		32	24	14	12	4	6
Small	80	30	32	—		32	24	14	9	4	6
Large	74	28	32	—		30	24	14	9	2	6
Small	74	28	32	—		28	18	14	9	4	6
	64	26	24	—		26	18	10	9	2	9
	50	22	24	—		22	12	4	6	2	6
	44	20	18	—		22	12	—		2	6
	40	—		—		28	18	8	9	4	9
	38	—		—		28	18	8	9	2	9
	36	—		—		26	18	8	9	2	9
Large	32	—		—		26	18	4	6	2	6
Small	32	—		—		26	12	4	6	2	6
	28	—		—		24	9	4	6	—	
	24	—		—		22	9	2	6	—	
	20	—		—		20	9	—		—	
Sloop	(ship rigged)	—		—		18	6	—		—	
Sloop		—		—		16	6	—		—	
Sloop		—		—		14	6	—		—	

THE CATBEAM

The function of this beam was to support the inboard ends of the cathead. The catheads had to bear considerable loads, therefore the scantlings of this beam were greater than the other beams of the forecastle. When a catbeam was fitted to a vessel with the traditional square beakhead bulkhead it served two other functions. Firstly, it gave support to the fore end of the forecastle deck. Secondly, it braced the stanchions that formed the frame of the bulkhead. When the catbeam was used for the latter function, it was scored to receive the stanchions at the required intervals.

Ships with round bows also had a catbeam, which served only as a support for the catheads. In all cases the dimensions of this beam can be estimated as 18in wider than the adjacent beams of the forecastle. Its depth was usually the same as the other beams, but occasionally it was about 2in deeper. It would be unwise to give any proportional length for this beam, due to the many variables during the period covered by this book. I have found that the length varied between three-quarters and three-fifths of the breadth of the vessel. This can be accounted for by three factors: the practices of the designer of the ship, whether the ship had a round bow or the beakhead bulkhead, and the degree of tumblehome in the hull.

The hanging knees and lodging knees were thicker than other knees in the vicinity. Generally the siding (thickness) was about 4½in greater than the other knees. Alternatively it can be estimated as 1in greater than the width of the forecastle beams. The length of the side arms and of the athwartships arms remained identical to those of the other knees. There was no variation in the manner in which the whole of the structure was secured together, apart from the increase in the diameter of the bolts (see Fig 3/4).

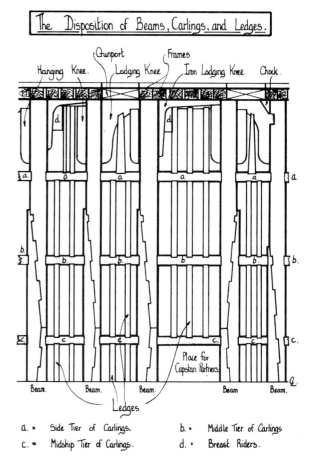

Fig 3/5

Fig 3/4

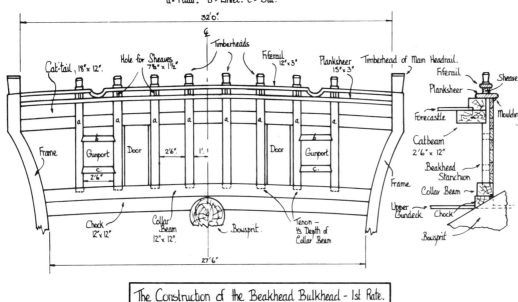

The Construction of the Beakhead Bulkhead - 1st Rate.

Victory. The poop deck undergoing restoration. The following features can be distinguished: the deck beams, the capping plank fitted over the timber heads, the stern counter timbers and their lining, and a lodging knee awaiting fitting. Other features visible are the hammock cranes (left), the crutch for the driver boom (on the taffrail) and the mizzen bitts temporarily removed (right).

THE CARLINGS

Carlings were short lengths of timber worked intercostally fore and aft between the beams. They were set out in specified lines known as tiers, each being a given distance from the centreline. These formed a series of longitudinal members, each consecutive tier having its own name: side tier, middle tier, or midship tier. Taking as an example the lower gundeck of a 74-gun ship: the side tier was 17ft from the ship's centreline, the middle tier 10ft, and the midship tier, 3ft 3in. The opposite side of the ship was exactly the same. The distance from the centreline varied with each deck, because the width of the decks declined due to tumblehome. The midship tier usually formed the athwartships boundaries of hatchways, etc.

Each separate piece was let into the side of the beams, with its upper edge flush with the topside of the beam. The depth to which it was let in varied between 1 and 1½in, and tapered down to ¼in at the bottom. Thus the carling was wedged in place, and it was then secured with nails from below.

The Lower Gundeck

The number of tiers varied with the size of the ship. It also differed at the fore and after ends of the deck, due to the reduction in breadth which occurred at the position of the fore hatch forward, and the mizzen mast aft. The number of tiers on 100- and 90-gun ships was reduced from four to three, on 80- to 32-gun ships from three to two, and on 28- and 24-gun ships from two to one. The

approximate width can be worked out from the following formula. The depth was always between ½ and 1½in less than the width.

$$Width \ of \ the \ carling \ = \ width \ of \ the \ beam \ \times \ \beta$$

Ship, number of guns (β) – 100, 90 (five-eighths); 84, 80, 74, 64, 60 and 44 (nine-sixteenths); (9); 38- and 36-gun frigates (five-eighths); 32- and 28-gun frigates (three-quarters); 24-gun frigates (four-fifths).

The Middle Gundeck

The number of tiers employed was three, being reduced to two at the fore and after ends. Their positions there were identical to those on the lower gundeck. The width was about two-thirds of the width of the beams of that deck, while the depth was 2in less than its width.

The carlings on this deck were fitted in the same manner as those of the lower gundeck. Some ships were fitted with additional half beams aft of the mizzen mast, in which case extra carlings were employed.

The Upper Gundeck

There were three tiers on this deck, in all ships except sloops and cutters, which had two. These were reduced to two and one respectively, forward of the fore hatch and aft of the mizzen mast. The width can be determined by the following equation:

$$Width \ of \ the \ carling = width \ of \ the \ beam \times \gamma$$

Ship, number of guns (γ) – 100 (eleven-sixteenths); 90 (three-quarters); 80–64 (five-eighths); 44 (eleven-sixteenths); 38–36 (nine-sixteenths); 32–24 (five-eighths); sloop and cutter (three-fifths).

The depth of these timbers was approximately 2in less than their width, on all vessels from 110 to 32 guns. Ships of the smaller classes had a depth of about 1½in less than their width. As on the middle gundeck, extra half beams and carlings were fitted aft of the mizzen mast. No carlings were employed on the quarterdeck, forecastle, or poop.

Orlop Deck and Platforms

There were four tiers on First Rate ships, and three on all other vessels. This diminished to three and two respectively at the fore and after ends. The position where this occurred was the same as on other decks. The carlings that formed the sides of hatchways, and those that formed the side tier, were set with their upper surfaces flush with top edges of the beams. This also applied to the carlings at the fore and after ends. The remaining tiers were set down from the upper face of the beams for a depth equal to the thickness of the deck planking. Thus the decking was level with the beams throughout the section.

The width of these carlings was determined as follows:

$$Width \ of \ the \ carling = width \ of \ the \ orlop \ beam \times \delta$$

Ship, number of guns (δ) – 100 (five-eighths); 90 (eleven-sixteenths); 84–64 (three-fifths); 44–32 (eleven-sixteenths).

The depth of these timbers was approximately 1in less than the width on First Rate ships, ½in less on 80-, 74- and 64-gun ships and 2in less on smaller vessels.

THE LEDGES

Shipwrights were not satisfied that beams and carlings alone gave enough support to the decks, and therefore worked additional lengths of timber of smaller scantling. These timbers, known as ledges, were fitted intercostally, parallel to the beams, and scored into the carlings for a depth of about 1–1½in depending on the width. Usually three were fitted between each beam. They were each equal in length to the distance between the tiers of the carlings.

Although measurements were stipulated, the scantlings of the ledges varied according to their position, especially where small, less important, hatches were fitted, and where only two instead of the normal three could be worked. This can be confirmed by close inspection of those of the *Victory* and the *Foudroyant*, where the difference in scantlings of the ledges is up to 4in in width and depth. Those that were worked between the side tier of carlings and the ship's side had their outboard ends let into either the lodging knees or the 'packing pieces' (see Fig 3/14).

The Lower Gundeck

The width of these ledges, except those wrought in the way of hatches and certain other features, can be determined as follows:

$$Breadth \ of \ the \ ledges = width \ of \ the \ carling \times \tfrac{2}{3}$$

This equation is suitable for 80-, 84-, 70-, 74-, and 64-gun ships. The ledges fitted on First Rates were half the width of the carlings. The remaining vessels of between 44 and 24 guns had their ledges fashioned to a breadth of seven-twelfths of the width of the carlings. The depth of these ledges was usually ½in less than the width. All were secured to the carlings with nails driven in from below.

Middle and Upper Gundeck

These were worked in the same fashion as those of the lower gundeck. Their breadth was half of that of their respective carlings, and their depth was ½in less than their width. Ledges were not fitted to the quarterdeck, forecastle or poop.

The Ledges of the Orlop Deck and the Platforms

The ledges were worked where necessary throughout this deck without hindering the access to the hold. The width can be calculated as follows:

Breadth of the ledges = width of the carlings × 7/12

This formula applies to ships from 32 to 44 guns. For First Rates the width was half of that of the carlings, for Second Rates and Third Rates substitute five-eighths for the seven-twelfths.

The Knees

THE HANGING KNEES

The hanging knees were thus named because they were fitted vertically at the ship's side, forming a 'bracket' between the ship's timbers and the beams, and making a tie between the frames each side of the ship. Throughout most of this period the hanging knee was made completely from timber, especially chosen from selected trees. This timber usually came from the part of the tree where a large bough grew out from its bole, with the grain at an angle of about 90 degrees. The knee was thus fashioned from both the bough and part of the trunk which gave them considerable strength. However, timber of those dimensions and shape was becoming more scarce towards the end of the eighteenth century. New methods and materials were needed – this opened up a complete new era in ship construction, paving the way to the later ironclads.

Many variations of iron knees were introduced by constructors such as Snodgrass, Roberts, Seppings, and Symonds, in which combinations of wood and iron, or iron by itself were used. The use of iron was not completely new, for proposals had been made as early as the time of Pepys by Sir Anthony Deane. The various types of iron knee are illustrated in Fig 3/9 and 3/10. Each type of knee will be explained in turn commencing with the normal timber type.

The Wooden Hanging Knee

Each of these knees was fitted adjacent to one of the ship's timbers and was positioned so that the head of the knee could be bolted to one of its side faces – whether fore or aft, depended on the position of the beam. This was very important, for the beams were also locked in place by lodging knees in the horizontal plane. Lodging knees will be explained later, but it is important to understand their effect on the setting out of the hanging knees. It was easier to fashion a knee that was a little over 90 degrees than less. Moreover, timber with grain running at an angle of less than 90 degrees was rare. The hanging knees were fayed and bolted to the opposite side

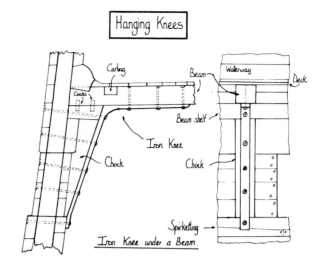

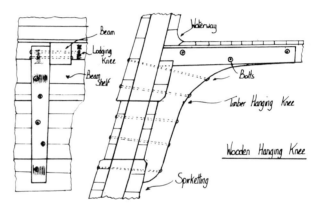

Fig 3/6

of the beam to the lodging knee. Therefore all the lodging knees were fitted to the after side of the beams in the fore half of the ship and to the fore side of the beams in the after half. The heads of the hanging knees were disposed so that those in the fore body of the ship were fitted to the fore side of the beams, and those in the after body were fitted to the after side. Sutherland wrote in *Shipbuilding Unveiled* of 1717 'The hanging knees are placed in the same position with the timbers, bolted both to beams and timbers for holding the beams to the sides.

'The beams ought to be placed one between and one under the ports of each deck, with this caution that the hanging knee may be placed clear of the ports and lodging knees abaft the beams forward and afore the beams abaft, for the benefit of making these knees as much greater than a square or as obtuse an angle as possible for the easiness of procuring them.'

The knees were made from oak cut to the required siding. Special care was taken to prevent too much wood being taken away from the area of the throat. This was because it was here that the knee had to be its strongest. Each was given a slight taper towards its toe, thus slightly decreasing its weight. The width at the throat was two

Victory. *The poop deck under reconstruction. Here the typical beam layout can be seen, with timber and iron lodging knees. On the left are the heads of the hanging knees and the mizzen topsail bitts, and on the right timber lodging knees. All are waiting to be fitted.*

and a half times the thickness or siding of the knee. The head or 'beam arm' of the knee was secured by three or four bolts, and two trennals or coaks. The bolts that fastened the side arm to the ship's side were disposed so that the top two were set as high as possible, and the remaining ones set at equal intervals down to the toe. All of the bolts that secured the side arm were driven through from outside, and clenched internally.

After 1748 longer bolts were employed, and were driven through the throat from within and clenched externally. Special care was taken to ensure that the bolts passed right through the timber. If this could not be achieved packing pieces were wrought between the timbers. Copper bolts, if used, had to be clenched with a ring or 'rove'. In this case, the copper bolts also had to have a ring fitted under their heads. Where the bolts were clenched externally, care was taken to have the end let into the planking, thus ensuring a flush finish after caulking. This was accomplished by boring out the plank to a small depth, to allow the rove to be fitted and the bolt to be riveted over it. Care had to be taken to ensure that the bolt, if driven from within, did not emerge at a planking seam.

After 1790, hanging knees were fayed to the underside of the beams, instead of one of the side faces. This meant that the lodging knees could be fitted to either side of the beam and thus in any position where abnormality in construction made strengthening necessary. The hanging knee thus took on the form of a 'chock', the length of the beam arm being shortened. This was to lead to the combination of timber and iron knee construction.

The Lower Gundeck (or Gundeck)

The siding or width of the hanging knee on this deck was equal to

$$Width\ of\ the\ beam \times \beta$$

Ship, number of guns (β) – 100 (two-thirds); 90 (eleven-sixteenths); 84–80 (two-thirds); 70–74 (three-fifths); 64-44 (five-eighths); 38- and 36-gun frigates (three-quarters); other smaller vessels (thirteen-sixteenths).

The length of the beam arm (or head) was a certain number of inches per yard of the ship's moulded beam.

$$Length\ of\ the\ beam\ arm\ of\ the\ knee = (moulded\ beam/3) \times \alpha$$

Ship, number of guns, (α in inches) – 110–100 ($3\frac{1}{2}$); 98–90 (3); 84–80 ($3\frac{3}{4}$); 74–70 ($3\frac{3}{4}$); 64–36 ($3\frac{1}{2}$); 32–24 ($3\frac{3}{4}$).

The side or vertical arm ran from the head of the knee to a position approximately in line with the top edge of the spirketting. This length was roughly one-third greater than the length of the beam arm or head, on all ships of 38 guns or more. On ships with less than 38 guns, the length was about one-quarter greater than the length of the beam arms.

Example: to determine the size of the hanging knee for a 50-gun ship with a moulded beam of 45ft.

The width of the beam = (moulded beam/3) × ¹⁷/₁₆ (from section on beams)

$$= {}^{45}/_3 × {}^{17}/_{16} = (15·94) = 16in$$

The siding of the knee = (width of the beam × 5)/8

$$= (16 × 5/8) = 10in$$

Length of the beam arm = (moulded beam/3) × 3½in

$$= {}^{45}/_3 × 3·5 = 52·5in = 4ft\ 4½in$$

Length of the side arm = (beam arm/3) + beam arm

$$= {}^{52·5}/_3 = 17·5 + 52·5 = 70in = 5ft\ 10in$$

Throat width = 2½ × the siding

$$= 2·5 × 10in$$
$$= 25in$$

Therefore a ship of 50 guns with a moulded beam of 45ft would have knees 10in thick, 4ft 4½in long at the head or beam arm, and 5ft 10in long from head to toe. Its width at the throat was 25in.

Bolts Securing Hanging Knees of Lower Gundeck

No of guns	No of bolts	Diameter of bolts (inches)	No of guns	No of bolts	Diameter of bolts (inches)
100 and 90	8	1½	38 and 36	8	1¼
80 and 74	7	1⅜	32	8	1
64	6	1⅜	28 and 24	7	1
50	6	1¼	20	7	⅞
44	7	1¼			

The Middle Gundeck

These were fitted in the same manner as those of the lower gundeck. The siding of these knees can be estimated by the following formula:

Siding of the knee = the width of the middle deck beams × ²¹/₃₂

The length of the beam arm or head of the knee was 3in for every yard of the ship's moulded beam. The length of the side arm was such that its toe terminated at the line of the upper edge of the spirketting. The throat had a width of two and a half times the siding. In all cases seven 1¼in diameter bolts were used for fastening the knee, to both the beam and the ship's side.

The Upper Gundeck

The knees of this deck were fitted and secured in an identical manner to those of the lower and middle gundeck. The siding of the knees can be calculated as follows:

Siding of the knee = width of the upper deck beam × α.

Ship, number of guns (α) – 100, 90, 38, 36, 32, and 28, (two-thirds); 84, 80, 74, and 70 (three-fifths); 44 (eleven-sixteenths); 24 and 20 (five-eighths); sloops and cutters (nine-sixteenths).

The width across the throat was two and a half times its siding. The length of the side arm was taken from the head of the knee to a position 6in below the upper edge of the spirketting. To calculate the length of the beam arm, the following formula can be used:

Length of the beam arm = (moulded beam/3) × βin

Ship, number of guns (β) – 110–90 (2⅝); 84–70 (2¾); 64–60 (2⅞); 50–44 (3¼); 38–24 (3½); sloops (4); cutters (3½).

The number of bolts employed was as follows: seven on all vessels of between 110 and 32 guns, six on the 20- to 28-gun frigates, and five on sloops and armed cutters. The diameters of these bolts varied: Ship, number of guns (diameter of bolts) – 110–64 guns (1¼in); 50–28 (1in); 24–20 (¾in); sloops and cutters (⅝in).

The Quarterdeck and the Forecastle

Fitted in the same way as the knees of the other decks, the knees of both these decks were more or less identical. Any difference in the beam size was reflected in the dimensions of the knees. During the first half of this period the scantlings of the forecastle beams were slightly less than those of the quarterdeck. This changed, and the continuous deck evolved, thus the knees became identical in their dimensions.

Siding of the knee = beam width × η

Ship, number of guns (η) – 110, 100, 90, 84, 80, 74, 70, 50, 44 and 38 (eleven-sixteenths); 64, 60, 36 (five-eighths); 32 and less (two-thirds).

The side arm of these knees was made so it terminated at the toe at the upper edge of the spirketting. The length of the beam arm was determined in the following manner:

Length of the beam arm = (moulded beam/3) × δin

Ship, number of guns (δ) – 110–80 (2½); 74–60 (2⅝); 44–24 (2⅞); sloops (3¼).

The throat was two and a half times the siding of the knee. All vessels of between 110 and 32 guns had their knees fastened with seven bolts, 20- to 28-gun frigates had six bolts and there were five on sloops. The diameters were as follows: all vessels of 44 guns and above had bolts of 1in diameter; those with between 38 and 28 guns ¾in bolts and the remaining smaller ships had ⅝in bolts.

The Roundhouse

Unlike other decks, only every other beam was supported with a knee on this deck, and these were placed where they would be most beneficial. The throat was made to a width two and a half times its siding, and the side arm was made so that it terminated at 6in above the spirketting. In all vessels there were five ¾in bolts for fastening the knees.

Siding of the knee = *roundhouse beam width* × γ

Ship, number of guns (γ) 110, 100, 64, 60, 50, 44, 38 (three-quarters); 90 (five-eighths); 84-70 (eleven-sixteenths).

Length of the beam arm = (*moulded beam*/3) × εin

Ship, number of guns (ε) – 110–98 (1¾); 90 (1⅞); 84–64 (2); 50–44 (2¼); 38 (2⅛).

The Orlop Deck

The construction of the knees on this deck differed from those on the other decks. Due to the curvature of the hull, turning towards the keel below the waterline, it was impractical to have hanging knees below the beams. This problem was also experienced in fitting the lodging knees at the fore and after ends of the decks. The builder thus inverted the knees, so that their vertical arms rose above the orlop beams. Apart from this, their disposition and attachment to the ship's structure was the same as that on other decks (see Fig 3/7).

Not all of the beams were supported with these inverted knees, or standards as they were more commonly known. Those that did not have inverted knees fitted were either those that received the heads of the second futtock riders or occasionally the fore or aftermost beams. Prior to the introduction of 'riders', when internal stiffening was by a series of 'cross pales', all the beams were supported by standards.

The number of bolts used for their fastening was as follows: 100- to 90-gun ships had 9; 84- to 70-gun ships had 8; 64-gun ships had 7; and the remaining vessels had 6. The diameter of the bolts varied between 1¼ and 1in. As with other knees, the throat was two and a half times bigger than its siding. The siding was determined as follows for ships of between 90 and 70 guns:

Siding of the knee = *orlop beam width* × σ

Ship, number of guns (σ) – 110, 100 and 64 (five-eighths); 90-70 (three-fifths); 44-32 (eleven-sixteenths).

The vertical, or side arm terminated at the lower edge of the upper strake of the gundeck clamp. The length of the beam arm was formulated in the following manner:

Length of beam arm = (*moulded beam*/3) × μin

Ship, number of guns (μ) – 110–70; (3¼) 64; (3½) 44; (3⅞) 38–32 (3⅞).

WROUGHT IRON KNEES

As timber became scarcer, it was necessary to use iron, either as an alternative to, or in combination with timber. These new methods had both advantages and disadvantages. The main disadvantage was that the iron could not be fastened as tightly as timber knees.

The Roberts Iron Plate Knee

This was introduced at the close of the eighteenth century, and was probably brought about because of a change in the construction of timber hanging knees. In the early 1790s, the hanging knee was set below the beam instead of to one side, a technique introduced to economise on the use of timber. This new type of knee, or chock as it became known, was fashioned with an inclined surface on its upper edge. The beam above was also given an inclined slot on its lower edge, into which the chock was put. The inclined faces were fashioned so that a horizontal slot, about 1½ to 2in wide, was left. Into this slot were placed two opposing iron wedges, of greater width than the hole. The purpose of these was to create a means of tightening up the structure when the ship was working in heavy seas, or to take up any slackness due to· shrinkage in the timber. Adjustment was simple, for all the ship's carpenter had to do was drive the wedges towards each other.

The chock, made from oak and sawn to the siding of the beam it supported, was tapered towards its toe, the reduction being about three-quarters of its siding at its head. Its length along its upper edge in the athwartships direction (the beam arm) can be estimated as 1⅞in for every yard of the ship's beam. The chock would be bolted to the ship's side with four or five bolts varying between 1¼ and ¾in in diameter.

The wrought iron plate was basically triangular in shape. The short length was set at right angles to the head. This ran along the ship's side, acting as a lodging knee. The angled portion of the plate was disposed so that it fitted in with the chock, thus ensuring that no part of the plate protruded beyond the boundaries of both beam and chock. The number of bolts used to fasten the plate varied according to the size of the plate. Each bolt was driven through the plate and the chock, and clenched on the side opposite the plate. If a plate was fitted to both sides of the chock, the bolts were driven through all three components, and clenched.

The dimension and shape of the plates varied according to where they were placed in the ship. Those fitted for the orlop beams were made to an angle of less than 90 degrees. Those on the gundeck were more or less right angled, and those further up the ship were more obtuse. When the iron plate was fitted, it was not unusual for the shipwright to set the plate into the timber to a depth of half its thickness. This was easily achieved by chiselling out the correct amount of wood after first drawing around the shape of the plate. This practice was used for all the iron knees described in the following sections.

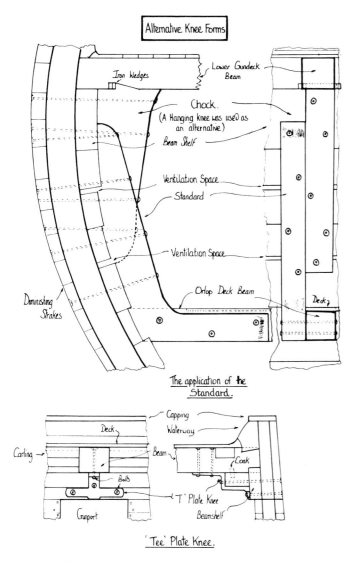

Fig 3/7

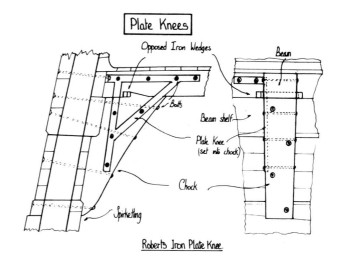

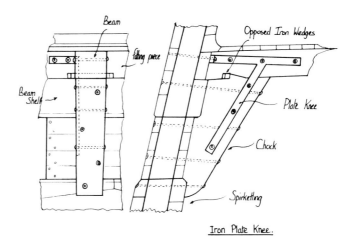

Fig 3/8

The Plates on the Gundeck

Although this section deals mainly with the gundeck, it also applies to those decks fitted where the ship's side was fairly vertical and not affected by tumblehome. It is not so easy to determine the sizes of the plates, therefore the data given in this part of the text must be treated as a rough estimate.

Proportional dimensions:

head or beam arm length = beam depth × 3
(or length of head of chock × 2)
side arm length = beam arm length × $\frac{7}{8}$
angled arm length = beam arm length × $\frac{5}{8}$
bracket length = deck beam wdth × $1\frac{1}{2}$
arm width = deck beam depth × $\frac{1}{3}$
number of bolts = 9 (2 set through bracket);
sometimes 11

The Plates Fitted on Other Decks

The plates mentioned in this section are those employed where the tumblehome was more pronounced, generally on upper gundecks.

Proportional dimensions:

beam arm length = deck beam depth × 3
(or length of head of chock × 2)
side arm length = beam arm length × $\frac{13}{16}$
angled arm length = beam arm length × $\frac{5}{6}$
bracket length = deck beam width × $1\frac{1}{2}$
arm width = deck beam depth × $\frac{1}{3}$
plate thickness = arm width × $\frac{1}{3}$
number of bolts = 7 (2 set through bracket)

Victory. The middle gundeck showing the following features: a chock type hanging knee with its associated Roberts plate knee, a side cast knee, and the upper gundeck beams and ledges. Also visible are various forms of internal planking, the deck clamp, lining, and spirketting. Packing pieces are worked above the deck clamp.

Victory. The carpenter's walk, starboard side looking aft showing fine examples of the chock type hanging knee braced with Roberts iron plate knees. Adjacent to each chock are the vertical portions of the inverted knees which support the orlop beams; these are generally called standards. Note the iron wedges set in the chock heads for tightening the structure, also the unusual 'weatherboard' planking on the near bulkhead.

The Plates Fitted on the Orlop Deck

The dimensions of these plates differ somewhat from those of the other decks, due to the curvature of the hull towards the keel. The data below gives the approximate sizes:

$$\text{beam arm length} = \text{deck beam depth} \times 2\tfrac{1}{4}$$
$$\text{side arm length} = \text{deck beam depth} \times 2\tfrac{7}{8}$$
$$\text{bracket length} = \text{deck beam width} \times 1\tfrac{1}{2}$$
$$\text{arm width} = \text{deck beam depth} \times \tfrac{1}{3}$$
$$\text{plate thickness} = \text{arm width} \times \tfrac{1}{3}$$
$$\text{number of bolts} = 10 \ (2 \text{ set through bracket})$$

Iron Plate Knees

This style of plate knee was nearly identical to the type designed by Roberts. The only difference was the absence of a side arm. A chock was still fitted beneath the beams, onto which the angled arm of the plate was secured. Estimated dimensions are as follows:

The plate:

$$\text{beam arm length} = \text{deck beam depth} \times 2\tfrac{7}{8}$$
$$\text{angled arm length} = \text{to beam arm}$$
$$\text{bracket length} = \text{deck beam width} \times 1\tfrac{1}{3}$$
$$\text{arm width} = \text{deck beam depth} \times \tfrac{1}{2}$$
$$\text{plate thickness} = \text{arm width} \times \tfrac{1}{3}$$
$$\text{number of bolts} = 7, 8, \text{ or } 9; \text{ their diameters being}$$
$$\tfrac{1}{6}\text{th the width of the arms.}$$

The chock:

$$\text{length athwartships of the head} = \text{deck beam depth} \times 2$$
$$\text{siding of the head} = \text{deck beam width}$$
$$\text{siding of the toe} = \text{head} \times \tfrac{2}{3}$$
$$\text{height of the chock} = \text{head} \times 3$$
$$\text{number of bolts} = 5$$

The Iron Knee

This type of knee was a bracket set between the lower face of the beam and a chock at the ship's side. This method of construction also included a 'beam shelf', which was a strake of planking wrought along the inboard face of the deck clamp. The beam shelf was made from oak, its width in the athwartships direction being one and one-third of the depth of the beam it supported. Its depth was approximately half its width. The beam shelf was both bolted and fastened with trennals throughout its length, to the deck clamp. The length of this strake was between 25 and 36ft, each length being joined by a flat scarph set vertically. The scarphs were given sufficient shift to those of the deck clamp. Special care was taken to ensure that the butts did not terminate beneath any beam.

The beam was bolted to both the deck clamp and the beam shelf. The bolts passing through the latter were driven upward and clenched above the waterway, through which they also passed. Between the beam and the beam shelf a pair of cylindrical coaks of either oak or lignum vitae were fitted to act as locating dowels. The inboard face of the beam shelf was angled so the iron knee could fit against it. Fayed to the ship's side below the beam shelf was the chock, which had a siding equal to the width of the beam. The athwartships width at its head was fashioned to fair in with the lower edge of the beam shelf. Its toe terminated at the upper strake of the spirketting.

The wrought iron knee was fashioned to the angle required, and made to the following specification: the bracket had a width of half the width of the beam (it was very rare for the width to exceed 6in because the iron was usually only made in widths of either 6, 4½, 3, and 2in). The thickness of the knee was about half its width at the throat, diminishing to between a half or a third at its extremities. The length of the upper arm was approximately 3in for every yard of the ship's beam for the larger vessels, and 3½in for ships of 44 guns and less. The length of the vertical arm was such that it terminated on the upper strake of the spirketting.

There were usually four or five bolts for the side arm, and three or four on the arm under the beam. The diameter of all these was one-sixth of the width of the knee. They were driven from within, passing through the chock and the ship's side and were clenched externally. Those driven through the upper arm were clenched on the top surface of the beam below the planking. No lodging knees were employed, therefore carlings were worked between the ends of the beams to preserve the rigidity of the structure. The athwartships width of these carlings was about the same as the depth of the beam, and their depth was usually half their width. They were positioned so that their outboard edge was in line with the inboard side of the beam shelf. For a complete explanation see Fig 3/6.

The Plate Bolt

This iron fastening was only employed for securing the roundhouse beams. It comprised three components: a beam shelf, a chock and a vertical iron plate. The beam shelf, made from oak, was fashioned with an athwartships width the same as the beam it supported. Its depth was half its width. This beam shelf was wrought along the inboard side of the deck clamps, and probably in one continuous length.

The head of the chock was fashioned to the siding of the beam,

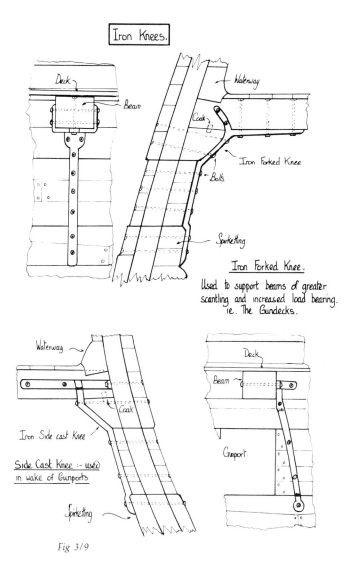

Fig 3/9

Foudroyant. *The carpenter's walk, port side looking forward. Chock knees and their respective plate knees were fitted throughout this deck. The modern valve set into a timber block occupies the same position as the original sea suction pump which was used for washing down decks and firefighting. Note the upper faces of the lodging knees on the deck and the iron wedges set into the heads of the chock knees.*

tapering slightly towards its toe. The width in the athwartships direction was the same as that of the beam shelf, and angled down to the spirketting where it terminated. Both the chock and the beam shelf were fastened to the ship's side by bolts driven through the iron plate, the number usually being five. The uppermost was driven through the beam shelf. The lowest bolt passed through the spirketting. All were clenched externally.

The iron plate was generally half the width of the beam, and its thickness at the head was half its width, tapering to half that at its toe. The head of the plate was fashioned with an integral bolt which passed vertically upward through the beam, and was clenched. It was this specially designed bolt that gave this fitting its name. The beam itself was secured by two bolts worked through from the underside of the beam shelf, and clenched above the waterway. A single coak of lignum vitae was employed for joining the beam to the beam shelf. This method of securing beams could only be used for lightly constructed decks, due to its weakness.

The Seppings Forked Knee and Chock

Like most of the other combinations of wood and iron used for supporting a beam's ends, a beam shelf, a chock and a form of iron bracket were used. The beam shelf was made to similar dimensions as those of the other designs. Its width was the same as the depth of the beam, and its depth half of its width. The chock was also made to exactly the same scantling as all those previously mentioned. The only difference was when the chocks were used for the support of the lowest gundeck beams, when their heels were continued down to be set on the top of the ends of the beams of the orlop. The inner face was not angled in towards the ship's side like those used on the other decks, but made more vertical. The purpose of this was to allow a 'side plate' to be fitted between the chock and the orlop beam; thus incorporating two features in one, and eliminating the standards of the orlop (see Figs 3/11 and 3/12).

The iron knee was forked into two curved arms that passed on either side of the beam. Both arms and the vertical plate (or side arm) were made to a width of either half or a third of the width of the chock, depending on which deck they were fitted to. Their thickness was approximately half their width. The number of bolts for the forked arms would generally be three, each being worked in the horizontal plane between each arm, through the beam and clenched to one side. The vertical arm was secured by four bolts, the uppermost passing through the beam shelf. All were driven from within, and clenched externally. Two other bolts were employed, one driven through the beam into the beam shelf, the other through both the waterway and beam into the beam shelf. These were fitted before the chock was placed into position, for the bolts had to be clenched underneath the beam shelf.

On larger vessels, where the dimensions of the beams were greater, five bolts were used to fasten the vertical or side arm. Also a single bolt was passed vertically up into the beam from the point where the iron knee was forked. This single bolt eliminated the need for the second bolt that went through the beam and the beam shelf.

One or two coaks usually made from lignum vitae, were set into the beam shelf and beam for location. If lodging knees were omitted, a tier of carlings, was wrought at a short distance from the ship's side. These were two-thirds of the depth of the beam in width, and in depth half their own width (see Figs 3/11 and 3/12).

Unicorn. *The port side of the berthing deck showing Seppings forked iron knees and their associated chocks. The beam shelf, deck clamp, lining and the spirketting can also be seen. Note the packing pieces fitted under the beam ends of the intermediate beams. The rectangular hole cut in the ship's side is not original. This fore part of the berthing deck was the living quarters for the common sailor, the table slung from the beams with a long stool being typical of a 'mess' during that period.*

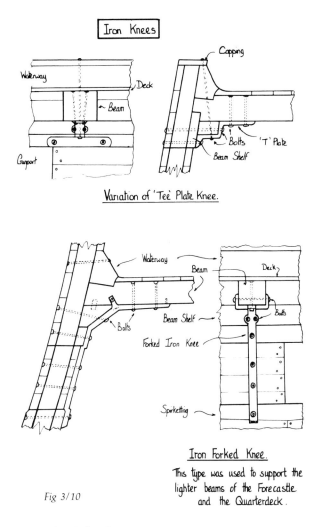

Fig 3/10

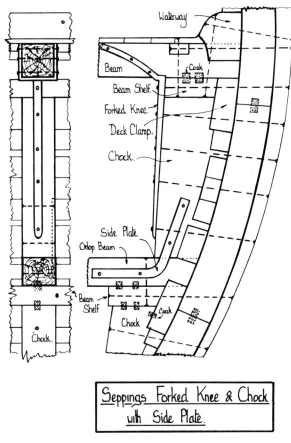

Fig 3/11

The Side Plate

This plate was the shape of a right angle, set across the chock that supported the gundeck beam and the beam of the orlop deck. Each arm was approximately twice the depth of the orlop beam in length, a third of the depth of that beam in width, and half of the width of the arm in thickness. Generally, four bolts were used for fastening, two to each arm. In all cases, a beam shelf was fitted below the beams, but it was of greater scantling than those used elsewhere in the ship. Its athwartships width was twice the depth of the beam, and its depth a third of its own width.

This shelf was fayed and bolted throughout the length of the hold to the orlop deck clamps. Two lignum vitae coaks were incorporated between the beam end and the beam shelf, for locating both members. One bolt was driven through both the beam shelf and the beam, and clenched underneath. Sometimes further support was given by the heads of the futtock riders, or by the heads of the trussed frame timbers that terminated directly below the beams (see Fig 3/11).

The Forked Knees

This type of construction was fashionable during the second quarter of the nineteenth century, and was introduced by Symonds. Unlike any of the other techniques where iron was used, this eliminated both the beam shelf and the chock. The knee itself was of a more complex design and was an iron knee in its own right. By the omission of the beam shelf, the deck clamp was increased in scantling. The deck clamp was either rounded or angled on its inboard face. When it was fashioned with a convex edge the whole clamp was wrought in one strake of timber down to the line of the gunport lintels. The athwartships width was increased to equal the depth of the beam it supported, and its depth was equal to the space between the beam and the lintels. Its inboard face was convex, fairing in to the quickwork below.

If the clamp was made with an angled face, it was usually wrought in two strakes, the lower being of rectangular cross-section. The upper strake was made to a depth and athwartships width equal to the depth of the beam. By this time the waterways had been increased in size, and were therefore scored on their lower edge in way of the beams, which slotted down onto them. This

83

Left: Unicorn. *The gundeck, starboard side, midships, showing three iron bracket knees and a diagonal timber truss worked between the frames giving additional longitudinal strength.*

Right: Unicorn. *The carpenter's walk, starboard side looking aft, showing the disposition of the beam shelf, deck clamp, thick stuff, chocks and iron knees. A diagonal iron rider plate is in the centre of the photograph.*

produced a more rigid fastening, preventing the beam from working fore or aft. All of the beams were fastened to the deck clamps with coaks of lignum vitae.

The iron knee was made in the form of a bracket, with two short side arms that clasped each side of the beam. The side or vertical arm was fashioned to fit the ship's side, and the shape of the inboard face of the deck clamp. The width of the arm was approximately one-third of the width of the beam, and its thickness was about a third of its width. The upper arm was secured to the beam by either two or three bolts driven up into the beam. The short side arms had either one or two bolts driven through in the horizontal plane, and clenched to one side of the beam. The arm at the ship's side was fastened with five or six bolts, and clenched externally, the uppermost passing through the deck clamp. The difference of one bolt in the side arm was because if the single strake of a rounded deck clamp was used, two bolts would be worked, and if the deck clamp was of two strakes only, one bolt went through the clamp and the other four were disposed of as the builder thought fit. A tier

of carlings was worked a short distance from the ship's side to give additional longitudinal strength, instead of having lodging knees fitted. The athwartships width of each was two-thirds of the beam width, and the depth of about half its own width (see Fig 3/9).

The Side Cast Knee

This type of knee was used where beams were fitted over the tops of gunports, where a normal straight iron knee could not be fitted. This could be incorporated with any type of deck clamp. The knee was fashioned with one beam arm, fitted to the side of a beam away from the port, and a side arm, that in one plane was made to the contour of the internal planking at the ship's side. A third arm or bracket was set at right angles to the beam arm, and formed a short lodging knee on the side of the beam away from the port.

The length of the beam arm was three times the depth of the beam, and the side arm was cut so it terminated on the upper strake

Details of a Seppings Designed Vessel – 'Unicorn' 1824

Chock and Iron Bracket Supports - sited at the Fore Platform.

Iron Forked Knee supporting the Gundeck Beams.

Fig 3/12

of spirketting. The right-angled bracket was made to a length the same as, or one and a half times, the width of the beam. The width of all arms was about one-third of the beam's width, and its thickness was half its own width. Three bolts were used to fasten the beam arm to the side of the beam. Two were driven through the bracket, and four through the side arm, the uppermost passing through the deck clamp. The number of bolts varied according to the size of the knee. Carlings were not needed since the right-angled bracket was constructed integrally with the knee (see Figs 3/9 and 3/10).

The 'T' Plate Knee

This form of knee was used on smaller vessels, and for the ends of the roundhouse beams on larger ships. It was also used for various small fittings throughout the ship. When it acted as a beam support, a beam shelf would be worked along the inboard side of the deck clamps. The beam shelf, as always, had a width the same as the

depth of the beam, and a breadth equal to half its own width (and in some cases two-thirds). The knee itself was fashioned in the form of an inverted 'T', its beam arm the length of the beam's width. The whole component was fairly small. The beam was continued and fashioned over the beam shelf, and formed a 'T' where it met the deck clamp. Six bolts were employed. Two were driven up into the beam and two from the ends of the 'T' into the ship's side. The other two bolts were set through the beam shelf, one driven horizontally to the ship's side, the other set up through the beam shelf and the waterway above (see Figs 3/7 and 3/10).

THE LODGING KNEES

The lodging knees were fitted horizontally between the ends of the deck beams at the ship's side, giving additional strength. Their primary function was to 'lodge' the beams longitudinally, preventing movement fore or aft, which could occur when the vessel was working in heavy seas. Like hanging knees, they were made from specially selected oak, which had grain with a turn of 90 degrees. This gave the knees much greater strength. Before 1748 lodging knees were only fitted to the beams of the orlop and the gundecks (they were not always fitted to the platform beams). After this date it was decided that they should also be fitted to the deck beams of the forecastle, quarterdeck and the poop. This further increased the strength of the vessel's upperworks.

The lodging knees were always fitted on the opposite side to the hanging knees on the same beam. The toe of the lodging knee was therefore butted against the face of the hanging knee on the adjacent beam. This was repeated throughout the length of the ship, the beams thus being locked longitudinally, giving rigidity to the structure. Due to the curvature of the ship's side towards the centreline at both the fore and after ends of the hull, the lodging knees were positioned so that those at the ends were given a more obtuse angle between the beam and the ship's side. If the knees had been made with a more acute angle they would have been weaker. Also, the procurement of timber for this would have been extremely difficult. Therefore the lodging knees fitted throughout the fore body of a vessel were fastened to the after side of the beams, whereas those in the after body were fastened to the fore side of the beams.

Usually knees were fastened with between nine and six bolts, three or four of which were driven through and clenched to the athwartships arm of the adjacent hanging knee. The remaining bolts were driven from without the hull at varying angles, and clenched internally. Like the hanging knees, the planking on the outside of the hull was bored to receive the bolt heads; the holes were plugged and caulked on completion. The side arms of these knees were fitted in one of two ways. By one method a packing piece of beech was lodged between the beam ends on the deck clamp and against the ship's timbers. The side arm was fayed to the packing piece, the bolts being driven right through. Alternatively the side arm of the lodging knee was made of sufficient scantling so it could be set in against the timbers and let down on to the deck clamp.

Many of the lodging knees employed during the latter years of the eighteenth century were made from two pieces of timber. This was due to insufficient supplies of suitable wood, and was aimed at reducing wastage by using up the off-cuts left from other parts of the structure. The corners of the lodging knee were built up with a triangular chock which made up for the deficiency of wood. In some cases this chock was omitted. The absence of wood at the corner made better ventilation to the beam ends possible, thereby reducing problems of rot. Secondly, there was no particular requirement at this point for strength, this being essential at the arms (see Fig 3/14).

When iron lodging knees were introduced at the end of the eighteenth century, they were first adopted on the beams of the poop. This was to reduce topweight, but over the next decade they were employed more extensively throughout the vessel. When fitted on the poop they were disposed on every other beam and in way of the gunports and doorways to the quarter galleries. There does not seem to be any pattern governing their position in other

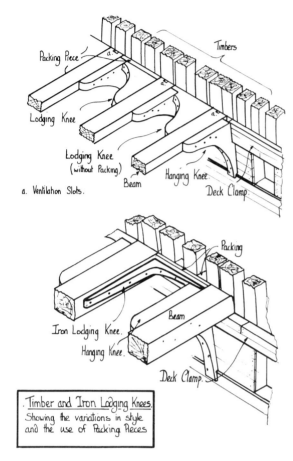

a. Ventilation Slots.

Timber and Iron Lodging Knees.
Showing the variations in style and the use of Packing Pieces

Fig 3/13

Fig 3/14

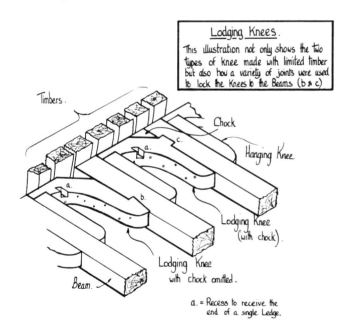

Lodging Knees.
This illustration not only shows the two types of knee made with limited timber but also how a variety of joints were used to lock the knees to the Beams (b & c)

a. = Recess to receive the end of a single Ledge.

Foudroyant. The curved lodging knees and beams of orlop (or platform) deck. The photograph was taken in the port side of the hold. This type of lodging knee was only used when the disposition of the beams made them necessary. Note the carling worked intercostally between the athwart arms of the lodging knees and the beams.

parts of the vessel. The draught of a 74-gun ship in Rees' *Naval Architecture* shows variations in their disposition on the gundeck. In places they are fitted at every other beam, and in other areas just as necessary. When Seppings introduced iron forked knees during the second decade of the nineteenth century, the necessity for lodging knees was diminished, due to the design of these new fittings.

Curved Lodging Knees

One of the most interesting aspects of lodging knee design can be found on the *Victory* and the *Foudroyant*. Here the side arms are fashioned with a downward curve, the toe terminating below the following beam. This method appears to be applied to the beams of the orlop and to those that support the platforms within the hold. Those on board the *Victory* are only fitted at one beam, which is situated next to the bulkhead at the fore end of the main hold (see Fig 3/15). The curved lodging knees on the *Foudroyant* are adjacent to all the beams amidships that support the cable tier (see Fig 3/15). This unusual design can be attributed to the disposition of the beams, the spacing of which was limited due to the design requirements of the vessel. The side arm had to be of sufficient length to give better loading distribution and greater surface area for security. It is safe to assume that this practice was applied only to ships where the disposition of the orlop or platform beam spacing was restricted. By the 1820s, this fashion had been superseded by the iron side plate, which served both as a standard and a lodging knee.

The Dimensions of the Timber Lodging Knees

On the orlop deck or platform, the length of the athwartships arm was exactly the same as that of the athwartships arm of the standards or hanging knees. The length of the side arm was equal to the spacing between the beams*. The siding can be estimated as follows: Ship, number of guns (proportion of moulded depth of beam) – 110–60 (five-eighths); 50–40 (seven-tenths); 38–20 (three-quarters). The number of bolts employed was: nine for ships of between 110 and 90 guns; eight or seven for those of between 84 and 60 guns; the remaining vessels had six, except sloops which had five. The diameter of these bolts varied from 1¼ to ¼in according to the ship.

On the lowest gundeck, the athwartships arm was likewise the same length as those of the hanging knees. The length of the side arm was equal to the spacing between the beams. The siding was as follows: Ship, number of guns (proportion of the moulded depth of beam) – 110–60 (three-fifths); 50–40 (two-thirds); 38 and 36 (three-quarters); 32–18 (four-fifths). The number of bolts employed was eight or seven, depending on the size of the vessel. These were made to a diameter of 1¼ to 1in.

On the middle gundeck, the length of the athwartships arm was from 3 to 6in greater than that of the athwartships arm of the adjacent hanging knee. The side arm fitted into the spacing between the beams. The siding can be calculated as either ½in less than the siding of the hanging knees, or three-quarters of the moulded depth of the beams. The number of bolts used was seven or six, and these were about 1in in diameter.

On the upper gundeck, the athwartships arm was approximately 6in longer than the hanging knees, on ships of 110 to 70 guns. The extra length for vessels of 64 to 36 guns was 4in, and on the remaining ships it was 2in greater than the length of the

*In the previous sections it is stated that the length of the side arm is equal to that of the given space between the beams. This rule only applies when packing pieces were omitted. It was also said that the scantlings of the lodging knee were increased to accommodate the absence of the packing pieces at the space above the deck clamp. In this case the toe of the side arm was fashioned with a rebate that enclosed the outboard top portion of the hanging knee. If a packing piece was employed, the length of the side arm is taken as the distance between the face of the beam which it supports and the face of the hanging knee on the adjacent beam.

athwartships arm of the hanging knee. The length of the side arm was equal to the space between the beams. The siding of the lodging knee can be calculated as ¾in less than that of the adjacent hanging knees, or as a proportion of the moulded depth of the beam as follows: Ship, number of guns (proportions of the moulded depth

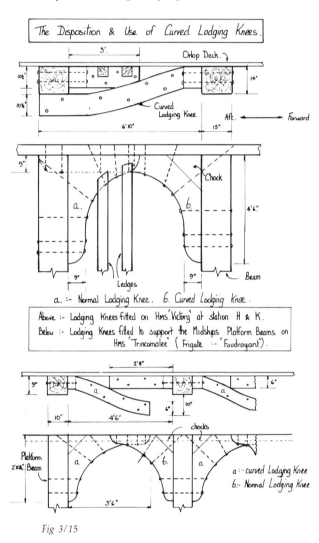

Fig 3/15

beam) – 110–80 (three-quarters); 74–64 (two-thirds); 50–40 (four-fifths); 38 and 36 (seven-tenths); 32 (four-fifths); 28–20 (two-thirds); sloops and cutters (five-eighths). The number of bolts used was as follows: ships of 110 to 32 guns had seven; the remaining vessels had six, with the exception of cutters, which had five. The diameter of these bolts varied between 1⅛ and ¾in.

On those fitted at the forecastle, the athwartships arm length was equal to that of the adjacent hanging knee. The length of the side arm was designed to fit the space between the beams. In most cases the siding of the lodging knee was equal to that of the hanging knee, but sometimes it was about ¼in less, mostly on ships of 74 guns and less. Alternatively the siding can be calculated as a proportion of the moulded depth of beam, as follows: Ship, number of guns

Foudroyant. *The port side of the hold with the lodging knees and beams of the orlop (or platform) deck. This photograph shows how the curved and straight lodging knees are worked between the beams. The side tier of carlings has been worked intercostally between the lodging knees and beams. The spaces between the strakes of planking aid ventilation of the timbers (or frames). In the foreground are pigs of iron ballast.*

Foudroyant. *Carpenter's walk, port side. The upper faces of both a straight and a curved lodging knee have been worked between the beams. Note the type of scarph used and the gratings giving both access and ventilation to the hold below.*

(proportion of the moulded depth of beam) — 110–60 (three-quarters); 50–40 (four-fifths); 38 and 36 (seven-tenths); 32 and less (four-fifths). The number of bolts was generally five varying in diameter from ⅞ to ¾in.

For those fitted to the quarterdeck, the dimensions given above for the forecastle can be applied. The siding was reduced when the quarterdeck was lightly armed.

On those fitted to the poop, the athwartships arm length was equal to that of the hanging knees, the side arms being made to fit the space between the beams. The siding of these lodging knees was approximately ½in less than that of the moulded depth of the beam, or equal to that of the siding of the hanging knees. In all cases, five bolts of ¾in diameter were employed.

IRON LODGING KNEES

Wrought iron knees were made to a width of 4 to 6in. They tapered from 4 to 6in thickness at the throat, to half of that at the extemities of the arms. When being fitted, it was essential that packing (made from beech) was worked between the frames and upon the deck clamp prior to their fastening. The clench bolts were driven from within, care being taken to ensure that the ends of the bolts did not terminate at a plank seam. If this was unavoidable then the bolt was made shorter, so that it could be clenched flush with the frames.

Although iron was used more extensively at the turn of the nineteenth century, many builders did not fully agree with its application. Some stated that the iron brackets did not cover a sufficient area for fastening and that they were not as flexible as timber. Another argument was that the bolts used in their fastening could not be clenched as tightly as those driven through timber, and these bolts often worked loose when the vessel was at sea. But over the next 40 years various types of iron fittings were employed, designed to give a vertical and longitudinal strength and security to the deck beams.

The Internal Stiffening

Although the internal stiffening timbers both fore and aft were collectively termed breast hooks, some confusion arises as to which these individual timbers actually were. For example, the timber situated at the fore end of the gundeck, acting as a support, is sometimes referred to as a breast hook when it was actually a deck hook. The difference will become more apparent later on in the text. To prevent confusion these timbers will be discussed under three headings: breast hooks, deck hooks, and crutches.

Victory. The forepeak, showing five breast hooks set across the stemson. At the top of the photograph is the orlop deck hook. Cross chocks, which are visible here, were not common during this period as specially selected compass oak had to be used. (Alternative types of timber and construction techniques are often used in conservation.)

THE BREAST HOOKS

These timbers were made from compass oak, because of the considerable strength in its curved grain. Once the timber was fashioned and sawn to its desired siding, it was fayed and bolted to the lining of the ship athwart the cant frames and hawse pieces. It was very important that these frames were strengthened internally, to ensure that they remained rigid against the impact of heavy seas. Breast hooks were also necessary because the hull at this point could not be stiffened by beams in the same manner as the hull at the ship's sides. From 1650 to 1800 breast hooks were usually made from timber, but after 1800 timber was in short supply and alternative materials were needed. Breast hooks of wrought iron were therefore introduced, and became widely used. There was of course a transition period where the timber type were braced with iron; examples of this can be seen on the *Victory*.

Below the Gundeck

These breast hooks were equally spaced between the step of the foremast and the deck hook of the gundeck. Five were fitted on First Rate ships, and four on all vessels of 44 to 84 guns. Three were employed on ships of 20 to 38 guns, excluding those of 36 guns which generally had four, while sloops and cutters had two and three respectively. The uppermost breast hook was longer than the rest.

Length of the Breast Hooks

No of Guns	Longest breast hook in	Remaining breast hooks in
110–100	12½	11¼
90–84	13½	12
80–70	14	11½
64–50	14¼	13
50–44	14½	9¾
38–32	14½	11½
28–24	13½	12
20–sloop	13½	12½
cutter	13½	11

For all vessels, the siding was three-quarters of the depth of the keel. The depth at the centreline had to be sufficient to accommodate the score at its lower face, that allowed the timber to be bedded down over the keelson. The score was made to the width of the keelson, and its depth was the depth of the keelson minus the thickness of the lining planks. The same applied where the breast hooks were fitted over the stemson. A score was also made to receive the limber strakes. The underside thus looked as if an inverted 'T' had been cut into it. The overall depth of the breast

Egmont. Looking forward showing the breast hooks wrought over the stemson and the deck hook, and associated ekeing of the lower gundeck fitted to the hawse pieces. The foremast step is built between the aftermost breast hooks and the stemson terminates below the head of the apron.

hook for all vessels can be estimated as 2¾in per inch of its width. The ends of the timber were finished with a rounded edge, the depth before this curve being approximately one-third of its depth at the centreline.

The number of bolts and their approximate size is given in the table overleaf. One bolt was situated at the centreline, driven through the stemson, apron and stempost, and clenched outside. The remaining bolts were spaced equidistantly throughout the length, alternating from side to side, these also being clenched from without. The placing of these bolts was important, for it was essential that they were driven through the frames. If the breast hook was set at a position over the keelson, the bolts were driven through to the underside of the keel.

Unicorn. The forepeak showing the stemson, hawse pieces, deck hook, ekeing and an iron breast hook. Wedges of timber are packed between the timbers (or frames) to create a solid floor to the hull in order to increase the vessel's strength. Rectangular pieces of iron ballast are in the foreground.

Diameter and Number of the Breast Hook Bolts

No of guns	100–70	64	50–36	32	28 and 24	Sloop
No of bolts	13	11	11	10	9	7
Diameter (in)	1½	1½	1¼	1	1	1

Example: to determine the dimensions of both long and short breast hooks below the gundeck of a 36-gun frigate with a keel of 15in and a beam of 37ft 3in:

Length of longer breast hook = (moulded beam/36) × 14½

Thus $(37.25/36) × 14.5 = 15$ft

Length of short breast hooks = (moulded beam/36) × 11½

Thus $(37.25/36) × 11.5 = 11.89$ft

$= 11$ft $10¾$in

Siding of the breast hooks = keel width × ¾

Thus $15 × ¾ = 11¼$in

Overall depth at the centreline = 2¾in for every inch of its siding.

Therefore depth = $2.75 × 11.25$

$= 30.9$in

$= 2$ft 1in

Depth at their extremities = overall depth/3

$= 31/3$

$= 10½$in (approx)

The equations for the next calculations are in chapter 1.

$$K^S = K^D - L$$

where K^S = depth of score for the keelson; K^D = depth of the keelson; L = thickness of the lining.

To determine the thickness of the lining:

$$L = S^D/2$$

where S^D = depth of the limber strake;

the limber strake is: $K^D × \beta$ (β for a 36-gun frigate is 0.4).

Therefore the full calculation is:

$$K^S = 15 - (K^D × 0.4)/2$$

Depth of score for the keelson = $4½$in.

Between the Decks

The breast hook between the lower gundeck and the middle deck of a three-decked ship was made to the same siding as the deck hook that supported the lower gundeck. Its moulded depth was that of the deck hook minus the thickness of the internal planking. This is important, for the deck hooks were fayed and bolted directly to the frames, whereas the breast hooks were fastened to the inner planking. The overall length was greater than the deck hook below it, but only by a fraction. This length can be easily calculated by finding the difference between the deck hooks of the lower and middle decks. For instance:

Length = lower gundeck deck hook + middle gundeck deck hook /2

Therefore if the length of the lower gundeck deck hook is 18ft and that of the deck above is 19ft, the length of the breast hook between is 18ft 6in. Although the breast hook at the fore end of the lowest gundeck, like all the others in the ship, was set halfway between the deck hooks, consideration had to be given to the position of the hawse holes. Due to this, it may be found that the breast hook was set at a slightly lower position. The number of bolts and their size was identical to the deck hook below. These were driven from within, the centre bolt passing through the stempost, the others through the centres of the hawse pieces and cant frames. The above information applies to the remaining breast hooks between the other decks, regardless of the vessel or how many decks she had.

THE DECK HOOKS

These timbers were made from compass oak, fashioned as required and fayed to the cant frames and hawse pieces at the level of each deck. Unlike the breast hooks these timbers were bolted directly to the frames instead of to the lining. The fore faces were given a slight cant, to allow the piece to lie with the sheer of the decks, whereas the breast hooks were set at right angles to the part of the ship they fitted to. Deck hooks had two functions. Firstly, they braced the cant frames and hawse pieces, secondly, they supported the fore ends of the deck planking. Sometimes it was not possible to find timber of a suitable length and the required curvature. Therefore a strake of timber known as the ekeing was worked between the deck hook and the foremost beam. The ekeing followed the curve of the ship's side, its after end butting on to the fore face of the beam, and the fore end was scarphed to the extremity of the deck hook. The length of the scarph was about one and a third times the width of the timber at the centreline (see Fig 3/16). The siding and width at the centreline were proportional to each other, as was the overall length of the deck hook. All the bolts that fastened the timber were driven from within, the centre one passing through to the stempost via the stemson and apron, the others being passed through the frames.

With suitable timber becoming short in supply, new methods were introduced, which finally resulted in the extinction of the timber deck hook. The first change occurred when the ekeing was increased in width and length towards the stemson or apron, where it was scarphed together where each side met. Abaft of this, a deck hook of smaller dimensions was fitted across the joint and bolted. Later an iron crutch was bolted abaft of the deck hook (see Fig 3/16(B)). Eventually, the width of the ekeing was reduced to that of the moulding of the apron, and an iron crutch was bolted across the structure (see Fig 3/16(C)). Each of these techniques will be explained in detail later.

As with the construction of ships of this period there was very little change in the design of deck hooks until the end of the eighteenth century. As a rule the length of deck hooks increased at each deck level of the larger vessels, but remained the same on other

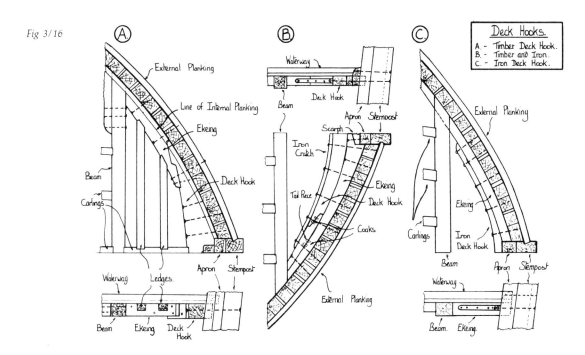

Fig 3/16

Foudroyant. *The forepeak. The position of the foremast partners is dictated by the two centreline pillars. The breast hooks are made from three pieces of timber, a chock piece being set down upon the stemson. The breast hook in the foreground forms part of the foremast step.*

ships. Their length varied from 12 to 16in for every yard of the vessel's beam. More precise figures are given in each of the sections below. To save repetition, the same formula for both the overall length and siding of the breast hooks can be applied, although the multiplying factors may differ.

The Lower Gundeck

The length of these deck hooks were as follows: Ship, number of guns (length, inches per yard) – 110–100 (12½); 90–70 (13½); 64–60 (14¾); 50–32 (15½); 28–20 (15). For ships with the above number of guns the siding of the deck hook was three-quarters the fraction of the keel depth.

The width of the deck hook at the centreline in the fore and aft direction was approximately 2in for every inch of its siding. The width at the extremities was one-third of that at the centreline. First and Second Rates had 15 bolts of 1½in diameter; Third Rates had 13 of the same size, and 11 bolts of 1¼in diameter were employed on vessels of 44 to 32 guns. Frigates of 28 guns and less were fitted with nine bolts of 1in diameter. The centre of the hook was scored to receive the apron and the stemson; the width of these being easily determined from the sizes of those timbers.

The Middle Gundeck

These were only fitted on ships with three complete gundecks, including those of 80 guns, which were abolished in about 1760. There were no apparent differences in the length and siding of any of the deck hooks, apart from on 110- and 100-gun vessels, for here their length was 13in per yard of the ships moulded beam. Thirteen 1½in diameter bolts were employed on all ships.

The Upper Gundeck

The length of these deck hooks were as mentioned above, and in some cases longer. Ship, number of guns (width in inches per yard of the ship's beam) – 110–100 (13½); 90 (14); 84–70 (13½); 64–50 (14¾); 44–36 (15½); 32 (16½); 28–24 (15½); sloops (16¾); cutters (14).

Ship, number of guns (thickness as a proportion of the keel depth) – 110–100 (five-eighths); 90 (two-thirds); 84–74 (twenty-three thirty-seconds); 64–50 (three-quarters); 44 (seven-tenths); 38 (three-quarters); 36–24 (seven-tenths); sloops and cutters (seven-twelfths).

The number of bolts used for First Rate ships was 15; Second and Third Rates, 13; 50 to 32 guns, 11. All these vessels had bolts of 1¼in in diameter. Frigates of 28 and 24 guns employed 9 bolts and smaller ships had 8, of 1in diameter.

METHODS OF STIFFENING THE HULL

Between 1650 and 1850 a number of methods were introduced to produce a stiffer hull, thereby eliminating two inherent problems. The first problem was relatively minor: the ship's timbers tended to move outwards away from the centreline due to the weight of the armament. This had more or less been rectified during the sixteenth century by the use of cross pillars, which were employed until the first decade of the eighteenth century. These also reduced racking – the tendency of the frames to move out of true when a vessel was working beam-on to a heavy sea. The second problem, 'hogging' and 'sagging', caused considerable concern. Hogging was caused firstly, by the amount of ornamentation which adorned the head and stern of the ship, which increased the loading of the keel at these points. Secondly, and more significantly, due to the narrowness of the hull below the waterline at both the fore and after ends, little support was given to the armament borne at these positions. This sometimes caused the fore and after ends of the keel to drop. This was further aggravated when the vessel was riding on the crest of a wave, which would lift her at the centre of her length, thus producing a droop at the fore and after ends. Even the reduction of top weight did not prevent hogging, for the general increase in the length of vessels in the eighteenth century had the same effect.

Sagging was caused by the reverse action of the sea. When a ship was riding across two wave crests, one forward and the other aft, the centre section of the keel would drop. Therefore it can be assumed that a ship riding relatively heavy seas would be continuously stressed by forces of compression and expansion. These problems were overcome by the use of either: internal frames set athwartships, known as riders; cross pillars; or the trussed frame, first introduced in timber, and later wrought iron and iron riders.

The Timber Riders

These had been in use since Tudor times, and appear to have been introduced around the second quarter of the sixteenth century. We are now very sure of this, due to information taken from Henry VIII's ship *Mary Rose*. Evidence is also given in Matthew Baker's *Fragments of English Shipwrightry*. It appears that the *Mary Rose* was fitted with these timber riders during her refit, and that this was to give additional strength to the hull due to her increased armament. Riders can be categorised into floor riders, set across the keelson and floors of the ship, and futtock riders that pass up the ship's side internally from the turn of the bilge to the orlop or lower deck.

It is not clear how many floor riders were fitted in vessels built during the latter half of the seventeenth century. A contract for the building of six Third Rates in 1666 specifically lists five. Therefore I assume that First Rates between 1650 and 1800 had about seven. A cross-section of a First Rate of 1680 shows that either eight or nine were employed, whereas a longitudinal section of the *Britannia*, a First Rate of 1682, only shows six. At this date the floor riders were of an individual nature and did not meet the futtock riders as was the practice in the eighteenth century.

These timbers were made from compass oak, sawn to the required siding, the under side fashioned and fayed to the varying thicknesses of the internal planking. The top surface was made flat for a specific length at the centreline and then conformed to the curve of the ship's hull towards the heads of the timber. It was bolted firmly with eight clench bolts, two of which were driven into the keelson. These bolts were about $1\frac{1}{4}$in diameter.

The scantlings for floor riders of vessels built between the seventeenth century and the first decade of the eighteenth century are a little obscure. I have calculated their proportional sizes from an illustration given in Deane's *Doctrine*. This shows a cross-section of a Third Rate vessel of 1670, from which I have deduced that there was some sort of proportional system related to the size of the principal timbers, which applied to all ships. The overall length of the floor rider was approximately $7\frac{1}{2}$in per foot of the ship's beam. The part above the keelson was flat for a certain length. To calculate this length, take 6in for every yard of the ship's beam. The timber was made to a fore and aft siding of one-eighteenth of its overall length (this was also approximately five-sixths of the moulded depth of the keel). The maximum depth of the rider at the centreline where it passed over the keelson was about twice that of its siding, while the depth of the heads (outboard extremities) was two-thirds of its fore and aft siding. Alternatively one can determine the latter

by either dividing the depth of the keel by two, or multiplying the depth of the rider at the centreline by three and dividing by ten.

Example: to calculate the dimensions of the floor rider for the 90-gun ship *Coronation* built in 1685 at Portsmouth by Isaac Betts. This vessel had a beam of 45ft.

The overall length of the floor rider $= (45 \times 7\frac{1}{2}\text{in})/12$
$$= 28\text{ft } 1\frac{1}{2}\text{in}$$
The length of the flat portion at the centreline $= (45 \times 6)/(3 \times 12)$
$$= 270/36$$
$$= 7\text{ft 6in}$$
The fore and aft siding $= (28 \cdot 125\text{ft}/18) \times 12$
$$= 18\frac{3}{4}\text{in}$$
The overall depth at the centreline $= 18 \cdot 75\text{in} \times 2$
$$= 3\text{ft } 1\frac{1}{2}$$
The depth at the heads of the timber $= (18 \cdot 75\text{in} \times 2)/3$
$$= 12\frac{1}{2}\text{in}$$

The whole timber was fastened down to the frames of the ship with eight clenches, which were generally made to a diameter of one-sixteenth of the siding of the timber. If it was secured with trennals these were made with a diameter of approximately one-eighth of the siding of the timber.

The number of floor riders fitted on eighteenth-century vessels again varies considerably. The 1789 edition of the *Shipbuilder's Repository* states that five were fitted on First and Second Rates and three on Third Rates. In the draught of a 74-gun ship in Rees' *Naval*

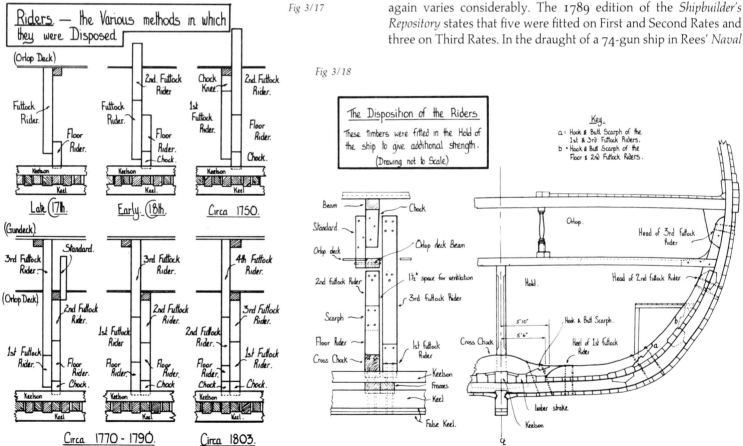

Fig 3/17

Fig 3/18

Victory. *Port side of the hold, above the wing platform, showing the orlop deck beams and lodging knees. The two vertical baulks of timber are the first and second futtock riders. The room and space of the timbers can clearly be seen above the internal planking, between the ventilation spaces and below the deck clamp.*

Architecture, five are fitted, whereas in J R Stevens' *The Embellishment of Old Time Ships* a longitudinal section of an 84-gun ship has seven instead of five. It is therefore important to be flexible in the use of lists of dimensions, for such rules must be treated only as a guideline.

Towards the last quarter of the eighteenth century a number of variations were made in the disposition of the floor riders in relation to the futtock riders (the latter will be explained later). Previously the futtock riders were placed at equal intervals between the floor riders. This changed, and the futtock riders were placed adjacent to the floor riders. It was at this point that the futtock riders had cross chocks fitted over the keelson, and the floor riders were extended further up the side of the ship by additional futtocks. The new method of rider construction did not even retain a set pattern throughout the length of the vessel. However each permutation will be discussed in full, after preliminary notes on the futtock riders themselves. The dimensions of the floor riders at the end of the eighteenth century did not vary much from those at the beginning. The only real difference was that the centre portion that originally had a level surface disappeared, leaving a more graceful hump. From dimensions given in 1775 I have produced the following method for determining the scantlings of these timbers.

The overall length of the floor rider was as follows: Ship, number of guns (inches per foot of moulded beam) – 110–100 (7·25); 90–80 (7·5); 74–70 (6·75); 64 and less (7·5). The siding of the floor rider fore and aft was as follows: Ship, number of guns (length in inches per yard of the rider's length) – 110–100 (1·75); 90–80 (1·625); 74–70 (1·875); 64 and less (1·75).

The overall depth of the timber at the centreline can be calculated by the following formula:

$$Depth = depth\ of\ the\ keelson + (the\ depth\ of\ the\ keelson) \times 2/3.$$

The above applies to First and Second Rates. For the other rates, use a multiplicaton factor of seven, and a divisor of eight.

The moulded depth at the heads of the floor riders was about 1in less than the siding for the First and Second Rates, and 2in less than the siding for the other rates. At this period (in around 1775) the riders were secured with twelve or ten clench bolts of between 1½ and 1¼in diameter.

The Futtock Riders

The futtock riders were single baulks of timber, fashioned to conform to the internal curvature of the ship's side below the waterline. They had their heels set at the line of the thick stuff over the rungheads of the floor timbers. During the seventeenth century these timbers did not extend beyond the level of the orlop or platform beams. Generally they were disposed so that their heads were fayed to these beams thus giving them some form of longitudinal bracing. By the end of the seventeenth century, they were extended to terminate half-way between the orlop and the lower gundeck. The fore and aft siding of these timbers were equal

to the siding of the floor riders, and their depth was equal to their siding. The depth diminished at the heads and heels by approximately one-third to a half. Then they were rounded off. They were fastened with clench bolts driven from within, and the roves set on the external planking in shallow borings and filled in with dowels. Usually between 10 and 12 bolts were used, with two driven laterally into the orlop beams. By the second quarter of the eighteenth century, the heels of the futtock riders had been extended to a short distance from the keelson, and they terminated at the level above the orlop beams. From this period, the fashion of construction began to vary, not only from ship to ship but even within one vessel.

The shortage of good sized compass oak led to the evolution of the complete rider system, made up of floor, first, second and third futtock riders. The floors also altered. They were now composed of two timbers with a cross chock set between them across the keelson. In some positions the first futtock heels were scarphed, and they too had a cross chock fitted between them. Fig 3/17 illustrates all the varieties employed and their approximate dates.

The number of futtock riders also varied, but in the late seventeenth century there was an identical number to the floor riders. Vessels built during the latter part of the eighteenth century seem to have more variation and according to the 1789 edition of the *Shipbuilder's Repository*, eight were used on First Rates, and six on other vessels. This list also states that only three or five floor riders were employed for those vessels, so it can be seen that there were differences in the number of floor riders and futtock riders. Some illustrations, including draughts of various ships, show an equal number of futtock riders and floor riders. Where a number of timbers were employed, each would be joined by a plain flat scarph set horizontal. The number of bolts used for fastening these timbers varied, as did the actual number of pieces making up a complete futtock rider. Usually there were 12 to 18 trennals giving additional strength at the scarphs.

The approximate dimensions for the futtock riders where a first (or lower) futtock and a second futtock were used were as follows: the lower futtock rider was sided equal to its respective floor rider. Its moulded depth at its heel was about fifteen-sixteenths of its siding, while its depth at its head was about eleven-sixteenths of its siding. The heel was set approximately 6in to one side of the keelson. The heads of these timbers reached the underside of the orlop beams if possible, and were also fayed and bolted to the floor riders with three bolts in the horizontal plane. If a floor rider was not fitted at this position, cross chocks would be fitted across the keelson. The scarph would thus be between 6ft and 7ft 6in in length.

The second futtock riders had a smaller siding, approximately seven-eighths of the siding of the floor riders. The depth at its heel was about fifteen-sixteenths of its own siding on First Rate ships, and thirteen-sixteenths of its own siding on other vessels. The depth at the head of this timber can be taken as two-thirds of its own siding on First Rates. For the other classes, it was about three-quarters of its siding. In some cases the scantling was increased in depth where it passed in way of the orlop beams. This was only by a few inches to allow more room through which the horizontal bolts could be driven. Between nine and eleven bolts were used to secure this timber, and a further three were driven horizontally into the first futtock, to which it was fayed.

The Cross Pillars (or Pointers)

This method of stiffening the hull, by 'tying' the two halves of the vessel transversely, had been in common use since the Tudor period. It is thought that this style of construction was employed in the *Mary Rose*. References to this technique are given in the works of Matthew Baker, a prominent Elizabethan shipwright. The construction, no matter how it was disposed (for there were a number of variations), consisted of a series of transverse pillars set diagonally, with their base at one side of the hold, and terminating with their heads at the beams of the lowest gundeck on the opposite side of the ship, (see Fig 3/19). Each cross pillar was set in the opposite diagonal to its counterpart, throughout most of the ship's length, thus distributing the expansive and compressive loading evenly to the hull. Usually there were two cross pillars per set of internal riders.

The heels of these timbers were usually placed at the thick stuff which was wrought over the rungheads of the floors, with one of its faces fayed and bolted to the heel of the lower futtock rider. Alternatively they were spaced equidistant between the floor riders and the futtock riders (see Fig 3/19). In most vessels these timbers would cross one another, either at the level of the orlop or platform beams or a little above or below them. In all cases they were firmly bolted to the beams where they crossed. This type of construction is well illustrated in the works of Edmund Dummer, who gives both a longitudinal view and a cross-section of a late seventeenth-century ship. He also shows a variation, where the pillars do not cross each other but are steeved at greater angles with their heads fayed to the underside of the gundeck beam. In this case the cross pillar does not pass the centreline axis, and therefore remains within the confines of that side of the vessel. I can only assume that this technique, illustrated in Fig 3/20, was adopted where the presence of the upper ends of the pillars on the gundeck would impair the working of the guns.

The well-known builders such as Deane, Shish, Tippets and Betts all employed cross pillars in their vessels. However, by the mid-1690s, the practice seems to have declined. This was due to improvements in frame construction, internal riders and extended futtock riders. The cross pillars obstructed the disposition of internal bulkheads, storage space and in some cases the working of the guns, and this led to the end of the practice.

It would be unwise to give exact figures for the length of these timbers, for this varied according to the cross-section of the ship, and depended on the breadth and depth of the hold. These factors altered the angle at which the pillars were steeved, and in turn either increased or decreased the length. The angle would be between 45 and 50 degrees, and for those vessels where pillars did not cross each other it was about 60 degrees. Their width fore and aft was about ½in for every foot in length, while their athwartships siding

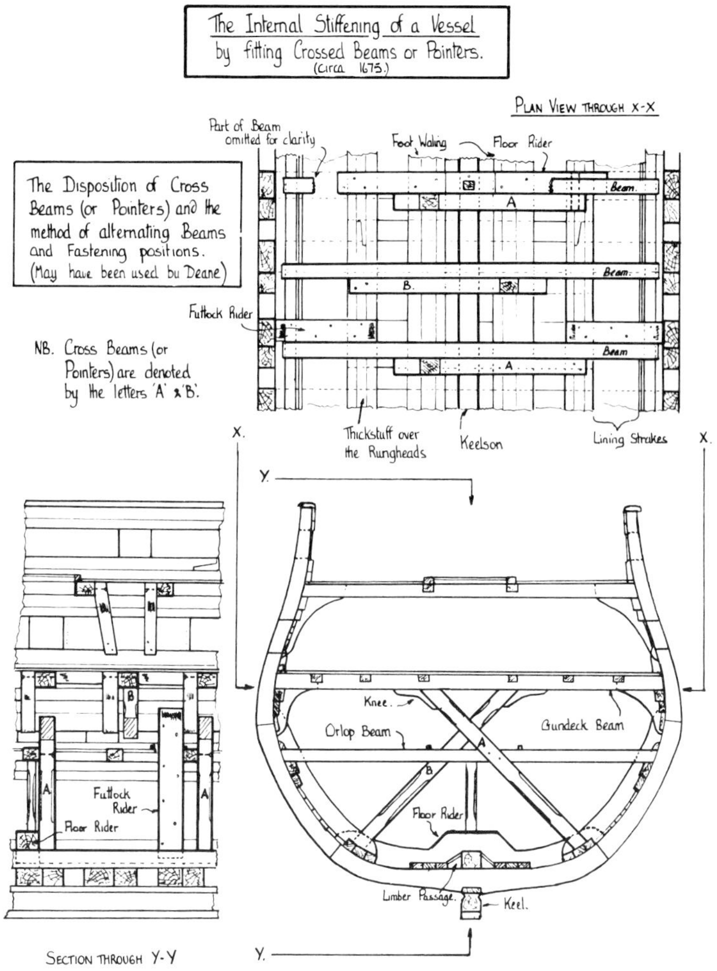

Fig 3/19

was seven-eighths of their fore and aft width. The bolts were between 1 and 1½in diameter. Strength at the fastenings was often increased by small wooden knees. If the heel was set on the upper face of a rider, it was fashioned with a tenon for locating it firmly.

IMPROVED METHODS OF HULL STIFFENING

Internal Hull Stiffening Proposed by Snodgrass

Towards the end of the eighteenth century, much research was undertaken to find alternative methods of strengthening ships against racking, the transverse stresses incurred at sea. This was the tendency for a ship's hull to move out of true when subjected to prolonged rolling in heavy seas. One of these proposals* was submitted to the Navy Board in 1792 by the Surveyor of the East India Company, Mr Snodgrass. His designs had been employed on

*Snodgrass' proposals were first put forward in 1771, and published by a House of Commons Committee.

a number of East Indiamen and included the use of iron pillars, iron plate knees, diagonal bracing timbers, and iron plate riders. The use of diagonal stiffeners was not new, similar methods having been used a century earlier by Deane and Edmund Dummer (compare Fig 3/21 with Fig 3/19 and 3/20).

The diagonal brace proposed by Snodgrass was set in a different fashion to those of earlier periods. The heel butted against the side of the keelson, while the head of the brace was fayed to both the underside of the lowest gundeck beam and the side of the deck clamp (or beam shelf) adjacent. Both head and heel of the timber brace were further stiffened with iron brackets fitted on the fore and after faces. The fore and aft arms of the brackets were bolted to the side of keelson, or to the deck clamp, all being secured with clench bolts driven from within. Amidships, an iron crutch was employed. This was fastened to the upper surfaces of the two braces, and secured to the keelson at its throat.

The diagonal braces were generally made from straight oak, square in cross-section. Their dimensions were approximately two-thirds of the depth of the keelson, their length varying according to the size of the vessel (see Fig 3/21).

The iron riders were either made from rolled plate, or were wrought. They were between 1 and 1½in thick and between 4 and 6in wide. The bolts used for fastening them were about 1in diameter. The riders were worked transversely across the faces of the inner planking or ceiling. The clench bolts were driven from within and passed out through the ship's timbers. Both these and the diagonal braces were introduced to replace the heavy floor and

futtock riders that were in use at the time. The iron brackets were placed at both the heads and heels of the square-sectioned pillars in the hold and orlop deck at the centreline; alternatively these were completely replaced by iron pillars. The plate knees in Snodgrass' designs were not dissimilar to those introduced by Roberts a few years later.

In 1983 the Foreman of Shipwrights, Mr Alec Barlow, and one of his assistants, Mr Terry Wallbridge, surveyed the Victory's hold, and believed they found evidence that Snodgrass' diagonal braces had, at some time, been fitted. I think this extremely unlikely for it was not until 1805 that this design was fitted on naval ships. During that year the 74-gun ship Orion was fitted out experimentally with the system proposed by Snodgrass. The insertion of braces was a time consuming process and could only be done during a major refit. The Victory had been on continuous sea-service since her refit in 1802–03 and thus at the time she would not have been available for such work. The insertion of diagonal braces involved the complete removal of all the floor and futtock riders, and the lifting of various sections of the orlop deck planking. They would then be fitted along with associated iron bracketing and the iron riders themselves. It now appears that the indication of some form of internal stiffening within Victory's hold may have been caused by some form of bracing used during her docking for restoration in 1922.

It seems that the methods proposed by Snodgrass were abandoned in favour of a far superior design introduced by Seppings a few years later. However, it appears that Seppings'

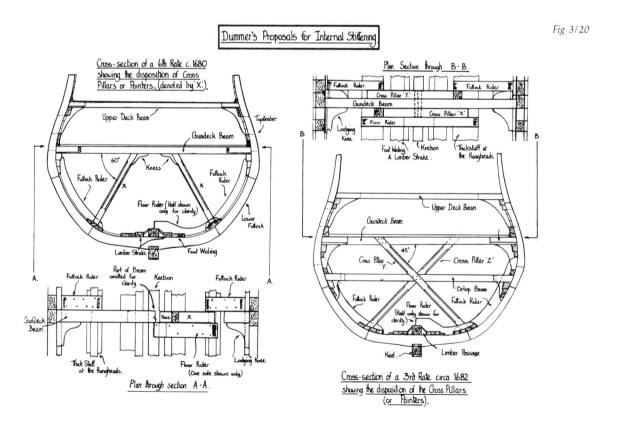

Fig 3/20

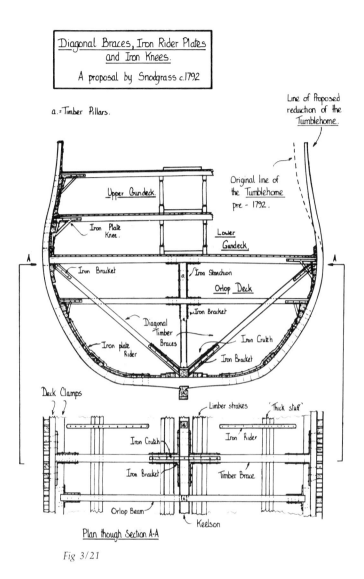

Fig 3/21

Unicorn. *A Seppings diagonal iron rider plate fitted in two sections, each 6in wide and 1in thick. This view shows it from the lower strake of thick stuff to the deck clamp of the berthing deck. The fore platform, in relation to the hold, is level with the uppermost bilge step.*

diagonal 'trussed' frame was influenced by Snodgrass' earlier proposals. This can be seen clearly by comparing their designs of the iron rider plates.

The Diagonal or 'Trussed' Frame

This revolutionary method of construction was introduced by Sir Robert Seppings and was first adopted on the 74-gun *Tremendous* in February 1811. This technique superseded the old method of stiffening the hull with floor and futtock riders. The trussed frame became common in all vessels after Seppings became Surveyor of the Navy in 1813, succeeding Sir William Rule. This new technique consisted of a series of diagonally worked timbers in three areas of the ship's hull. Firstly, they were fitted throughout the entire length of the hold between the beam shelf of the lower gundeck and the keelson. Secondly, they were fitted between the deck beams of the gundecks, replacing the older system of carlings and ledges. Lastly,

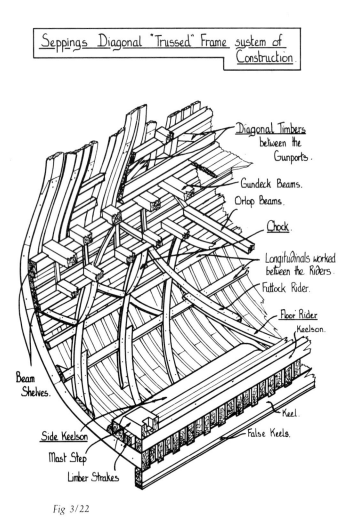

Seppings Diagonal "Trussed" Frame system of Construction

Diagonal Timbers between the Gunports.
Gundeck Beams.
Orlop Beams.
Chock.
Longitudinals worked between the Riders.
Futtock Rider.
Floor Rider
Keelson.
Beam Shelves.
Keel.
Side Keelson
False Keels.
Mast Step
Limber Strakes

Fig 3/22

diagonal timbers were wrought between the frames of the gunports along each of the complete gundecks. A fine example of the latter can be seen throughout the decks of the 46-gun frigate *Unicorn* and there is also an excellent longitudinal section model of her at the National Maritime Museum, Greenwich, showing the entire layout of diagonal framing.

There were a number of advantages inherent in the trussed frame, which not only overcame existing problems but advanced the introduction of steam propulsion. The ship's side planking did not tend to open quite so freely when the vessel was working in heavy seas. Thus ships were much drier, which was better for both the ship's company and the perishable stores. Greater rigidity to the hull form meant that the overall length of ships could be increased, which was beneficial in three ways. Firstly, more guns could be mounted on each of the gundecks, thereby reducing the number of decks, whick in turn lowered the centre of gravity, producing a greater righting moment for the ship. The result of this can be seen on the 92-gun *Rodney*, built in 1833 and the 90-gun *Albion* launched in 1842. Both vessels carried their main armament on two decks. Fine examples which showed the length to which a wooden hull could be built are the *Gibraltar* of 1856 and the *Victoria* of 1859,

both had gundecks 250ft long. Secondly, the problem of hogging that had persisted throughout the last two centuries was more or less eliminated. Thirdly, the hull could now bear a greater weight. Thus heavier armaments could be carried and it had the ability to support large components like boilers and steam reciprocating engines, thereby paving the way for a modern steam navy.

Later, wrought iron plates were used instead of timber for the diagonal timbers in the hold. These plates were generally between 6 and 9in wide and between 1 and 1½in thick. This system can be seen in the lower regions of the *Unicorn*. She is a classic example of the improvements made by Seppings and a monument to both the man and to the twilight of the completely timber-built man-of-war.

The 'Trussed' Frame as Fitted in the Lower Body of the Vessel

This consisted of a series of timbers divided into three categories: the diagonal riders (or timbers), the longitudinals, and the trusses. With these were a number of chocks, and a side keelson on each side of the main keelson. The riders were generally composed of three individual lengths, the lower two being either scarphed or fayed together where they overlapped. These timbers were known as the lower, middle and upper riders. The lower rider crossed diagonally. Its heel was set at the line of the limber strakes, and terminated approximately 2ft 6in above the line of the heads of the actual floor of the ship's framing. Those that were fitted in the after body were set with a rake forward, while those in the fore body were set with a rake aft. These timbers were generally laid at 45 degrees.

The middle riders' heels were approximately 2ft 6in below the line of the floor heads, thus giving a shift of 5ft to the lower riders. The heads of these timbers terminated about 1ft below the thick strake immediately under the beam shelf of the orlop deck. These timbers were fayed to the fore side of the lower riders in the fore body, and to the after side of the after body and were secured with bolts driven through both timbers. The upper riders butted end on to the heads of the middle riders, with their heads terminating about 6in below the beam shelf of the lower gundeck. The head was fashioned with a snipe to allow it to be fayed with the chocks that supported the beams of the gundeck. In the fore body the head was fayed to the fore side of these chocks, and to the after side in the after body.

Only two riders were employed on frigates, due to the shallower depth in the hold. In this case the upper rider extended from the longitudinal at the floor heads to within 6in beneath the beam shelf of the lower or berthing deck.

There was a specific bolting sequence to these timbers. The lower rider had one bolt driven in 6in from the end of the timber, and the next 12in from that. The remaining length was secured every 18in, on alternate sides. The middle rider had one bolt at each end, 6in in, and the next a further 6in in. The remainder were 12in apart, on alternate sides. The upper rider was secured with the aid of an iron plate fitted about 1ft from the top end, fastened with two bolts. The

Unicorn. *The intersection of the fore and after diagonal iron rider plates at midships. Note that the two heavy bands of thick stuff are wrought in top and butt fashion and that the beam shelf supporting the carpenter's walk above is of relatively light construction.*

next was set below this at the level of the beam shelf. The remainder were set 18in apart. If this timber was not scarphed to the middle rider (or lower rider in frigates), an iron plate would probably have been used to secure it.

The longitudinals were baulks of square-sectioned timber, fore and aft between the diagonal riders. They were wrought directly over the floor heads and the first futtock heads. Their purpose was to ensure the heads and heels of the floors and futtocks were securely fastened, in much the same way as the thick stuff in the old system. The ends of these timbers were fitted with coaks, which passed between them and the diagonal riders, thus locking them in position. One bolt was driven at about 9in from the end of the longitudinal and one halfway along its length; they were driven from within the ship and clenched externally. The remaining bolts were set on alternate sides every 18in, driven from the outside of the hull and clenched within.

The trusses were fitted at the opposite angle to the riders, between the corners where the riders were met by the longitudinals. The purpose of the trusses was to lock the other timbers in a manner that would prevent distortion. The heads and heels were fashioned with snipes, so that they would fay well with the edges of both the riders and the longitudinals. Made to the same scantling as the riders, they were secured with a bolt, approximately 9in from each end. The next was set 21in from the end. The remaining bolts were set about 15in apart. All the bolts were driven from within and clenched on the outside of the hull.

Chocks were fitted in the way of the orlop beams, to give support. They were set at an angle to the riders, thereby distributing the loading along these timbers. A side keelson was wrought parallel to the main keelson at the vicinity of the step of the mainmast. This timber was approximately one-fifth of the length of the keel, and was positioned so that the step for the mast was half way along it. The function of this timber was to produce a base for the mast step, and distribute the weight. It also served as a well for the pumps. The lower riders at the fore and after ends were made progressively deeper towards the centreline of the ship, and acted in the same manner as the breast hooks and crutches of the old system.

The 'Trussed' Frame as Fitted Between the Gunports and Laid Between the Beams

In Seppings' design, short lengths of timber were wrought diagonally between the frames that formed the fore and after sides of the gunports. Their function was to give additional support to the area of the hull, where the break in the fore and aft planking left it weak and prone to distortion. The angle at which they were set was determined by the width between the ports. Throughout most of the ship's length, only one timber was employed at each position, except between the two ports at the halfway position. Here, two were fitted at opposite angles. Those that were fitted in the after body of the vessel were inclined upwards towards the after end of the ship, and in the reverse direction in the fore body. These timbers were as thick as the 'in and out' width of the frames, and in depth were half their thickness. The ends of the timbers were mitred for fitting, and the space above and below was planked up with boards of thin deal. The trusses were fastened to the frames with iron spikes, driven from the top or bottom of the truss. If two trusses were used, as in midships, each was scored to form a simple 'cross halving' joint at the desired angle, two bolts being driven through to make it secure (see Fig 3/23).

The trusses that were wrought between the deck beams of continuous gundecks were always set at 45 degrees to the centreline. Only the midship tier of carlings remained in use with this system, so that the butts of the trusses could be set against them (see Fig 3/23).

The dimensions of these angled timbers were not dissimilar to those of carlings used in the old method of construction. Their siding was approximately three-quarters that of the beams to which they were fitted, and they were about seven-eighths of their own width in depth. A shallow mortice was cut in the face of the beam at the desired position, to receive the butt of the truss. They were then secured with iron spikes driven through where it was most accessible.

These trusses appear to have been omitted on some vessels and there are only two possible reasons for this. Firstly, the diagonal frame construction required a vast quantity of timber which increased the ship's overall weight, but by omitting deck trusses the

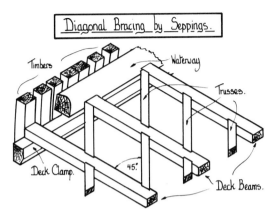

A. Diagonal Trusses set between the Deck Beams.

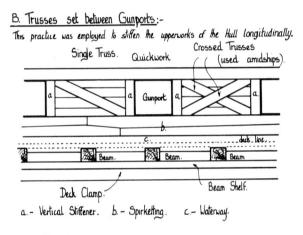

Fig 3/23

weight was slightly reduced. Secondly, the overall cost of timber would be reduced.

The Diagonal Frame With Iron Riders

By 1820 timber diagonal riders were superseded by those made from wrought or rolled iron. This method of construction reduced the weight of vessels considerably, for not only were they less bulky, but it was no longer necessary to have the trusses set in the opposite angle, as iron was less likely to distort. The idea of using iron for riders was not new. Snodgrass proposed diagonal construction employing either timber or iron riders as early as 1771.

These iron riders were generally between 6 and 9in wide, and between 1 and 1½in thick. Usually two riders were used, the lower extending from the line of the floor heads to a little below the beam shelf of the orlop. The upper rider was laid adjacent to the lower, with an overlap of 4 to 6ft. The bolts were driven from within and clenched externally, and were disposed so that they passed through the strakes of thick stuff which was wrought over the floor and futtock heads. The topmost end of the upper rider terminated just below the beam shelf of the lower deck. This method of

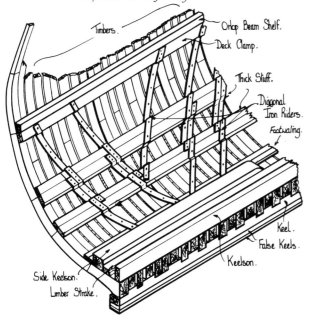

Note 1 :- In some cases the Heels of the Riders were worked below the Footwaling whereas in other cases they were worked under the Lower strakes of the Thickstuff wrought over the Floorheads.

Note 2 :- The spaces between the Floors and the 1st Futtock Riders were filled up with short timber wedges forming a solid Hull.

Fig 3/24

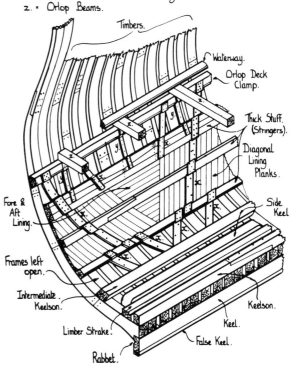

x. = Iron Plates (6"wide x 1" thick). y. = Iron Knees.
z. = Orlop Beams.

Fig 3/25

construction can be seen on the *Unicorn*. The riders in the after body were always inclined aft, and those in the fore body, forward. If the ceiling planking was omitted from the spaces between the strakes of thick stuff in the hold, the iron rider was fashioned to the contours of the ship's internal sides. When the riders in the fore body met those at the after body, they generally crossed each other (see Fig 3/24).

The Composite Diagonal Frame of Iron and Timber

At the National Maritime Museum, Greenwich there is a model of a longitudinal section of a man-of-war which displays two unusual features. The diagonal bracing is of both timber and iron and an intermediate side keelson is fitted. As can be seen from Fig 3/25, a series of longitudinals was worked up to the beam shelf of the orlop. The area between the keelson and the thick stuff over the floor heads was left unlined, except for the side keelsons. Here iron floor riders were laid in their familiar inclined pattern, and firmly bolted through the frames and to the intermediate side keelson and thick stuff. The areas between the strakes of thick stuff and the beam shelves were boarded up with diagonal planking, the angle of that

in the after body opposing that in the fore. Where this planking met midships, the space left was boarded up with fore and aft laid planks. At reasonable intervals an iron futtock rider was laid diagonally between the lower strake of thick stuff and a position a little above the orlop deck. The number of futtock riders did not correspond to the number of floor riders employed, because more of the latter were used.

ADDITIONAL METHODS OF STIFFENING THE HULL

The Crutches

The function of the crutches was to strengthen the hull internally at the position of the after cant frames. The manner in which they were fashioned was not dissimilar to the breast hooks that served a similar purpose in the fore body of the vessel. The only noticeable difference was the greater angle to which the arms were set, due to the sharper rise of the floors in the after body. The *Shipbuilder's Repository* states that two crutches were fitted on all ships of 36 guns or more, and one in the lesser classes. This was not strictly so, for there were many vessels fitted with one or two more. One of the

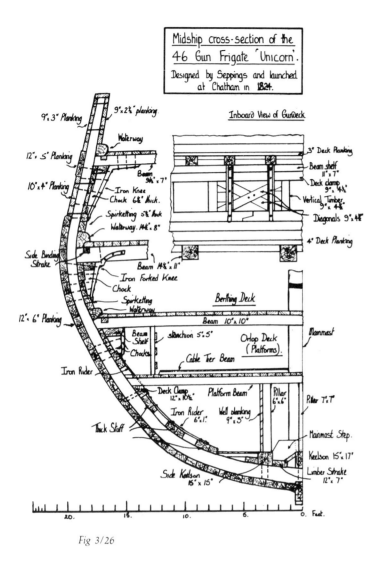

Midship cross-section of the
46 Gun Frigate 'Unicorn'.
Designed by Seppings and launched
at Chatham in 1824.

9".3" Planking
9".2½" planking.
Waterway
12".5" Planking
10".4" Planking
Beam 9¾".7"
Iron Knee
Chock 6½" thick.
Spirketting 5½" thick.
Waterway 14½".8"
Side Binding
Strake
Beam 14½".11"
Iron Forked Knee
Chock
Spirketting
Waterway
12".6" Planking
Beam 10".10"
Beam
Shelf
Chocks
stanchion 5".5"
Iron Rider
Deck Clamp
12".10½"
Iron Rider
6".1".
Thick Stuff
Side Keelson
15"x 15"

Inboard View of Gundeck
3" Deck Planking
Beam shelf
11".7"
Deck clamp
9".4½"
Vertical Timber.
9".4½"
Diagonals 9".4½"
4" Deck Planking

Berthing Deck

Orlop Deck
(Platforms).

Mainmast

Cable Tier Beam

Platform Beam
Pillar
6".6"
Pillar 7".7"
Well planking
9".5"

Mainmast Step.
Keelson 15".17"
Limber Strake
12".7"

Fig 3/26

main reasons for this was that the foremost crutch was employed as a part of the mizzen mast step. This was the normal practice until 1807, when it was decided to raise the mizzen mast step to the level of the lower deck.

These timbers were made from compass oak, the underside being fashioned to fit over the keelson and the limber strakes. Once it was complete, it was set across the keelson at right angles, and secured with bolts that were clenched externally with roves.

The length of each arm of these timbers can be calculated by the following equation:

Length of the arm from centreline, in feet = moulded beam/6

The siding of these timbers are estimated in the following manner:

(The length of one arm in feet × 12)/y

Ship, number of guns (y) – 110–60 (seven and one-quarter); 50–32

(seven); 28–20 (seven and one-quarter); sloops and cutters (eight).

Example: to estimate the size of the crutch for a 36-gun frigate with a moulded beam of 34ft.

Length of one arm is $34/12 \times 2 = 5.66\text{ft}$ (5ft 8in)
Siding of the crutch $(5.66\text{ft} \times 12)/7 = 9.7\text{in}$ (9¾in)

The diameter of the bolts used to fasten these timbers varied from 1½ to 1in. The number employed also varied: ships of 60 guns and over had 12 and those of 36 to 50 guns had eight. Other vessels had about seven, excluding sloops and cutters which generally had five.

The shape between each of these timbers varied from 6ft 6in on the larger vessels to 4ft 9in on the lesser classes. This of course was dependent on the amount of room in the after body which was itself governed by the underwater shape and the rise of the floors.

The use of crutches was eliminated upon introduction of the diagonal frame by Seppings in 1811. In some cases two crutches were fitted in the fore body acting as the step for the fore mast. (This is discussed separately in the section on the step on pages 171–172.)

The Breast Riders

Prior to the final development of the floor and futtock riders in the lower part of the hull, experiments had been made on the use of timbers to stiffen the structure above the waterline. These timbers, known as breast riders, were fayed and bolted to the inner lining of the hull from the level of the beams on one deck, to the lower strake of spirketting on the deck below. At first these timbers were set vertically and generally adjacent to a beam on the deck between its extremities. The scantling was increased at this point in the athwartships direction so that it formed a hanging knee at the beam (see Fig 3/27). In the lower tier of breast riders, the heels of the timbers were a little above the level of the orlop, and terminated at the deck clamp of the lower gundeck. If the vessel had three decks, the second tier started at the lower strake of spirketting on the lower deck, and terminated at the deck clamp of the middle gundeck. Generally, twelve breast riders were employed on each tier. The heads and heels were fashioned in a similar manner to those of the hanging knees, and the standards used at the beams.

A note must be made here regarding the uppermost run of riders, which span either the lower and upper decks of two-decked ships, or the middle and upper decks of three-decked vessels. These are not breast riders, but top riders which although serving the same function did have a few subtle differences (these will be explained later).

It is not very clear when breast riders were first used. They are certainly not mentioned in the lists given in the *Shipbuilder's Repository*. Thus I assume that they were fitted on some ships at the builder's discretion both before and after 1790. After a while, the manner in which they were fitted altered, and they became angled in the fore and aft plane. There does not appear to be any hard and fast rule on whether they should incline forward in the fore body or aft in the after body. One illustration shows at least two timbers inclining aft in the fore body while one timber inclines forward in the after body. The 74-gun ship in Rees' *Naval Architecture*, distinctly shows all the breast riders inclining forward, whereas the top riders incline forward or aft as required.

These timbers were increased in scantling where they passed beside a beam, to act as a hanging knee. Now that they were inclined, they were also increased in width at the level of the beam in the fore and aft plane (see Fig 3/27).

The approximate dimensions of these timbers, whether vertical or canted, were as follows: their width in the athwartships plane (the increased scantling at the beam excluded) was generally 1¼in for every foot of the timber's length; the fore and aft siding was approximately three-quarters of its athwartships width. The timber was secured with bolts driven from within and clenched externally.

The Top Riders

These timbers served the same function as the breast riders, but were wrought on the upper part of the hull. On ships of two decks the heels of these timbers were set at the lowest strake of the lower deck spirketting, and terminated at the deck clamp of the upper deck. When fitted on three-decked vessels, the heels were set at the spirketting of the middle deck. When first introduced they were vertical, and like the breast riders increased in athwartships scantling where they were adjacent to a deck beam. The heads of these timbers did differ, insomuch as they were fashioned exactly like hanging knees throughout the deck. Thus these timbers fulfilled two functions (see Fig 3/27). Later, these timbers were canted like breast riders, and were disposed in a similar manner, either inclining aft or forward as the builder wished. With this the scantling was increased in the fore and aft plane at the position of the deck beams, while the knee fashioned at their heads was dispensed with. The way in which the top riders were secured was the same as that employed for the breast riders. The proportional dimensions can be assumed to be exactly the same as the breast riders. The decision to incline the breast riders and top riders to stiffen the hull longitudinally was to lead to the design of the diagonal frame construction introduced by Seppings in 1811.

The Knee at the Head of the Sternpost

Although the sternpost was supported at its fore side by the deadwood and the sternson knee, it was additionally strengthened by an inverted knee or standard at its head. This standard was made from selected compass oak. The fore arm was long enough to span at least three deck beams, and was often scored on its underside to allow it to sit down onto the beams. The height of the after end on

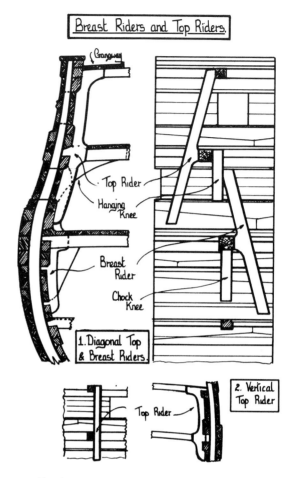

Fig 3/27

the vertical arm was such that it finished at the upper edge of the helm port transom. Its overall length, including the rake aft of the vertical arm from the fore face of the third aftermost beam, was approximately one-eleventh of the length of the gundeck. Its athwartships siding was about half of that given for the width of the head of the sternport. The depth at the foremost part of the fore arm was the same as its siding, plus 2 or 3in for the depth of the scores, thus allowing it to be set down 2 to 3in on the beams. It was fastened with trennals of 2in diameter, and iron clench bolts of about 1¼in diameter. The standard was always fitted prior to the laying of the deck planking. These timbers appear to have been used only on ships of 44 guns and above. I assume that this standard was employed when the sternpost was of considerable length, and would therefore require extra support.

This timber does not appear to have been used on vessels of the seventeenth century and is thought to have been introduced around 1730. One possible reason for its introduction could have been to overcome the 'drop' of the sternpost produced by hogging, for there can be no other reason for making the fore arm of such considerable length, unless the aim was to spread the stress loading over a large area, hence overcoming any apparent pull aft.

Foudroyant. Berthing deck, aft, port side, showing the transom knees (or sleeper beams) supporting the after structure. The tiller sheave block set in the deckhead is of particular interest as it is fitted with two sheaves to increase its mechanical advantage. Vertical iron brackets support the deck beams.

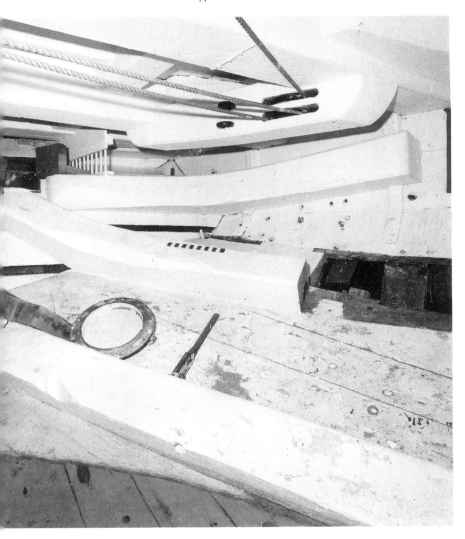

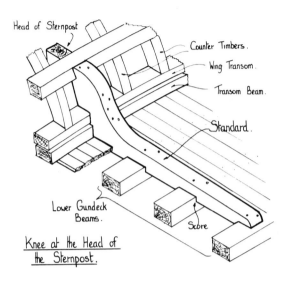

Transom Knees

Head of Sternpost
Counter Timbers.
Wing Transom.
Transom Beam.
Standard.
Lower Gundeck Beams.
Score

Knee at the Head of the Sternpost.

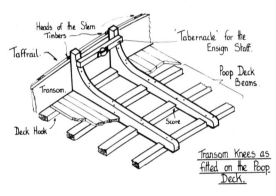

Heads of the Stern Timbers
'Tabernacle' for the Ensign Staff.
Taffrail.
Poop Deck Beams
Transom.
Score
Deck Hook

Transom Knees as fitted on the Poop Deck.

Fig 3/28

Standards (or Inverted Knees)

The use of standards for stiffening the hull of a vessel, had been general practice since the Tudor period. They were fitted at the sides of the beams, and bolted to the ship's side. They were employed as an alternative to the normal hanging knees. They must have helped prevent racking, or movement of the hull out of square with the centreline.

During the seventeenth century they were fitted extensively throughout the gundecks, and used to support the orlop deck beams. However, those used for the orlop were fitted for a completely different reason, and are discussed separately on page 78. By the end of the third quarter of the eighteenth century the number of standards had been reduced, and they were found only on lower decks. The evolution of the breast and top riders seem to have made standards redundant and by 1790 they were only found on the orlop.

In the seventeenth century, standards were fitted to all gundecks. The vertical arm terminated at the line of the deck clamp, while its athwartships arm was approximately one-eighth of the vessel's moulded beam in length. The siding of these timbers was proportional to the beams which they supported. These varied with both the size of the ship and the deck to which they were fitted. The proportions given below have been estimated from figures listed in Deane's *Doctrine of Naval Architecture*. There does not appear to be a specific number of standards, though a contract for six Third Rates of 1666 demands 'four pairs of substantial standards with shoulders of two inch plank under them, and to bolt them with six bolts in each, with an inch and a half quarter auger.'

The siding of the standards on the lower gundeck: Ship, rate (proportion of the width of the deck beam) – First (three-quarters); Second (three-quarters); Third (eleven-sixteenths); Fourth (two-thirds);

Unicorn. *Looking aft showing the centreline support pillars and the gratings covering the limberways. The pump well, without its side planking, can be seen in the background. To the left are iron ballast pigs.*

Fifth (four-sevenths); Sixth (half).

The siding of the standards of the middle gundeck: Ship, rate (proportion of the width of the deck beam) – First (nine-sixteenths); Second (nine-sixteenths); Third (half).

In the eighteenth century the height of the vertical arm was exactly the same as above, and it was made to the same length athwartships as the hanging knees of that deck. Although the standards were fitted on only one deck, there seem to have been more. Ship, number of guns (number of pairs of hanging knees) – 100–90 (twelve); 84–70 (eleven); 64–50 (ten); 50–40 (eight); 38–36 (six); 32–24 (four).

These timbers were fastened to the ship's side with iron bolts, driven from within and clenched. First Rates were usually fitted with eight bolts, the remaining ships having seven, except for the 28- and 24-gun frigates which were secured with six. The diameter of these bolts varied from 1½ to 1¼in.

The Stern (or Transom) Knees

The knees, or more correctly, standards (inverted knees), discussed here must not be confused with those employed in the lower part of the hull. Those described here were fitted to give support to the upper ends of the stern timbers of vessels with a square or flat stern. Their second function was to give support to the 'tabernacle', a baulk of timber that housed the foot of the ensign staff.

The fore and aft arm was made to span the three aftermost deck beams of the poop and the height of the vertical arm was sufficient to terminate just below the taffrail. The width of the fore and aft arm was 7 or 6in, and the vertical arm tapered to about 1in less at its head. The lower edge was scored to allow it to be set down onto the deck beams, where it was firmly bolted. The vertical arm was fayed and bolted to the inner lining of the transom, and fastened to the stern timbers with clench bolts.

The number fitted varied according to the size of the ship. Contemporary models show that either two or four were used, the latter for the largest vessels. However, *Shipbuilder's Repository* clearly states that three are fitted on all ships of between 100 and 60 guns. I presume this is a mistake because usually two were employed on ships of 80 guns or less.

There are a few models that differ from the norm. These include the 74-gun ship *Ajax* of 1767, which has only three, the centre one being made to a greater height, its head supporting a large lantern. There is also a model in the National Maritime Museum of the

Victory at the time of her launch in 1765. Here there are five fitted, the centre one being taller so that it can support the ensign staff. Very few of the smaller vessels were fitted with these knees, for the stern timbers were not sufficiently long to require additional bracing. These knees were fashionable from no earlier than 1745 to no later than 1803. It was only in the first 20 years of this period that three knees were used.

CHAPTER 4

The Construction of the Bulkheads

In this chapter the principal methods of bulkhead construction are discussed, including the manner in which certain compartments, for instance the magazines, were fabricated. Throughout most of the period covered by this book, the bulkheads above the waterline were portable and could be removed prior to engaging the enemy. These bulkheads were of very light build, fitted in sections to facilitate speedy dismantling for stowage in the hold, or for jettisoning overboard in a hurry. This was done to minimise the dangers of splinters from enemy shot, thus reducing the number of casualties in the ship's company. The number and layout of these bulkheads did vary somewhat throughout the period, according to the size of the vessel.

It was not unusual for the light bulkheads of the gundecks to be made from nothing more than a framework of battens supporting canvas screens. This method was generally used between 1680 and about 1780, though during the latter twenty years it was confined to the construction of the more minor divisions, such as officers' cabins. The removal of bulkheads prior to action meant that the gundecks were completely free from obstruction, thereby making the working of the guns easier. The expression 'clear for action' no doubt originates from this task. The bulkheads below the waterline, on the orlop or platforms and in the hold, where division was required for stowage of stores, victuals, shot and powder, were of a more permanent nature. Unlike the vessels of today's navy, these did not form gas-tight or watertight compartments, neither did they act as transverse stiffeners to the hull, this function being performed entirely by the beams.

Each deck is discussed individually. However, the magazines are described separately because of the complexity of their construction. The layout of the more general compartment divisions that is described is typical of naval vessels, but it must be noted that the positioning of individual cabins varied, especially on the gundecks of ships in Pepys' navy.

The Types of Bulkhead

THE BULKHEADS SUBDIVIDING THE HOLD

On First, Second and Third Rate ships the layout of the hold was standard, only varying if an after magazine was fitted. The aftermost bulkhead was placed at the position of the aftermost beam of the orlop deck, the space abaft being used as the bread room. In some cases a partition was made right aft at the sternson and crutches, producing a triangular void known as the 'lady's hole'. Access to this space was by a scuttle on the gundeck, or an 18in square doorway from the bread room, allowing the ship's carpenter to make regular inspections of the timbers in the vicinity. The unusual name of this space probably originated from the 'lady' of the gunroom, a nickname given to the gunroom cleaner who used this area for storage. Another, somewhat implausible, explanation for the name of this area is that if a woman was on board (an unlikely circumstance) and the ship came under fire, she would be sent to this space where it was relatively safe.

The fore bulkhead of the bread room either formed the after bulkhead of the after magazine (if fitted) or the after bulkhead of the fish room. If there was an after magazine, this bulkhead was constructed in the manner described in the section on after magazine construction. If there was no after magazine a series of vertical stanchions was worked transversely across the hold between the ceiling and the orlop deck beams. These were generally made from straight oak, and later pitch pine (which was cheaper and more abundant). Their dimensions varied from 6 to 4in in square section. The heads and heels were tenoned into the fixed positions, above and below. Pine planking of about 3in × 6in was worked up the stanchions and secured with iron spikes. The edges of these planks were rabbeted to form a watertight seal, battens being worked along the seams. The fore bulkhead of the fish room was

Foudroyant. The port side of the carpenter's walk, looking forward. Pillars line the cable tier. None of the bulkheads are original because the support pillars are scored in order to carry the horizontal battens to hold the cable.

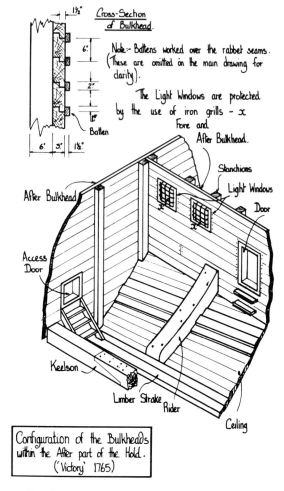

Fig 4/1

made in a similar manner. However, if an after magazine was fitted, the after bulkhead of the fish room was made to the requirements of a magazine. In some instances around 1650 a small steward's room was fitted in the vicinity of the bread room.

The remainder of the bulkheads fitted throughout the hold were of similar construction, except those which formed the boundaries of the fore (or main) magazine. Quite a number of vessels were built with a form of suspended compartment aft of the main magazine. There is one on the *Victory* at Portsmouth which is about 5ft in its fore and aft width and spans the complete width of the hold. The 'flooring' is set approximately 4½ to 5ft above the ceiling of the hold, thus allowing one to walk beneath it to gain access to the forepeak via a scuttle about 18in square cut in the adjacent bulkhead. The decking is supported on beams about 8in square, the outboard ends of which are fayed and bolted to the thick stuff which is wrought along the line of the first futtock heads. These are

supported by a series of square pillars set across the ceiling of the hold, generally in two or three lines. The planking of the bulkhead is 2½ to 3in thick, and 6 to 7½in wide, the edges being rabbeted together. The planking that formed the deck was not always secured, thus each slat could be removed to give access in order to move whatever was stored below. Access scuttles were often placed on this deck if the decking was fixed permanently. This compartment was generally used for stowing either coal or wood for the galley fire.

The layout of the bulkheads in the hold of Fourth Rates and below was not as standard as on larger Rates. This was because most of these vessels were not fitted with an orlop deck, the space in the hold being subdivided by bulkheads and platforms. Platforms were built where required, to ensure that the maximum space was retained. These vessels did not have the same depth in the hold as the larger ships, thus the fitting of an orlop was impractical. Also,

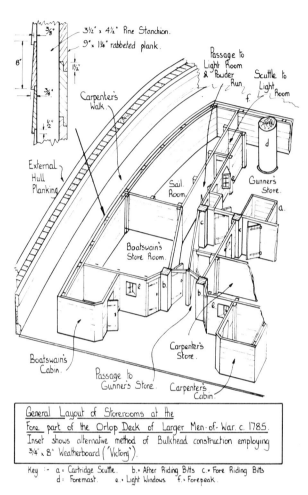

Fig 4/2

Labels on Fig 4/2:
3½" × 4½" Pine Stanchion.
9" × 1¼" rabbeted plank.
Carpenter's Walk.
External Hull Planking.
Passage to Light Room & Powder Run.
Scuttle to Light Room.
Sail Room.
Gunner's Store.
Boatswain's Store Room.
Boatswain's Cabin.
Passage to Gunner's Store.
Carpenter's Store.
Carpenter's Cabin.

General Layout of Storerooms at the Fore part of the Orlop Deck of Larger Men-of-War. c. 1785. Inset shows alternative method of Bulkhead construction employing ¾" × 8" Weatherboard ('Victory').

Key :- a.- Cartridge Scuttle. b.- After Riding Bitts c.- Fore Riding Bitts d.- Foremast. e.- Light Windows f.- Forepeak.

Typical Layout of the Cabins and Bulkheads, Storerooms etc fitted throughout the after end of the Orlop Deck.

(Illustration adapted from a Draught of a 74 Gun ship circa 1785.)

Labels on Fig 4/3:
Lady's Hole.
After end of the Orlop.
External Hull Planking.
Bread Room.
Steward's Store.
Carpenter's Walk.
Purser's Cabin.
Slop Room.
Chaplain Apothecary.
Spirit Room Hatch.
Surgeon's Cabin.
Captain's Secretary.
Marines' Clothing Store.
Pillar.
Cable Tier Beam.

Key:- a.- Scuttle to Light Room.
b.- Scuttle to After Magazine.
c.- Steward's Bed Space. d.- Support Pillars for Mizzen Mast Step.
e.- Access Door. f.- Ladder from Gundeck.

Fig 4/3

there was generally less space, for the smaller ships were sometimes sharper in their section, due to their sailing requirements. The hold layout varied throughout the many classes, though the construction was very similar to that of larger ships. Stanchions of between 4 and 6in in square section supported rabbeted planking between 2 and 3in thick and 6 to 9in wide. The structure was secured with iron spikes, except in way of the magazines. The best way to understand the general disposition of these bulkheads is to study individual draughts.

On brigs and cutters, the hold space was very small, for most of the room was taken up by individual compartments subdividing the area both transversely and longitudinally. These were used for cabin accommodation, provision rooms and stores. This layout also applies to bomb ketches and to gun vessels, the latter being introduced in about 1800 and employed primarily in the Napoleonic Wars. Vessels built in the latter half of the seventeenth century and first 30 years of the eighteenth century, were built with

fewer platforms and subdivisions than those built later.

THE BULKHEADS ON THE ORLOP DECK

Most of the bulkheads fitted on this deck were of very light construction, and usually made from fir. The planks were approximately 8in wide and 1½in thick and the edges were rabbeted. The vertical bulkhead stiffeners were also made from either fir or pitch pine, about 4in square, spaced between 3 and 4ft apart where necessary. It was often the practice to rabbet these stiffeners, so that the ends of the planking could be set flush. This enabled shorter lengths of timber to be used, thereby reducing wastage.

The area in the vicinity of the mainmast was sectioned off to form a stowage place for sails. The sails required ventilation to prevent

Left: Unicorn. *Looking aft into the compartments fitted on the after platform. The passageway on the right which led to the bread room also gave access to the after magazine and its light room.*

Below left: Unicorn. *The cable tier set upon the middle platform above the hold, seen from starboard. Slats of timber are fitted transversely across the deck to allow the cables to drain into the bilges. To the fore side of this tier was the sail room.*

Right: Unicorn. *The wardroom and cabins. Although these cabin bulkheads are of typical lightweight portable construction, they were never removed for action because of their level in the ship. In the background is the iron tiller. The louvered doors enhanced the ventilation of the cabins.*

mildew, or even more dangerous, spontaneous combustion precipitated by dampness. Ventilation was obtained by having the bulkheads made in a louvre fashion, the boards being about 2in thick and 9in wide. The vertical stiffeners did not differ greatly from those employed throughout the rest of the deck. This method of construction was altered in 1819, the louvre boards being replaced by vertical gratings which gave a better course of ventilation. *Foudroyant*'s sail room is on the midships platform and its construction is unusual. The bulkheads are flat but only 3ft 6in high. The space above them is fitted with vertical iron bars of about ¾in diameter. The ends are driven into the uppermost plank and a light carling at the deckhead.

Most of the compartments on this deck were either fore or aft, the section amidships being open to accommodate the cable tier. The cable tier had a series of beams, about 4 to 6in square, placed athwartships across the deck, to allow the anchor cables to drain after being hove in. To contain these cables a semi-bulkhead, made in a series of vertical gratings of stout build, supported by stanchions, was constructed longitudinally. This bulkhead was set about 4ft from the ship's side, the gratings being fitted to give ventilation. In earlier vessels, this division may have been made by a line of pillars only.

The compartments aft were mainly for accommodation for personnel such as the surgeon, junior lieutenants, master's mates etc. These cabins were not placed directly against the ship's side, for a longitudinal bulkhead was fitted about 4ft from the hull. The passageway produced between this bulkhead and the ship's side was called the carpenter's walk. It allowed the ship's carpenter and his mates to continually inspect the hull for damage and leaks below the waterline. Their task was to plug any shot holes with soft wedges and wooden bungs. This bulkhead was constructed either by the simple method described above or by a method, introduced in about 1770, that resulted in a double skin.

THE BULKHEADS ON THE BERTHING DECK

Ships that were not fitted with an orlop usually had a berthing deck or lower deck. Generally there were no bulkheads fitted in the fore

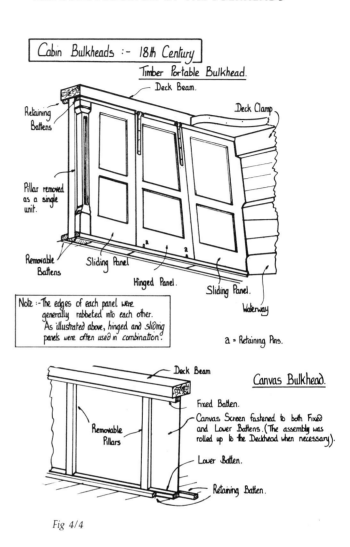

Fig 4/4

half of this deck. The after section was not dissimilar to that of the orlop deck of the larger vessels. The only real difference was that the cabins were set adjacent to the ship's side without having a carpenter's walk in between. A single screen bulkhead was fitted a little to the fore side of the mizzen mast, to act as a division between the senior and junior officers. The number of individual cabins fitted throughout this deck was greater than that fitted on the orlop of the larger ships. This was due to the fact that with only one gundeck, very little room was available to accommodate a large number of officers. The construction of the cabins was very simple: either panels of deal, or on earlier vessels, canvas fitted on a light framework.

The layout for brigs and cutters was more complex, for due to the limited space most of the berthing deck was fitted out with cabins and storerooms. There was a sail room amidships, between the fore and main hatches, and officers' accommodation was aft. Forward of the fore hatch were the cabins and storerooms for the boatswain, gunner and carpenter, the remainder of the crew having their mess situated on either side of the sail room. The bulkheads of these vessels were generally more robust, and permanent. The gun vessels that were introduced around 1800 had no actual deck below the upper deck, thus the accommodation and storerooms were fitted within the confines of the ship's underwater body.

The best way to appreciate the layout of a frigate's berthing deck is to visit the *Foudroyant* at Portsmouth, or the *Unicorn* at Dundee. These vessels give a good idea of the construction of the lower deck, of ships built in the first quarter of the nineteenth century.

Seventeenth-century ships, and probably those built in the first half of the eighteenth century, had berthing deck cabins made and subdivided with canvas partitions, the only fixed bulkheads being those set athwartships.

THE BULKHEADS ON THE GUNDECKS
The Lower Gundeck

No bulkheads were fitted on the lowest gundeck (disregarding ships with a single gundeck). This ensured that the deck remained completely unobstructed from stem to stern, thereby giving maximum room to work the heaviest armament. Nevertheless it was often the practice to divide off the after section with a canvas screen. The area enclosed accommodated the gunner and his mates, and was called the gunroom. The canvas bulkhead could be rapidly dismantled prior to action. The only other division on this deck was the 'manger', a 'dwarf' bulkhead situated well forward. The function of this barrier was to contain seawater, which drained either from recently hove-in anchor cables, or entered the ship through the hawse holes. The water was channelled to the scuppers at the ship's side. The manger is discussed in detail in Chapter 6.

On single-decked vessels, the after end was fitted out for the captain's accommodation. This included his day cabin, sleeping quarters, and the dining cabin. Forward of this there was additional cabin space for the first lieutenant and other senior officers. All the

Left: Unicorn. *The berthing deck, looking forward from the bulkhead that divided off the wardroom. The cabins shown here were usually used by the warrant officers and senior tradesmen such as the carpenter.*

Right: Foudroyant. *The captain's day cabin with a typical portable bulkhead. The diamond shaped inserts in the deck beams cover the boltheads.*

bulkheads were of the portable type, that could be unshipped in sections, leaving the gundeck clear fore and aft. The bulkheads were similar to those fitted on the middle and upper decks of First, Second, Third and Fourth Rates, described in the following section.

The Middle and Upper Gundecks

Throughout most of the period, the wardroom on two- and three-gundecked vessels was situated above the lower gundeck and the captain's quarters, below the poop – on frigates and sloops the captain's quarters were on the main deck while the wardroom, which on these vessels was known as the gunroom, was on the berthing deck below. Prior to 1740, the wardroom was at either the after end of the middle, upper, or lower gundeck. In the latter position, it was often referred to as the gunroom. The officers' cabins were also fairly well dispersed before 1740. Therefore the wardroom as we know it was not a confined accommodation space. Vessels with three gundecks generally had the Admiral's accommodation at the after end of the upper gundeck.

Until about 1730 the major transverse bulkheads that were fitted at the break of the forecastle, quarterdeck and poop, were generally permanent. The remaining cabin partitions on these decks were usually made from either canvas or thin wooden panels that could be easily unshipped and stowed below in the hold.

In 1673 Pepys authorised a reduction in the number of cabins to be fitted throughout the decks, in order to improve ventilation below decks and to decrease the time taken for a vessel to prepare for action. The number of partitions prior to this date was

considerable, and impaired the air flow. In addition to the deck plans in this book which illustrate general layouts, draughts and models can be studied at the National Maritime Museum. In order to avoid confusion permanent and temporary bulkheads are described separately.

THE TEMPORARY OR REMOVABLE BULKHEADS

These were usually made from oak or mahogany, until such woods became too expensive. Thereafter plain deal was used to reduce costs. Bulkheads on earlier vessels were made in sections varying from 6 to 10ft in length, and stiffened with carved stanchions of fir. The width of the stanchions varied from 2 to 4in and they were about 1in thick.

Later, bulkheads were made in light, short-length panels. Each section was made to the appropriate height, and to a width of 2ft 6in or 3ft. In all cases the lower half was made from a plain panel. The upper portion was either in the form of a panel, or was louvered. The advantage of the latter was ventilation. Where these bulkheads were fitted under the break of the poop, the upper section of each panel was fitted with small windows to illuminate the master's cabin and chart room. Each pane of glass was approximately 7 × 4½in.

Each individual section was located at its bottom edge by a retaining sill, which spanned the entire length of the required bulkhead. Holes were bored vertically at intervals to receive the sliding bolts fastened to each panel. The sill was made from fir or a similar wood to that used for the deck planking. It was about 7in wide, and about 3in deep. This was secured to the deck with Muntz keybolts.

The manner in which the top of each section was secured varied. In some cases a retaining lintel with similar scantlings and fastenings was secured to the deckhead. The sections of the bulkhead were either held with sliding bolts, let into the lintel or the upper part of each section hinged at the deckhead, so it could be unbolted at the bottom and swung up, and rebolted in its horizontal position.

False carved pillars were set on the vertical edges of each section, to overlap the next section, thereby reducing draughts. Alternatively, detachable pillars were fitted between each section and rabbeted to receive the panels on either side. Considerable thought must have been given to the design of removable bulkheads, for most vessels could clear for action in less than ten minutes.

SCREEN BULKHEADS

This type of bulkhead was only found on vessels with a stern walk. It was generally fitted about 4ft forward of the stern timbers, and was originally made in the double sash form. However, this was found to be too heavy, and difficulties occurred in the removal of the screen when going into action. This problem was overcome by changing the construction to the single sash method, which was far lighter. Authorisation for this was given in 1757. Screen bulkheads remained in fashion until the introduction of the closed stern in 1795. The double sash bulkhead was approximately 7½ to 8in thick and the sash was equal in depth to the panels.

THE FIXED OR PERMANENT BULKHEADS

Bulkheads were fitted under the break of the forecastle quarterdeck and poop in most vessels until the introduction of fore and aft gangways in 1744. Prior to this, the waists of naval ships were completely open with only the high bulwarks at the ship's side. It is not known exactly when the permanent bulkheads were superseded by more temporary ones, but it seems probable that they had become obsolete in most classes of vessel by 1760. Those at the break of the poop may well have changed to the portable type at a much earlier date.

Generally (excluding those fitted under the poop) these bulkheads were not flat but incorporated a number of projections

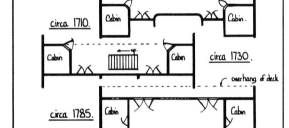

Fig 4/5

(usually three), produced by the cabins in the vicinity. The more individual features of these bulkheads were determined by the actual position of the bulkhead in question.

The Bulkhead at the Forecastle

During the latter half of the seventeenth century, this bulkhead was lavishly decorated with carving, and considerable gilt-work. There were three convex projections, the one at the centreline being the greatest. This was the after side of the galley on larger vessels. It was only recently that the belfry had been transferred from its original position aft, to the forecastle. This area was transformed into an elaborate architrave highlighting the ship's bell. A fine example of this can be found on the model of the *Prince* of 1670. The other two projections situated on either side of the ship were formed by the after bulkheads of the cabins allotted to the bosun and carpenter.

The construction of the forecastle bulkhead was probably fairly simple, although not obviously so, beneath the façade of richly carved pillars and mouldings. The basic vertical support stanchions were evenly dispersed, with their heads and heels tenoned into specially shaped beams produced to give the desired contoured effect. Most of these were made from oak and were 4 to 6in in square section. The spaces between the stanchions were filled in with oak panelling. The bulkhead was then ornamented with carved pillars and elaborate mouldings.

By 1700, on most ships the outer two projections were square, although they were still rounded on some vessels as late as 1720 (model of a 60-gun ship at the National Maritime Museum at Greenwich). There was slightly less elaborate carving on the belfry which had been raised to sit on the forecastle (for example the *Mordaunt*, 1682). Between 1675 and 1695, double doors gave access at the bulkhead. Each pair of doors, when closed, contained a divided aperture, the cover of which could be opened to run out a gun facing aft. This feature was also found on bulkheads that faced forward. Should the vessel be overcome by boarders, defence could be maintained from the other areas of the ship.

Internally, the partitions forming the other boundaries of the galley and the cabins were more likely to be of the removable type, and made from either canvas (cabins only) or of a light panelled timber. There were quite a number of variations in the construction of the forecastle bulkhead. A model of a 40-gun ship of 1685 shows a rectangular hinged 'flap' fitted at the centreline of the bulkhead at the level of the deck. The hinges are placed along the upper edge so that the flap opens in the same manner as a gunport lid. The flap would be raised for the passage of the anchor cables, as the riding bitts are fitted aft of the forecastle at the waist, and the hawse holes were on the same deck. (Both of these features are unusual, for most vessels had them fitted on the lower gundeck). The capstan was also fitted on this deck, a little aft of the mainmast.

Some ships did not have any form of bulkhead fitted at the break of the forecastle – especially those with a very short forecastle. This was the case on a number of Sixth Rates. Such 20-guns ships built between 1719 and 1727, are often referred to as the 'Blandford' or 'Lyme' class. The belfry is set to the port side, while a square-section flue for the galley is set to starboard. This design seems to have been adopted from Fifth Rates of 32-guns that had been built earlier. Although these vessels were built with a round bow, small roundhouses were retained.

The *Dolphin*, a 20-gun sloop built in 1731, was built without a bulkhead at the break of the forecastle. Although she is listed as carrying 20 guns, in fact she probably carried 22, for her hull is pierced with eleven gunports on each side. She was not dissimilar to the 24-gun sloops built ten years later, their dimensions being similar. The aforementioned was built without a forecastle bulkhead, but was fitted with a flat beakhead bulkhead with roundhouses, a fashion that had been superseded in this class ten years previously.

Models of the above mentioned are on display at the National Maritime Museum at Greenwich. The *Dolphin* model is also in the Transport Museum in Glasgow. This, however, shows the ship with a somewhat shorter quarterdeck.

Victory. *The fore part of the hold. The area in the foreground was originally the main magazine, the divisional bulkhead between the powder room and the filling room was situated at the beam marked 'z' and the fore bulkhead of the filling room terminated at beam 'y'. Access to the filling room was through the small scuttle marked 'x'. The internal planking consisting of the limber strake, footwaling, ceiling and thick stuff, is on the left. Also shown are the orlop deck clamp, the keelson and the breast hooks.*

Victory. The main magazine viewed from the port side. This photograph shows the after bulkhead of the magazine, the timber hooks for cartridges set into the beams and the varying thickness of the internal planking and strakes of thick stuff. Note the scarphs in the beams and the top and butt fashion employed for the orlop deck clamp.

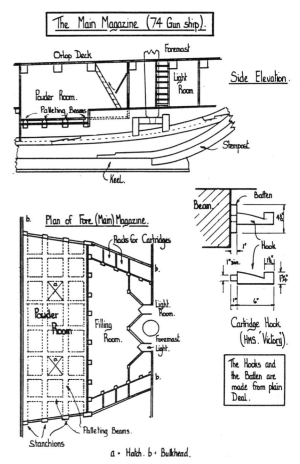

Fig 4/6

The Bulkhead at the Quarterdeck

This was constructed in a similar manner to the bulkhead at the break of the forecastle. Its general layout was also in the form of three projections produced by a centre and two outboard cabins. These bulkheads were originally concave but like those at the forecastle the outboard cabins were square by the end of the seventeenth century. The former style is finely reproduced on a model of a 44-gun ship of 1660. This also shows some small cabins placed to the fore side of the bulkhead under the gangways, a feature which will be explained fully later.

The first sign of a change to squarer cabins is evident on a model of a 90-gun vessel of 1703. By 1720 the centre projection began to disappear, and the side cabins remained for only a short period afterwards. A model of a 60-gun ship of 1720 shows this development. It also has a few unusual features: double cabin doors are fitted at the corners of the cabins and the companionway leading to the quarterdeck is set athwartships at the centreline. All of these models can be seen in the National Maritime Museum at Greenwich.

By 1735, the bulkhead had become flat, and all the cabin accommodation was aft of the bulkhead. Like the forecastle bulkhead the quarterdeck bulkhead was built in the portable fashion in all vessels by 1760. The access doorways were generally double. Between 1675 and 1695 they were pierced with a divided aperture through which a gun could be pointed.

The Bulkhead at the Poop and the Coach

These were built in the same way as those previously mentioned, except that they were generally flat, with no projections. Because they were higher up in the ship they were lighter. The stanchions were 2½ to 3in square section, panelled with either oak or mahogany. They were often built with windows in place of the top panels. The coach was only fitted on a few First Rates. It was a very short deck built above the poop at the after end. Sometimes this deck was called the flying poop or poop royal. The *Victory* of 1737 (often referred to as Balchen's *Victory*) was one of the few vessels fitted with this deck. These bulkheads were probably the first to be made in the portable style.

Towards the end of the eighteenth century the bulkhead at the poop was set back further aft, and small compartments were fitted on each side under the overhang. These were used to accommodate the captain's clerk, and the sailing master; the latter's cabin also acted as the chart room. The ship's steering wheel was set within the recess formed between these cabins. During the last 25 years of the sailing warship, a few of the larger vessels had these cabins made with circular corners, a characteristic that was also common to ships of the latter half of the seventeenth century.

The Magazines

THE MAIN MAGAZINE IN THE EIGHTEENTH CENTURY

By 1750 the construction of this magazine had become quite complex. It was generally fitted deep within the hold of the ship, where it could not be penetrated by enemy shot. It was normally situated in the fore part of the hold, where the shallow rise of the floors gave the maximum amount of space to accommodate it. The larger vessels also had additional 'hanging magazines' for ready use supplies; these are discussed on pages 124–25. The smaller warships did not have the additional room for hanging magazines, and therefore had an after magazine fitted in the hold. This also is discussed on pages 122–23 in the text.

The position of the main magazine was determined by the station at which the after bulkhead was situated – it was constructed a set distance from the fore perpendicular. The figures that follow were taken from the *Shipbuilder's Repository* of 1789: Ship, number of guns (distance from fore perpendicular) – 100 (42ft 9in); 90 (41ft 4in); 74 (42ft 6in); 64 (38ft 6in); 44 (33ft 6in); 38 (34ft 9in); 36 (33ft 9in); 32 (24ft 6in); 28 (20ft); 24 (18ft).

Construction

The floor was supported by a series of transverse beams, about 9in in cross-section, set at a height of 2ft 6in to 3ft above the ceiling of the hold. This was to prevent any ingress of damp or water, and to produce an even deck. Across these beams a platform was constructed, with planks of pitch pine 12in wide and 3in thick. It was secured to the beams with copper dumps. A small access scuttle was generally fitted at the centre of this deck, to allow loose powder to be removed as a precaution against fire.

On top of this deck a second platform was constructed, called the palleting flat. First a series of beams and carlings were fitted to the platform already formed, set out both longitudinally and transversely. This divided up the platform into 3ft square sections. The approximate sizes of these beams were as follows: Ship, number of guns (beams and carlings in square cross section) – 100 (7in); 90, 74 and 64 (6in) 44 and 38 (5in); 36 (4¾in); and 32 (4½in).

A rabbet was cut along each side of the upper edges of the beams and carlings, to receive the butts of the deck planking. These were 1 to 1½in deep and wide. The transverse beams were laid directly over the lower beams that supported the first platform, and were fashioned with a mortice to receive the tenoned ends of the carlings. Once all was in place it was all secured to the lower beams and the deck with bolts (see Fig 4/7).

Next the palleting deck was laid. This was made up of a number of planks, 9in wide and 1½in thick, each plank being 3ft long. Four of these planks were fastened together by two stiffeners and set down into the square apertures formed by the palleting beams and carlings. This is where the term palleting is derived from, because

Unicorn. *The entrance of the main magazine viewed from starboard.*

pallets formed the deck. These were not fastened down, but were portable to allow loose powder to be removed, and to enable an air flow to keep the magazine cool.

The fore and after bulkheads of the magazine were constructed on a series of vertical stanchions set transversely across the ship, extending from the ceiling of the hold to the beams of either the orlop or the berthing deck. The distances between these stanchions are given in the table overleaf. The bulkhead planks were generally made from pitch pine. They were set horizontally, and each edge was rabbeted, thus allowing each plank to overlap the joints. The rabbet was half the thickness of the plank in depth, and equal to the thickness of the plank in width. The alternate edges of each plank were rabbetted, so that when fayed together a reasonably watertight seal was achieved. Strips of deal were worked over the seal both internally and externally, a practice was used extensively on the bulkheads in the hold. This type of sealing can be seen on board the *Victory* at Portsmouth. The *Victory's* hold is not generally open to the public but I am sure that if you are specifically interested the staff will oblige (see Fig 4/7).

The bulkheads at the wings were constructed in a different way and consisted of a series of panels fitted into rabbets on the inner surfaces of the stanchion. These stanchions were set approximately 2ft 3in apart, each being 12in in the fore and aft plane and 6in athwartships. The rabbets cut for the panels were 3in wide and equal in depth to the thickness of the plank they received. See the table overleaf for dimensions.

Foudroyant. Fore side of the main magazine bulkhead. Here short lengths of planking have been worked between the bulkhead stanchions. In the centre of the photograph is a light box. These were fitted when there was not enough room for a lamp room.

The forward half of the magazine was known as the filling room. It was here that the cartridges of powder were filled and stowed ready for use, on the racks lining the bulkheads. By the end of the eighteenth century the whole of this compartment was sheathed with either lead or copper, to prevent sparks being produced by any iron, such as nails on shoes, belts etc. This is why the gunner and his mates wore felt slippers when entering the magazine. This lining also served to prevent the rats that often lived in the lower regions of the ships from gnawing their way into the magazine and eating the cartridges.

The division between the filling room and the palleting flat was made by fitting a series of stanchions, about 6in in cross-section, set approximately 2ft apart. Battens were then fitted across these stanchions, thus preventing the kegs of powder in the palleting flat from moving about during heavy weather. Access to the filling room was usually on the port side of the orlop deck. Here, through a small hatch about 18in², cartridges were passed to the 'powder monkeys' waiting in the passageway above. The deck of this passageway was lined with lead about ⅛in thick.

Access to the whole of the magazine was through a scuttle fitted to the starboard side, leading from the orlop deck. The sizes of these access hatches are given in the list below. The scuttle also led to the light room adjacent to the magazine. Here a lantern was placed at a window which shed the light into the magazine, thus avoiding the presence of a naked flame in the magazine. This prevented fire and explosion, which would occur if the lantern be overturned in action or by accident. By the end of the eighteenth century, an iron grill was also fitted over the window as an added precaution. The sizes of the scuttle to both magazine and light room are as follows: Ship, number of guns (size of scuttle) – 100 (3ft 3in); 90 (2ft 9in); 74 (2ft 6in); 64 and 44 (2ft 4in); 38 (2ft 3in); 36, 32, 28 and 24 (2ft 2in).

On the *Victory*, I found that on the sides of the beams of the orlop (which formed part of the deckhead of the main magazine) a row of shallow square mortices cut into a batten that was fastened to the beam. In places a few remaining wooden hooks set into the mortices can be seen. This is evidence that cartridges were suspended from these hooks for stowage. Both access hatches are still present, as is the after bulkhead, but although the fore and side bulkheads are missing there is still evidence of their original positions. For details of the hooks, see Fig 4/6.

THE AFTER MAGAZINE

The after magazine, or powder room as it was often called, was only found on vessels that were not fitted with hanging magazines. The after bulkhead was generally set at a particular position forward of the after perpendicular. This was often at the station of the aftermost beam of the orlop or platform deck, and formed the division between the magazine and the bread room. The position of the fore bulkhead varied from ship to ship according to either the whim of the builder or to whether the mizzen mast was stepped on the gundeck or in the hold. One draught of the *Victory* shows the

Fore and After Bulkheads of the Main Magazine

No of Guns	Stanchions, square in section in	Distance set between stanchions ft	Distance set between stanchions in	Thickness of the bulkhead planking in
110–100	8 × 8	2	11	3½
90–80	7½ × ½	2	10	3
74–70	7 × 7	2	9	3
64–60	6 × 6	2	8	3
50–44	5½ × 5½	2	6	3
38	5 × 5	2	4	2½
36	5 × 5	2	4	2½
32	4¾ × 4¾	2		2
28	4½ × 4½	2		2
24	4 × 4	2		2

Right: Unicorn. *Pump well viewed diagonally across the hold.*

Below right: Unicorn. *The after end of the hold and the pump well. The doorway cut into the well is not original and would have once been occupied by the bulkhead of the shot locker. Above is the after end of the platform forming the cable tier.*

mizzen mast stepped aft of the magazine, whereas another draught of the same ship shows it passing through the compartment*. The *Agamemnon*, a 64-gun ship built by Adams at Bucklers Hard on the river Beaulieu, definitely had the mizzen mast stepped in the centre of the magazine. The list below gives the length of the magazine between the fore and after bulkheads. These figures are taken from the *Shipbuilder's Repository* of 1789: Ship, number of guns (length, fore and aft) – 74 (9ft 8in); 44 (7ft); 38 (7ft 4in); 36 (7ft 3in); sloop (8ft); cutter (9ft 11in).

Ships of 100, 90, and 64 guns have been omitted. These were generally fitted with hanging magazines, although the draught of the *Agamemnon*, built only 8 years previously shows an after magazine, and there is no indication of hanging magazines. The fore and aft length of her powder room is shown as 8ft.

Below are the principal dimensions of a 74-gun ship, taken from a draught dated 1 October 1805, which is from Rees' *Naval Architecture*:

The length between the fore and after bulkheads 12ft
Width between the wing bulkheads (athwartships) 17ft
Thickness of the bulkhead planking 3in
Vertical stanchions made square 7 × 7in
Width of the deck or platform beams 9in
Depth of the deck or platform beams 7in
Thickness of the deck or platform planking 3in
Width of the deck or platform planking 12in
Height between deck and underside of the orlop deck 8ft.

Construction

Construction of the powder room was similar to that of the fore or main magazine, except that palleting beams were omitted. The method of construction differed, for two possible reasons. Firstly, there was less room in the ship's after body due to the rise of the floors. Secondly, this was primarily a powder room, as cartridges were not filled in this area and thus there were none of the problems associated with loose powder. All the bulkheads were constructed in the same manner as the fore and after bulkheads of the main magazine. The edges of the planks were rabbeted and strips of deal worked along the seams. This also applied to the wing bulkheads,

*One draught of the *Victory* shows both hanging magazines and an after magazine. Apparently this was altered in her later life, for she has been restored so that the compartment in this vicinity has a long narrow light room, fitted along the port side, with three windows at which the lanterns were hung. It is important not to adhere to any hard and fast rule regarding compartment layout as practices changed over the years.

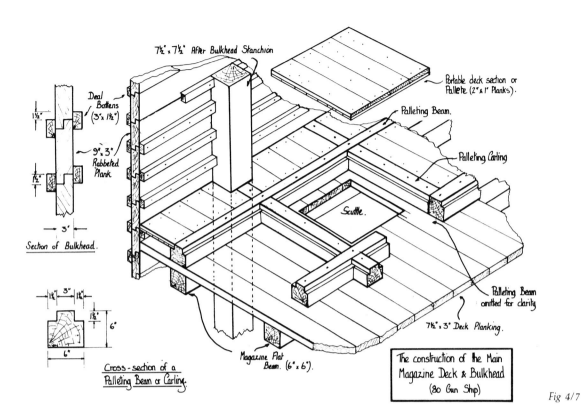

Fig 4/7

which were not of panelled construction like the wing bulkheads of the main magazine. The figures given below are taken from *Shipbuilder's Repository*.

Fore and After Bulkheads of the After Bulkhead

No of Guns	Sections of stanchions in	Distance between the stanchions ft in		Thickness of the bulkhead planking in
74	6 × 6	2	9	3
44	5 × 5	2	6	3
38	4½ × 4½	2	4	2½
36	4½ × 4½	2	4	2½
32	4½ × 4½	2	2	2½
28	4½ × 4½	2		2½
24	4 × 4	2		2½
Sloop	3½ × 3½	2		2
Cutter	3 × 3	2		2

For vessels without hanging magazines, the powder room was fitted out to allow for the filling of cartridges (although there were no palleting deck or beams). This was because the after magazine supplied the after guns of the ship in action. By the end of the eighteenth century these bulkheads were lined with either lead or copper, and all fastenings were copper (bolts, dumps and nails).

The position of the light room varied. It was generally in a midships position, and constructed in a triangular shape within the boundaries of the compartment. This allowed light to be cast to both port and starboard of the magazine, the lantern being placed in the next compartment forward. There does not appear to have been any strict pattern governing the exact layout, for the *Victory* has a light room running the full length of the magazine on its port side, with access from both the spirit room forward, and aft. Access to the light room when fitted on the centreline was from the deck above, via a scuttle to one side, another scuttle being fitted adjacent giving passage to the magazine itself.

THE HANGING MAGAZINE

This type of magazine was generally fitted on vessels that had insufficient room to accommodate an after magazine, due to the rise of the floors, and in First, Second and some Third Rates. There were two advantages to this type of magazine. Firstly, due to its position on the orlop deck, the cartridges could be dispatched more speedily to the gundecks above. Secondly, because of its unique design it was drier and cooler due to the air that circulated around the bulkheads. This was achieved by having the whole magazine suspended between the orlop deck and the hold.

The deckhead of the compartment was about 2ft below the deckhead of the orlop, thus allowing air to pass over the top. This also ensured that no water would penetrate from faulty or badly maintained seams in the planking of the gundeck above.

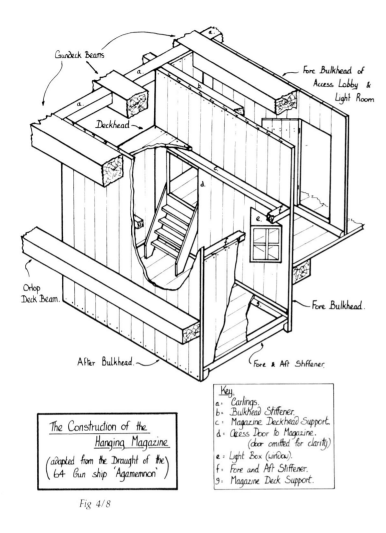

Gundeck Beams

Fore Bulkhead of
Access Lobby &
Light Room

Deckhead

Orlop
Deck Beam.

Fore Bulkhead.

After Bulkhead.

Fore & Aft Stiffener.

Key.
a : Carlings.
b : Bulkhead Stiffener.
c : Magazine Deckhead Support.
d : Access Door to Magazine.
  (door omitted for clarity).
e : Light Box (window).
f : Fore and Aft Stiffener.
g : Magazine Deck Support.

The Construction of the
Hanging Magazine
(adapted from the Draught of the
64 Gun ship 'Agamemnon')

Fig 4/8

Construction

The fore and after bulkheads were constructed from pitch pine planking, 8in wide and 3in thick. Unlike the bulkheads of the other magazines, and bulkheads of the hold, the planks were set in a vertical plane. The edges of the planks were rabbeted so that they would form a watertight seal, half the thickness of the plank in depth and equal in width to the plank. The heads of these planks were secured to the sides of the gundeck beams, and where they passed to the beams of the orlop deck they were secured with copper spikes.

Set across the fore and after bulkheads were a series of oak stiffeners, 4in wide and deep. These supported the deck and deckhead of the magazine. The bulkhead that supported the deckhead was set at a specific distance below the level of the gundeck (given in the table adjacent). Likewise fore and aft stiffeners of the same scantling were fitted, on to which the fore and after bulkheads were secured. The planking for these bulkheads was identical to that used for the forward and the after bulkhead. The forward bulkhead was pierced for a small access door, and a window with two faces. This window was fashioned with a ledge so that a

lantern could be placed on the other side to illuminate the magazine from the adjacent access lobby and light room. A short ladder was fitted in the magazine, to reach the deck from the level of the orlop deck. (See Fig 4/8.)

The access lobby and light room were generally fitted to the fore side of the magazine. The athwartships width of this combined compartment was equal to that of the magazine, and was from 2ft 6in to 3ft in width, fore and aft. Fig 4/8 shows the lobby and light room as one compartment. This is different to the most common layout, in which the light room was separate, but enclosed within the lobby area, with its own access door. The door from the orlop to the lobby was hung so that it opened into the compartment, the door to the magazine itself opening away from the magazine. This was done so that in the event of an explosion on the orlop adjacent to the lobby, the first door would be blown open by the blast. The door to the magazine itself (which was opposite) would thus be shut by the blast, and the magazine isolated from the danger. All the access doors were made with their planks rabbeted in the same fashion as those of the bulkhead, and were generally about 2ft 3in wide and 3 to 3ft 6in high.

The doors and bulkheads were usually lined with lead, and later with copper, to prevent sparks. Below I have produced a table which gives the principal dimensions, taken from the *Shipbuilder's Repository*. Dimensions varied very little, as can be seen from the second table which gives the dimensions of the hanging magazines of the *Victory*, which was completed some 24 years earlier.

Dimensions of Hanging Magazines

Dimension	No of guns					
	100		90		64	
	ft	in	ft	in	ft	in
After magazine – fore bulkhead from after end of main hatch	27*		25	6*	25	
Fore magazine – fore bulkhead from after side of fore hatch	3	4*	4*		–	
Fore and after magazine:						
Length fore and aft	6	2	5		6	
Width athwartships	9		8	6	9	
Height between deckhead of the magazine and underside of gundeck planking	3	2	4	3	3	5
Depth of the magazine deck below the underside of the orlop deck planking	2	3	3	7	2	8

*This measurement can also be taken as the following: the fore bulkhead of the after magazine was approximately one-third of the length of the gundeck from the after perpendicular. The fore bulkhead was set one-third of the length of the gundeck from the fore perpendicular.

It appears from the above table that only one hanging magazine was fitted to a 64-gun man-of-war. In fact, some vessels had none at all.

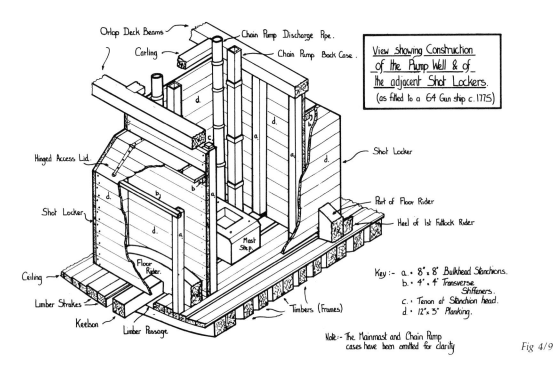

Orlop Deck Beams
Carling
Chain Pump Discharge Pipe.
Chain Pump Back Case.

View showing Construction
of the Pump Well & of
the adjacent Shot Lockers.
(as fitted to a 64 Gun ship c.1775)

Hinged Access Lid.
Shot Locker
Shot Locker
Part of Floor Rider
Heel of 1st Futtock Rider
Mast Step.
Floor Rider.
Ceiling
Limber Strakes
Keelson
Limber Passage
Timbers (Frames)

Key :- a.= 8" x 8" Bulkhead Stanchions.
b.= 4" x 4" Transverse Shiffeners.
c.= Tenon at Stanchion head.
d.= 12"x 3" Planking.

Note:- The Mainmast and Chain Pump
cases have been omitted for clarity

Fig 4/9

Dimensions of the Victory's Hanging Magazines

Dimension	ft	in
After magazine – fore bulkhead from after end of main hatch	27*	
Fore magazine – fore bulkhead from after side of fore hatch	3	8*
Length fore and aft	6	
Width athwartships	9	7
Height between deckhead of the magazine and underside of the gundeck planking	3	
Depth of the magazine deck below the underside of the orlop deck planking	2	9

*One-third of the depth of the gundeck from the after perpendicular.

THE SHOT LOCKERS

Throughout the period covered by this book, the shot lockers were fitted by the well in the hold, adjacent to the mainmast step. The reason for this was that by having them down in this part of the vessel, weight was kept low, ensuring that the ship had a low centre of gravity. The construction of the shot lockers was relatively simple, and in most cases the fore and aft side were a continuation of the sides of the well itself. The number of lockers fitted, depended on the size of the vessel. Usually there were two, one forward and one aft of the well. This can be clearly seen in a number of illustrations, such as Dummer's *Draughts of the Body of an English Man-of-War* which shows a longitudinal section of a First Rate of 1680. Nelson's *Victory*, the *Agamemnon*, a 64-gun ship of 1781, and the 74-gun ship in Rees' *Naval Architecture* all have two lockers. It

seems that only one was fitted on the smaller Fifth and Sixth Rates. The *Unicorn*, which was built in 1824, has only one locker, and this was fitted aft of the well. This appears to be the norm for vessels built with platforms instead of an orlop deck.

Construction

Before discussing the shot lockers, the construction of the well will be explained. Four stout stanchions were set up between the ceiling of the hold and the beams of the orlop, or platform, two aft and two forward of the mainmast step, forming the corners of the well. These generally measured from 6 to 8in², and were made from oak. The ends were tenoned into the beams and the ceiling planks. On larger ships, where the length of the well was considerable, an additional pillar was fitted on each side, between the others, to stiffen the bulkhead planking. The frame was then planked up on the fore and after bulkheads with oak boards 9 to 12in wide and 3½ to 1½in thick.

Three to five pillars were set up both fore and aft of the transverse bulkhead of the well; these formed the framework of the shot lockers. The pillars were the same scantling as those used for the well, though they were shorter because they were not continued upward to the beams of the orlop, for the shot lockers were usually only two-thirds of the depth in the hold. The heads of these pillars were stiffened with transverse timbers of oak, of 3 to 4½in square section. Similar pieces of timber were worked horizontally across the transverse bulkheads of the well, to support the top and its hinged access hatches.

Dimensions of the Well and Shot Locker Planking

No of guns	Plank thickness in	Plank width in
110–100	3½	12
90–84	3¼	12
80–50	3	12
46–40	2½	10
38	2	8
36–32	2½	9
28–24	2	8
Sloops and cutters	1½	6

The sides of the well and shot locker were then planked up with boards of the dimensions already given above. Finally the transverse bulkheads of the shot locker were planked. All the planking was laid in the horizontal and care was taken that the nails were driven in canted to ensure that the planks did not work loose due to the weight of the shot.

The tables opposite give the approximate size of these lockers including the dimensions of the pump well, which was integral to their construction. The complete assembly is shown in Fig 4/9. The method of building shot lockers for ships without an orlop deck and with just a series of platforms will be discussed separately.

The Shot Lockers of Ships with a Platform

Although the bottom table covers shot lockers fitted on smaller vessels, the construction of shot lockers did vary slightly. It appears that often only one was fitted, aft of the pump well. This fashion was most common on the 40- to 46-gun frigates built after 1810, and was probably adopted on smaller vessels at the turn of the nineteenth century. The platform deck terminated at the fore end of the shot locker, the deck being canted down to the stanchions of the after bulkhead of the locker. Unlike eighteenth-century shot lockers these were completely planked in with two small hinged access lids, not unlike those of the gunports. This can be seen clearly on the *Unicorn* at Dundee, although a great deal of the bulkhead planking is missing in the vicinity, and on the *Foudroyant* at Portsmouth.

Dimensions of the Well

No of Guns	Length, fore and aft ft	Length, fore and aft in	Width athwartships ft	Width athwartships in	Plank thickness in
100	11	8	10		3½
90	9	6	8	6	3¼
74	10		8		3
64	8	6	7	3	3
44	7	4	6	10	3
38	7		6	9	2
36	7		6	8	2½
32	6	8	6	8	2½
28	6		6		2
24	6	10	6		2
Sloop	5		5		1½
Cutter	3		4		1½

Dimensions of Shot Locker

No of Guns	Length, fore and aft ft	Length, fore and aft in
110	2	10
90	2	5
74	2	6
64	2	1
44	2	
38	2	
36	1	11
32	1	10
28	1	9
24	1	8
Sloop	1	6
Cutter	1	6

The width athwartship and the plank thickness were as for the well.

Foudroyant. *The berthing deck with an example of a Seppings iron tiller and a double sheave tiller block fitted to the deckhead. Although this vessel had been modified with an eliptical stern it can be seen that the original transom pieces and their associated knees (or sleepers) were retained.*

CHAPTER 5

The 'Machinery' of the Ship

The Steering Arrangements

This book will deal with two methods by which the ship's rudder was controlled: the whipstaff and the steering wheel. Common to these were the rudder and the tiller, to which there were little alteration between 1650 and 1850.

THE RUDDER

The function of this 'board' was to steer the ship by being rotated about a fixed point, the sternpost, by means of a travelling beam called the tiller. The tiller itself was moved by either the whipstaff or the steering wheel. The overall length of the rudder taken from the inclined fore edge, was determined from the height at which the tiller or upper tiller was placed. Its fore and aft width at its 'sole' was approximately one-seventh of its height in First Rate ships, one-sixth in Third Rates, and one-fifth in the smaller classes. The whole of the rudder was comprised of the following pieces of timber: the main piece, the bearding and the back boards. All of these baulks were fayed and bolted together producing a flat plate.

The main piece was made from oak. Its siding at the head was equal to that of the sternpost at that point, whereas the siding at the heel was equal to that of the after end of the keel.

To the fore edge of the main piece the bearding was fayed. This was a relatively thin strip of elm fayed, dowelled and bolted along the entire length from the heel to the point where the sternpost terminated. It was triangular in cross-section, with the angles set at 30 degrees between 1650 and 1720, and 45 degrees from 1720 onwards. An identical piece was fayed and secured to the after edge of the sternpost, with similar angles. The combined angles thus produced a turning motion of either 60 or 90 degrees in one direction (see Fig 5/2).

The after side of the rudder was completed with a number of fir baulks. It was stepped with either one or two hances, which reduced the overall width fore and aft, to allow the head of the rudder to pass through the helm port in the lower counter. Finally, two thin strips of elm were fastened to the bottom and after edges. These were called the 'sole' and the 'back'. Various timbers were used according to their individual properties: straight oak, for the main piece, primarily for its strength; English elm for its durability in sea water and its ability to withstand shock; and fir for the after part due to its low cost, as it was at this point that damage was a great possibility, and fir was easy and less costly to replace.

The rudder head (or stock) was generally rounded, though sometimes it was three-sided, with the corners rounded. Most ships had their rudders designed to accommodate two tillers, one fitted on the level of the lower gundeck, the other a little over the planking of the deck above. This applied to most ships above the Fifth Rate. The reason was that a second tiller could be shipped in the event of damage to the lower tiller in action or through strain in heavy seas. The tillers were let into fore and aft mortices cut through the rudder stock. The mortices were fashioned with a taper running aft, diminishing by about one-sixth of the width and siding of the end of the tiller. The dimensions of the mortice for the upper tiller, if fitted, were generally 1 or 1½in less than the lower tiller.

The rudder stock was bound up with wrought iron hoops and strapping, to strengthen the points around the tiller mortices, thus eliminating any strain caused by the leverage of the turning motion of the tiller itself. The wrought iron was generally about 3 to 4in wide, and ½ to ¾in thick. First, two lengths of strapping were laid across the head of the rudder, and then passed vertically down each side to a position just below the lower tiller mortice. Over this was placed a series of iron hoops, four being used on vessels with two tiller positions, and two on those with one. Each of these hoops was

Scantling of the Rudder and its Components (see Fig 5/1)

No of guns	*A* *ft*	*A* *in*	*B* *ft*	*B* *in*	*C* *ft*	*C* *in*	*D* *ft*	*D* *in*	*E* *in*
100	6	6	4	6	2	6	2	4	4
90	6		4	4	2	4	2	3	4
74	5	7	4		2	4	2	2	3
64	5	5	3	10	2	3	2	1	3
46	5		3	6	1	10	1	8	3
38	4	8	3	2	1	10	1	8	3
36	4	6	3		1	9	1	7	3
32	4	1	2	11	1	8	1	6	3
28	4		2	10	1	7	1	5	2½
24	3	9	2	9	1	6	1	5	2½
Sloop	3	6	2	7	1	3	1	2	2
Cutter	3	5	2	7	1	3	1	1	2

Dimensions of the Pintles and Braces (see Fig 5/1)

(all dimensions in inches)

No of Guns	*A*	*B*	*C*	*D**	*E*	*F*	*G*	*H*	*J*	*K*	*L*	*M*	*N*	*P*	*Q*	*R*
100	5½	2½	4½	18	9	a	7½	b	¾	c	¾	c	d	3	e	f
90	5	2	4	16	8	a	7	b	¾	c	¾	c	d	2¾	e	f
74	4½	1⅞	3½	14	8	a	6¾	b	¾	c	¾	c	d	2½	e	f
64	4½	1⅞	3	12	7½	a	6¾	b	¾	c	¾	c	d	2½	e	f
44	4	1¾	3	12	7	a	6½	b	¾	c	½	c	d	2¼	e	f
38	4	1½	3	12	7	a	6½	b	¾	c	½	c	d	2¼	e	f
36	3¾	1½	2¾	11	6¾	a	6¼	b	½	c	½	c	d	2	e	f
32	3½	1¼	2¾	10	6¾	a	6¼	b	½	c	½	c	d	2	e	f
28	3¼	1¼	2½	9½	6½	a	6	b	½	c	½	c	d	1¾	e	f
24	3¼	1¼	2¼	9	6½	a	6	b	½	c	½	c	d	1¾	e	f
Sloop	3	1¼	2	8½	6¼	a	5¾	b	½	c	½	c	d	1½	e	f
Cutter	3	1¼	2¼	8½	6½	a	6	b	½	c	½	c	d	1½	e	f

*The dimensions given here apply to the majority of pintles. However, the lowest was always 2in greater than those listed here.

a This dimension is variable, due to the position on the rudder at which the pintle is placed.

b This dimension was always ½in less than the diameter given in column C.

c This dimension varies with the size of the sternpost, and with the positions at which the components were sited.

d This angle varies according to position and to the underwater shape of the hull.

e This dimension is the combined fore and aft width of the sternpost and the bearding fitted to it.

f This dimension varied according to the height at which the brace was set. The length of the arms tended to decrease progressively towards the uppermost one. The table on page 131 gives the length of the lowest taken from the end of the sternpost. Therefore to calculate the correct length deduct the figure in column Q.

set about 3in above and 3in below the mortices, both the strapping and the hoops being fastened with iron bolts.

The letters in the two tables above correspond with the dimensions marked in Fig 5/1. The dimensions are taken from the *Shipbuilder's Repository* of 1789.

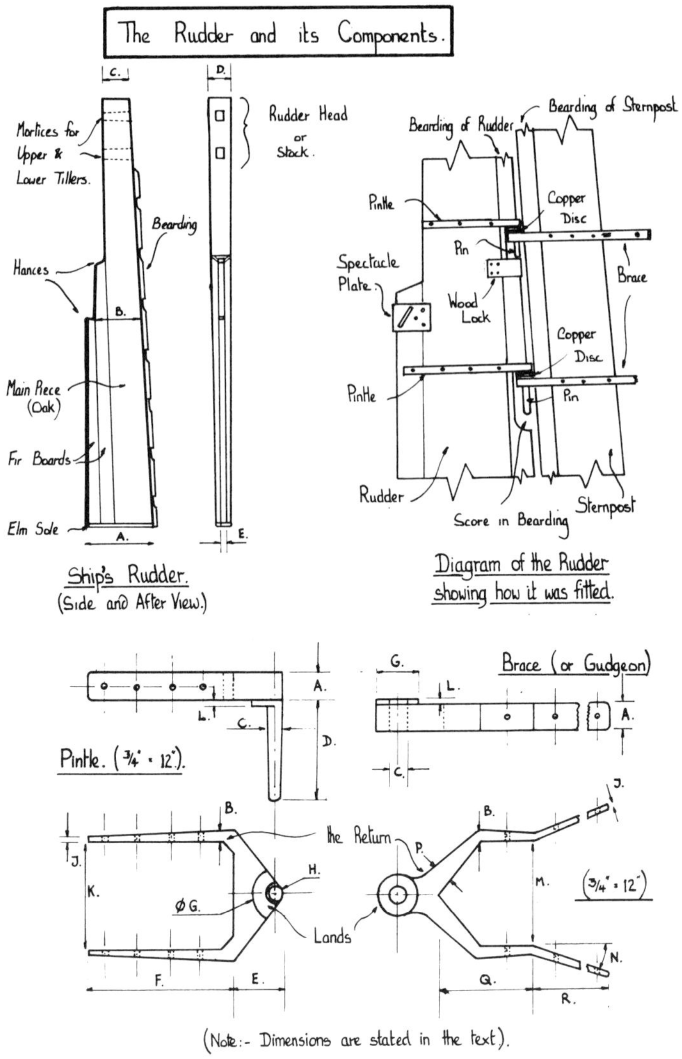

Fig 5/1

The Pintles and Braces

These formed the hinges on which the rudder was suspended. The braces are often referred to as gudgeons (see opposite page). The pintles were made from bronze and later iron, in the form of a yoke that embraced the sides of the rudder. At the 'return' (see Fig 5/1) which passed over the bearding, a vertical pin was incorporated, to pass through an eye of the same diameter on the after end of the brace. The bearding itself was cut away at the vicinity of these pins, so that the rudder could be unshipped. All of these scores were made to a length equal to that of the lower pintle, for this was generally a couple of inches longer than the others. The score in the bearding nearest the waterline was also fashioned with a recess to one side. This was to allow the fitting of the wood-lock, which was fitted once the rudder had been shipped, and prevented the rudder lifting out of its braces. The arms forming the yoke were secured to the rudder with copper or iron bolts, which passed right through to the other arm opposite and were clenched. The length of the arms varied according to the fore and aft width of the rudder at the points where they were fitted. The number of arms for various sizes of vessels are as follows: ships of 110 to 70 guns had seven; 64 to 36, six; the remaining rates had five. The table on page 130 lists the dimensions of the pintles, the letters refer to Fig 5/1.

Overall Length of the Arms of the Lowest Brace from the After End of the Sternpost, and Second Uppermost Brace from the Rabbet

No of guns	Lower brace		Second uppermost brace	
	ft	in	ft	in
100	8		5	4
90	7	6	5	
84	7	3	4	9
74	7		4	8
64	6	6	4	3
50	6		4	
44	5	6	3	6

No of guns	Lower brace		Second uppermost brace	
	ft	in	ft	in
38	6	6	4	2
36	5	10	3	8
32	5		3	2
28	4	10	3	
24	4	9	2	9
Sloop	4	6	2	6
Cutter	4	6	na	

Although generally regarded as synonymous, it can be argued that the brace and gudgeon differed. The gudgeon can be considered as the eye through which the pin of the pintle passes, and the remaining strapping or housing that retained the gudgeon to the ship as the brace. The dimensions of braces varied very little from those of pintles, as the previous table shows. The only major differences were that the arms of the braces were considerably longer, and that the angles to which they were set altered to conform to the underwater shape of the after end of the hull. These too would be fastened with copper or iron bolts, but due to the distance between the arms, they could only be clenched within the hull where possible.

When the rudder was shipped in position, thin pieces of dressed copper were inserted between the 'lands' of both the pintles and gudgeons. When copper plating was introduced, provision had to be made for the thickness of these plates when fitting the pintles, to allow clearance. During the second half of the eighteenth century, a spectacle plate was introduced as a fitting on the rudder. This acted as a firm securing position for a secondary steerage system that could be adopted should the ship's steering wheel or tiller be damaged in action. This plate took the form of an inverted U-

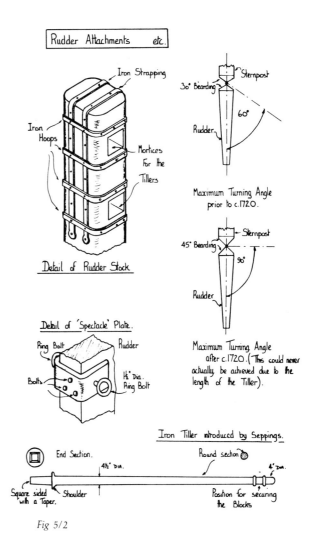

Fig 5/2

shaped iron casting with a ringbolt about 1½in in diameter fastened to each side. The whole component was bolted onto the upper hance of the rudder. The steering ropes passed from the ringbolts to eyes set on the corners of the lower counter, then up the ship's side to the quarterdeck, via a fairlead in the bulwark (see Fig 5/2).

THE TILLER

This was a horizontal lever that traversed to left and right, producing the turning motion for the rudder. It was generally made from oak, ash or pitch pine. Ash was preferred due to its flexibility, as it would not crack under normal conditions. Tillers of wrought iron were introduced by Seppings, around 1814.

The length of the tiller was relative to the extreme angle that was required on the rudder, and to the width of the ship at the point where the steering blocks were fitted. At this point the hull was approximately four-fifths of the moulded beam, and the full angle turned in one direction was 45 degrees. Thus the length of the tiller was taken from the after end of the rudder stock to the steering block when the rudder was turned hard over at 45 degrees (see Fig 5/2). This only applied to ships steered by the wheel, or by blocks and tackles. When a whipstaff was employed, the length of the tiller was relative to the position of the whipstaff beam from the after end of the rudder stock; the whipstaff was attached to the fore end of the tiller.

Tillers made from timber remained square in cross-section throughout their length. At the after end, where it entered the mortice in the rudder stock, it would measure approximately half the athwartships width of the rudder stock, whereas at the fore end it was proportionally less. The proportions were as follows: for vessels of 60 to 100 guns, three-quarters of its scantling at the stock; ships of 20 to 50 guns, four-fifths; sloops and cutters, eleven-sixteenths.

The secondary tiller, if fitted, was generally shorter, due to the position of the cabin bulkheads of the upper deck. The dimensions at the stock were usually about 1 to 1½in less than those of the lower tiller, and its fore end tapered down to the proportions already given.

Iron tillers were introduced by Sir Robert Seppings in the second decade of the nineteenth century. Iron was used both for its strength and its low cost, and with the advancement of the iron industry it became easily obtainable. Fine examples of this can be seen aboard the *Unicorn* and the *Foudroyant*. On both these vessels, the tiller is about 12ft long and 4½in diameter, tapering to 4in at the fore end. The extreme after end was square in section, with a shoulder to butt against the fore side of the rudder stock (see Fig 5/2 and 5/7).

THE WHIPSTAFF

This method of steering a ship had been in common use since well before the Elizabethan period.* Basically this system of operating the rudder consisted of two principal levers, the tiller and the whipstaff proper. The former was generally made from ash, a wood that could withstand shock. This beam was set in the horizontal plane, the after end being fitted into a mortice fashioned in the head of the rudder stock. The fore end of the tiller had freedom of movement. The function of this beam was to produce the transverse movement of the rudder upon the latter's own axis of rotation.

The whipstaff was a shaft set in the vertical plane. This beam was made from either ash or pitch pine, the former being the most suitable. The whole structure revolved about a fixed point situated at a height which gave the mechanical advantage required for easy operation. The lower end engaged with the fore end of the tiller, completing the network of levers between the helmsman and the rudder.

The maximum angle of rudder that could be achieved was 20 degrees in either direction. Any advance on this limitation would

*The description of the whipstaff's operation is a reconstruction of the most likely method, based on the available information.

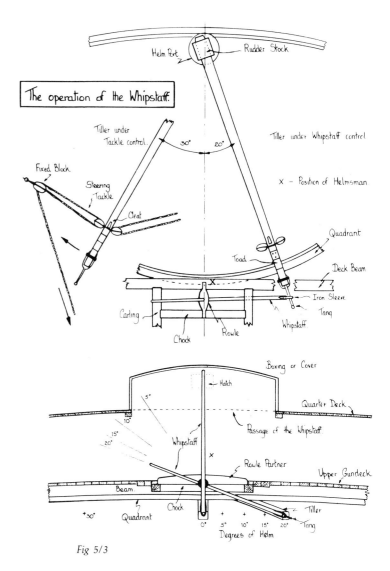

Fig 5/3

have been impractical for it would have been necessary to increase the length of each lever. To attain greater angles of helm, the tiller could be moved a further 10 degrees by the use of blocks and tackle. This additional gear was permanently fitted for use in the event of damage or disengagement of the whipstaff. When the vessel was steered in this manner the orders were relayed between the decks.

Operation of the whipstaff was simple. If the helmsman wished to turn the ship's head to starboard he pushed the beam to the right. Likewise if a movement to larboard was desired the whipstaff was moved over to the left.

The overall length of the whipstaff was roughly 4in for every foot of the ship's extreme breadth. It was circular in cross-section throughout its length, tapering towards the top end. The diameter at its lower end can be calculated as follows.

Heel diameter = (length of the whipstaff/12) × π (π = 3·142)

The diameter of the uppermost end was generally two-thirds of that

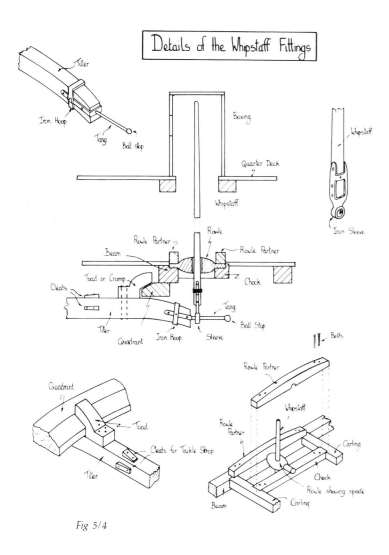

Fig 5/4

Unicorn. *The after end of the berthing deck showing the iron tiller, the tiller sheave block, the stemson and the iron crutches. Also visible are Seppings iron bracket knees and the head of the aftermost diagonal iron rider plate.*

of the heel. Attached to the lower end was an iron sleeve, the bore of which was set fore and aft. This sleeve engaged with the tang of the tiller, however, its diameter was such that the fit was relatively slack to allow for the opposing movement between both the tiller and the whipstaff as they traversed further from the centreline.

The rotary motion of the whipstaff was achieved by what was called the rowle. This was fashioned from a block of elm into a cylinder tapered at each end. The rowle was approximately 2ft long and 9in diameter. A hole was bored centrally through the side half way along its length, through which the shaft of the whipstaff passed. The diameter of this hole was such that the whipstaff shaft could pass freely without binding at any point on its taper. The whipstaff slid to and fro through this hole when the helm was pushed across. It was thought that the whipstaff lever remained fixed to the rowle, but this has recently been proved a misconception.

The ends of the rowle were turned down into short shafts to allow rotation. These were about 4in long and 3in diameter. Alternatively iron spindles were driven in the ends, these were 1½ to 2in diameter. The whole assembly was set between the deck

beams or special partners, depending on the disposition of the whipstaff. The rowle was generally situated on the deck above the tiller regardless of the size of the ship. From this it can be realised that vessels having three gundecks had the whipstaff set low in the ship in relation to the upper deck.

To support the ends of the spindles or shafts of the rowle, bearing blocks, called chocks were fitted athwartships at each end. These were made from oak, fashioned to fit between the carlings. In some cases only one chock was used, the other bearing being formed in the adjacent deck beam either fore or aft, this being governed by the position of the whipstaff.

To prevent the rowle from rising out from the chocks or bearings a second inverse chock was fitted and bolted firmly in position. The underside of this chock, or rowle partner as it was called, was fashioned with a semicircular groove equal to half the diameter of the spindle. This acted as the top half bearing for the rowle. Generally the upper face of the rowle partner was trimmed to produce a cambered surface.

The dimensions of the chocks generally corresponded to the respective carlings of the deck concerned. The only variation from the norm was where the depth of the carling was less than twice the diameter of the rowle spindle. In this case the chock would be fashioned deeper at its centre of length.

The rowle partners were made to a length that spanned the carlings below. In width they were generally sawn to a siding equal to that of the length of the rowle spindle. The depth at their centre of length was approximately equal to either twice the diameter of the rowle spindle, or, more commonly, equal to the diameter of the rowle.

Fitted to the fore end of the tiller was an iron tang. The function of this fitting was to engage with the sleeve fitted to the lower end of the whipstaff. The length of the tang varied between 18 and 24in, while in diameter it varied between 1½ and 2in. The fore end of the tang was 'up-set' into a ball stop with a diameter approximately twice that of the mean diameter. The purpose of this stop was to prevent the whipstaff disengaging from the tiller. The opposite end of the tang was formed into a yoke, each arm of which embraced the tiller. Provision was made to allow the yoke arms to be bolted to the tiller, the whole assembly being further secured by fitting an iron hoop over the end of the same.

Due to its length the tiller had to be supported at its fore end. Initially this was done by a beam fitted below the tiller. The position of this beam was such that support was given throughout the complete travel of the tiller. However, this method was very impractical, for having a beam set at a height of about 5ft fitted across the lower gundeck was an encumbrance. The more successful method later adopted comprised two members, a toad and a quadrant. The quadrant was a curved beam fitted to the deck beams above the tiller. The curvature of this beam followed the arc created by the sweep of the tiller. Due to its complex shape, the quadrant would have been made up of several segments of timber, scarphed and bolted together. The after top edge was bearded to form a land for the toad.

The toad, named because of its similarity in shape to the amphibian, was a specially fashioned block of wood fitted on the upper side of the tiller. The fore edge of the toad was positioned upon the bearded portion of the quadrant, thus the weight of the tiller was distributed. (See Fig 5/4.) It is interesting to note that both of these components were to later evolve into regular fittings within the steering system which incorporated the steering wheel. The toad was transformed into the iron gooseneck of the second half of the eighteenth century, while the quadrant remained as it was.

Understandably the length of the whipstaff made it necessary to omit a section of the deck planking in way of its travel at both the level of the rowle and in the deck above. This slot was generally referred to as the passageway for the whipstaff. In those vessels where the upper end of the whipstaff protruded above the upper deck or the quarterdeck a box-like structure was built over the top to protect it from the weather. Usually a small hatch was fitted in the top of this box through which the pilot could relay orders to the helmsman. Alternatively a small window was fitted to the fore side through which the helmsman could see.

The finer points of the whipstaff system are shown in the accompanying illustrations (Figs 5/3 and 5/4). It can be clearly seen that when a considerable angle of helm was required much effort was needed on the part of the helmsman, for the amount of leverage obtained was reduced the further the tiller was put over. Steering in this manner must have been very difficult in heavy seas and I am of the opinion that at such times the assistance of blocks and tackle would have been necessary. The apparent frailty of the whipstaff system also made headsails necessary for manoeuvring the ship, the rudder only being used for the finer point of sailing and steering.

THE STEERING WHEEL

The steering wheel was not a completely new concept when first introduced to British ships during the first decade of the eighteenth century. It was probably adapted from the relatively simple affair that had been in use on Arab dhows for many years. The earliest form of steering wheel fitted on British vessels can be seen on a model of a 60-gun ship of 1703, at the National Maritime Museum in Greenwich. This model displays a windlass set with its axis athwartships, mounted on iron brackets. Detachable crank handles were fitted at each end of the spindle, for turning the drum of the windlass. Transmission from the windlass to the fore end of the tiller was achieved by a single continuous rope. This rope was secured at one end to the tiller, and was then passed to a single purchase block fastened to the ship's side. This block was at a point where the tiller finished, at its maximum traverse. The rope then continued from the block to a sheave set vertically in the deckhead. From here it passed vertically to the drum of the windlass. It then went around the drum for about seven turns, and returned to the tiller in a similar manner.

This was obviously a step in the right direction. This system's advantage over blocks and tackle was simply that due to its position on the quarterdeck, there would be no delay in relaying orders. The advantages over the whipstaff were more numerous. As the system relied on ropes and blocks, control was both easier and more exact, due to the improved mechanical advantages. The angle of helm was far greater, and was as much as 60 degrees in one direction. Again, due to its position on the quarterdeck, response to orders was far speedier. Lastly, should the ropes be severed by shot in action, replacement was simple, whereas to replace the beam of the whipstaff was not easy.

There were of course a number of disadvantages. Although greater control was possible, those manning the crank handles could not keep an eye on the ship's heading when manipulating the windlass. Therefore a third party was always necessary. Also, the rudder sometimes tended to 'whip' in heavy seas, and this action was relayed throughout the system to the windlass. This would often result in the drum turning violently, thus jerking the crank handles, which could injure those manning them. The diameter of the drum was relatively small and therefore the number of revolutions required to move the rudder was considerable. This was not helped by the small turning circle of the crank handles.

Very shortly after the introduction of this wheel, it was decided to turn the whole assembly through 90 degrees and modify the drum. The crank handles were dispensed with, and a large spoked wheel was fitted in their place, a second wheel being introduced a few years later. The wheel had a number of advantages. Firstly, its greater turning diameter allowed far better control, and did not

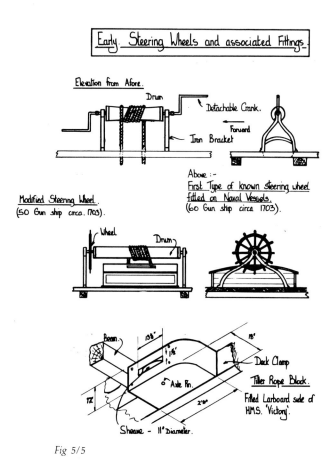

Fig 5/5

for 6in outside the diameter of the rim.

From the time of its introduction a number of additional fittings were added to the steering wheel. These were the quadrant, the gooseneck, and the sliding foot assembly.

The Quadrant

The function of this was, with the aid of the gooseneck, to support the far end of the tiller. It appears that it was only fitted on larger ships, due to the length and weight of the tiller. It comprised a series of timbers scarphed together, forming an arc equal to that of the sweep of the tiller. The assembly was firmly bolted to the underside of the beams above the gundeck (or berthing deck). Teak was generally used in its construction, although it is possible that pine was sometimes used for the upper piece. The lower piece was usually wider, and was rabbeted on both its fore and after faces, the fore face to receive the small vertical rollers, and the after face to support the gooseneck. The rollers were of either lignum vitae or

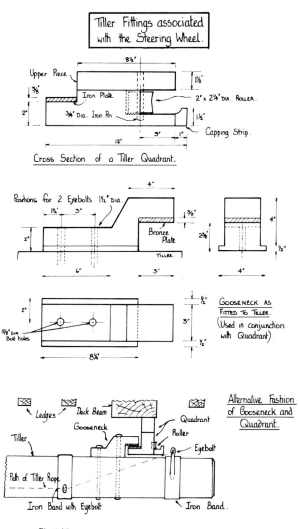

Fig 5/6

cause injury in the event of whip to the rudder. Secondly, as the helmsman remained upright, he could watch the ship's heading and the sails. The drum was a greater diameter, thus fewer revolutions were required to turn the rudder. The ropes were run in a similar manner to those on the windlass. This type of steering mechanism can be clearly seen on a model of a 50-gun ship of around 1703 at the National Maritime Museum, Greenwich. This model also shows provision was maintained for the fitting of a whipstaff. It seems that like so many new inventions, the first well-tested idea was retained due to lack of faith in the new. Although a whipstaff is not fitted, the rowle is present on the lower deck, and the transverse slot can be seen on the upper deck. Both of the above types of wheel are illustrated in Fig 5/5.

The dimensions of a ship's steering wheel differed very little from one vessel to the next. It seems that the only variation was the fore and aft length of the drum (or barrel), the maximum length being about 3ft and the minimum 2ft 6in. The diameter of the drum was generally 1ft 9in, and probably 1ft 6in on Sixth Rates. It seems that by having a standard diameter of wheel, a helmsman would find little difference between steering a ship of 100 guns and one of 20 guns. The diameter of the wheel itself also varied little from vessel to vessel. The standard outside diameter was 4ft 6in for the rim, the internal measurement being about 4in less. The rim was 4in thick and the spokes were between 1½ and 2in diameter. These extended

iron, their function being to ensure smooth running for the tiller rope. The rabbet on the after face was lined with an iron seating to prevent wear from the iron gooseneck. I will not attempt to estimate any measurements, for there appear to have been a number of variations in the design, two of which are shown in Fig 5/6 (the dimensions of these are approximate only).

The Gooseneck

This was a specially designed iron casting, bolted to the upper surface of the tiller. Its fore lower edge was designed to sit down on the iron seating on the quadrant. To prevent sparks being produced by the iron surfaces rubbing together, a bronze facing plate was shrunk onto the shoulders of this face (see Fig 5/6).

The Sliding Foot

To prevent sea water etc, from seeping down from the upper deck where the rope passed from the drum to the sheaves below, a sliding foot was constructed. This consisted of a shallow housing, fitted over the fore and aft slot cut in the deck through which the rope passed. The housing was designed to allow a piece of timber to slide fore and aft. This was bored to allow the rope to pass through it at one end. The identical fitting, for the other rope, was fitted to the other side of the wheel. The only difference was the position of the hole, which was at the opposite end (see Fig 5/7).

A number of small modifications were made to the steering wheel in the fifty years following its introduction. The single purchase blocks on the gundeck were replaced with a solid housing containing the sheave, which was bolted to the ship's side.

Alternatively the sheave was incorporated with the outboard ends of the tiller quadrant. The sheaves fitted at the deckhead, which adjusted the direction of the rope from horizontal to vertical, were also made in a stronger fashion. The sheaves in diagonal carlings were set at the centreline. The carlings were set to the angle necessary to lead the rope to the blocks at the ship's side. This was far more rigid than the previous method, in which normal blocks were secured to eyebolts. The carling method seems to have been adopted about 20 years after the introduction of the wheel. Both this and the housings method can be seen on the *Victory*.

Around 1750 a secondary steering system was introduced, to replace the normal method should it be damaged in action or bad weather. This was made up of ropes fastened to the rudder at the spectacle plate (see section explaining the rudder), passing through eyes fitted at the outboard extremities of the lower counter, and up to a fairlead on the quarterdeck. In earlier examples, the ropes passed through the lower counter to the lower gundeck. In some ships, the ropework in the vicinity of the rudder and near the waterline was replaced with chains, which did not deteriorate so rapidly. Then, for a number of years, both rope and chain were employed. The model of the *Royal George* of 1756 at the National Maritime Museum, Greenwich is an example of a ship fitted with chains; these can also be seen on the *Victory*. Prior to the introduction of the secondary steering system, the chains fitted to

Fig 5/7

Fig 5/8

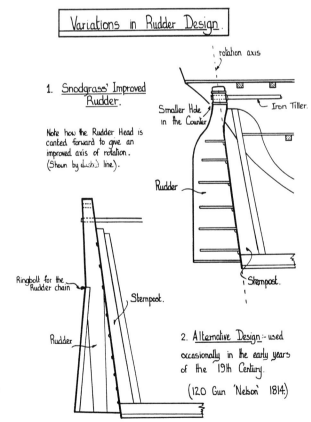

136

the rudder were used to hold the rudder in the event of the pintles breaking.

Some vessels built after 1830 had two round ports cut in the upper counter, each a short distance from the centreline. Passing from each of these ports were chains which terminated at the spectacle plate on the rudder. By this time the after edge of the rudder had taken on a more graceful appearance, being fashioned in a gentle curve towards the stock. I do not believe that these chains were part of a secondary steering system, but that they may have been used for securing the ship to a buoy. The two ports are too near the centreline to produce a satisfactory turning motion for the rudder. If these chains were used for mooring the ship, then I would assume that they were detached from the rudder and paid out to the buoy. The shackles that secured the chain to the rudder would be also used for attaching to the buoy. The chain would then be warped taut by the capstan. Chain anchor cables had been in use since 1811, and capstans had been adapted to take them. The best example of this can be seen on the model of the *Albion*, a 90-gun ship of 1842, in the Science Museum in South Kensington.

STEERING GEAR FITTINGS

The Tiller Locating Plate

As previously mentioned, the tiller was housed into the mortice cut into the rudder stock. This was a simple affair, consisting of a tapered mortice which received the similarly tapered end of the tiller. This was not altogether satisfactory, for the tiller could be easily unshipped, resulting in a complete loss of steering. To prevent this, a more efficient appliance was introduced at the end of the eighteenth century.

The plate was an iron binding hoop, with a specially fashioned eyeplate projecting from two sides. It was fitted approximately one and a half times the fore and aft width of the rudder stock from the end of the tiller. Holes of the appropriate diameter were bored horizontally through the rudder on each side of the tiller mortice. A bolt was then driven through each eyeplate to the after side of the rudder, and firmly clenched, thus locking the whole assembly (see Fig 5/7).

The Iron Bands (or Hoops)

These were fitted at intervals throughout the length of the tiller, to prevent splitting. Generally they were made from wrought iron 3 to 4in wide and about ½ to ¾in thick. Although some were of the simple square hoop design, others were fashioned with eyes or ringbolts. They served two purposes. One was fitted at the fore end of the tiller, to which the loose ends of the tiller rope were secured. They also acted as guides or 'fairleads' for the tiller rope after the introduction of the tensioning tackle towards the end of the eighteenth century (see Fig 5/7).

Foudroyant. *The counter with the improved rudder introduced by Gabriel Snodgrass. It is easy to see how the counter was planked. The eyebolts on both the hull and the rudder are for the secondary steering system.*

The Tensioning Tackle

It had been found that the tension of the tiller rope varied with both temperature and humidity, which altered the response of the wheel. If the rope was wet or damp it became more taut, and when the weather was warm and dry, it tended to slacken considerably. To overcome this, blocks and tackle were secured to the end of the tiller rope so that adjustments could be made according to the conditions. This tackle was set up on both sides of the tiller to the two ends of the tiller rope, a single purchase block being seized to the rope at this point. At the after end of the tiller a double purchase block was secured to an iron band with an eye. The appropriate tackle was rove through the blocks, and the loose end belayed round a cleat fitted to the tiller (see Fig 5/7). Alternatively, the double purchase block was secured to a plain ringbolt driven into the side of the tiller. This innovation was in general use by the mid eighteenth century and can be seen on the *Victory* at Portsmouth.

In 1815 the hemp tiller rope was replaced with rawhide. It had been found that, when wet, rawhide did not stretch as hemp did, thus play was reduced.

SNODGRASS' IMPROVED RUDDER

One of the major problems of the conventional form of rudder was the ingress of seawater through the helm port which was cut in the lower counter. At the beginning of the eighteenth century, the angle of the lower counter had been altered, the head of the rudder extended and a tarred canvas apron fitted over the orifice. This, however, did not prevent water being shipped when a vessel was in heavy seas, the smaller classes being particularly vulnerable in this respect. In 1779 a solution was finally found and introduced by Gabriel Snodgrass, the Surveyor of the East India Company. His design was very soon adopted on the East Indiamen, but it was to be another three decades before the Admiralty approved of its application.

The new design was produced by altering the cross-section of the head of the rudder, and by fashioning it in such a manner that it was cranked forward over the head of the sternpost. Prior to this, the cross-section of the rudder head was either square or triangular, neither of which produced an adequate seal against water at the helm port. The new form, with a circular cross-section, permitted a smaller hole to be cut in the counter, effectively reducing the clearance, and increasing watertight integrity. Also, the cranked effect altered the axis of rotation, to a point where it passed through the axis of the gudgeons and pintles. The canvas apron was still retained for good measure.

It is not known exactly when this improved rudder was introduced to naval vessels, but evidence suggests that it first appeared on the smaller ships as early as 1814. Both the *Foudroyant* (1817) and the *Unicorn* (1824) were fitted with this form of rudder. One exception is a model of an 84-gun ship of 1815 at the National Maritime Museum, for the new design was not generally adopted on larger vessels until about 1838. One fine example of a Snodgrass rudder can be seen on the model of the 90-gun ship *Albion* (1842) at the Science Museum in South Kensington.

It can be seen from Fig 5/8 that the general external appearance was altered. The stepped hances on the after face of the rudder were replaced by a curved surface. This diminished the overall width of the head of the rudder towards the point of entry at the helm port.

The Ship's Pump

Pumps were fitted in all vessels for several purposes: removing water from the bilges and discharging it overboard to keep the ship dry, washing down the decks, and fire-fighting. Water accumulated in the bilges because of natural leakage from the seams of the hull and defects caused by decay or damage caused during action or sustained during heavy weather. Water was sometimes pumped into the hold to displace the foul air, and then pumped out again, this practice being exercised around 1720. Water was also required for domestic appliances such as the boiler at the galley.

Throughout most of the period the most common pumps in naval use were the main chain pump (often called a yard pump), and the elm tree pump, and later the lift pump of the nineteenth century.

THE MAIN CHAIN (OR YARD) PUMP

This type of pump was used primarily for removing water from the bilges. Although it is referred to as a single pump, it generally consisted of either two or four pumps combined. This type of pump had been in use from about the turn of the seventeenth century and probably earlier as its use was mentioned by Sir Walter Raleigh. It could move one ton of water in one minute with eight men manning the crank handles. Naturally its design and performance improved over the years, and by 1650 most vessels of substantial size had two fitted. There were, of course, many disadvantages in the design, but it was improved greatly by Cole, under the instructions of Captain Bentinck, during the second half of the eighteenth century. The improvements were as follows: the design of the chain was simplified by lengthening the links, reducing friction at the sprocket wheel and reducing damage. The chain had a tendency to disengage from the wheel so was subsequently fashioned with hooks. This reduced the jerking effect when operating under high loads. The materials used for the sprocket wheel were also improved, to facilitate repair. One other factor that made the original pump inefficient was that it was easily choked with rubbish from the bilge itself. The modified type of pump was given trials on the frigate *Seaford*. The comparisons of the old and the modified pumps are as follows: On the old pump 7 men pumped 1 ton of water in 1 minute 16 seconds and 4 men pumped 1 ton of water in 1 minute 21 seconds. On the modified pump 4 men pumped 1 ton of water in 44 seconds and 2 men pumped 1 ton of water in 55 seconds.

Fig 5/9 illustrates the action of the pump. The crank handles were turned to rotate the sprocket wheel towards the centreline of the ship. Thus the chain would travel down the back case. At the bottom of the back case a second wheel reversed the direction of the chain. As the leather washers affixed to the chain passed into the limber passage the water accumulated there was scooped up and lifted up through the working chamber, where the washers acted as lifting pistons. The water was lifted and discharged into the cistern, from which it overflowed into the fixed or temporary pump dale, the function of which was to carry the water to the scuppers at the ship's side. The function of both the back case and the working chamber was to prevent the water returning to the bilge.

This non-return facility was achieved by having the heads of both the back case and the working chamber set about 1ft above the bottom of the cistern. In some cases a 'poppet' valve was fitted at the head of the return side, to act as a non-return valve. There is little information on the design of this valve but I would think that it

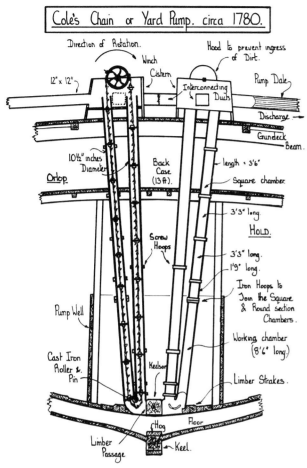

Fig 5/9

The Cistern

This was basically a box-like structure that was placed on the gundeck or first deck above the waterline. It served two functions, firstly it provided an overflow chamber for the water discharged up through the working chamber, secondly, it supported the bearings of the sprocket wheel. The 'box' was generally made from elm and was supported at each side on blocks which raised the whole cistern about 1ft above deck level. The underside was pierced with two square holes, through which passed the casings of the back case and the working chamber. The overall length of the cistern, measured athwartships, was 4ft 4in, the width 18in, and the height 3ft 3in. Provision was made for pump dales and connecting chambers on the desired side of the cistern. An iron bearing at both the fore and after end was let down into the timber for the axle of the windlass.

The Windlass

The sprocket wheel which was integral to the windlass comprised two separate wheels set parallel to each other and joined by tie rods of 1in diameter. The overall diameter of the wheels was 2ft, with a hub of 6in diameter. The tie rods not only served to maintain the two wheels at the desired distance (1ft) apart, but also acted as the

Egmont. Chain pump cisterns, crank handles and the main jeer capstan on the lower gundeck. To the left is the internal planking consisting of the spirketting, lining and waterway. Note the standards abreast the mainmast partners.

was made in the form of a circular plate, with an orifice of a slightly smaller diameter than that of the leather washers that were fitted on the chain. The whole assembly was secured at a position just below the head of the working chamber and would have been made from either iron or leather, most probably the latter, which would reduce the wearing effect on the leather on the chain itself.

The efficiency of the chain pumps on the *Victory* was relatively low, the pump output being determined more by the number of revolutions produced in a given time. However, due to the simplicity of its general construction and design, the maintenance required was minimal, with problems only arising from breakages in the chain links, or wear on the leather washers. The total estimated output of all four pumps on the *Victory*, when running for a considerable period employing 150 men at once to operate the cranks, was about 120 tons of water an hour.

The dimensions given in the following descriptions are taken from the pumps at present fitted on the *Victory*. For clarity only one pump is explained. The alternative name, yard pump, was derived from the distance between the leather washers, but following improvements, the spacing was reduced.

sprockets to which the hooks of the chain would engage. Passing through the hubs was the axle, which was made from wrought iron bar 1½in diameter, the ends being of square section for the engagement of the crank handles. The whole of this assembly was forge-welded together after the initial fabrication of each component. The sprocket wheel on earlier pumps consisted of a cylindrical elm block fitted with iron crutches about its periphery.

The Back Case

This was a fabricated casing of 10½in square section, passing from the cistern to the limber passage at one side of the keelson. The back case was always fitted nearest the centreline. Elm was used for its construction, the whole case generally being made up in sections so that if damaged it could easily be repaired. The sections were connected to each other by iron transition pieces, lead or copper being used on earlier pumps.

The Working Chamber (or Return Case)

This was manufactured in the same manner as the back case, except that the lowest section was of circular cross-section. It was this tube that can be truly termed the working chamber, for it was inside this that the leather washers of the chain lifted the water. The return case was 10½in square in cross-section, and the working chamber 7in internal diameter. Iron, lead or copper transition pieces held each section together, with iron hoops holding the working chamber. The length of the working chamber was about 8ft 6in.

At the point of intersection between both the back case and the working chamber was a fitted roller of 6in diameter, made of iron. The function of this was to reverse the direction of the chain. The lower ends of each case were open to the bilge, but fitted with a guard to prevent the pump being fouled with rubbish.

The Connecting Chambers

Whether two or four pumps were fitted, the cisterns were connected to each other by sectioned ducts made from elm. Their function was to enable any pump to discharge from any cistern as required. The pumps on *Victory* have only two discharges, both of which are adapted to the two cisterns forward; they are only about 8in diameter. They were fitted to a portable hose to carry the water to the scuppers. The alternative was to have pump dales permanently fixed between the cistern and the ship's side, thus discharging directly overboard. The connecting chambers were about 12in square section, made from planking 1in thick. The pump dales were of the same construction, or were round; the width or diameter being about 10in, with a wall about 1in thick. If round, they were often made from lead or iron piping.

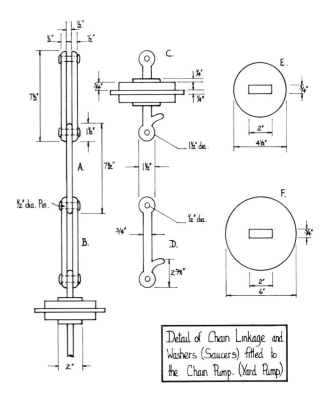

Detail of Chain Linkage and Washers (Saucers) fitted to the Chain Pump. (Yard Pump)

A.= Single Link.   B.= Double Link.   C.= Saucer Link.
D.= Double Link - side view.   E.= Saucer or Backing Plate.
F.= Leather Washer.

Fig 5/10

The Chain

This was made from iron or bronze on earlier pumps. Two types of links were employed, single and double, each type being joined together by ½in diameter pins, riveted over once passed through. The length of the links, whether single or double, was 7½in, the width ¾in, and they were ½in thick. Each end was made to an outside diameter of 1½in, with a ½in hole for the link pin. To one side of each link a hook was fastened, the purpose of which was to engage with the sprockets or tie rods of the windlass.

To some links were also fitted the backing plates, and washers that retained the leather washers. The backing plates were 4½in diameter and 1in thick, while the leather washers were 7in diameter and ¼in thick. The combined component was generally termed the piston. These were at approximately 3ft intervals, hence the term yard pump.

The Hoods

To prevent the ingress of rubbish to the cistern, lightly constructed timber hoods of semi-circular shape were placed over the top of the windlass. These were designed to give clearance so that the pump could be operated without any hindrance from the leather washers, when being passed over the windlass.

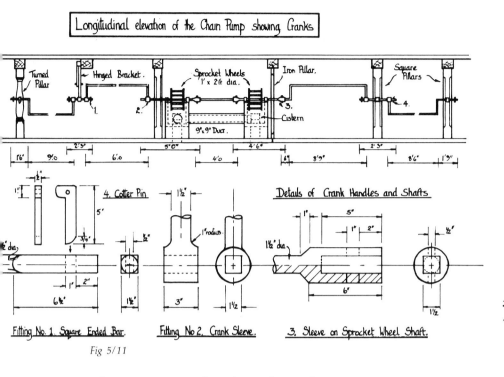

Fig 5/11

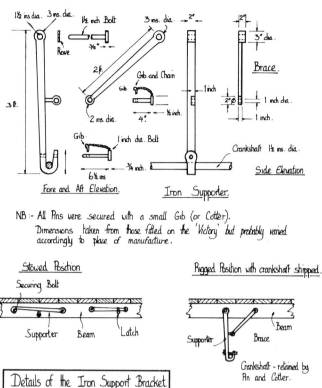

Fig 5/12

The Connecting Rods and Crank Handles

The pumps were worked by crank handles manipulated by the crew. These handles were either engaged directly to the axles of the windlasses, or indirectly by means of connecting rods, which were fitted to the axles. If both fore and after pumps were fitted a connecting rod was placed between them. This allowed both pumps to be worked simultaneously, with all the crank handles on each side of the ship. Should the crank handles of the fore pump be damaged the fore pump could still be operated with the crank handles of the after pump, and vice versa.

The crank handles were all designed to produce a turning circle of 3ft (18in throw); their lengths varied according to their relative position along the gundeck. The connecting rods and the crank handles were fitted to one another by a simple arrangement of sockets and square-ended bars, all fashioned to receive a retaining pin or tapered gib. It is not possible here to explain all the variations of these connections. They are shown with dimensions in Fig 5/11. The manner in which the crank handles and connecting rods were supported along their length also varied, the most common methods being stanchions (either timber or iron) or retractable iron brackets fitted to the beams (see Fig 5/11 and 5/12).

Most of the components were of universal dimensions, except for the cistern, the back case and the working chamber (the latter two depending on the height of the pump from the bilge).

The dimensions in the following table do not correlate to those of the cisterns fitted on the *Victory*, which show that the back case and the working chamber were fitted with their own individual cisterns. This arrangement appears to be a modification made to chain pumps after the *Victory* was built in 1765. The draught of a

74-gun ship in Rees' *Naval Architecture* shows that on the lower gundeck the back case and the working chamber are not united with a common cistern at their heads (see Fig 5/13).

This modified design did not have all the benefits of its predecessor. With the new pump it was impossible to discharge from a starboard pump via that fitted to port, and hence over the port side of the ship. Also, no provision was made to discharge to the fore pump from the after pump. There were no connecting chambers fitted to the fore or after pump (unlike the original pumps), though there was no reason why this should not have been done. The only advantage of keeping the back case and the working chamber separate was that, should the vessel have a considerable

Dimensions of Cisterns fitted to Vessels Built around 1780

No of guns	Width athwartships		Depth		Breadth		Height from deck to underside	
	ft	in	ft	in	ft	in	ft	in
100	2	6	3	3	1	2	1	1
90	2	2	2	9	1	0	1	2
74	2	1	2	8	10		1	1
64	2	0	2	7	8		1	0
44	1	11	2	6	8		1	1

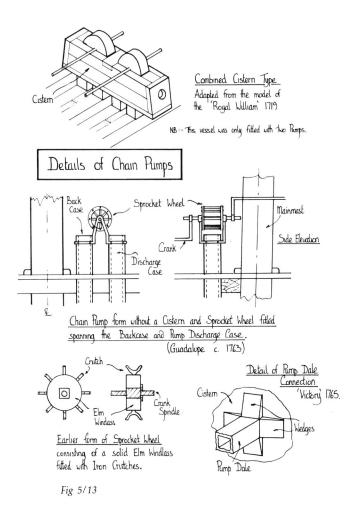

Fig 5/13

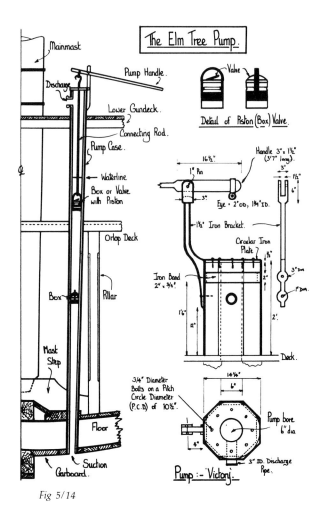

Fig 5/14

list due to flooding or the vessel rolling in heavy seas, no water could return down the back case. Alternative arrangements had to be made for the support of the bearing for the windlass. This was achieved by fitting an iron bracket with its feet set down on each of the cisterns.

Contemporary lists mention only one or two pumps per vessel. It is evident that when referring to one pump, they were also taking into account its counterpart on the other side of the vessel. Thus all ships of the Third Rate and above were fitted with two pumps (two afore the mainmast and two abaft) and vessels below Third Rate had one pump (two abaft the mainmast).

THE ELM TREE PUMP

Due to its simple design, this type of pump was used throughout the fleet, in large and small men-of-war. In vessels of Fourth Rate and below it was used as the main bilge pump, in preference to the chain pump used on larger ships. It was also employed on the largest men of war as a domestic pump, for washing down decks, fire-fighting and for providing water for the distillers, if fitted.

There were two methods by which this pump received water. In

the first, the lower end of the pump passed through the ship's hull, adjacent to the keel, which gave direct suction. In the second, a cistern was fitted somewhere below the waterline. The end of the pump was within this cistern which was filled by two pipes passing to either side of the vessel, and through the hull below the waterline. Both these pipes were fitted with a form of non-return valve, that could be shut when necessary or when the cistern was full. It was on 29 August 1782, while the shipwrights were working on one of these pipes at the waterline that the 100-gun *Royal George* turned over and sank with a loss of over 800 lives. However, the loss of this vessel was not due to the pipework, but to an error in the manner in which she was heeled to allow the work to be done.

The advantage of this type of pump lay in its simple construction which required little maintenance, except for the occasional renewal of the non-return clapper valves fitted to the pistons (or boxes as they are often called). However, they were not very efficient. Approximately 25 gallons could be pumped per minute, forty strokes being applied to the handle per minute (one complete pumping action was equal to one up and one down stroke every 1½ seconds). The number of elm tree pumps fitted to each vessel varied. Ships that had them fitted as bilge pumps had four or more, plus one for domestic use. Ships like the *Victory* had two for domestic services, one terminating at the lower gundeck and the other on the middle gundeck. *Victory* had direct sea suction pumps, the pump casing being filled with water to a height level with the waterline.

Construction

The pump consisted of a long wooden tube or case, with its lower end either at the limber passage, outside the ship's bottom, or within a cistern, depending on its purpose. The case or tube was made from a hollowed out elm tree, furnished with a number of iron hoops to prevent the timber splitting. Elm was used because of its ability to withstand long periods of immersion in salt water. Alternatively the pump case was made in two halves, fayed and caulked together, and retained with iron hoops shrunk upon it throughout its length. This ensured it remained watertight.

Two pistons or 'boxes' were fitted within the tube, one of them fixed and the other allowed to move in a reciprocating fashion. The lower box, which remained stationary, was fitted with a non-return 'clapper' valve, which allowed water to pass from below to above the box at the appropriate time in the pump cycle. A staple was secured to its upper surface so that it could be hooked and drawn up for examination of the clapper. It would be technically wrong to describe this item as 'fixed', for it only remained at its desired position by virtue of being jammed in, aided by the swell of the timber of the case when wet.

The moving piston or 'box' was also fitted with a clapper valve on its upper surface, which acted in the same manner as that of the piston below. Provision was made for the attachment of the connecting rod or 'spear' as it was known. The upper end of the spear was fastened to the end of the pump handle or brake, by means of a loose iron bolt. The spear was long enough to ensure that the piston remained below the waterline. The pump handle was usually made from ash, and pivoted about a fulcrum formed by two cheeks or 'ears' fitted to the top of the pump case. A cap basket was usually placed over the lower end of the pump, if employed as a bilge pump, to prevent any rubbish entering and choking the pump.

The Action of the Pump

When the pump handle was pulled downwards, the spear and upper piston lifted. The water above the piston was raised, and overflowed out of the discharge, while the vacuum below the piston drew water from below the lower piston via the non-return clapper valve. The clapper valve opened automatically during this action. The weight of the water above the upper piston kept the clapper valve in the shut position. On the upward stroke of the handle, the spear and upper piston moved downward. The clapper valve on the upper piston was opened by the force of the water below, which was thus transferred to above the piston. The compressive force also closed the clapper valve fitted to the lower piston, preventing any flow back to the suction side of the pump, and thus the cycle continued. For full details of its construction see Fig 5/14.

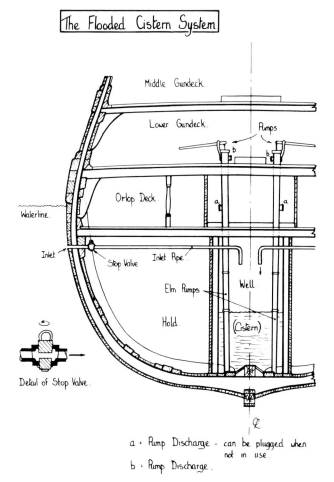

Fig 5/15

The Flooded Cistern System

When these pumps were employed for domestic purposes, the water was drawn either by direct suction from the sea or from an internal cistern flooded from the sea. The latter method consisted of a closed cistern within the confines of the well in the hold. Passing from this 'tank' to either side of the ship's hull were copper or lead pipes each of which were fitted with a stop valve which was a short distance inboard from the side. Both pipes emerged externally about 3ft 6in below the vessel's load waterline and therefore remained continuously submerged even when the ship heeled. By the opening of the valves the cistern could be filled as required or continuously fed if the valves were left open. The water was pumped from the cistern by one of two elm pumps whose suction ends remained below the surface of the water at the bottom of the well. The height of the cistern was such that the water level remained constant to the waterline when the valves remained open. This system appears to have been used only during the latter part of the eighteenth century. By the turn of the nineteenth century improvements were introduced in which the pipes led directly to the elm pump casing while provision was also made to fill the cistern if necessary. This incorporated the fitting of a filling plug on the inboard side of the elm pump casing, the plug being retained by a chain or lanyard (see Fig 5/15).

NINETEENTH-CENTURY PUMPING ARRANGEMENTS

The chain pump was finally superseded by the more efficient lift pump. This form of pump was more reliable, and had few moving parts, therefore maintenance was relatively low. One such pump was the Downton Patent Pump, which was introduced in 1825. An original can be seen aboard the *Unicorn* at Dundee. The pump itself is still intact but much of the original suction pipework has been removed or modified. Therefore its general layout can only be guessed at. This pump served two purposes: to discharge water from the bilges, overboard, and to take water from the sea for washing down decks and fire-fighting.

It appears that the suction side of this pump could be connected to a suction manifold, probably by the use of a short hose or 'jumper pipe'. The manifold consisted of a circular plate fitted in the deck adjacent to the pump out of which protruded seven stub pipes. Each stub pipe was closed off with an end cap, which was threaded onto the pipe. The stub pipes were set in the plate, with one at its centre and the others set around it on a pitch circle diameter, the opposing ends passing off to the required suction position within the hold. The only obvious layouts of pipework I have found led to the pump well, and to the ship's side on the level of the orlop. The latter was obviously used for drawing water in from the sea, for it was fitted with a non-return valve. Most of the pipework was made from lead, with an internal bore of 2in and a wall thickness of ³⁄₈in.

The pump was operated by a large handwheel, which rotated a short crankshaft to which the pump piston or plunger was attached, via a connecting rod. To ease the operation, extra labour could be used by engaging an extension crank handle. This was done by lowering a stanchion from its housing in the deckhead, to which one end of a crank handle was fitted, the other end engaging the handwheel. When not in use the stanchion and the crank handle were stowed in a similar manner to the old chain pump. When the stanchion was released and lowered down, its heel was located within a retaining plate fitted into the deck. Judging by the size of the pump's cylinder, a large number of revolutions was required to ensure efficiency.

A similar type of pump was employed on the *Vanguard* of 1841 though they were used primarily for pumping out the bilges, and their layout was like that of the old chain pump. Four pumps were fitted, two to each side of the vessel, one abaft the other. The heads of the pumps terminated within cisterns on the lower gundeck. The cisterns were inter-connected by tubular iron dales which in turn were joined to a common discharge which passed to each side of the vessel, and then overboard. The suction pipework was taken from the well, around the base of the mainmast. Each pair of pumps (port or starboard) was operated by a common crankshaft, which in turn

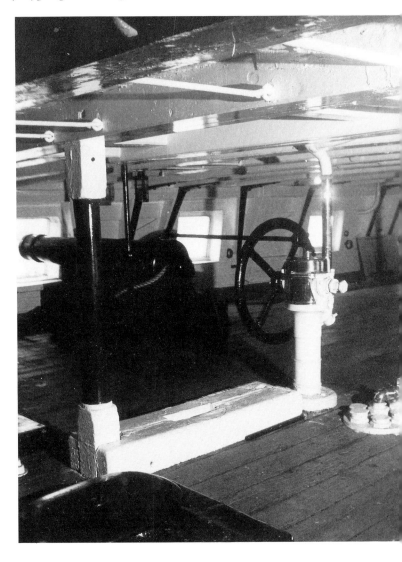

Unicorn. *The Downton Patent Pump was introduced in 1825. This photograph shows how the crank handle and its support pillar were rigged (one side only). A pump suction change-over plate is fitted on the deck adjacent. This meant that there could be suction from various points throughout the vessel, as well as directly from the sea, for fire-fighting and washing down decks.*

was rotated by two handwheels. Extension crank handles could be connected to thse handwheels if required, in the manner previously used on the chain pump. The only difference in operation was that the driving crank was fitted on the deck above the pump itself, with long iron connecting rods passing to the deck below. Water for washing down decks and fire-fighting was obtained from a separate lift pump, similar to the elm tree pump that was fitted on the *Victory* seventy years earlier.

Cable Handling Gear

THE CAPSTAN

A capstan is a mechanical device for veering and hauling heavy cables such as anchor hawsers. The term capstan was derived from the Latin word 'capistrum', and the Anglo-Saxon word 'capster', which mean halter. A capstan consisted of a vertical spindle with a number of square sockets around the periphery at the head, into which the capstan bars fitted. These bars, when fitted, projected like the spokes of a wheel and when force was applied in one direction the whole assembly rotated, either hauling in or veering out the cable to which a load was attached. Besides their primary function of weighing the anchor, capstans were also used to lift or lower a ship's boats, masts, yards, and other heavy equipment.

Between 1650 and 1850 alterations were made to the design, improving the ability and construction, and also enabling the capstan to work with the chain cables introduced in the second decade of the nineteenth century. Before explaining the general construction, a brief outline of its development is given. Scantlings of the earlier versions are rare and are therefore omitted unless reasonable assumptions can be made.

The capstan of 1650 was relatively simple. It consisted of a single spindle, octagonal in its cross-section, while the lower part was rounded and tapered towards its heel, which was fitted in the step. The step was on the deck below that on which the capstan was fitted. At this time most capstans were of the single-tiered type, but double-tier capstans were introduced later in the century. Either four or eight whelps were fayed and bolted to the flat faces of the spindle, the length of which was approximately one-third of the overall length of the spindle. The width of the whelps was approximately half that of the flat of the spindle. The upper end of these whelps was stiffened with a disc of timber fitted over the top of the spindle, and was bolted to both the whelps and the spindle. The disc was further retained by a number of brackets fitted directly above each whelp. The sockets for the bars were cut directly through the spindle, the bars being passed right through, thus providing two of the 'spokes' (see Fig 5/16).

Over the next 20 years the head of the spindle became circular in section, and the whelps were given additional lateral support by a series of chocks fitted between their faces. One of the most important changes was the introduction of the drumhead. On the older capstan the bars passed through the spindle. This produced excessive torque, weakening of the wood grain in the vicinity of the sockets, and the spindle split along its length. The drumhead, which was circular, was fashioned to receive the capstan bars, which were bolted to the spindle and to the heads of the whelps. Should any damage be done to the drumhead, it could be easily repaired or replaced without the complete removal of the spindle.

The whelps had a twofold function. Firstly, their width increased the diameter of the capstan, so that the number of times the capstan was turned was reduced, while the length of the cable actually hauled in was increased. Secondly, the faces of the whelps were

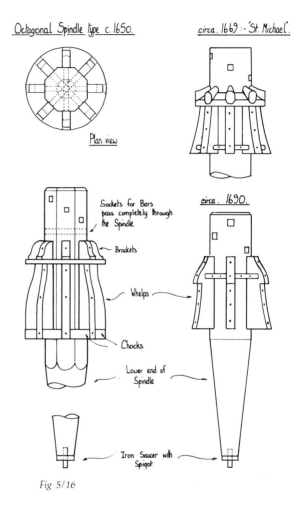

Capstans :– 17th Century

Octagonal Spindle type c. 1650.

Plan view

circa. 1669 :- 'St. Michael.'

Sockets for Bars pass completely through the Spindle

Brackets

Whelps

Chocks

Lower end of Spindle

Iron Saucer with Spigot.

circa. 1690.

Fig 5/16

angled inwards towards their heads by 8 to 10 degrees. This was called the 'surge', the purpose of which was to move the cable up or down as it turned onto the capstan. This would tighten it, thereby increasing the frictional hold, and reducing any slip.

To prevent the capstan from 'walking back' when the cable was under strain, a ratchet appliance was fitted, consisting of a series of pawls and a pawl ring. The lower ends of the pawls were allowed to move or lock automatically, by the virtue of their weight, into the racks of the pawl ring. The pawl ring was fixed to the deck, while the pawls were pivoted so that they could be reversed, should it be necessary to veer instead of haul on the cable. Pawl rings were rarely fitted before about 1790. Prior to this two pawls were fitted on the deck, one end pivoted on a bolt, the free end engaged with the heels of the whelps. The introduction of the iron pawl ring greatly enhanced the rigidity, and reduced wear on the whelps.

The double tier capstan was in use by 1680. On this type, two capstans shared a common spindle, which was therefore extended. The advantage of this was that, as the cable turned on the lower capstan, the upper capstan could be turned without the feet of the

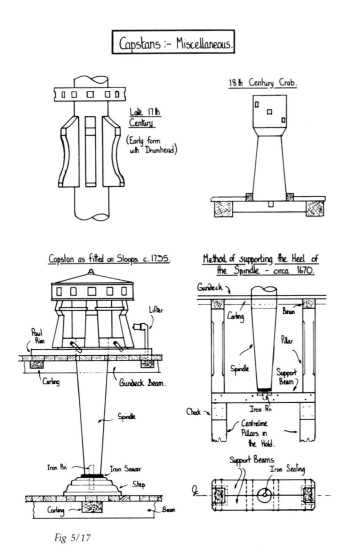

Fig 5/17

men being hindered. However, this was not always the case, for after about 1740* both capstans could be manned to reduce the individual work load for each man. This type of capstan became common, and by 1701 the larger First Rates often had one single capstan and two of the double type. All of these were fitted with drumheads, the lower capstans being fitted with a similar feature called the trundlehead. The first move towards standardisation of the dimensions is given by Sutherland in *Shipbuilding Unveiled* of 1717. The scantlings are as follows:

Overall width of the whelps = diameter of the barrel ÷ 2

N.B. In this case the barrel is taken as the spindle.

Maximum height of the surge = height of the whelps × ⅔

The width of the whelp at the maximum height of the surge = 2⅔in for every foot of the whelp in height.

*After about 1740 double capstans had trundleheads on both parts.

The above figures are fairly accurate; the angle produced was approximately 9 degrees for the surge. However, these calculations are not valid for capstans fitted in the second half of the eighteenth century. Apart from a general increase in capstan dimension, little change occurred until 1795. The Navy Board order of that year, dated 27 February, authorised the introduction of a modified capstan with a removable spindle to enable repairs to be made to the bearings. By 1830, modifications were made to allow capstans to take the chain cables. Also it was found that the double tier type had a number of disadvantages. The main problem was that if a second capstan was required when weighing anchor, it was not available until the completion of the first task. This was overcome by designing the double tier capstan, with a facility to disengage the upper capstan from the lower. This was achieved by the use of two plates, one fitted to the spindle the other to the trundlehead of the lower capstan, the two being engaged with drop pins.

The following description is based on a main jeer capstan fitted to a First Rate ship of 1785. Although I have given the various scantlings, these should not be applied to all vessels.

The Spindle

This was made from a single baulk of timber, usually oak, 2ft 4in diameter and 13ft long (the height of two decks). The upper section was twelve-sided, and the lower half ten-sided, leaving a short centre portion of rounded cross-section between them. The head of the spindle was fashioned with a tenon 18in square and 4½in deep, bound with a wrought iron hoop (¾in thick) let into the faces. Iron bands of similar dimensions were also fitted at the top and bottom of each dodecagon and decagon sections. At the heel of the spindle an iron plate with an integral pin was fitted, which acted as the bearing shoulder for the actual bearing inlaid in the step. In some cases the spindle was greater in length, and continued to a position on the orlop deck. This fashion was very common in vessels fitted with a single tier type, the step being on the berthing deck (see Fig 5/18).

The Step (or Partners)

The step which sat between the beams fore and aft of the capstan was usually made from oak, varying in width from 20 to 24in, and in depth from 18 to 22in. Both the fore and after ends were set into the adjacent beams to a width of 1¾in, and a depth of half the depth of the beam. Often the step was slightly proud of deck level to a distance approximately equal to that of the pawl ring. Fastening was achieved by bolts driven through the beams horizontally, into the step itself. At the centre of the step, an iron bush was inlaid, into which the pin on the bottom of the spindle was received. This component, the saucer, was about 6in deep and 12in diameter.

Foudroyant. *Main jeer capstan, showing the drumhead, whelps, chocks and the different types of bolting arrangement.*

The Drumhead

The construction of the drumhead was somewhat complex in comparison to the remainder of the capstan. English elm, with its irregular grain, was found to be the most suitable timber for its manufacture, due to its strength and torque-loading capabilities. The whole assembly was made up from four semi-circular pieces, each pair forming a single layer. The lower layer was cut with a recess 3in deep on its bottom face and was 12-sided, so it could be set down upon the similarly shaped part of the spindle. A second recess was made centrally, of sufficient depth and size to receive the tenon at the head of the spindle. On the upper surface, 12 tapered slots were cut radially, from the periphery. They were about 9 to 12in long, their width equal to and depth half that of the capstan bars. The upper layer was made with identical slots for the capstan bars, on its bottom surface, and given a round up on the top. The slots for the bars were, like those of the lower layer, made to half the depth of the capstan bars. Once all the pieces had been fashioned, they were matched together and fixed with eight bolts set vertically on a pitch circle with a diameter six-sevenths of that of the spindle. After the whole component was fitted in place on top of the spindle,

it was further secured with vertical bolts driven into the heads of the whelps.

The sockets for the bars were given a taper of 1in per foot. This only applied to the top and side, for the lower faces were made flat. Generally a lightweight cover was fitted over the top of the drumhead, with a little decoration. When the capstan was required, it was removed, and it was on top of the drumhead that the 'shanty man' would sit playing suitable jigs. Towards the end of the eighteenth century, it was not uncommon for small drawers to be fitted in the sockets for the bars. Each of the drawers contained a small piece of lint, a block of salt and some twine, which was first aid equipment for minor injuries sustained during action. The drawers were removed when it was necessary to house the capstan bars.

The Trundlehead

This was made in exactly the same manner as the drumhead, except that the centres of the four segments were designed to fit around the ten faces on the spindle. Once in position it was bolted down onto the heads of the whelps. The diameter of both the drumhead and the trundlehead was twice that of the spindle. However, the depth of these two components differed and can be determined as follows:

$$Drumhead\ depth = (drumhead\ diameter \times 3)/14 + 2in$$

$$Trundlehead\ depth = trundlehead\ diameter/5$$

The size of the sockets for the capstan bars varied from 3½ to 4½in, according to the size of the capstan. Although they were completely square in section, the sockets tapered 1in in every foot.

The Whelps

The function of these was to increase the sweep of the capstan and to 'surge' the cable. Throughout most of the period they were made from oak, but with ever-increasing shortages, African oak and sabicu were used. Generally six were fitted to the upper capstan, and five to the lower, though this varied if the capstan was of the single tier type. Each was fayed radially to the flats of the spindle, all being set equidistantly apart, and fastened to the spindle with three bolts. The top of each whelp was fayed with the lower edge of the drumhead (or trundlehead), and terminated with a free end either above the partners or into the pawlhead. This depended on whether the capstan was of the single or double tiered type. The bolts used were of 1 to 1½in diameter, the heads being driven well in, and covered with a diamond-shaped or circular wooden cap. The following equations give the approximate proportional sizes, the diameter of the spindle being the criterion for all the required scantlings, directly or indirectly. The diameter of the spindle was five-ninths of the vessel's beam.

The width of the whelps (distance between the periphery of the spindle and the extreme edge of the whelp) can be calculated as follows:

$$Width = spindle\ diameter \times 2/7$$

$$Thickness = width\ of\ the\ whelp \times 3/2$$

$$Height\ of\ whelps\ (upper\ capstan) = spindle\ diameter \times 6/5$$

$$Height\ of\ whelps\ (lower\ capstan) = spindle\ diameter \times 7/5$$

Having determined the principal dimensions, the next part to be fashioned was the surface forming the surge. The width of this was diminished at a given height on each individual whelp, which varied according to the number of whelps fitted. If six whelps were employed, then the angle required for the surge was about 9 degrees; if there were only five whelps it was between 8 and 10 degrees.

The height of the surge varied according to the part of the capstan concerned. Thus if the capstan was of the double tiered type

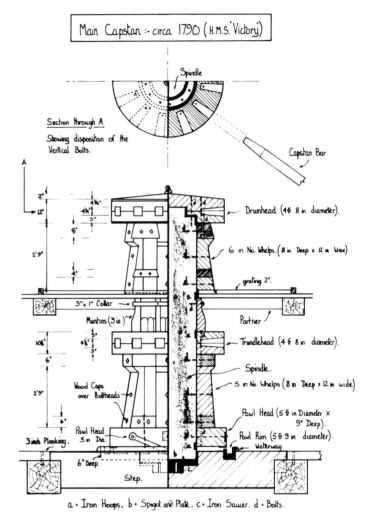

Main Capstan :- circa 1790 (H.M.S. 'Victory')

Fig 5/18

two formulae must be used. Should the capstan be of the single type, then the second of these formulae should be used.

$$Upper\ capstan = height\ of\ the\ whelp \times 2/3$$

$$Lower\ capstan = height\ of\ the\ whelp \times 3/4$$

The smallest width of the whelp was governed by the angle of the surge, which has already been mentioned. The width of the surge can be calculated as follows:

The upper capstan whelps:
$$W^s = (W - H) \times \tan 9°$$

The lower capstan whelps:
$$W^s = (W - H) \times \tan 10°$$

where W^s = width at the height of the surge; W = overall width; H = height of surge

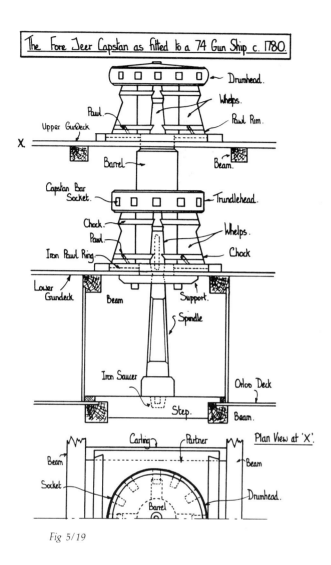

The Fore Jeer Capstan as fitted to a 74 Gun Ship c. 1780.

Drumhead.
Whelps.
Pawl.
Pawl Rim.
Upper Gundeck
X
Barrel.
Beam.
Capstan Bar Socket.
Trundlehead.
Chock.
Pawl.
Whelps.
Iron Pawl Ring.
Chock
Lower Gundeck
Beam.
Support.
Spindle.
Iron Saucer.
Orlop Deck
Step.
Beam.

Plan View at 'X'.
Carling
Partner
Beam
Beam
Socket
Drumhead.
Barrel

Fig 5/19

The Chocks

These were segments of timber set horizontally between the heads and heels of the whelps, to give them further support thus preventing them twisting under strain from the cables. They also gave additional support to the drumhead or trundlehead. The uppermost chocks of the upper capstan were made to a depth equal to the width of the whelps, with their periphery conforming to that of the same. A second set of chocks was set at the heels of the upper capstan's whelps. The depth of these was generally half that of those fitted above. The chocks on the lower capstan were both of the same depth, and approximately half the thickness of the whelps. All were bolted horizontally and those at the drumhead, trundlehead and pawlhead were bolted additionally with vertical bolts. The heads of these bolts were covered with caps, as previously mentioned. Oak was normally used for the construction of chocks until the early years of the nineteenth century, when African oak or sabicu was adopted.

The Pawlhead

This was fitted at the lower part of the capstan, below the whelps. Its function was to house the pawls which were bolted around its periphery. English elm was the most suitable timber for its construction. It was made in two or four segments, fayed and bolted to the flat faces of the spindle. It was also bolted vertically into the heels of the whelps. The bolts were 1 to 1½in diameter. The size of the pawlhead in comparison to the spindle was as follows:

$$Pawlhead\ diameter = spindle\ diameter \times {}^{32}\!/_{15}$$

$$Pawlhead\ depth = pawlhead\ diameter \times {}^{3}\!/_{20}$$

The Pawls

Four pawls were usually fitted, each being spaced equidistantly around the pawlhead. They were made from wrought iron bars, about 2½in square in section, with an eye at one end, through which a 1½in bolt passed. The pawl on the capstan of a First Rate ship was 2ft 9in long. Using this dimension, it can be determined that the length of the capstan was approximately nine-sixteenths of the diameter of the pawlhead. The pawl itself could be rotated to reverse the ratchet effect, to reverse the capstan for veering.

The Pawl Rim (or Ring)

This was generally made from cast iron, fashioned with a series of 'stops', into which the pawls engaged. The dimensions of this ring on a First Rate ship were as follows: the external diameter 5ft 7in and the internal diameter 1ft less. The width and overall height of the rim was 6in, although the two rims were a different size. The space between these rims was half the width. Each stop was 4in in height from the base and 6in in length, all being spaced equidistantly around the circumference. The complete ring was set down into the recess in the upper surface of the step, and bolted at every space between a stop. The depth at which it was let into the step was normally five-sixths of its height. A small waterway made from elm was fayed around the ring, it protruded above the step and was about 1½in wide.

$$External\ diameter = (diameter\ of\ the\ pawlhead + pawl\ width) \times 2 + 2in$$

$$Internal\ diameter = external\ diameter - 12in$$

$$Cross\ sectional\ width = (external\ diameter - internal\ diameter)/2$$

$$Height = the\ width.$$

$$Height\ of\ stops = five\text{-}sixths\ of\ overall\ height.$$

Unicorn. The main capstan made from iron for hauling in chain anchor cables. Pawls and a pawl rim are fitted at the base.

The Collar

Where the capstan was double tiered the portion of the spindle between the upper and lower capstans was often of a smaller diameter, therefore it was necessary to increase the width. Once the capstan had been put in place during building, the spindle was retained radially by the partners. However, these did not retain the spindle axially. This problem was overcome by fitting small wedge-shaped pieces of timber between the trundlehead and the partners themselves. Generally eight were used, each being approximately 18in long (the difference between the top of the trundlehead and the deckhead) and 3in thick, all being spaced equidistantly around the circumference. They were fastened by iron spikes, and stiffened further by an iron collar, 3in wide and 1in thick. This collar was retained by the wedge shape of the eight mountings. Thus the whole capstan was maintained in its lower bearing.

The Capstan Bars

The most suitable timber for the capstan bars was English ash, which had the desired springiness. The length of a single bar was one-third of the vessel's extreme beam (those of the *Victory* are 16ft 9in long) and the width varied from 3½ to 4½in. A small slot was cut at one end, its width being one-third of the width of the bar and it was two-thirds of the width of the bar in depth. This was used for the 'swifter'. The opposite end was tapered to fit into the sockets of the drumhead or trundlehead. A swifter was a rope used to secure all the bars in place once they were housed in the capstan, passing completely around the ends of the bars within the slots, giving the whole an appearance of a spider's web.

THE IMPROVED CAPSTAN

Towards the end of the eighteenth century the capstan was subjected to a number of improvements to increase the mechanical advantage and to adapt to the introduction of chain cable a decade later. The first modification enabled the upper capstan to operate separately from the lower. Until then, both the upper and lower capstans shared a common spindle, which formed the barrel of each capstan. This design only allowed both capstans to be turned together, which was found impractical for certain tasks, and the effort required was too great. It must be understood that the combined weight of both capstans, plus that of the object being moved, had to be taken into account when power was needed to turn the capstan.

To alleviate this problem, the design had to be altered to allow the upper capstan to be turned either separately or together with the lower capstan as required. The restricting factor was that the spindle, common to both, also formed the barrel of each capstan. Therefore independent barrels had to be used. This was done by substituting the wooden spindle for one of wrought iron, the barrels being built separately. It was now possible to rotate the barrel while the spindle remained stationary. Likewise, the spindle could be revolved with the barrel stationary. By having the spindle permanently fixed to the upper capstan, the lower capstan could be employed independently. All that was needed was some means of engaging the lower capstan to the spindle. This was achieved in the following manner: first, a circular plate of iron with 3 or 4 vertical holes for the engaging pins was bolted to the spindle above the trundlehead. A second plate which was similarly drilled, and free to revolve around the spindle, was bolted to the trundlehead. Engagement was carried out by lining up the holes in each plate to one another and fitting the drop pins. Disengaging was also simply done, by their removal.

The construction of the capstan varied very little from previous designs, apart from these modifications. Because the spindle was now made from wrought iron, iron bushes or bearings had to be fitted to ensure the alignment of the spindle and to prevent wear to the wooden barrel. The step was made from a different material, cast iron. The following description refers to a capstan of ships of 52 to 36 guns.

The Spindle

This was manufactured from best quality wrought iron. It was 11ft ½in long, with a diameter of 5in at the uppermost bush and 8in at the lower. The lower end was fashioned with a locating spigot set into the step. The diameter of its middle section (which passed through the barrel) was approximately 12in.

The Step

The step was made from cast iron, with a bush to receive the spigot of the spindle. The step was octagonal, to prevent it moving within its timber bed. At its upper side it measured 10½in and at its base 9in. The integral bush for the spindle was 4½in deep and ¾in diameter. The overall depth of the casting was 7in.

The Barrels

Unlike the timber spindled capstan in which the barrels were formed by the spindle, the barrels of the modified capstan were built up around the iron spindle. The barrel was made from segments of English oak, which when combined formed a twelve-sided cylinder, the diameter of which was 2ft 2in across the flats; the overall length was 3ft 4½in. Its upper end was fashioned with a tenon 17in square and 4in deep. Binding the whole barrel together were two iron bands or hoops, made to fit the twelve sides, and let into the timber producing a flush outer surface. Each band was about 4in wide and ½in thick.

Once the barrel was bound, it was bored through vertically to the diameter of the spindle (in this case 5in), and the spindle was driven through. To secure the barrel to the spindle, two iron bushes were fitted to the barrel, one at the top and the other at the base. Each bush was fastened to the barrel with rag-bolts, and to the spindle with a horizontal bolt passing radially through it. The major components of the upper capstan were thus complete.

The barrel for the lower capstan was made in a similar manner to that of the upper, except that the spindle was not attached. The diameter of the barrel was 2ft 1in, and its length 4ft. It, too, was fashioned with a tenon at the top, 20in square and 5¾in deep. The other difference was that the barrel was shaped with ten sides as opposed to the twelve of the upper capstan. In a similar manner the segments were bound together with iron hoops, of identical dimensions. Because the spindle passed directly through the barrel, no bushes were required.

The Bushes of the Upper Capstan

The upper bush was 2½in thick, and the lower bush 3¼in. No specifications are given of their diameter, except for the bolt sizes.

Foudroyant. *A nineteenth-century modified capstan adapted for use with chain cables. The spindle is wrought iron. The two iron pins set on the trundlehead are used for disengaging this capstan from the one fitted on the deck above. One pin is shown raised in its disengaged mode, the other is engaged. This view also shows the pawls and pawl rim.*

The overall width and breadth of the bushes must have been about 12in, for by including the diameter of the spindle, the external diameter of the bush and the extreme diameter of the plate accounted for the pitch circle diameter of the bolts. The plate was not circular, but 'lobular'. The upper bush was retained, with four bolts 7in long and ⅝in diameter, while the lower bush was held with four bolts, 12in long and ¾in diameter.

The Drumhead

This was made from English elm, and given a diameter of 4ft 2½in. It was 11in thick with a round up of 2in. It was fashioned from four semi-circular segments fayed together to form a disc, the joints of the top half being set at 90 degrees to those of the lower portion. The whole assembly was bound together with two iron hoops, 3in wide and ⅝in thick, each set flush with the outer surface. The internal diameter was about 3ft 10½in. The segments were further secured to each other with vertically driven bolts 12in long, and ⅝in diameter. The lower half was fashioned with a mortice to receive the tenon of the barrel, and once set down upon the barrel was retained by four vertical bolts 14in long and ¾in diameter passing down through to the upper chocks.

Prior to the assembly of the drumhead, the square sockets for the capstan bars had to be fashioned. It cannot be assumed that they were cut after assembly, for despite the skills of the men at that period this would have been a difficult task. It would seem reasonable that half of each socket was cut out by chisel before matching the segments, each slot being cut radially. The taper of each slot was confined to top and side surfaces, and was approximately 1in per foot. Twelve bar holes were cut, each 4¼in square, tapering to 3¼in because they were 1ft long. Provision was also made to 'let in' the heads of the whelps to the bottom surface, to a depth of 1¼in.

The Whelps of the Upper Capstan

Six whelps were fitted to the barrel of the upper capstan, made either from sabicu or African oak. They were 3ft ½in long, and 7¼in wide. Their breadth was 11in at the sole and 7in at the head. Each was secured to the barrel, with two 12in long bolts, ⅞in diameter. The flat surface of the barrel to which they were fayed had a recess of about an inch into which the whelps were set. The 'angle of surge' was 9 degrees 30 minutes from the vertical.

The Whelps of the Lower Capstan

These were, like the whelps of the upper capstan, made from sabicu or African oak, but only five were fitted. The overall length was 2ft 9½in and they were 7½in wide. The breadth at the head was 8in and at the sole it was 10½in. In a similar manner they were let into the barrel and the trundlehead, but in this case they were also let into the upper surface of the pawlhead, to a depth of about 1¼in. Each was fastened to the barrel with two bolts, 12in long and ⅞in diameter. Due to the fact that there were only five whelps, the angle of the surge was different and was nearer 10 degrees to the vertical.

The Chocks

These, like the whelps, were made from sabicu or African oak. The chocks of the upper capstan were as follows: the top chocks were 3in thick, while the lower ones were 7in thick, both sets being cut to the required width between the whelps. The actual height at which the top chocks were set was approximately ¾in above the surge, and they were rabbeted into the whelps for a depth of half the thickness of the chock itself (1½in). The lower chocks were set 6in from the soles of the whelps, and checked in for a depth of 2in. Each chock was secured with two bolts, 15in long and ¾in diameter, the bolts for the upper chock were about 1in shorter. The chocks fitted

to the lower capstan were identical both in dimension and the manner in which they were secured. The only exception was that the lower faces of the bottom chocks were fayed and bolted vertically to the pawlhead.

The Trundlehead

This was made from English elm, and fashioned in the same manner as the drumhead, except for the dimensions and some minor details. It was 4ft 2in thick and 10½in diameter. In this case there was no round up on its top surface. Similarly, two iron hoops were employed to bind the assembly together, but due to its difference in thickness they were only 3in wide. The major difference was the form of the tenon and mortice joining the trundlehead to the barrel. In this case the underside of the trundlehead was cut out to conform to the ten sides of the barrel, for a depth of about 5in, the trundlehead fitting down upon the barrel. It was then fastened with four bolts driven vertically, each 19in long and ¾in diameter. Before the assembly, 12 bar holes were cut, 4½in square and 11in long, with the same degree of taper as the drumhead. One of the connecting plates, which was used for disengaging was fitted to the top surface of the trundlehead.

The Connecting Plates

The overall diameter of the lower connecting plate was 2ft and it was 4in thick at its centre, tapering to 3½in at the extreme diameter. The whole plate was manufactured from iron, and was bored through at its centre for the spindle. The diameter of the spindle at this point was 1ft. The plate was not in the form of a complete disc, but had three flat arms radiating from its centre. Each arm was bored vertically to receive the drop pins. A similarly shaped iron plate was forge-welded to the spindle above the lower connecting plate, and set 1in above it. This plate was also bored to receive the drop pins.

The Drop Pins

The drop pins were made from wrought iron and were 9in long and 2¾in diameter. A small hole of about ¼in diameter was bored horizontally through the bolts near their lower end. A pin was fitted in the hole when the drop bolt was disengaged, to prevent it from dropping into the lower plate. These pins were 6in long and about ¼in diameter. The lower capstan was engaged by removing the retaining pins, lining up the consecutive holes in both plates, and driving the large drop pins into the hole of the lower plate.

The Pawlhead

This was made from two semi-circular pieces of English elm, of 4ft 6in diameter and 6¾in thick, bored through at the centre for the spindle. The two halves were held together with iron hoops, one at the top and one at the bottom, each 3in wide and ½in thick. Both hoops were secured with 16 bolts, 6¾in long, and ¾in diameter. Like

Left: Unicorn. *View of the epicyclic gearing fitted on the deckhead of the berthing deck below the main capstan and above the step. This arrangement produced a working ratio of 3:1, thus reducing the energy required to haul in the chain cables.*

Right: Unicorn. *Close-up view of the whelps of the main capstan showing a chain fitted vertically, secured at the upper chock and passing through the lower chock. I have yet to discover the purpose of this. This arrangement is duplicated on the opposite side of the capstan.*

all the other iron hoops, these were set flush with the outer surface. The pawlhead was also fastened with vertically set copper bolts driven through from the lower chock. These bolts were 13¾in long and ¾in diameter.

Around the periphery of the pawlhead were six rectangular iron castings set into the wood. Each was 11in long, 3½in wide and 1in thick, and they were fastened with four bolts, 9in long and ½in diameter. To the plate was fitted the iron pawl, 1ft 7in long and approximately 2½in square in section. The pawl was secured with a single bolt 16½in long and about 1½in diameter.

The Pawl Rim (or Ring)

The pawl rim was similar to that employed on the older type of capstan. The external diameter was 4ft 10in, with an internal diameter of 4ft 4in, giving a width of 3in. The inner and outer rims were 5in and 6in respectively, the ratchet stops being of the same heights. The whole rim was set down into the wood of the step.

An example of this type of capstan can be seen on the *Foudroyant* at Portsmouth. On this capstan the maker's plate gives the name T D Brown, and the design is given as 'Grylls Patent: Wheles of London'. No date is given, but it is known the vessel was launched

in 1817. I am not sure whether the capstan was fitted at the time of building or as a later modification. If it was installed initially, it is reasonable to assume that this form had been in general use for a number of years. Further evidence supporting this dating comes from the fact that there are no adaptations to accommodate the recently introduced chain cable. It appears that modifications for chain cables were first made on the riding bitts, and it was a number of years before they were introduced to the capstan (see Fig 6/7).

The next improvement in capstan design was aimed at increasing the power advantages required to raise chain anchor cables. The capstan fitted to the *Unicorn* is modified with epicyclic gearing at its base, giving a 3:1 advantage. The gearing consists of a centre-toothed wheel, integral with the spindle, around which revolve three planetary wheels of larger diameter. Enclosing all of these gears is a single wheel, which is toothed on its inner surface. The effort required to raise a chain cable was greatly reduced. It is thought that this design was introduced initially by Captain Phillips. However, many technically minded people were forwarding improvements at this time, therefore its origin is a little uncertain. During this period, naval construction was swamped with inventions, due to the rapid acceleration of the Industrial Revolution.

THE WINDLASS

This piece of equipment was generally used as an alternative to the capstan on such vessels as cutters, schooners, luggers and the smaller classes of gun brigs. Unlike the capstan, its barrel was set horizontally between two vertical bitts, and turned with either handspikes or a ratchet and crank device. The barrel was usually made from oak, it was eight-sided and tapered towards its extremities. An iron spindle was driven into each end, and located by radial bolts passing through both the barrel and the spindle. The ends of the spindle were set into bronze, and later iron, rhodens (or bushes), and these were located in holes between the faces of the bitts and the cheeks.

To prevent the windlass reversing when either hauling or veering, a pawl and pawl rim were fitted. The pawl was made from cast iron and was located at the centre of the length of the barrel, with securing bolts that were flush at their heads. This was done to prevent the pawl action being impaired by fouling. In some cases two pawl rims were fitted at the extremities of the barrel, instead of at the centre. This appears to be a later style. In most cases the internal diameter of the pawl rim was eight-sided, to conform to the shape of the barrel, and also to prevent any slip.

The whelps were made from oak. They were fayed and bolted on the alternate faces of the barrel, and secured with bolts or dowels. The purpose of the whelps was the same as when used on capstans: to increase the surge for the cable. Square sockets which held the handspikes for turning the windlass were cut into the barrel around its periphery. This method was superseded in the second quarter of

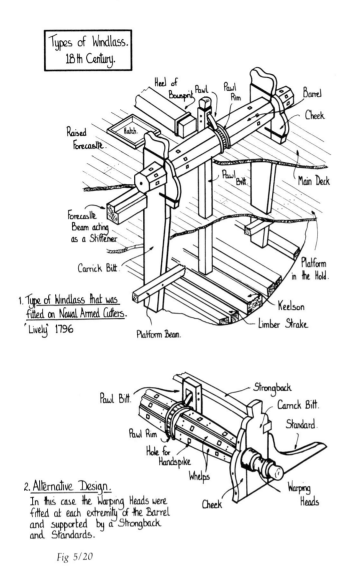

Types of Windlass.
18th Century.

Heel of Bowsprit Pawl Pawl Rim Barrel

Raised Forecastle Hatch. Cheek

Forecastle Beam acting as a Stiffener Pawl Bitt Main Deck

Carrick Bitt. Platform in the Hold.

1. Type of Windlass that was fitted on Naval Armed Cutters.
'Lively' 1796

Keelson

Platform Beam. Limber Strake

Pawl Bitt. Strongback

Carrick Bitt.

Standard.

Pawl Rim

Hole for Handspike

Whelps Cheek Warping Heads

2. Alternative Design.
In this case the Warping Heads were fitted at each extremity of the Barrel and supported by a Strongback and Standards.

Fig 5/20

Windlass for Chain Cable.
('Hornet' 1832).

Crank Handle

Pawl Bitts Carrick Bitt

Standards

Square Section Spindle

Pawl Rims Cheek

Carrick Bitt Scored & Bolted to Beam

Iron Housing

Pawl in its disengaged position

Pawl

Pawl

Detail of a Pawl Head. Cross-Section Front View.

The Pawl is disengaged from the Pawl Rim by removing the Retaining Pin 'A' and raising the Pawl by rotating it up around Pivot 'B' then re-inserting the Retaining Pin.

Fig 5/21

the nineteenth century when the barrel rotated by means of crank handles. The end of the crank handle had a toothed pinion, which engaged with a toothed wheel on the barrel itself.

The carrick bitts supported the barrel at the spindle ends. These were made from oak, in such a fashion that their heels extended to the deck below, and were rigidly bolted to both sets of beams. They were also supported by standards, made from oak. These standards were scored on their lower faces to enable them to be let down onto the deck beams, to which they were bolted. They were always bolted to the side of the bitts that received the strain of the cable being hauled, and therefore are always to be seen to the fore side of the windlass. On the opposite side of the standards were the cheeks which gave additional support to the spindle. These were made so that they could be removed to allow the bush in which the spindle was located to be refurbished. Provision was therefore made in the method of bolting the cheeks to the bitts, to allow for easy dismantling.

It was often the practice to fit a transverse strongback between the two bitts, to give extra support. At the centre, to one side of the barrel, a vertical baulk of timber known as the pawlhead was fitted to the deck. A square hole was cut through it fore and aft, into which was fitted a wrought iron pawl, which pivoted on an iron pin set vertically through the housing. A second hole was bored horizontally at the vicinity of the pawl, through which a retractable bolt could be inserted, which, if engaged, would hold the pawl clear of the pawl rim, allowing the windlass to veer. For windlasses that had the pawl rims fitted at the end of the barrel, a similar arrangement was made for the pawls, which in this case were fitted to the carrick bitts. Some windlasses were made with the barrel extending beyond the confines of the carrick bitts, where the end of the barrel was fashioned into an additional appliance known as a warping head. This was located upon the spindle by means of a radial bolt. Details of the various forms of windlasses are given in Figs 5/20 and 5/21.

THE CRAB

The crab is a form of capstan that was generally employed for lesser tasks until the end of the eighteenth century. It was mainly used for setting up the less heavy standing rigging, warping and for hoisting relatively lightweight stores. Unlike most forms of capstan, the wooden bars for turning the crab passed directly through the head or drum. This was done in much the same manner as the earlier forms of capstan. Therefore the possibility of the barrel splitting governed its use. The length of the bars varied but general opinion is that they were half the vessel's extreme beam. Sutherland, in *Shipbuilding Unveiled* of 1717, states that they were to be thirteen times the radius of the crab itself.

The type of crab illustrated in Sutherland's work indicates that it was portable. Such a device was obviously a great asset to a ship. Other illustrations, taken from various sources, show the crab as a permanent fixture. If this was the case, their absence from models remains a mystery. It can therefore be assumed that they were classified as an additional fitting, that could be removed and stowed below when not in use. The two variations are illustrated in Fig 5/22.

Fig 5/22

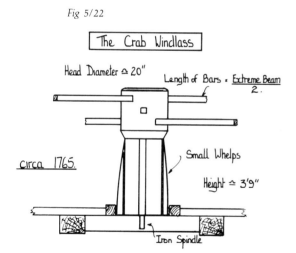

Crab as shown in Sutherland's 'Shipbuilding Unveiled' (1717)

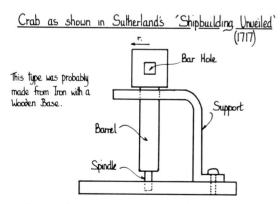

ADDITIONAL ANCHOR CABLE HANDLING GEAR

In addition to the capstan and the riding bitts, a number of fittings were employed to assist in the movement of the anchor cable. These were: messenger rollers, cable lifters and cable compressors. It must be noted that these fittings were not used on vessels with windlasses, as the circumferences of the cables were too small, and they could be turned around a windlass barrel without any difficulty.

Before discussing each fitting in detail, the various methods by which the anchor cable was retrieved must be understood. The factor that governed these methods was the size of the anchor cable itself. In most cases the circumference of the cable was too great for it to be wound around the capstan. This was overcome by the use of a loop of rope (half the size of the anchor cable) which was wound around the capstan and easily manipulated. In 1811 chain cables were introduced. This meant that new methods of cable recovery had to be introduced. It can be assumed that a chain cable could be passed around a capstan easily, by virtue of its smaller diameter, but until modified capstans were introduced, some form of additional cable was employed. The two methods commonly used in the Navy were the vyol and the messenger, the latter being introduced in 1744, although the former was retained as a standby until the end of the eighteenth century.

The Vyol (or Voyol)

By referring to Fig 5/23 it can be seen that this continuous cable was partially under tension between where it was 'married' to the anchor cable and the capstan. To assist in reversing the direction of the vyol relative to the ship, a large single-sheaved snatch block was secured to the mainmast. The anchor cable was released from the vyol at the

Fig 5/23

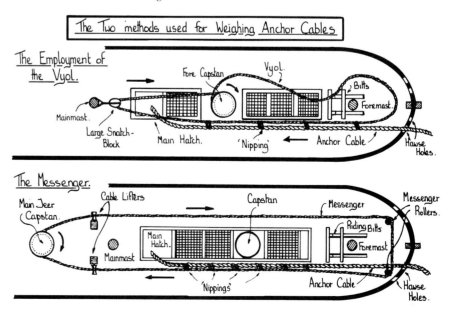

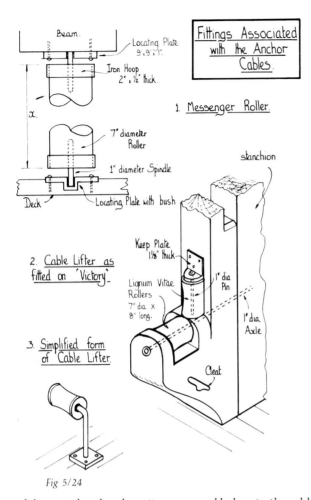

Fig 5/24

point of the main hatch, where it was passed below to the cable tier. This method of 'warping' the anchor cable was used up to about 1750, but was superseded by the messenger, which was introduced in the 1740s. The disadvantage of a vyol was that its configuration had to be altered if it was necessary to haul in the anchor cable on the other side of the vessel. This entailed the vyol's removal from the capstan and the snatch block. The vyol would then be re-run with the alternative bight of the rope wound around the capstan, and led through the snatch block.

To weigh the starboard anchor, a clockwise rotation of the capstan was required, the reverse movement being needed to weigh the larboard cable. It must also be noted that the direction in which the vyol was wound on the capstan barrel was also altered when changing over from the starboard to the larboard side, and assumed the same direction as the rotation of the capstan.

The Messenger Cable

In Fig 5/23 it can be seen that the messenger was taut throughout its entirety. This was helped by the addition of two vertical messenger rollers, set in the fore part of the manger. These were introduced in 1792. A simple snatch block may have been used before this date. Like the vyol, the messenger was half the size of the

anchor cable, and was made as a continuous rope. The messenger was wound four times around the capstan, in a clockwise direction. When weighing the starboard anchor cable, the capstan was turned in a clockwise direction and reversed for the larboard. As the anchor cable entered the ship it was temporarily lashed or 'nipped' to the messenger, and released as it passed below. The 'nipping' was carried out by the ship's boys, who would bind the two cables together with a piece of small line and walk with the 'married' cables to the point of release – hence the term 'nipper' which is often used in reference to youngsters. Any boy thought to be adept at this task was called a 'smart young nipper'.

The Messenger Rollers

The function of these rollers was to assist in the movement of the messenger cable when the anchor cable was hove in. They were first introduced in 1792. Usually two were fitted, both within the confines of the manger. Each one was set in line with a pair of hawse holes, at a suitable distance abaft the stemson. Oak of about 7in diameter was used for the rollers, because of its hard-wearing qualities. The whole assembly was set in the vertical plane, between the deck and the deckhead. To prevent the wood splitting at each extremity, an iron hoop, 2in wide and ½in thick, was shrunk over it. Into each end was driven a 1in diameter iron bar which acted as a spindle. Each spindle was retained in its own locating plate, made from iron and fastened to the deck and deckhead with bolts. This plate was approximately 9in square and 1in thick, with a 1¼in diameter hole for the spindle at its centre.

The Cable Compressor

The function of the cable compressor was to act as a brake, to check the rate of movement of the anchor cable as it was run out. It also served to control the rate that the anchor cable was passed down to the cable tier, making it more manageable when being laid out to drain off. The earlier designs were relatively simple, and consisted of a curved or angled arm made from wrought iron, which could be rotated around a fixed axis. This was generally situated on the underside of the main hatch, through which the cable was sent below. One compressor was fitted for each respective cable, one to larboard and one to starboard. Movement of the arm was made by a single purchase block and tackle, fastened by a pendant to an eye which was integral to the compressor. The anchor cable was 'checked' by the compressor being moved to 'choke' it between itself and the corner formed by the side of the hatch. To prevent wear to the head ledge and coamings, an iron chafing piece was fitted (see Fig 5/25).

By 1800 more versatile designs had been introduced. In all of these the arm of the compressor was given a more pronounced curve, to reduce wear on the cable. The practice of passing the cable through the main hatch was abolished and a separate navel pipe was used. This took the form of an orifice cut through the deck, with a block of timber with a similarly sized hole fitted over the orifice (see Fig 5/25). Some of these had the arms more curved than others.

Victory. *The starboard messenger roller on the lower gundeck. The cable passing through the hawse hole is the bower anchor cable, the other is the messenger itself. There is also an iron breast hook with its 'filling' timber and a heavy waterway. The hawse holes shown here are not as they were originally when they were lined with beech instead of iron sleeves, as shown here.*

Below: Foudroyant. *Berthing deck. This type of cable compressor was introduced around 1800. This photograph also shows the mainmast partners with the underside of the wedges protruding below the deck planking. To the left is the cylindrical form of the original chain pump casing.*

Right: Unicorn. *Cable compressors with their respective hawse pipes passing from the gundeck above. The compressor fitted to starboard is temporarily jammed in its present position hence the unusual angle. To the right is the main companionway leading to the gundeck and in the background the warrant officers' cabins.*

However, those fitted on the *Unicorn* were relatively straight, but this form was probably used for the chain cables introduced after 1811. By 1840, a cable compressor had been specially designed to handle chain cables. This was fashioned so that, no matter which way a chain link was set, it was clenched as necessary. This was done by the use of a sliding block of iron, which could be manipulated by a square-sectioned lever set in a bearing. At the other end of this lever was a block and tackle, which functioned in the same manner as in the other designs (see Fig 5/25).

The Cable Lifter

The function of this fitting was to raise the messenger cable to a suitable height, so that it passed directly onto the capstan. Two types were used, one being built integrally with support pillars, the other being simpler. The latter type was generally situated quite close to the capstan and consisted of a lignum vitae roller, supported by an iron stanchion. The rollers were usually about 7in diamater, and of a suitable length for the cable size (see Fig 5/24).

The Drop Keel

Very few naval vessels were ever fitted with a sliding (or drop) keel, which was mainly used on the smaller men-of-war employed for inshore work. The idea of this device was not entirely new when it was first introduced to the British Navy in the late 1780s by Captain John Schank. Schank was serving as a master's mate aboard a British warship off the North American colonies in 1773 when he first noticed that a number of the local craft were fitted with a form of drop keel. The advantage of this device was that it could be raised when the vessel was in shallow coastal waters, and dropped when going deep sea. Using his natural engineering genius, Schank improved the design and successfully adapted it to some experimental craft in 1774. Impressed with his results, he forwarded his proposals to the Navy Board ten years later. The Board finally accepted his idea, and ordered the building of a Sixth Rate aptly named *Trial*. This ship was fitted out with three drop keels, placed equidistantly along the length of the keel. A fine model of a vessel with this layout can be seen at the National Maritime Museum at

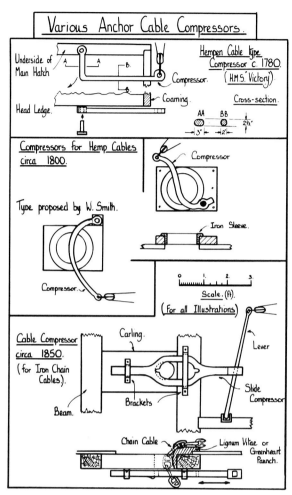

Fig 5/25

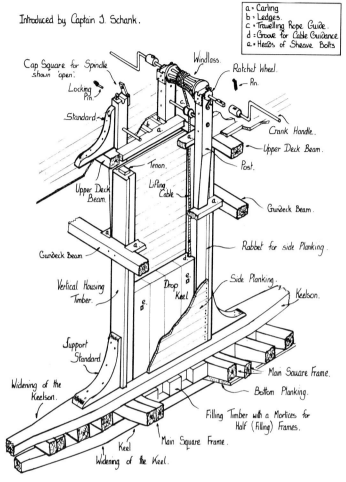

Fig 5/26

Greenwich. In 1798 the *Lady Nelson*, also built with drop keels, was sailed in Matthew Flinders' exploration of Australia and Tasmania. Here the practicality of this device was proved. When the *Trial* was employed for blockade work off French ports, she too proved her worth in confined waters.

THE CONSTRUCTION

The construction was relatively simple, consisting of a vertical watertight housing extending from the keel to the open upper deck in which the sliding keel was contained.

The Housing

Because the drop keel was set directly on the ship's centreline, modifications had to be made to the keel and keelson. This could only be achieved by increasing the scantling of both the keel and keelson to twice their normal athwartships width, thus enabling a

slot to be cut vertically through them. The drop keel was designed to pass freely through this slot. The width of the slot was equal to that of the drop keel, while the fore and aft length of the slot was governed by the 'room and space' rule applied to the particular vessel. The faces of the main square frames formed the fore and aft boundaries of the construction. The space between these frames was filled with two horizontal baulks of timber (one each side of the ship's keel) which were also sandwiched between the keel and keelson. The function of these baulks was primarily to receive the tenoned heels of the half (or filling) frames, and secondly to maintain a watertight boundary from the flooded portion of the housing. Both the upper and lower edges of the timbers were lined with tarred flannel, ensuring the watertight integrity.

Above the keelson, forming the fore and after sides of the housing, were two vertical oak timbers. The heels of these were tenoned into the keelson, and the upper ends into the deck beams of the upper deck. The overall breadth of the timbers was equal to the width of the slot for the drop keel, plus twice the thickness of the housing's side planking. The fore and aft width was equal to the

159

width of the beams to which the head was tenoned. The sides were fashioned with a rabbet, into which the side planking was set. The depth of this rabbet was equal to the thickness of the planking, while in width it was approximately three-quarters of the width of the timber, fore and aft.

Each side was planked up with oak boards, 8 to 10in wide, and equal in thickness to the planks used for the ship's bottom planking. Each plank was secured to the vertical timbers with two copper bolts at each end, the bolts being driven from one side of the housing to the other and clenched. All of the seams were caulked and payed, as were the rabbets into which the planks were received, which were lined with a layer of tarred flannel. These measures were to ensure that the housing remained completely watertight. In some cases a builder would work battens along the seams as an extra precaution against leakage. Externally the sides were braced with vertical stiffeners of pitch pine, cut to about 6in square. These were not made from a continuous length of timber, positioned at the height of the housing, but were worked in relatively short lengths at each deck level.

The Windlass

On the upper deck two pairs of stout timber posts were erected at the fore and after end of the slot in the deck for the drop keel. A spindle was set between these posts in the athwartships plane, carrying the drum of the windlass. The drum had a diameter of 15 or 18in. The surface of the cylinder was concave to produce a 'surge'. The 'surge' acted on the lifting cable in the same manner as it would on a capstan. The ends of the spindle were made square to fit into the crank handle. The latter could be removed for stowage when not in use. Just outboard of the posts, a ratchet wheel was fitted to the spindle, a pawl being fitted adjacent to this wheel and bolted to the post. These were incorporated to prevent the drum reversing when the drop keel was being raised. Small standards were fitted to support the posts, and were placed at either the fore or after ends, depending on which posts they were fitted to.

The Drop Keel

The drop keel was made from either oak or lignum vitae. The separate baulks of timber were fayed and bolted to each other. A slot was cut horizontally fore and aft across the drop keel at a pre-determined height, to accommodate the sheaves through which the lifting and lowering cable ran. The two sheaves were about 12in diameter and 4in wide, and were made from lignum vitae, bronze or iron. They were held in position with either copper or iron bolts of 2in diameter. The fore and after edges of the drop keel had grooves running between the upper edge and the sheaves. Their function was to produce a 'run' for the lifting cable to the sheaves from the windlasses. Alternatively these grooves had a hole of sufficient diameter bored vertically from the upper edge of the sheaves. Despite extensive research I have failed to find any reference to

whether weights would have been fitted to the drop keel or not. These would certainly have helped in the lowering process. If weighting was ever adopted, then I assume that the lower part of the drop keel would have been shod with iron. For a detailed illustration of the drop keel housing assembly (shown as fitted to a sloop) refer to Fig 5/26.

The Domestic Arrangements

THE GALLEY

Between 1650 and 1850, the overall construction of galley firehearths altered considerably. The major factor that influenced design was the fire risk that was forever present on wooden vessels. Because of this, over the years the construction changed from a brick-built hearth to a self-contained iron stove, which had a number of additional features. Another factor that may have influenced the design of hearths was the change in the crew's diet. However, it may have been that diet improved because of better facilities.

During the first half of the seventeenth century, it appears that the firehearth was situated low down in the vessel's hold. This practice seems to have been quite common, and is found on the Swedish ship *Vasa* (1628), which was raised and restored in the 1960s. This type of hearth consisted of an enclosed fireplace in the form of a pit over which cauldrons were suspended or set on an iron grill (see Fig 5/27). There were a number of advantages in this type of fireplace. Firstly, the whole structure was set well below the waterline, and was therefore free from damage by shot. Secondly, because it was low down it greatly enhanced the stability of the vessel by maintaining a low centre of bouyancy and thus gravity. There were of course some disadvantages, the major one being that the fire was close to the ship's magazines, the danger of which is obvious. The other problems were that the smoke had to find its own course out of the ship, which must have been very unpleasant for the crew and (although damp was the major factor) the heat of the fire could damage provisions in the hold.

By 1670, moves were made to relocate the galley under the forecastle or at the fore end of the middle gundeck on ships with three decks. This had a number of advantages and disadvantages. It was far more practical from the crew's point of view in that the galley was both above and near their accommodation. Secondly, it was far easier to incorporate a flue for the smoke to be removed from the ship. Also, the firehearth was well away from the magazine. There were major disadvantages. Firstly, the firehearth could be damaged easily during action, and secondly, its position higher up in the vessel would have influenced the stability of the vessel. This was not a great problem, for it was during this period that structural changes were made to the low parts of the ship's bow. The bow was given broader floors, thus providing more support to the forward guns.

Construction details for this period are scarce. The only clues to the design are in the building contracts which are a little obscure in

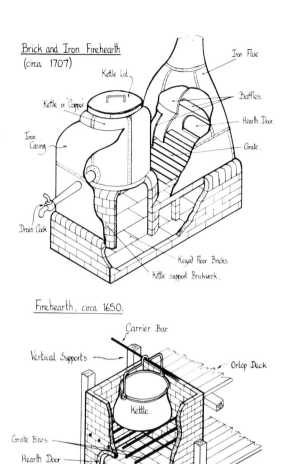

Brick and Iron Firehearth (circa 1707)

Fig 5/27

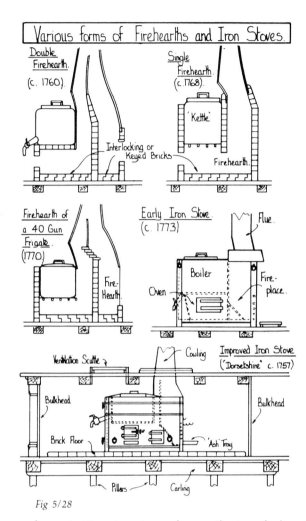

Fig 5/28

their content. The contract for the building of the *Biddeford* in 1692 (given in Appendix 1b), refers to the bricklayer's work, oak stiffening, and what could be described as plaster of lime. The type of brick used varied, for the shipwright or contractor would have had to rely on local businesses to supply materials. Generally the firehearth was constructed with a platform on which the cooking cauldrons were placed. The lower part of the smoke stack was also of brick, with an iron flue fitted above, passing up to the forecastle. Oak stiffeners are also mentioned. These, I assume, were fitted vertically at each corner of the brickwork, to brace the whole structure. The brickwork was often further braced with iron strapping, probably about 1½in wide and ¼in thick. This strapping was worked intercostally between the oak stiffeners. Iron strapping was also likely to have been worked vertically, forming a lattice work. Thus the brickwork was prevented from working loose. One other factor that does seem a little obscure is the reference to 'plaster of lime'. It is not known precisely how this was applied but it can be assumed that it was used as a form of 'lagging' or 'cladding', to reduce radiated heat, thereby reducing the risk of fire.

Design of the brick firehearth varied over the years. The various styles are shown in Fig 5/27. Around 1750 the iron firehearth or stove was introduced, and was to become popular. After this date the use of brick firehearths declined. In 1781 the Brodie stove was introduced, and revolutionised the design of iron stoves. Subsequently this type became the general pattern for naval ships. The Brodie stove itself varied in design according to the vessel on which it was fitted. A fine example can be seen on the *Victory* in the form of a wooden replica, though some of the special features of the design have been omitted. These features are clearly shown in Fig 5/29. In 1811 an improved stove under the patent of Lamb and Nicholson was introduced. This was similar to the iron stoves that were common for domestic use as late as the 1940s.

The construction of iron stoves was relatively simple, and consisted of iron plates and lengths of iron stiffening. The iron plates were bolted to heavier vertical stiffeners, set at each corner. Further bracing of the whole structure was achieved by a series of intercostal stiffeners, work both internally and externally. These were set in the horizontal, perpendicular and diagonal planes. The whole assembly was fastened together with bolts. The stove consisted of three parts: the firehearth, the boiler and the oven. The firehearth was set at either the fore or after end, the latter being most common. It had suitable grate bars, to prevent the coals falling out. Usually an iron catch or 'ash' tray was put nearby as an added precaution, and to facilitate ash removal when the fire was extinguished. The heat generally passed directly up the flue, but on the larger of the Brodie stoves an ingenious system for driving the spit was incorporated. This made use of an impeller or fan, fitted in the uptakes and geared to a horizontal spindle. This passed outside the flue and was fitted with a wheel at the end, designed to drive two chains. Each spit (if two were employed) was furnished with wheels, with a chain drive connected to that of the spindle above. The spits were rotated by the hot flue gases turning the impeller. They were mounted on an adjustable rack, which could be moved towards or away from the heat source.

Usually two boilers were incorporated in the design, either of the same or differing capacities. Those fitted on the *Victory* are of 250 and 150 gallons capacity. Each was covered with a lid, and drain cocks on the underside. Another feature was the distiller. This consisted of an open ended stub pipe, protruding from the top of each boiler, into which was connected the inlet pipe of a simple form of distiller. Distillers are discussed separately in another section. The stub pipes were furnished with caps, which were fitted when not in use.

Beneath the boiler, and adjacent to the heat source, were two ovens, each of which had a door on either side. The capacity of each varied according to the overall size of the stove. Those of the *Victory* had baking room to produce 80lbs of bread.

Within the confines of the firehearth, two pot holders were usually fitted. These were made in the form of hinged bars set horizontally, and fixed to the side of the hearth. The upper surface was fashioned with a series of scallops, into which the handles of the pots were set, the bar being swung over the heat as required. At each top corner of the stove were iron rings, which were used for lifting the stove when it was installed. The surrounds were generally furnished with iron rails, on which utensils could be hung.

One unusual fitting, probably only used as an experiment, was that which can be seen on a drawing of *Sovereign*'s hearth (See Fig 5/29). This has a facility to ventilate the deck below, using the convection currents set up by the flue gases. This was achieved by means of a vent pipe, passing up from the deck below to the flue. The convection of heat up the flue caused a venturi effect on the vent pipe, drawing air with it from the deck below (see Fig 5/29). It is not known whether this was a standard means of ventilation but during this period there were many experiments aimed at reducing the humid conditions of the lower decks.

The Area Around the Galley

Generally the area around the firehearth was either fully or partly enclosed in a similar manner to the arrangements for temporary bulkheads. A series of portable panels were located in bearers at the deck and deckhead, with some vertical stiffeners. Within these confines, suitable working surfaces were fitted for the use of the

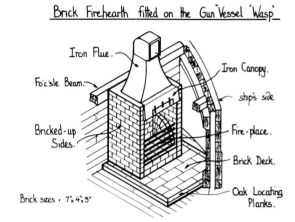

Galley Firehearths Late 18th Century.

Brick Firehearth fitted on the Gun Vessel 'Wasp'

Iron Flue. Iron Canopy. Fo'c'sle Beam. ship's side. Bricked-up Sides. Fire-place. Brick Deck. Oak Locating Planks. Brick sizes · 7"x 4"x 3"

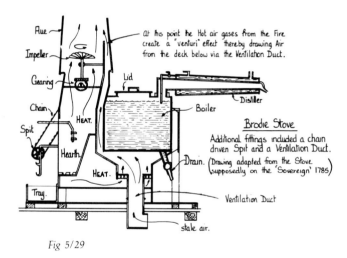

Flue. Impeller. Gearing. Chain. Spit. HEAT. Hearth. HEAT. Tray. Lid. Boiler. Distiller. Drain.

At this point the Hot air gases from the Fire create a "venturi" effect thereby drawing Air from the deck below via the Ventilation Duct.

Brodie Stove

Additional fittings included a chain driven Spit and a Ventilation Duct. (Drawing adapted from the Stove supposedly on the 'Sovereign' 1785)

Ventilation Duct

stale air.

Fig 5/29

cook. The common type of partial enclosure can today be seen on the *Victory*.

Throughout the whole of the period the deck on which the firehearth was placed was usually lined with brick as a further precaution against fire. Again we cannot be too sure on the details of this brickwork, for it was most likely of local origin. Due to the additional weight of the firehearth or stove and the brick, additional carlings and pillars were placed below to give support. The only difference in the carlings was that they were usually deeper in scantling, and instead of being worked between the beams, were fitted below and scored on their upper face to fit into the beams.

The Cowlings

The upper end of the flue on the forecastle varied in design, ranging from a single conical shape to an angle head with a cover plate. Some were of square section, tapering towards the top. The later types, with the angled head (which can be seen on the *Victory*), could be rotated to prevent the wind driving the smoke back down the flue. Another improvement was the adoption of a flat cover plate, that could be adjusted by simply sliding it back and forth on the two locating rods. I have often wondered if this facility was used in relation to the impeller fitted within the flue for turning the spit. It would seem that any adjustment made to the cover plate would alter the flow of hot flue gases, thereby increasing or decreasing the speed of the impeller and effecting the rate of rotation of the spit.

THE DISTILLERS

One of the main factors affecting the well-being of the ship's crew was the lack of fresh water. Most of the water was contained in barrels filled from rivers before embarking on a voyage. One of the foremost roles of the Navy during this period was blockading enemy ports, which required ships to spend long periods at sea without entering port. The water very soon went bad, and it was supplemented with beer, spirits and wine, the allowances of which were considerable by today's standards.

The idea of producing fresh water at sea is not new, and the first signs of this can be traced back to 1684 when the first seagoing distiller was filled experimentally. There are few details of this distiller and the way it worked, but it can be assumed that it was very simple in form.

Evidence of this experiment was found in the following letter, forwarded to the captain of the vessel on which the trial took place.

Charles R.

Whereas a Proposal has been made to Us of an Engine to be fixed in one of Our Ships for the making an Experiment of producing Fresh Water (At Sea) out of Salt. Our will and Pleasure is, That, upon application to you by ye Persons concerned in ye said Engine doe receive ye same on Board and cause it (at their Charge) to be fixed in some convenient place in Our Ship, in Order to youre making ye said Experiment in ye present Voyage and Reporting to Us yor Observations upon it, for Satisfaction, upon your Returne: Provided that you be first satisfyed that ye same may be put up and made without any sort of danger to Our Ship by Fire or otherwise For w'ch this shal bee your Warrant Given at Our Court at Windsor this third day of August 1684.

To Captaine William Gifford.
   Command'r of Our Ship the
      Mermaid.   By his Majesty's Command.
                                         S. Pepys

It would appear from the above that the distilling engine was a self-contained unit fitted above a heat source. Condensing of the steam take-off from boiling sea water was likely to have been obtained by passing the condensate through a coiled pipe cooled by air. Otherwise some form of cold water cooling jacket could have

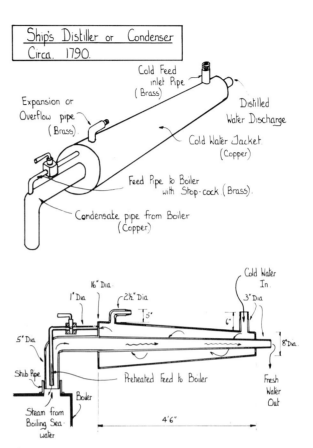

Fig 5/30

been employed. The distilling apparatus used towards the end of the eighteenth century was of an even simpler form. The actual output was probably meagre, and often the surgeon was given most of the water produced.

The distiller or 'condenser' installed on the *Victory* consisted of a single copper pipe, with one end connected to the boiler of the Brodie stove. Surrounding this pipe was a tapered cooling jacket. The taper allowed for the expansion of the cooling water as it absorbed the latent heat from the steam from the boiling sea water. At one end of the jacket was an inlet pipe which emitted cold sea water. At the other end there were two connections. One of these was used primarily as an overflow for expansion. The other, smaller, pipe passed into the boiler, thereby allowing the pre-heated water to pass via a stopcock. This simple means of pre-heating was an early form of ensuring efficency but the overall gain must have been negligible. Details of a typical distiller are given in Fig 5/30. The dimensions may have varied from one distiller to another, but the principles remain the same. All of the fittings were made in copper or brass. The cold water fill arrangements are a mystery, but it can be assumed that some form of leather hose with a brass screw connection was employed. Whether a continuous feed arrangement was also used is still not known, as some form of tank would have been needed, situated above the distiller, operated by gravity.

Foudroyant. *Gundeck showing the mainmast partners with the main topsail and jeer bitts. An iron cable lifter and the cable scuttle to the cable tier are in the foreground.*

CHAPTER 6

Internal Fittings

The Position and Rake of the Masts

When a naval vessel was designed and constructed it was of the utmost importance that the masts were placed at specific points along the length of the vessel. These positions helped to determine the best sailing qualities for men-of-war, and had been perfected over many years. By 1650 most positioning had become standardised and from this date, apart from some small modifications, the positions remained unchanged until the end of the era of the sailing navy. The desired rake (angle the masts were inclined aft) had also been developed to a specification which produced the maximum performance of each individual sail in drawing, dispelling or spilling the wind. On the whole a more pronounced rake was found on such vessels as cutters and schooners, which had one or two masts, whereas ship-rigged vessels had different degrees of rake on each mast. Although documents of the period show rules for each mast, it was not unusual for a seasoned master to adjust the rake to his own requirements, to gain a little advantage in speed and manoeuvrability.

The builder therefore had to consider both the standard rules and the wishes of the master when placing the mast steps and the partners at each deck level. He would also be required to calculate the positions for the channels, to ensure that the masts were well stayed by the shrouds. Each mast was given a specific position at the level of the lower deck.

MAST POSITIONING 1650–1700

The Foremast

On most vessels the foremast was positioned on the lower deck, approximately three thirty-seconds of the length of the lower gundeck abaft the fore perpendicular. This is only an average, as details for this period are a little sparse. The apparent change in the position of this mast was due, in fact, to alterations made to the stem. The rake of the stem was reduced over a number of years, by extending the fore end of the keel forward which made it appear that the foremost had been moved considerably.

On most vessels built prior to 1665 the mast was placed about two-thirds of the distance between the fore perpendicular and the fore end of the keel, in front of the keel. From 1665 until 1700–10 it was positioned about half of the distance between the fore perpendicular and the fore end of the keel, in front of the keel.

The Mainmast

The position of this mast leads to some controversy, for the works of this period show many schools of thought. On inspection of draughts, I have found many minor variations. On average the mainmast was placed on the gundeck seventeen thirty-seconds of the length between the fore and aft perpendicular. Again evidence shows varying ideas from different builders. On Deane's ships the mast is placed at the middle of the length of the gundeck, or a little aft of this. Elsewhere it is stated that it should be placed exactly 3ft forward of the middle of the length of the keel.*

The Mizzen Mast

The positioning of this mast varies considerably. R C Anderson in *Seventeenth Century Rigging* gives positions based on visual

---

*The finer points of sailing, and the discussion of the mainmast as a 'pivot' on ship-rigged three-masted vessels are given in Darcy Lever's *Young Officer's Sheet Anchor*, 1819.

inspection of contemporary models in the National Maritime Museum and other sources. He states that the mizzen should be between a third and half the distance between taffrail and the mainmast. This, although reasonably accurate, appears to rely purely on the construction of the ship, and does not take into account the aspects of sailing itself. It is important to consider the distance between the masts. If two masts were placed too close together, the sails of the aftermost mast could starve the sails of the other mast of wind. This of course would reduce the sailing qualities of the vessel. On the other hand, if the distance between the main and the mizzen mast was too great, the advantage of using the mainmast as a pivot would be lost. This could result in the vessel trying to 'crab' to leeward. With these two aspects in mind, a compromise was reached. During this period the mizzen mast was placed on the level of the lower gundeck, nine thirty-seconds of the length between the fore and after perpendicular abaft the mainmast.

MAST POSITIONING 1700–1750

These years were a transition period. The Establishments maintained set dimensions for all classes of vessels, and also regulated the position for each mast, proportional to the ship's length. Until about 1720 the mast positions were not dissimilar to those prior to 1700, although the new rules were also being put into practice. For example, it is stated that the mainmast of ships built after 1725 were to be placed one twenty-fifth of the length of the lower gundeck abaft the mid point of that deck. This can be calculated using the following formula.

Mast position = (gundeck length/2) + (gundeck length/25)

This is taken from the after side of the stempost.

Towards 1750 the positions become more standard and are given below.

The Foremast

For all classes of vessel with over 24 guns the foremast was positioned seven sixty-fourths of the length of the gundeck abaft the fore perpendicular. For vessels with 24 guns or less the distance was approximately one-eighth.

The Mainmast

On ships of 110, 100, 90, 84, 80, 74, 70, 64, 60, 36, 32, 28 and 24 guns the mainmast was positioned nine-sixteenths of the length of the gundeck abaft the fore perpendicular. On vessels of between 50 and 40 guns the proportion is thirty-five sixty-fourths, and on 38- and 20-gun ships and sloops, nineteen thirty-seconds.

The Mizzen Mast

On all ships of 110 to 38 guns, the position on the level of the gundeck was as follows: five thirty-seconds of the length of the gundeck *afore* the after perpendicular. This also applies to sloops. On the remaining vessels the distance was nine sixty-fourths.

MAST POSITIONING 1750–1800

In some written sources the position of the centre of each mast at the lower deck is given as follows: the foremast placed one-ninth of the length of the deck abaft the fore perpendicular; the mainmast five-ninths of the length of the deck abaft the fore perpendicular; the mizzen mast one-seventh of the length of the gundeck afore the after perpendicular. However, the actual position of the masts did differ from the theoretical measurements as the list below shows.

The Foremast

For all vessels, except 74- and 70-gun ships and sloops, this mast was one-ninth of the length of the lower gundeck abaft the fore perpendicular. For the 74- and 70-gun ships this distance was one-eighth, while on sloops approximately one-sixth.

The Mainmast

On ships of 100, 90, 64 and 60 guns the mainmast was placed five-ninths of the length of the lower gundeck abaft the fore perpendicular, while for those of 84, 80, 74, 70 and 38 guns it was seven-twelfths. On remaining ship-rigged vessels, of 50, 44, 36, 32, 28 and 24 guns, the distance was approximately nine-sixteenths. The figures for the 20-gun ship and the sloop was three-fifths, and for a cutter three-eighths.

The Mizzen Mast

On vessels of 100, 50 and 44 guns, the mizzen mast was positioned approximately one-sixth of the length of the lower gundeck abaft the fore perpendicular and one-seventh for ships of 90, 84, 80, 74, 70, 64, 60, 38 and 36 guns; for ships of 32, 28 and 24 guns three-twentieths, while for sloops and some 20 gun ships two-thirteenths.

Most of the above figures allow for a maximum error of about 4in. Some may argue that in some cases my calculations appear a little too specific, when considering the actual difference in some of the fractions. For instance the difference between five-ninths and nine-sixteenths is as little as one thirty-sixth, which at first seems negligible. If however, one relates this fraction to a ship's gundeck length, of for instance 186ft, the total error produced is 5ft 2½in. This margin would have had some effect on the sailing qualities of the vessel concerned.

THE RAKE OF THE MASTS

Having determined the position for each mast, it was important for the designer and constructor to know the required rake for each to enable them to position the partners at each deck, and to ensure that the correct angle was achieved. It was also necessary to fix the exact position for the mast step along the fore and aft axis. As we have seen, in most cases the mast position was given at the level of the lower gundeck. Below this point, the heel of the mast was often set a little further forward due to the rake.

The mast of a First Rate ship extended approximately 21ft below the gundeck. If the rake of the mast was 1⅛in per yard, then the difference in position between the gundeck and the step would have been 7⅞in. On first sight this may seem negligible, but in some places about 41ft of mast passed through all of the decks. This would have given an overall movement along the fore and aft axis of 15in, 7½in forward below the gundeck, and 7½in aft at the quarterdeck. Generally the rake of the mizzen mast was greater than this. Therefore the difference in position was greater. The angle of rake was always measured off against the horizontal of the keel.

Mast Rake 1650–1720

There are no precise figures for mast rake during this period. Contemporary models are not very reliable, due to the masts warping through age, and the possible misalignment caused by overtaut rigging. Deane's draughts provide various angles of rake. Generally the foremast and mainmast were set at 90 degrees to the keel, though in some cases they inclined aft at an angle of about 1 degree. This angle would give a rake of ¾in per yard. The mizzen masts of these vessels varied from 4 to 5 degrees, giving a rake of between 2⅝ and 3⅛in in the yard.

Mast Rake 1720–1750

During this period the masts appear to take a more uniform aspect. The foremast was set vertical, while the mainmast was inclined further aft at about 2 degrees, or 1 to 1¼in in every yard. The angle of the mizzen was reduced, to approximately 2¾ degrees or 1⅞in in the yard. The angles of the masts of smaller vessels were made slightly greater, to improve sailing qualities.

Mast Rake 1750–1830

By this time, mast rake was included in the lists of principal dimensions laid down by the Navy Board, and therefore it is easier to differentiate between sizes and types of vessel.

The Rake of the Masts (1750–1830)

No of guns	incline per yard (inches)	Angle, degrees (1750–1850)
FOREMAST		
110–44	⅛	¼
38–24	1/10	⅛
20	⅞	1½
sloops and brigs	⅞	1½
MAINMAST		
110 and 100	1⅛	1⅞
90–60	1	1¾
50–40	⅞	1½
38–24	⅝	¾
sloops and brigs	¾	1
cutters	1½	2¼
MIZZEN MAST		
110 and 100	1⅝	2½
90–80	1½	2¼
74–70	1⅝	2½
64–60	1½	2¼
50–40	1¼	2
38–24	1	1¾
sloops and ketches	1⅛	1⅞

The Position and Rake of the Bowsprit

THE POSITION OF THE BOWSPRIT

The precise position of the bowsprit could not be calculated in a similar manner to the other masts, which were almost vertical. The following factors had to be considered: the height of the stem head, the manner in which the mast was stepped and the angle at which it was 'steeved'. The height of the stem head can be considered as part of the ship's main construction, so this can be regarded as the fixed criterion. It served as a support to the bowsprit.

Next to be accounted for was the manner in which the mast was stepped. Throughout most of the seventeenth century the bowsprit was placed to the starboard side of the foremast and stem head. In this case it would be passed through the respective deck and the beakhead bulkhead to one side of the centreline. The heel of the bowsprit was fashioned to fay flat upon the deck adjacent to the foremast, or a little aft of it. The hawse pieces on the starboard side of the stempost may have been lengthened to give support to the mast at this point (see Fig 6/1).

Over the years a transition was made, and the bowsprit was brought directly on the centreline. This was probably introduced to the smaller vessels first, and by 1677 was common on larger ships. I presume this change was made because, firstly, the weight of this mast and the force of the wind on the various sails set on it, would no doubt have had an effect upon the timbers which supported that side of the hull. Secondly, having the mast stepped to one side of the foremast must have limited the space available for working the guns, and impeded their recoil. It is not known exactly when the

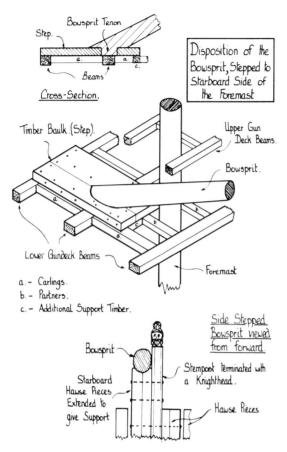

Fig 6/1

Victory. Looking forward and upward at the partners of the bowsprit. The fore and aft partners and cross partners are clearly visible with the incorporated angle chocks. The shoring is temporary.

change was complete. Even the draughts by Deane do not clarify this matter entirely. Examples of the 'off-set' bowsprit can be found on the models of the *St Michael* (1669) and the *Prince* (1670) built by Tippets and Pett respectively.

Another factor that must be considered is the point where the mast passed into the hull. This depended on both the construction of the ship and the angle to which the mast was 'steeved'. Some of the larger men-of-war, built prior to 1676, had a deep beakhead bulkhead, the height of which varied between one and a half and two decks. To the fore side of this bulkhead was a platform known as the prow deck. This was built at the same level as the middle gundeck, or approximately 2ft above it. The advantage of the deep beakhead bulkhead was that it could be pierced with gunports for chase guns. The bowsprit either passed through this deck, a little forward of the bulkhead, or through the bulkhead. This depended entirely on the height at which the prow deck was built in relation to the bulkhead. After 1676, the prow deck was always raised to the height of the upper gundeck, thus the general appearance altered with the bowsprit now passing through this deck only.

The position where the bowsprit entered the ship was again altered during the eighteenth century, for the prow deck was raised about 2ft above the level of the upper deck. This alteration was carried out on the *Victory*.

THE STEEVE OF THE BOWSPRIT

The angle or steeve of the bowsprit varied considerably between 1650 and 1850 and it differed according to the type of vessel. Between 1650 and 1700 the angle was about 30 degrees to the horizontal of the keel. In some cases this angle was less. On draughts by Deane, I have found variants of 27, 28½, 29 and 30 degrees. These angles were probably influenced by the manner in

The Steeve of the Bowsprit

Date	No of guns	Angle to the keel	Vessel
1670	70	29	
1670	70	28	
1670	60	27	
1670	40	28	
1670	16	25	
1670	100	36	Prince
1701	96	36	St George
1719	80	36	
1719	60	32	
1732	64	36	Centurion
1734	22	36	Tarter
1737	100	35	Victory
1765	100	30	Victory
1781	74	24	
1781	64	30	Agamemnon
1795	74	26	
1796	38	20	
1798	40	21	
1800	80	26	
1805	36	28	
1815	84	32	
1817	46	18	Foudroyant
1824	46	19	Unicorn
1840	50	25	
1842	90	30	Albion
1846	50	24½	Constance

which the bowsprit was stepped, the height of the stem head, and the general disposition of various parts of the construction in this vicinity.

By 1700, the angle of the bowsprit appears to have been increased. This was due to the abandonment of the spritsail topsail and possibly the relationship between the position at which the mast was stepped and the stem head. To understand this we must return to the factors discussed in the previous section. By 1680 the head of the ship was reduced in length, and its angle increased. Therefore the distance between the foremast and the stem head was reduced. By this date the bowsprit was stepped on the centreline a little afore the foremast. Therefore to clear the now raised head (including the figurehead) the angle had to be increased. The steeve of the *St George* (1701) was approximately 36 degrees. This angle became common in most of the larger vessels for the next 45 years, after which it tended to be reduced to the original 30 degrees. The angle for the smaller vessels varied considerably, between 20 and 28 degrees. As in all cases, the steeve was dependent on the size and type of vessel. The table above shows how inconsistent these angles were between 1650 and 1850.

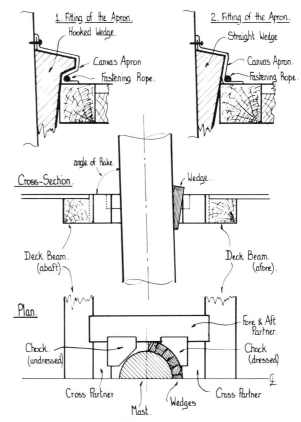

The Partners of the Masts.

NB:- When the Chock was initially fitted its angled face remained undressed. After the mast had been stepped the angled face of the Chock was then dressed to make its surface concentric to the circumference of the mast. Once this was complete, fitted wedges were then driven into the annular space between the mast and the Chocks.

Fig 6/2

The Masts' Partners

The partners were the constructions at deck level, through which each mast passed, and which supported the mast. The partners were made by fitting carlings of increased scantling, baulks of timber, and wedges. The space between the beams at these positions was often referred to as the mast room. The disposition of the carlings in the athwartships direction was governed by the diameter of the mast itself. To this was added a further 10 to 12in, for the fitting of wedges around the periphery of the mast.

With the above criteria in mind, it is essential that the diameter of each mast be evaluated. This determined the distance that the carlings were set apart. The information was also required for placing the timber baulks fore and aft of the mast, these being fayed and bolted to the adjacent beams. The diameter of a mast was proportional to its overall length; likewise its length was indirectly proportional to the size of the ship to which it fitted. The mainmast was proportional to the size of the vessel, whereas the other masts, the foremast, mizzen and bowsprit were proportional to the mainmast.

THE MAST DIAMETERS

The factors for calculating mast diameters varied between 1650 and 1850, and each must be considered when determining the width between the carlings of the partners. The rule alterations were as follows:

The Mainmast

where M = length of mast in feet; D = diameter of the mast in inches; K = keel length; W = extreme breadth of ship in feet; Y = depth of ship in feet; G = length of gundeck in feet, taken between the rabbet of the stem and the rabbet of the sternpost.

then:

1650
$$M = W \times 2{\cdot}4$$
$$D = M/3$$

1670
for ships exceeding 27ft in breadth (W)
$$M = 3[(K + W + (W/2)/5) - (W/3 - 27/3)]$$
$$D = M/3 \times {}^{15}\!/_{16}$$

for ships less than 27ft in breadth (W)
$$M = 3[(K + W + (W/2)/5) + (27/3 - W/3)]$$
$$D = M/3 \times {}^{15}\!/_{16}$$

1711
$$M = (G + W)/2$$
$$D = M/3 \times {}^{15}\!/_{16})$$

1719
$$M = (G + W)/\alpha$$

where α in: First, Second and Third Rates of 80 guns = 2·28; Third Rate of 70 guns = 2·32; Fourth Rate of 60 guns = 2·34; Fourth Rate of 50 guns = 2·36; Fifth Rate of 40 guns = 2·38; Fifth Rate of 32 guns = 2·40; Sixth Rate of 20 guns = 2·42.

$$D = M/3 \times {}^{15}\!/_{16}$$

1745
$$M = (G + W)/\beta$$

where β in: First Rates = 2·24; Second Rates = 2·26; Third Rates = 2·27; Fourth and Fifth Rates = 2·22; Sixth Rates = 2·28.

$$D = M/3 \times {}^{15}\!/_{16}$$

1773
$$M = (G + W)/2{\cdot}23$$
$$D = M \times {}^{9}\!/_{10}$$

1794
$$M = (G \times W)/2$$
$$D = M/3$$

The Foremast

The length and therefore the diameter of the foremast was proportional to the mainmast. The length of the mainmast can be calculated by multiplying the factor in brackets by the length of the foremast. Year (factor) – 1650 (0·87); 1670 (0·90); 1711 (0·90); 1719 (0·90); 1745 (0·90); 1773 (0·93); 1780 (0·90); 1794 (0·90).

The Mizzen Mast

Like the foremast, the mizzen mast was proportional to the mainmast. In some cases the mizzen mast was stepped on the lowest gundeck. All the calculations that determine the length of the mizzen are taken from the point where the mast was stepped upon the keelson. It is also from this point that the diameter of the mast was formulated, not from the length taken from the gundeck. The height of this mast from the gundeck is calculated by deducting the height of the hold and orlop from the predetermined length. From 26 January 1807 it was ordered that the mizzen be stepped on the gundeck instead of on the keelson. The factor to give the length of the mizzen mast in relation to that of the mainmast is:

1650	0·74
1670	0·67
1711 and 1745	0·86
1719	0·85 except in the Sixth Rate, when the factor is 0·80
1773	0·84
1794	0·85
1815	First Rate: 0·87; Second and Third Rates: 0·86; Fourth Rate and below: 0·83
1836	as for 1815 except for sloops when the factor is 0·75.

The diameter of the mizzen mast in inches is one-third of the length of the mast divided by 12, and the result multiplied by the appropriate factor:

1650	1
1670	0·94
1711 and 1732	0·66
1719 and 1745	First, Second, Third and Fourth Rates: 0·68; Fifth Rate 0·67; Sixth Rate: 0·62
1749, 1815 and 1836	First, Second and Third Rates: 0·6; Third Rate and below: 0·67

FITTING THE PARTNERS

Having calculated the diameter of each mast, their relation to the positions of the carlings or partners can be understood. The inner faces of the carlings were set a specific distance from the centreline. This distance was equal to half the diameter of the mast, plus 4 or

5in (for one side only). In general the breadth of these timbers was half the diameter of the mast but their depth varied. For all vessels of 40 guns and above, the depth was usually 1in greater than the breadth. On ships of 38 guns and below, the depth was generally 1 to 1½in less than its breadth. For specific regulations for different periods see opposite.

The way in which the fore and aft partners were set varied between 1650 and 1850. In some cases the upper edge of the partner was set level with the upper surface of the adjacent deck beams. Later, the lower edge of the partner projected below the beams. The more common practice was to set the partners with their upper surface raised above the upper edge of the beams. When this was done, the desired height was three-sevenths of the depth of the partner, on ships of 80 guns, and approximately half the depth for other classes. The length of the partner fore and aft was the distance between the centres of the deck beams adjacent to the mast. Each end was secured with two bolts of approximately 1in diameter, driven from above and clenched on the underside of the beam. Fitted athwartships between the partners were the cross partners. These baulks of timber were fayed and bolted to the inner faces of the deck beams, and were about 1in diameter. The depth of the cross partners was the same as that of the fore and aft partners, but their width was more variable. Their exact width was determined by the disposition of the deck beams, leaving a space of 4 to 5in clear of the mast.

The area around the mast was octagonal, due to the addition of the angle chocks. These were triangular, and made from oak. Each was set into rabbets cut in the faces of the fore and aft partners and cross partners. The depth of these rabbets was approximately half the depth of the angle chocks. When these were first fitted they were made a little oversize and were then rounded out to the finished diameter, equal to that of the mast plus about 10 or 12in.

Once the mast was in position, the 4 or 5in annular space remaining was fitted with wedges of oak, ash or elm. These wedges were driven in from above to secure the mast in position, and were set around the entire periphery. Special care had to be taken in fitting these wedges, and some had to be 'tailor made', especially at the fore and after sides of the mast, for the rake of the mast had to be taken into consideration. Their design varied, and was either of the normal plain shape or fashioned with a hook at the top.

On completion it was often the practice to fit a canvas 'apron', which was nailed, or more generally secured with rope, to the mast, and pulled in at the bottom with a second rope. If the wedges were of the hooked type, the rope that secured the lower part of the apron was pulled in under the hooks. The function of the apron was to ensure watertightness, the canvas usually being coated with tar. The lower part could easily be removed for inspection. This was very important after a ship had been through heavy weather, for it was these conditions that tended to work the masts out of the ship. Thus it would be necessary to tighten up the wedges. This was also done when the ship had been sailing for a prolonged period on a single tack, when the mast would strain in the same direction. (See Fig 6/2).

The rules for calculating the scantlings of the partners fitted at the gundeck or lower gundeck are as follows:

1700–1770

The width of the partner was half the diameter of the mast which it supported, whereas the depth was more variable. The depth of the carling for vessels of 40 guns and above was about 1in greater than its width. On ships of 38 guns and less, the depth was approximately 1–1½in less than width.

1770–1830

On draughts of this period the size of the partners vary somewhat and tend to be proportional to the adjacent beams, instead of the mast sizes. It also appears that variations were made for each mast. This is indicated by the scantlings laid down in the 1789 edition of the *Shipbuilder's Respository*. From these figures I have produced the following approximate dimensions.

The partners of the mainmast:
  Width = 2in greater than the adjacent beam width
  Depth = 3in greater than the adjacent beam depth

It can also be stated that the depth was 1in greater than the width.

The partners of the foremast:
  Width = 1in greater than the adjacent beam width
  Depth = Approximately 3⅝in less than the beam depth.

Stepping the Mast and Bowsprit

THE MAST STEPS

In general the step for each mast consisted of a large baulk of timber, usually oak, fashioned in such a manner that it straddled the keelson. A mortice was cut vertically into its upper surface, in which the tenon at the heel of the mast sat. Both the mortice and the tenon were proportional to the diameter of the mast. The mortice and tenon were always made to the following dimensions: the tenon at the heel of the mast was half the diameter of the mast in the fore and aft plane, and had a width two-thirds of the diameter of the mast athwartships. The depth of the tenon was usually about half the diameter of the mast. It was a general practice to cut it slightly smaller, to allow for shrinkage of the wood.

The manner in which each mast was stepped varied according to both the period and to the disposition of the breast hooks and crutches. The mainmast was always stepped on a block of timber set over the keelson, whereas the foremast and the mizzen mast steps were constructed in conjunction with the existing breast hooks and crutches. Alternatively, the step for the mizzen mast was placed on

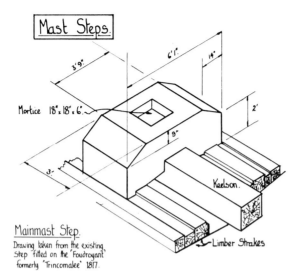

Mast Steps.

Mortice 18" x 18" x 6".

Keelson.

Limber Strakes

Mainmast Step.
Drawing taken from the existing
Step fitted on the 'Foudroyant'
formerly 'Trincomalee' 1817.

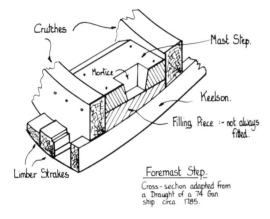

Crutches

Mast Step.

Mortice

Keelson.

Filling Piece :- not always
fitted.

Limber Strakes

Foremast Step.
Cross-section adapted from
a Draught of a 74 Gun
ship circa 1785.

Fig 6/3

The Foremast Step

The foremast step consisted of a baulk of timber fitted between two breast hooks, or crutches. Another method was used on vessels of 36 guns and less in which a single crutch was employed, which either acted as the step itself or as an after support for the step.

The overall length of the crutches varied from 11 to 12ft on ships of between 110 and 40 guns, and 8 to 10ft 6in on Fifth and Sixth Rates. The fore and aft sidings of the crutches were as follows; Ship, number of guns (siding in inches) – 100 (11); 90 (10½); 74 (10½); 64 (12); 44 (10); 38 (10); 36 (23); 32 (23); 28 (21); 24 (20); sloop (18). From these figures, it can be seen that the crutches of the lesser rates were fairly wide. From this, it can be assumed that the crutch served as the step.

On ships where two crutches were used, a suitable block of timber, similar to that for the mainmast, was fitted between them. Its dimensions varied very little from that of the block for the mainmast, except that its fore and aft siding was equal to the space between the crutches, which was approximately as follows: Ship, number of guns (space between the crutches in inches) 100 (3ft 9in); 90 (4ft); 74 (3ft); 64 (3ft); 44 (1ft 11in); 38 (2ft). The step was bolted with eight or six bolts of 1in diameter. (For details see Fig 6/3.)

The Mizzen Mast Step

Details of this fitting are scarce, but it appears that the step was formed by one of the crutches, fitted at the after end of the hold. The foremost crutch was used for the step and a mortice related to the dimensions of the mizzen cut in the upper surface. The fore and aft siding and depth and length of the crutch corresponded to those fitted nearby.

The Mizzen Mast Step Upon the Lower Gundeck

Until 1807 it was common practice to have the mizzen mast stepped upon the keelson. However, there were a few exceptions to the rules mostly in smaller craft and vessels built in the seventeenth century. In these the masts were generally of relatively low weight. The *Boyne* of 1693 had her mizzen stepped on her upper gundeck but this was unusual. The reason behind the Navy Board order of 1807 was that there was no real need to have this mast made to such a length that it extended to the keelson. If the mast was stepped higher this would not only reduce the weight of the mast, but also allowed more room for stores etc below the deck. Vessels with a single gundeck often had the mizzen mast stepped upon the berthing deck.

The step itself comprised a baulk of oak made to a length that would span three deck beams below the position of the mast. In a 74-gun ship the timber would be approximately 11ft long, 20in broad and 16in wide. The whole structure was lowered into the beams below, to a depth of 2 to 3in, and secured with clench bolts

the level of the lower gundeck, or berthing deck. This practice became general after 26 January 1807. In this case the design incorporated additional support members fitted beneath the step. It is discussed separately later.

The Mainmast Step

The fore and aft siding of the step was usually approximately twice the width of the keelson, less 1in. The overall length athwartships was such that the step could slide clear of the stanchions of the well. The depth of the step was quite considerable, in some cases as much as 2ft 6in. The overall depth was the height between the upper face of the footwaling and limber strake and the upper face of the keelson, plus sufficient height to form a suitable mortice for the heel of the mast. This can be taken as equal to the depth of the keelson, minus 2in. The size of the mortice itself has already been discussed. (See Fig 6/3).

and trennals. A mortice was cut for the mast stepping, into which the heel was received. The rules governing the size of the mortice were as follows: the size (fore and aft) was half the diameter of the mast, while in the athwartships direction it was one-third of the diameter. In all cases the step would be positioned one-seventh of the length of the gundeck from the rabbet of the sternpost. Thus in a 74-gun ship with a gundeck length of 182ft, the step would be set 26ft forward of the sternpost. The shipwright would in all cases dispose of the gundeck beams in a manner that would allow one beam to be set directly below the mizzen mast, to give maximum support.

To give additional support, an extra carling was fitted below the beams that supported the step. This carling was made with increased scantling, and was further supported by stout square pillars, the heels of which were set down onto the orlop deck beams. In ships that were too small to have an orlop deck, the mast step itself would be fitted on the berthing deck and the carling with its pillars fitted below, their heels set down onto the keelson.

The carling would be made between 12 and 14in deep, and 10 to 12in wide. Its length was measured from the fore side of the first beam forward of the mast to the sternson knee. The upper surface was scored to a depth of 6in at intervals, to receive the beams above. The after end was secured to the sternson knee by two iron plates, fitted on each side and fastened with clench bolts passing from one plate to the other. This fitting may have varied according to the builder, with either wrought iron strapping or specially designed brackets.

The supporting pillars varied in length, depending on their disposition, but they were always made of square-sectioned oak, tapering from 9in at their heads to 12in at the heels. Three pillars were generally employed, one set immediately below the step, and

Unicorn. *The compartment on board which also served as the bread room. This photograph illustrates the mizzen mast step and support pillars, the after part of the keelson, the cant frames, two bands of thick stuff, an iron crutch, and diagonal iron rider plate.*

Fig 6/4

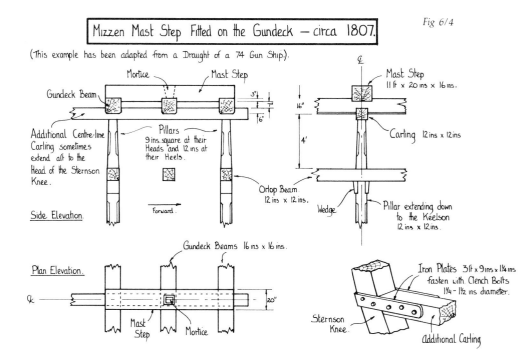

173

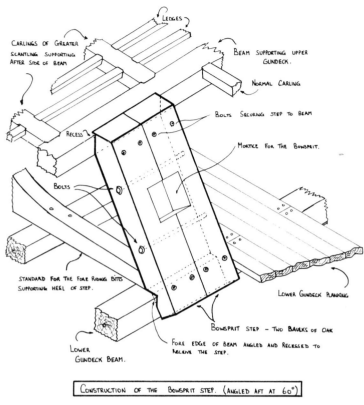

Fig 6/5

Unicorn. *The fore end of the gundeck showing the step for the bowsprit and on the right, two iron sleeved hawse holes with their plugs. The vertical structure to the fore side of the step is believed to have been fitted for the mooring cables when the ship was laid up 'in ordinary'.*

one under each beam directly forward or aft of the step. The pillar below the step was made longer on ships that had an orlop deck, and this pillar passed through the orlop, where its heel sat down into the keelson's mortice.

On the ships with an orlop deck, the beams that supported the fore and aft pillars were further supported by stanchions, forming frames for the bulkheads that divided the hold into compartments. These stanchions were also tenoned into the keelson. Ships that did not have an orlop had the pillars set directly into the keelson.

The stanchions were fashioned in such a manner that loading was spread over a greater area. A piece of timber was removed from the outboard sides of the stanchion at its head. This was 2in thick and 18in long. Into the space left, a piece of wood 6in wide at the top and 2in wide at the bottom, and 18in long was inserted. These wedges were then fastened with iron spikes. Most of the stanchions and pillars were bearded along their lengths, except at their heads and heels.

STEPPING THE BOWSPRIT

There were various methods used for stepping the bowsprit. Some vessels were 'ship-rigged', and the steeve of the bowsprit was between 25 and 33 degrees. Ships of the smaller classes, such as cutters, schooners and brigs, had their bowsprits more or less horizontal, and stepped into a block on the upper deck. In ship-rigged vessels, the step was located according to the number of gundecks that the ship had. Ships with three gundecks had the step on the middle gundeck, whereas on those with two decks, the step was on the lower deck. The step in frigates and sloops was either on the gundeck or on the berthing deck below the gundeck.

The step was made from two baulks of oak, fayed vertically together and bolted athwartships with two bolts, and clenched. One bolt was set a little above the mortice, the other a little below. I would imagine that each piece of the mortice was cut to the size required prior to being bolted together. This would certainly have made the work a lot easier for the shipwright.

The step was set with a rake aft of approximately 60 degrees, thus giving the correct angle for the steeve of the bowsprit, which tenoned into the step at right angles. As previously mentioned, the angle of the bowsprit could vary, and the rake of the step would vary accordingly. The rake of the bowsprit can be calculated by taking 5in for every foot of the bowsprit's length.

The length of the step was taken from the upper edge of the deck beam above to the lower edge of the deck beam below. These beams were fashioned with a slope corresponding to the rake of the step on their fore side, for a width equal to that of the step. The step was secured to these beams with clench bolts, the diameter varying from 1⅜in on a 100-gun ship to ⅞in on a sloop.

Extra strength was added by fitting extra carlings to the after side of the beams adjacent to the step. Alternatively, the carlings were made with increased scantlings. Planking of greater thickness than the deck planks would sometimes be fitted aft of the heel of the step, when it was fitted on the middle gundeck. When it was sited on the lower gundeck one of two methods for increasing the rigidity of the heel were used. Either a thick plank was run forward from the toe of the fore riding bitt standard to the heel of the step or the fore riding bitt standard was extended forward of the fore mast to the heel of the step.

The Riding Bitts

These large timbers acted as a securing point for the cables which held the ship while riding at anchor. They were positioned along the centre, the fore set abaft the foremast and the after set approximately 12ft aft of the fore bitts. They were always found on the lower gundeck of two-decked ships, and on the gundeck of frigates and sloops. Both the fore and after bitts were of identical construction, except that the fore bitts had their supporting standards longer at their feet.

The strain on the bitts was considerable. Therefore, to ensure that the strain was not confined to one deck, the bitt pins extended downward to the orlop deck beams and were secured with clench bolts to the after side of these beams. As frigates and sloops did not

have an orlop, the bitt pins were secured to the berthing deck beams. Two clench bolts were used at each deck level, the diameter varying from 1¼in on larger ships to ¾in on sloops. Each bitt pin was scored at deck beam level, to receive the beam. Again the size of the pins varied (see table overleaf).

The bitt pin was tapered from the lower edge of the gundeck beam to its heel, on the after face only. The reduction was about one-third less than its thickness fore and aft at the head. I assume that this was done to reduce its weight, without reducing its strength.

The after face of the bitt pin was scored to receive the cross beam, the depth of which was about one-sixth of the width of the beam (which was equal to the depth of the beam). The height of this score was different in each size of ship, but averaged about 1ft 8in from the deck to the bottom of the beam.

The cross beam was made from a single baulk of oak, its width and depth not varying much from the bitt pins. It was attached to the bitts with iron clench bolts (on in some cases forelocks) and it was not uncommon for it to be fastened with long trennals 2½in in diameter. The beam was made longer than the span of the bitts, its extremities being given a slight bearing. Earlier vessels often had more ornate riding bitts, with heads carved on the tops of the pins

Fig 6/6

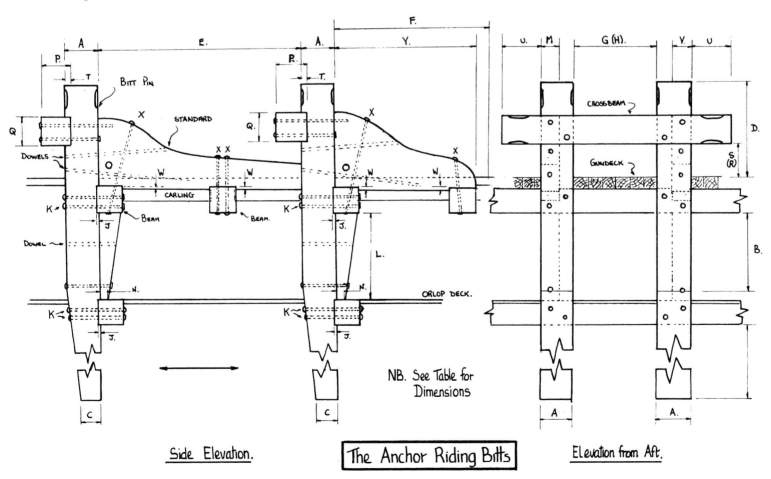

Side Elevation.   The Anchor Riding Bitts   Elevation from Aft.

and the outer ends of the cross beams shaped like a cylinder.

Each bitt pin was supported on its fore side by heavy standards, made to a thickness approximately two-thirds the width of the pins, and to a height which corresponded to the upper edge of the crossbeam. The foot of the standard was let down below the upper face of the gundeck beams. The fore riding bitts were of a smaller athwartships width, because the middle tier of carlings on that deck tended to close in towards the centreline from about this point. The after bitts had their standards running forward to butt onto the after face of the fore bitts, while the foot of the fore bitts was a little longer.

A 4in hole was bored through the throat of each standard, for the attachment of the 'cable stoppers' which helped secure the anchor cables when they were paid out. The standards were fastened to the deck beams by clench bolts, and dowelled to the bitt pins.

During my research I found that on the *Victory* there are two 2in holes, bored vertically through the outer ends of the cross beam of the fore bitts, 6in from the ends. I assume that these acted as some form of securing arrangement.

I have produced some drawings of the riding bitts in Figs 6/6, 6/7 and 6/8. Fig 6/6 illustrates the measurements in the table below.

Table of Dimensions for the Riding Bitts (see Fig 6/6)

Dimensions	No of guns											
	100		74		44		36		28		Sloop	
	ft	in	ft	in	ft	in	ft	in	ft	in	ft	in
A	1	10	1	8	1	4	1	2	-	1	-	10
B	4	3	2	6	1	6	-	6	-	6	-	6
C	1	3	1	1½	-	11½	-	10½	-	9½	-	8
D	5	2	5	2	5	0	5	0	4	3	3	6
E	11	5	11	4	10	4	15	3	14	0	9	6
F	31	8	31	5	23	5	18	6	16	10	12	6
G	4	10	4	4	3	8	5	2	4	10	4	0
H	4	0	3	8	2	11	3	1	3	1	3	0
J	-	2½	-	2	-	2	-	2	-	2	-	1½
K (dia)	-	1½	-	1⅛	-	1	-	1	-	⅞	-	¾
L	4	9	4	6	4	0	2	6	1	9	1	6
M	1	1	-	11½	-	10	-	8½	-	7	-	6
N	-	8	-	7	-	5½	-	4¾	-	4¼	-	4
P	1	8	1	6½	1	3½	1	2¾	1	1	-	10
Q	1	7	1	5½	1	2	1	2	-	11	-	9
R	1	10	1	9	1	6½	1	10	1	5	1	5
S	1	9	1	8	1	5	1	10	1	6	1	6
T	-	4	-	3½	-	3	-	2¾	-	2¼	-	2
U	2	3	2	3	2	3	1	11	1	11	1	10
V	1	1	-	11½	-	10	-	8½	-	7	-	6
W	-	2	-	1¾	-	1¼	-	1	-	¾	-	½
X (dia)	-	1¼	-	1¼	-	1⅜	-	1	-	⅞	-	¾

Y This was made to a length that would run to the beam forward of the foremast, or to the beam aft of the foremast. This varied with the designer of the ship, and would not reduce the strength and security of the timber.

Z This measurement also varied, as it ended a little below the orlop beams, or was set down to the ceiling of the hold.

AA The height of this standard was Q + S (from above).

BB The height of this standard was Q + R

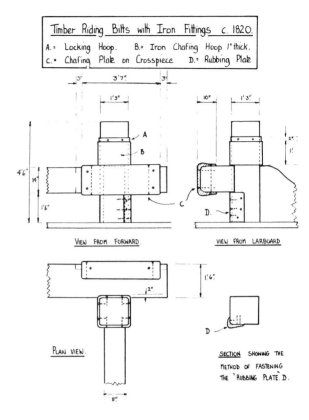

Fig 6/7

IRON AND TIMBER RIDING BITTS

In 1811 iron chain cables were experimentally introduced for the anchor cables in preference to those made from hemp. The main advantage of this type of cable was that it was more durable and less expensive. It did, however, present a few problems, for the iron cables imposed considerable wear on the timber riding bitts and timber-lined hawse holes. This was overcome by a series of modifications, which eventually evolved into the cast iron bitts that can still be seen today on board the *Foudroyant*. In 1817 chain cables were introduced and most ships in the fleet were fitted with conventional timber riding bitts. To reduce the expense of conversion, a number of adaptations were made, by fitting specially designed iron plates and cylindrical hoops where necessary.

At first these modifications were made on a temporary basis, allowing the riding bitts to be used for both chain and hemp cables. It can be seen from this twofold function that chain cables were regarded with reservations by many captains. The kind of difficulties that often occurred were described by Captain Griffiths whose views are quoted in Captain Liardet's *Recollections of Discipline* of 1849.

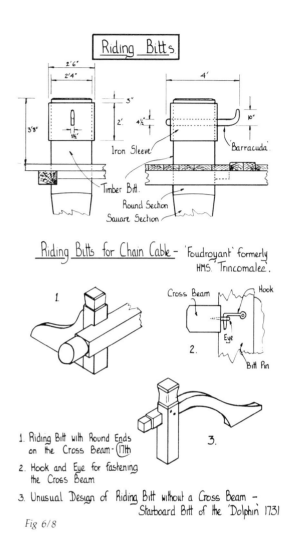

Fig 6/8

Foudroyant. The gundeck. The cast iron riding bitts introduced in the nineteenth century, shortly after the introduction of chain cables. Note the curved 'Barracuda' and the shoulder plates.

The scepticism of the Navy was overcome by adopting a 'belt and braces' system that allowed only the port side bitts to be furnished with iron linings to prevent excessive wear. These were fashioned in a manner that permitted the iron fittings to be removed when the use of hemp cables was desired. Further evidence supporting this is given in the warrant issued by the Navy Board in 1819.

> We transmit herewith a drawing showing the mode of fitting the Bitts of His Majesty's Ships for the reception of an Hempen or an Iron Cable; and pursuant to an Order from the Lords Commisioners of the Admiralty of the 10th ultimo, we direct and require you to conform thereto; observing that this plan is to be adopted to the after Larboard Bitt of such ships as have two pairs of Bitts; and in vessels that have but one pair, the Larboard side of the Bitts is to be fitted.
>
> For this shall be Your Warrant. Dated at the Navy Office 9th March 1819.
>
> W. Legge.
> J.D. Thomson.
> Respective Officers of His Majesty's Yard at Chatham.

This type of design is shown in Fig 6/7, the drawing of which is adapted from the original draughts reproduced in Volume 1 of the *Sheerness Records*. Most of the iron plates and hoops were secured with alloy screws, which permitted easy removal of the plate when hemp cable was used. The only exception was that of the chafing piece, which was fitted to the cross piece. This was located with trennals only. This permitted a similarily shaped portion of timber to fitted in lieu.

By the 1830s the iron attachments of the bitts took on a more permanent nature. A later design by Captain Elliot is illustrated in the *Sheerness Records*, and on inspection it can be seen that they are not dissimilar to those that were later fitted on the *Victory*. A reference to this is given in *The Engineer* of 1891, which discusses the Royal Naval Exhibition. The article is entitled 'H.M.S. Victory, Her History and Construction', by Captain C Orde Browne RA and H J Webb, and Fig 6/8 is adapted from a drawing of this work. It can be seen that some alterations were made, to adapt the iron fittings, which altered the general design of the bitts.

The heads of the bitts were cylindrical and a flat iron ring of about 3in in thickness was passed over them. The ring was set down into the upper surface of the cross piece and supported on the opposite side by the top of the standard that supported the bitts. The overall diameter of the ring was approximately one-third greater than that of the bitt head. I have some reservations on the validity of the drawing, for it would have been more practical to have an iron 'top hat' fitted over the bitt head, instead of a simple flat ring. The after face of the cross piece was rounded, instead of the conventional square cross-section. Over this face was fitted a cast-iron plate, to prevent injury to the wood. In some cases the centre portion of the cross piece was square between the two plates. The final design was a completely cast-iron riding bitt, as mentioned earlier (see Fig 6/8).

The Manger

The manger was the partition or 'dwarf bulkhead' that was fitted transversely across the deck on which the hawse holes were situated. Its primary function was to prevent any sea water that entered through the hawse holes, from passing aft along the entire expanse of that deck. It also retained water that drained from the anchor cables as they were hauled inboard and washed down. Also, this enclosure was found to be a convenient place for keeping livestock, hence the name.

The general construction of the manger was as follows: two vertical stanchions were set up a little forward of the step of the bowsprit (or directly below on three-deckers), and positioned athwartships in line with the midship tier of carlings. Every stanchion had a scantling of 6 to 9in in square section, and they were bolted to the beams at their heads. Their heels were either tenoned into the deck or fastened with iron brackets. The inboard edge of each stanchion was rabbeted to receive the ends of the after transverse bulkhead planking. The outboard faces were similarly rabbeted, but at an angle of between 30 and 45 degrees, to receive the edges of the planking of the bulkheads that ran to the ship's side.

Another stanchion was fitted at the ship's side (one per side). This, too, was rabbeted for the bulkhead planking. The dimensions of these two stanchions were identical to those fitted near the centreline. Their height, however, was only that of the bulkhead. All the rabbets were made to a width and depth equal to half the thickness of the bulkhead planking.

The planks of the bulkhead were made from oak, and sometimes fir, the latter due to its cheapness. Each plank was 10 to 8in wide and 3 to 4in thick. On vessels of 64 guns and more, 4in plank was generally used, and 3in plank was used on the remaining rates. The exception was the sloop where 2½in planking was used.

Each plank was slotted into its appropriate rabbets, and was built up to a height not exceeding 3ft 6in at the outboard ends. The uppermost plank was often stepped in two places, diminishing the height to about 3ft. To achieve this, the top plank was usually made a greater width. The after transverse bulkhead was made to the minimum height of 3ft. In other cases the top plank was not stepped. Therefore it is reasonable to assume that the steps were given clearance for the anchor cables and the messenger cable as it passed from the vertical rollers. The after side of the bulkhead was fitted with a waterway at deck level, to ensure that the whole enclosure was watertight. It was made from oak, of about 3 or 4in cross-section.

Any water that accumulated within the manger was drained away through lead scuppers. There were usually four which were greater in diameter than those on the rest of the deck. The following list gives the diameters of scuppers around 1790. These figures are taken from the *Shipbuilder's Repository*: Ship, number of guns (diameter in inches) – 100 (6½); 90 (6¼); 84–70 (6); 64–50 (5); 44–32 (4¾); 28, to sloops (4½).

The dimensions of the timbers that made up the manger varied very little from one vessel to another. The scantling laid down in a

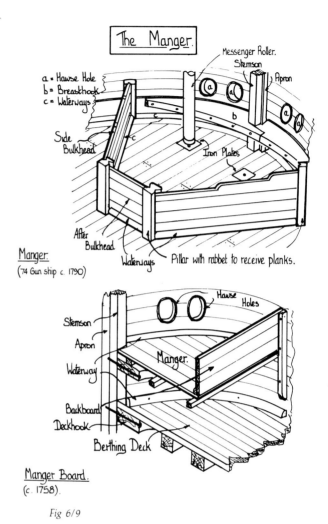

Fig 6/9

building contract of 1692 (the Sixth Rate *Biddeford* – see Appendix 1b) states that the manger was constructed with oak planks, 3in thick, and of 'sufficient compass around the hawse'.

An alternative arrangement was to have a box-like structure fitted above deck level, abaft the hawse holes. This method was not common, and was probably only used on vessels which had the hawse holes entering the berthing deck just below beam height (see Fig 6/9).

The Hawse Holes

In all vessels, the hawse holes were at the head of the ship, equidistant of either side of the stempost. The name 'hawse' is derived from the Anglo-Saxon noun meaning throat. Throughout most of the period, naval vessels usually had hemp anchor hawsers, therefore few problems arose from wear.

As with most aspects of construction, the shipwrights did not simply cut a hole for the passage of the anchor cable, but worked to a rule. The diameter of the hole to be cut was proportional to the size of the cable passing through. The rough and ready rule for

HAWSE HOLES

Hawse Hole design for Hemp Cables.

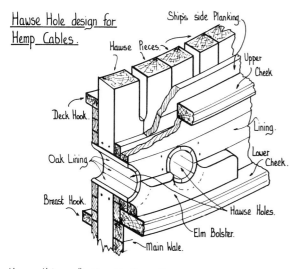

Ships side Planking.
Hawse Pieces.
Upper Cheek
Deck Hook.
Lining.
Lower Cheek.
Oak Lining
Breast Hook.
Hawse Holes.
Elm Bolster.
Main Wale.

Hawse Holes with Wrought Iron Sleeves

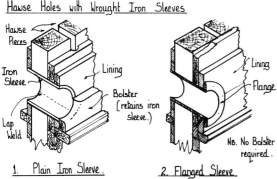

Hawse Pieces
Iron Sleeve
Lining
Bolster (retains iron sleeve.)
Lap Weld
1. Plain Iron Sleeve.

Lining
Flange
NB. No Bolster required.
2. Flanged Sleeve.

Fig 6/10

determining the size of cable for a particular ship, prior to the introduction of chain cables was as follows:

Vessel's extreme breadth ÷ 2

This gives the circumference of the cable in inches. (This is the nominal size given for any rope dimension.) To calculate the diameter of the hawse hole (in inches) first calculate the diameter of the cable.

Diameter of the cable = cable circumference/ 3*

From the above equation the diameter of the hawse hole can be calculated.

Diameter of the hawse hole = cable diameter × 9⁄4

*Although Pi = 3.142, for this calculation Pi = 3 is accurate enough as cables were all manufactured to specific sizes and the constructor would choose the one most suitable.

It would of course be simpler to use one equation to determine the diameter of the hawse hole directly from the given vessel's beam. The answer as above is given in inches. The maximum error is ½in, therefore in all cases this figure should be added to the sum.

Diameter of the hawse hole = vessel's extreme breadth × 9⁄24

Prior to the introduction of chain cable, lining the hawse holes was done by the following method. A series of oak segments were placed around the internal periphery of the hole, in 'barrel stave' fashion. Between eight and twelve segments were used, depending on the size of the hole. This was then lined with either lead or heavy gauge copper, the latter being used in the second half of the eighteenth century. In some cases, it seems that the practice was to have the hole sheathed in lead only. The thickness of the lead varied for various classes of vessel. On ships of 100 to 70 guns, the lead was 1¼in thick; 64 to 32 guns, 1in thick, and ¾in for smaller vessels.

In 1817 chain cable was introduced throughout the Navy.* It was obvious that provision had to be made to prevent the chain damaging the lining of the hawse holes. The problem was overcome by inserting a wrought iron sleeve. These sleeves were rolled from a single plate, 1in thick, the ends of which were joined together by a lap weld which was carried out on the forge. The length of the sleeve was such that it fitted flush with the internal and external planking. No flanges were used until later years. The sleeves were retained by the use of oak bolsters fitted externally, and set down upon the lower cheek. The thickness of the ship's side determined the length of these inserts. Those fitted to the *Victory* are 20in internal diameter, 1in thick and between 28 and 30in long. Whether the hawse holes were of the timber or the iron sleeved type, the angles at which they were set from the centreline in one plane, and the angle set down forward, seem consistent. The angle set downward was between 8 and 10 degrees, while that in the horizontal plane varied. On inspection of a variety of draughts, I have found that some builders gave a small deviation of about 8 degrees off the centreline whereas other placed them directly fore and aft.

*Chain cable had previously been used experimentally.

Unicorn. *The head of the ship, showing the round bow, planked head rail, figurehead and knee of the head. The 'diagonal' type cathead with its support knee is on the right.*

CHAPTER 7

The External Fittings

The Ship's Head and the Head Rails

It would be difficult to explain the construction of the head of the ship without including the many other fittings in its vicinity. Any alteration to the design of the knee of the head resulted in alteration to the head rails, cheeks, hair bracket and the brackets which supported the head rails throughout their length.

THE PARTS OF THE HEAD

The Knee of the Head

The knee of the head was a large knee made from pieces of oak, bolted together. The whole knee projected forward from the stempost, to which it was secured. Its function was not to provide strength, but its graceful lines concealed the otherwise bluff 'apple-cheeked' bow of the ship. I can recall a time when the *Victory* was being restored extensively at the head. The complete knee of the head, along with the head rails etc had been removed, leaving the extremely ugly bow of the vessel exposed. The construction of the knee of the head is explained in Chapter 1.

The Head Rails

These rails were made from a number of pieces of oak, which formed a series of serpentine curves running aft from the hair bracket to various points on the hull. Besides giving graceful lines to the head of the ship, they also provided transverse support to the upper part of the knee of the head. The uppermost rail was usually extended up the side of the beakhead bulkhead (if fitted), and terminated a short distance above the cathead. Its head was in the shape of a knighthead, and later it was fashioned to a tapered block, generally

five-sided to conform to the converging angles of the beakhead bulkhead and the ship's side. The second rail followed a similar path, but terminated at the heel of the bracket that supported the cathead. Throughout most of the period it was faired in and fayed to the ship's side at this point, thus giving the impression that the knee below the cathead continued right to the hair bracket. The remaining rails terminated at the side of the hull, to which they were fayed and bolted.

The Cheeks

These were made from compass oak in the form of a knee. Their function was to support the knee of the head in the transverse plane. It was very important that the knee of the head was stiffened in this way. The surface area of the knee was considerable, whereas the point where it joined the stempost was relatively small, and therefore weak. The action of a large moving volume of water against one side of the head imposed considerable strain on that area, hence the necessity for stiffening knees or cheeks.

The Hair Brackets

These were merely an extension to the fore arm of the uppermost cheek, which produced a good finishing line to both the figurepiece and the figurehead itself.

The Brackets

Curved timbers were fayed and bolted at their heels to both the lacing and the upper edge of the hair bracket. Usually they were made from oak. The function of these brackets was to give support to all the head rails along their lengths, their outboard faces being scored to receive the head rails. They also served to support a

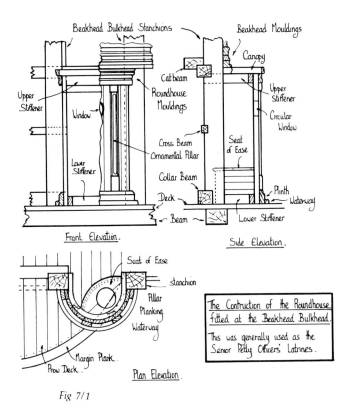

Front Elevation.

Side Elevation.

Plan Elevation.

Fig 7/1

The Contruction of the Roundhouse fitted at the Beakhead Bulkhead.

This was generally used as the Senior Petty Officers' Latrines.

number of lightweight beams which were set at intervals between the extremity of the hull and the after face of the figurehead. Across these beams were placed a number of gratings, forming a light deck area from where parts of the rigging of the bowsprit and jib-boom (spritsail topmast in the earlier vessels) could be worked. It was on this deck that the ship's heads were situated.

THE ROUNDHOUSES AT THE BEAKHEAD BULKHEAD

Roundhouses were first introduced at the turn of the eighteenth century, and were to remain a feature on naval vessels until the beginning of the nineteenth century, when the round bow became common. The function of this semi-circular projection, fitted to the fore side of the beakhead bulkhead, was to accommodate the heads for the senior rates, such as the boatswains, mates, artisans, etc. It gave more privacy and more comfort than the 'seats of ease', which were exposed to wind and weather, and were used by the lesser seamen.

When roundhouses first made their appearance it is thought that only one was fitted, to one side of the beakhead bulkhead. This can be clearly seen on the model of the 50-gun ship *Ripon* of 1712, on display at Edinburgh Castle. The roundhouse is set on the starboard side while the normal 'seat of ease' is fitted on the opposite corner. Soon after the introduction of the roundhouse, two were fitted, making the beakhead more symmetrical. This change was made as early as 1703, for a model of a 90-gun ship of this date at the

National Maritime Museum shows two. Another unusual feature on this model is a square window on the inboard side, in addition to the small circular light set on the fore side.

This model has a number of unusual characteristics that are worth noting. Firstly, there is a canopy fitted athwartships across the roundhouse, constructed in the form of a long grating. This I assume is to provide a platform to allow men to operate the rigging of the headsails and spritsails. Secondly, there is an additional set of knightheads fitted directly aft of the figurehead. Again these are probably for the running rigging of the headsails. One very important feature is the windlass type mechanism that appears to be the forerunner of the steering wheel. This is discussed more fully in the section on the ship's machinery. Another interesting feature is the presence of two entry ports, on each side of the ship. This practice was only common for a short period.

The construction of the roundhouse was relatively light, considering the exposed position at the ship's head. The internal diameter was approximately one-tenth of the length of the bulkhead on First and Second Rates and one-twelfth on remaining ships. The base was made from timbers about 4in in square section, fashioned to the desired curve. The top was identical. The space between was boarded up with vertical planks, 3 to 4in wide and 1½in thick, the edges being bevelled to produce the curved surface required. The roundhouse was usually built between the two stanchions of the beakhead bulkhead that were furthest outboard. This tended to make the base overhang the ship's side to a small degree. The advantage of this is explained later. The base frame was secured to the deck with iron spikes, while the top frame was supported by a number of light stanchions, to which it was secured. The deckhead planking was similar to that of the sides, and on completion the top and side were well payed, seamed, and caulked.

Externally, a waterway was fitted which was about 4in deep around the base. The top was fashioned with a series of mouldings that corresponded to those along the beakhead bulkhead, thus maintaining uniformity in the décor. The area between the top and the base was divided into a number of panels by ornately carved pillars, which either extended to the top or to supporting arches. These panels were painted with stylish frieze work during the first 60 years of the eighteenth century, but became quite plain towards the end of the century. The after sides of these roundhouses were closed off with panelled partitions, with an access doorway. The actual 'seat of ease' was fitted to the outboard side, this allowing the refuse to pass straight out, for the base of the roundhouse overhung the ship's side.

Some roundhouses were fitted on ships that did not have a beakhead bulkhead. As early as 1720 it was seen that there were many disadvantages associated with the flat bulkhead at the bow of the vessel, and because of these the round bow was introduced, to smaller ships such as sloops and small frigates before it was fitted to all vessels at the beginning of the nineteenth century. The fitting of roundhouses on round-bowed ships can be seen on a model of a 20-gun Sixth Rate of 1719 at the National Maritime Museum. These roundhouses are relatively small in diameter, their bases being the

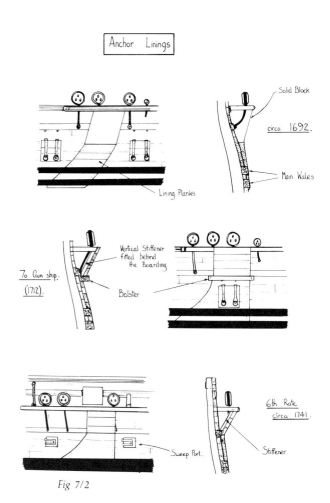

Fig 7/2

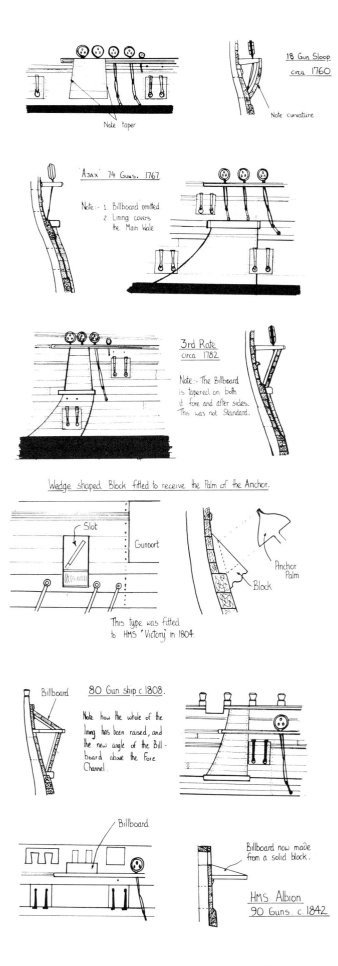

shape of inverted domes, fairing in with the ship's side planking. Another fine example, also at the National Maritime Museum, is the *Dolphin*, a 20-gun ship built at Deptford in 1731. This model is of particular interest, for one side is built as she was launched while the other is as the vessel was fitted out as a fire ship in 1746. There is another model of this vessel at the Transport Museum in Glasgow. This model differs for the quarterdeck is very much shorter, terminating aft of the mizzen mast.

One vessel which does not correspond to the normal pattern is a 24-gun ship of 1741. This retains the square beakhead bulkhead, roundhouses being fitted either side. This is unusual, for most vessels of this size were fitted with the round bow by this date, although it was not until 1760 that the round bow was fitted to frigates of 32 and 36 guns.

The Anchor Lining

The anchor lining was a layer of planking laid over the ship's side planking to prevent damage to the hull during catting (explained below) and fishing the anchor. This layer of planking could be easily removed and replaced without extensive work being carried out on the hull. When the anchor had been hove short and had broken the surface, the hook of the catblock was put through the anchor ring. Then, by hauling in on the catfall, the anchor was swung up to the cathead. This process was called catting, and once the anchor was suspended from the cathead it was said to be catted. The next action was to swing the anchor upwards and aft, to bring the shank parallel to the upper deck. This was done by rigging a fish davit from which hung a fish pendant with a hook at its lower end. The rope then passed up to a block. The hook was secured to the inner arm of the anchor, which was swayed up and finally secured with a chain called a shank painter, which was made fast to the timber heads. The possibility of damage from this heavy weight was great, with the bill of the anchor being allowed to swing.

The position for the anchor lining was determined by the arc produced by the length of the shank as it was swung up from its catted position. The arc gave the centreline of the width of the lining. The planks used were made to the same width as those of the ship's side, but their thickness was equal to the difference between the normal planking and the thickness of the wales. If this difference was 3in, then the planking of the lining would be 3in thick. Therefore a completely flush surface was given to the ship's side. To protect the chains and preventer plates for the shrouds, a billboard was adopted, its heel set into a bolster, and its head fastened to the outboard edge of the fore channel. The sides of this board remained parallel, whereas the lower lining was wider at its base than its top (see Fig 7/2).

There were many variations of anchor lining. Some had gunports cut into them, others had additional billboards fitted above the channels. The illustrations in Fig 7/2 show the many types. Some ships were not fitted with anchor linings, and others had alternative arrangements. The *Victory* had a large wedge-shaped block bolted to the ship's side in which there was a groove for the bill of the anchor. Sometimes a block similar to this was set temporarily on top of the bolster of the conventional linings, once the anchor was fished.

The Fenders

The function of these timbers was to prevent stores from fouling on the raised edges of the wales and drift rails during their embarkation. They were usually made from oak or elm, woods that could withstand a high degree of wear and shock. Each timber was set vertically, fayed and bolted to the ship's side, conforming to the tumblehome. These fenders evolved from vertical hull stiffeners that were common on fourteenth- and fifteenth-century ship types, such as the carrack. By 1650 they protected the hull at midships, and generally abreast the major hatchways at the waist. Usually four or five were fitted on First, Second and Third Rates, with three on the remaining rates. The use of a fifth fender had been dispensed with by 1706, the remaining four being set at equal intervals between the after end of the fore channel and the fore end of the main channel. The next change was made in about 1736, when all vessels had the number of fenders reduced to three, two of which were fitted closer together, forming a parallel haulage guide. This was to remain the general pattern throughout most of the eighteenth century, with a

pair of fenders set approximately 2ft 9in apart, abreast of the main hatchway. About 1780, the single fender forward was shortened, and fashioned to receive sheaves for the main tack, and therefore adopted as a modified chesstree. This was set at a point equal to the extreme beam of the ship afore the mainmast; its position was critical to the sailing qualities of the ship.

During the early part of the nineteenth century, all vessels became smooth-sided, the external planking being faired in with the wales by means of diminishing strakes. Therefore the fenders were no longer necessary.

The depth of the fender timbers, between the ship's side and their outboard edge, was between 14 and 16in, which was sufficient scantling to ensure that they remained proud of the variations of the ship's side plank thickness. Their width was approximately one-third of their depth. For example, if the depth of a fender timber on a Second Rate ship was 14½in, the width would be about 4¾in. The length was as required, taken from the top of the ship's side to the upper edge of the main wale. When the foremost fender was converted to a chesstree, its length was reduced according to the vessel to which it was fitted. If fitted on a three-decked ship, it terminated at the upper edge of the middle wale. On ships of two decks, it terminated at the upper edge of the channel wale, and for those with a single gundeck, a little above the main wale. They were fastened with iron bolts or trennals, the bolts being between ¾in and 1in in diameter. Three or four bolts were used to secure the fender used as a chesstree.

The Channels

The channels were the long horizontal boards fitted to the ship's side, which acted as the securing point and spreader for the lower ends of the shrouds that transversely stayed the lower masts. They are often also called chain wales or chain plates, the name channel being an abbreviated version of the former. Channels were generally made from oak planks, fayed, bolted and sometimes dowelled together, giving an overall width of 3ft on smaller vessels, and 3ft 6in to 3ft 9in on larger ships. Three or four planks were employed, the thickness at the ship's side varying from 6½ to 4in, depending on the size of the vessel. The edge of the outermost plank was approximately 1 or 2in thinner than the innermost edge of the plank adjacent to the ship's side. The overall length of each channel was governed by two considerations: the number of shrouds, and the positions of the gunports in its vicinity. The latter was important because the shrouds had to be spaced between the ports. The former was governed by the period in which the vessel was built. In 1700 the number of shrouds was increased.

Before 1700, the number of shrouds per side was as follows: foremast, nine shrouds and one backstay; mainmast, nine shrouds and one backstay; mizzen mast, five shrouds and one runner. After 1700 the number of shrouds per side was: foremast, twelve shrouds and two backstays; mainmast, twelve shrouds and two backstays;

mizzen mast, six shrouds and one backstay.

The fore end of the channel was a set distance afore the centreline of the lower mast. This altered little between 1650 and 1850. The following table gives dimensions sufficient for the modelmaker.

Distance in Inches between the Fore End of the Channel and the Centreline of the Mast

No of guns	Fore channel	Main channel	Mizzen channel
100	6	6	3
90	10	10	12
74	8	8	6
64	6	6	3
50	6	7	4
44	6	9	4
38	5	6	5
36	6	6	3
32	11	7	3
28	6	6	5
24	5	5	6

The level at which the channels were disposed in relation to the ship's side height was more variable, and altered quite a number of times between 1650 and 1810. One of the major factors that influenced the raising of the channels was the reduction in tumblehome. The manner in which the channels were supported also altered due to the change in angle of the shrouds.

THE HEIGHT OF THE CHANNELS

Ships of Three Decks

Before 1703 the fore and main channels of these vessels were located just below the middle deck gunports. The tumblehome was quite pronounced, and therefore it was necessary to have the channels placed as low as possible, to produce a suitable angle for the shrouds. Around the turn of the eighteenth century the tumblehome was reduced. Therefore it was possible to raise the channels above the middle deck ports, which had the great advantage of reducing sea damage. The fore end of the main channel had, until this time, been extended to facilitate a 'landing' at the entry port, but after 1703 other arrangements were made. It seems that the mizzen channel, which was already set at a greater height, may also have been raised by one deck level, to a position above the upper deck ports, if this had not already been done.

The main and fore channels of some three-deckers were raised again in 1745 to a position above the ports of the upper deck, but by 1756 they had been reverted to their previous level. The only reason that I can see for this is that the ships of three decks were considered to have had enough freeboard, and sea damage was less likely.

Finally, around 1787 the main and fore channels were raised above the upper deck ports, and remained in that position. It has been argued that this occurred earlier, for it is believed that the

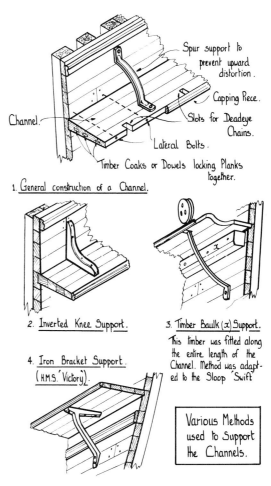

1. General construction of a Channel.

Spur support to prevent upward distortion.

Channel.

Capping Piece.

Slots for Deadeye Chains.

Lateral Bolts.

Timber Coaks or Dowels locking Planks together.

2. Inverted Knee Support.

3. Timber Baulk (x) Support. This timber was fitted along the entire length of the Channel. Method was adapted to the Sloop 'Swift'

4. Iron Bracket Support. (H.M.S. 'Victory').

Various Methods used to Support the Channels.

Fig 7/3

Royal George, that sunk at Spithead in 1782, was the first First Rate ship to have channels above the upper deck ports. In 1803 the mizzen channel was raised to above the quarterdeck ports, as on other rates of vessel fitted with a poop deck.

Ships of Two Gundecks and Remaining Smaller Classes

The raising of the fore and main channels appears to have taken place between 1745 and 1750. In all cases, whether the vessels were of one or two decks, the channels were raised to a level above the upper (or gundeck) gunports. The position of the mizzen channels was altered in 1803, on vessels with a poop deck. One of the major advantages of having the channels above the gunports was that the rigging and deadeyes did not obstruct the guns. When they had been fitted below the ports it was found that sparks and smouldering wadding could easily set fire to the rigging in the vicinity of the cannons' blast. This was prevented by having the gunport covers opening in a single or a double slit door fashion.

The channels were supported at the ship's side by inverted knees, iron spurs or brackets, or a combination of both. Between 1650 and

Egmont. The forecastle of the model illustrating the external features: the cathead, fore channel and chains, bower and sheet anchors and billboard. Also shown are the fish davit, galley flue and belfry as well as the many other typical fittings and fastenings of the period.

1736 the common practice was to have either five spurs or five knees at the fore and main channels and three at the mizzen channels. These fittings were secured on the upper side to prevent the channel being raised upwards under the strain imposed by the shrouds. The oak knees, which were initially used, had to be supplemented by spurs. This was done because of the increase in the tumblehome, which made the angle of the knees more obtuse, rendering them weaker.

The iron spurs were made in the form of an arch, the upper end being bolted to the ship's side and the other to the outermost plank of the channel (see Fig 7/3). By the end of the seventeenth century the tumblehome had been reduced, which meant that the width of the channels had to be increased to maintain the correct angle for the shrouds. The use of spurs did not compensate for this, consequently a superior method was required.

This was achieved by a combination of changes, around 1705. One solution was to raise the channels to a higher position on the ship's side. The second was to modify the chain plates which secured the deadeyes themselves. Until then they had only been secured to the ship's side at a single point, on the lower strake of the wale to which the channel was fitted. Once the channels had been raised by a deck, the chain plate was lengthened so that it was still fastened at the same point on the ship's side, and made firmer by having two points of attachment. This gave greater support and therefore the practice of employing spurs disappeared by 1736. The use of a bracket, fitted to the underside of the channel, was to be found more successful, at first being used in tandem with the knees. The latter eventually disappeared, and by the end of the eighteenth century the remaining brackets were made from iron instead of oak.

The chains had originally been made in the form of a flat iron strap, with a hooked section to receive the deadeye. Around 1720 this fashion changed to the chain link method. Initially chain link was fitted for every second shroud (making a total of three or five), with backing links aiding the chain plates. By 1800 all the shrouds were fitted in this manner. The number of chain plates for vessels of 1720 can be calculated from Sutherland's work *Shipbuilding Unveiled*.

The Number of Chain Plates on Vessels of 1720

Rate of ship	Fore channel	Main channel	Mizzen channel
First	8	9	6
Second	8	9	5
Third	7	9	5
Fourth	6	8	4
Fifth	5	7	3
Sixth	4	6	3

In 1771 an improvement was made to facilitate removal of the deadeyes, for replacement or maintenance. This modification required slots to be cut into the outer edge of the channel, in place of the original holes through which the chain plates passed. Over these slots, along the edge, a thin capping was nailed, to prevent the chain plates and the deadeyes being unshipped. This batten was made to a width of two-thirds of the thickness of the outer edge of the channel, and was generally fashioned with a plain moulding. The fore and after ends of the channels were made in a scroll or flourish, or simply squared.

By the end of the eighteenth century, the number of shrouds was increased, probably due to the fact that the height of the masts had also increased, with the general lengthening of all vessels. The figures given in the following tables are taken from the 1789 edition of the *Shipbuilder's Repository*.

The Dimensions of the Main Channel

No of guns	Length		Thickness at inboard edge	Thickness at outboard edge	No of bolts	Diameter of bolts
	ft	in	in	in		in
100	39		6½	4½	11	1⅜
90	38		6	4½	11	1⅜
74	38		5¾	4¼	11	1¼
64	27	8	5¾	4	9	1¼
44	26	10	5½	3¾	8	1⅓
38	25	9	5¼	3¾	8	1⅓
36	27	6	5¼	3¾	8	1⅓
32	24	9	5¼	3¾	7	1
28	24	4	5	3½	7	1
24	20		5	3½	6	1
Sloop	15		4½	3	5	⅞
Cutter	12		4	3	4	⅞

The Dimensions of the Fore Channel

No of guns	Length		Thickness at inboard edge	Thickness at outboard edge	No of bolts	Diameter of bolts
	ft	in	in	in		in
100	33	6	6½	4½	9	1⅜
90	34		6	4½	9	1⅜
74	37		5¾	4¼	9	1⅜
64	23	2	5¾	4	8	1¼
44	25	4	5½	3¾	8	1¼
38	25	6	5¼	3½	8	1⅛
36	24		5¼	3½	7	1¼
32	21	10	5¼	3½	6	1
28	17	6	5	3½	6	1
24	17	6	5	3½	6	⅞
Sloop	13	6	4½	3	5	⅞

The Dimensions of the Mizzen Channel

No of guns	Length		Thickness at inboard edge	Thickness at outboard edge	No of bolts	Diameter of bolts
	ft	in	in	in		in
100	19	6	5¾	3¾	7	1¼
90	19	6	5½	3¾	7	1¼
74	13		4½	3½	6	1¼
64	14		5	3½	6	1⅛
44	15		4	3	6	1⅛
38	12		4½	3½	6	1
36	9	6	4½	3½	5	1
32	11	6	4½	3½	6	⅞
28	9	6	4	3	5	⅞
24	9	6	3¼	2¼	5	¾
Sloop	8	6	3	2	4	¾

The above dimensions are fairly accurate for all vessels built in the second half of the eighteenth century, providing they had the same number of shrouds. These scantlings can be compared with

Unicorn. *The after end of the quarterdeck. The distribution of the gunports around the transom made an all round arc of fire possible.*

those of the *Victory* launched in 1765, which are as follows: length of the main channel 29ft 6in; the fore channel 36ft; and the mizzen channel 16ft 4in. These figures correspond to those of a 74-gun ship of 1805, which show that the length of the channels had increased in proportion to the length of the vessels. The stools used for securing the back stays had been abolished by 1770, and they were now secured by increasing the length of the channels at their after end.

Unlike other fittings very few alterations were made in the design of the channels. The only variation was that used on the sloop *Swift*, built in 1721. Instead of using the more conventional knees and spurs to support the channel, a baulk of timber was fitted beneath, adjacent to the ship's side (see Fig 7/3). This may have been practical on a smaller ship, with hardly any tumblehome, but was probably of little use on larger vessels. It may have been this experiment that resulted in the use of brackets on all ship's channels.

CHANNEL KNEES

These were inverted knees made from oak, fitted between the upper sides of the channel and the ship's side. Their function was to brace the channel boards against the upward strain imposed by the shrouds. The arm of each knee was sufficiently long to stand clear of the deadeyes, and give suitable landing at the ship's side. The number of knees depended on the overall length of the channel itself. Each knee was fitted equidistantly along the length of the channel, except in way of gunports where they were brought as close as possible. Contemporary figures give the spacing of the knees as follows: Ship, number of guns (spacing between knees in inches) – 100–70 (2ft 9in); 64–38 (2ft 3in); 36–28 (2ft 9in); 24 guns and less (2ft 6in).

The siding of these knees was relatively small, ranging from 5½in on First Rates to 3in on Sixth Rates. Each knee was bolted with four bolts of ½ to 1in diameter. Some of the First and Second Rates had five or six bolts. According to the figures, channel knees were not fitted on the cutters, probably due to the size of such vessels.

Ports

GUNPORT LIDS

Generally all gunport lids were made in a double layer construction, each layer worked at 90 degrees, forming a two ply system. The outer layer was equal in width and thickness to the ship's side planking, and it conformed to the plank sheer of the vessel. The inner layer was made from four relatively thin boards (about 1½in thick), all set in the vertical plane. Those at the centre were generally of equal width while those on each side were made to a suitable width in order to make up the difference in total width. Once all the various planks were placed together, they were fastened with trennals or iron dumps, a combination of both often being used after 1735. The whole assembly was further stiffened by the bolts that fastened the hinges and the rings (see Fig 7/4 and 7/5).

Most gunport lids were of the upward opening type, with the hinges on the upper edge. However, some variations were adopted, due to their position relative to rigging, channels, and other features. These types can be divided into the following categories: the single door, the double door, half lids and drop lids.

Fig 7/4

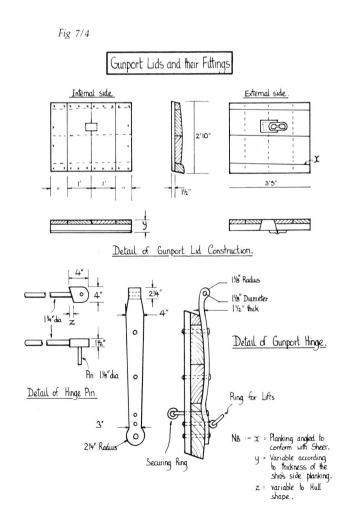

Single Door Port Lids

These were not often used after 1690. Being made in the form of doors, they had to be positioned where space was available on one side and thus were usually found in such places as the beakhead bulkhead, where they served as access doors as well as ports for the chase guns. On some early vessels they were in the vicinity of the cabin accommodation. Sometimes this type of lid was fitted at the foremost gunport of the upper deck, where it was adjacent to the anchor gear (see Fig 7/9(3)).

Double Door Port Lids

This form was common prior to the raising of the channels. The advantage of having two half doors, opening outwards, was that the shrouds and deadeyes could be protected to a certain extent from the heat and sparks discharged from the guns. This form was also used in the cabin areas, where it served as a window, for ventilation without undue draughts.

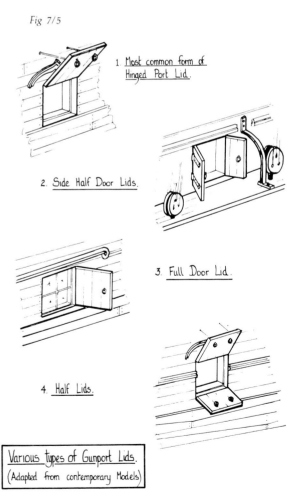

Fig 7/5

1. Most common form of Hinged Port Lid.

2. Side Half Door Lids.

3. Full Door Lid.

4. Half Lids.

Various types of Gunport Lids.
(Adapted from contemporary Models)

Half Lids

This type was generally found at the stern chase-ports, and appears to have been introduced around 1797, though very probably earlier. Previously the lids for the stern chase-ports were of the normal type but had proved difficult to raise fully. This was because the angle of the lower counter was quite obtuse. By halving the lid horizontally, the difficulties of opening were overcome. The hinges were fitted to both halves as necessary, the lower half hanging downward when open. The rings for the halliards were fitted for raising and lowering. This fashion was found to be very adaptable, especially when the circular stern was introduced, for due to the varying contours of the ship's side at the vicinity of the quarter ports, a normal lifting lid would have been difficult to manufacture. This type is clearly reproduced on the model of the 90-gun *Albion* of 1842, at the Science Museum in Kensington. This model also appears to have them fitted along the upper gundeck, and at the level of the quarterdeck.

Drop Lids

Until the nineteenth century full-sized lids that opened downwards seem to have been fitted only to fireships. The advantage of having this type of port was that the flames from the incendiaries stowed on the lower decks could rise more easily to engulf the ship and the unfortunate enemy vessels being attacked. The model of the 20-gun sloop *Dolphin* of 1731, at the National Maritime Museum, Greenwich, portrays this vessel as a sloop and as she was when converted to a fireship in 1746. One point of interest is that, apart from the extra ports cut on her lower deck, one of these ports is somewhat deeper. It was closed by two half doors and a half drop lid. It is possible that it was used both to embark the incendiary devices and as an exit for the crew once they had set the vessel on fire. (see Fig 7/6).

The use of drop lids appears to have become common in a number of vessels during the nineteenth century. On the model of the *Albion* they were fitted along the upper deck ports.

Gunport lids were sometimes fitted below the cabin lights at the stern of a vessel. These lids were concealed in the planking below the windows, and were used only as a last resort, when attacked from aft. The implication of this was revealed to me on a visit to the *Victory*. On inspection of most ships' draughts there is no indication of this, and they show only two or four guns that could be brought to bear facing aft. However, on *Victory* provision was made for mounting extra guns on each deck above the lower gundeck. First the panelling from the main stern timbers between the windows was removed. This panelling was made in a 'box' form to facilitate this. This revealed the ringbolts to which gun tackle could be secured. Next the whole bench seat that spanned the after windows, including the panelling above it was removed. The actual gunport lid was then exposed by raising the deadlights on their lead-weighted sashes, which covered the windows entirely. The gunport lid was opened by sliding back two bolts and giving the lid a hearty

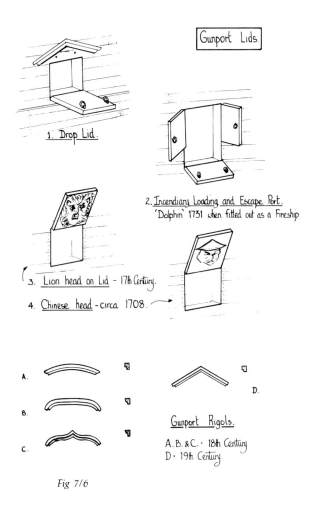

Fig 7/6

timber, port lids fitted at the waist of the ship were abolished. However, these lids were reintroduced in the nineteenth century when the upper deck was closed in completely.

THE EMBELLISHMENT OF THE GUNPORTS

From the Commonwealth period to the turn of the eighteenth century, the gunports of the upper gundeck and the quarterdeck were generally adorned with wreaths, which were either painted bright or gilded. This practice did not usually apply to vessels with single gundecks, except Royal yachts. Throughout most of these years, the inner faces of the lids were painted red, and the outer side was either payed or painted to conform with the surrounding friezework. The alternative was to have a lion's head painted in gold on a red ground, this being more common on First, Second and Third Rates. Some vessels also had carved lion's heads, but this was

Fig 7/7

Gunport fitted Astern in Cabin Quarters - Victory.

1. Diagram of the Stern Construction showing the Gunport when not in use.

2. First stage in attaining access to the Gunport Lid was achieved by raising the Deadlight and removing the Panelled Boxing to expose the Ringbolts and the Gunport retaining bolts.

3. Bench seat removed giving clearance for the Gun. the retaining bolts thrown back to allow the Gunport Lid to be lowered open.

kick, which swung it out and down on its hinges. When these ports were opened the 'gingerbread' at the stern was invariably damaged, a small price to pay for the defence of the ship. Using the *Victory* as an example, it can be seen that with provision for another three guns on each deck, her after fire-power was increased to eleven guns (including the two stern-chaser guns on the lower gundeck). Due to the comparatively light construction of the stern timbers, the rate of fire had to be kept low, consideration being given to the effect of recoil on the timbers. No additional guns were carried for these gun positions, but if required they would have been taken from those on the broadside, and manhandled into position (see Fig 7/7).

GENERAL FEATURES OF GUNPORTS

Apart from a tendency to simplify the design and appearance of the hinges they remained unchanged between 1650 and 1850. The number of rings to which the lifting halliards were secured did vary, either one or two being fitted depending on the weight of the lid itself. From about 1708, two were fitted on most vessels, due to the overall increase in size of the lids. Rings were also fitted on the internal face, to enable the lid to be pulled shut (see Fig 7/4 and 7/5). When, in 1703, the Navy Board ordered a reduction in the use of not common, except on vessels of foreign navies.

In 1703, in the interests of both cost and timber conservation, the Navy Board ordered a reduction in carved and gilded works. The result of this was not as dramatic as first intended, and was merely a limitation. The only change was that the wreaths that surrounded the upper gundeck ports were abolished, but those on the quarterdeck remained. These, too, finally disappeared by 1710 (to be replaced with plain circular mouldings), along with the carved lion heads on the port lids. The circular mouldings and painted lion heads remained fashionable for a further fifteen years, until they disappeared by 1730. A model of the 100-gun *Royal George* of 1756 in the National Maritime Museum depicts a painted lion head. It is not known for certain whether this ornamentation was still used at this late date; it may simply have been an idiosyncrasy of the modelmaker.

During the second decade of the eighteenth century, an alternative fashion in décor was chinoiserie. Here the undersides of the gunport lids were painted with either Chinese cat heads or mandarin heads. An excellent example of this can be seen on a model of a 90-gun ship of 1706, at the Science Museum. The date of this model does, however, seem a little early for the Chinese style.

For the next 75 years, very few changes were made to the decoration of the gunport lids and gunports. The internal faces of the lids remained the 'blood red' colour, and the external side was payed or painted as necessary. By the end of the century some captains had the external faces of the lids painted black, as a contrast to the ship's other side, which was painted with bands of yellow ochre. This style was universally adopted under Nelson's influence, and was therefore known as the Nelson chequer. The external faces remained black from then on, even on the false gunports painted on the tea clippers of the 1860s and later.

In 1815 the inboard works of some ships were changed from dull yellow or red to green. The inner faces of the lids were painted similarly, although the red colour still remained usual. By 1830 it was decided that the inboard works should be painted white to brighten up the living quarters. The inner faces of the gunport lids were either kept red, or painted white.

THE SWEEP PORTS

The use of sweeps (oars) was quite common on smaller vessels between 1670 and 1846. Sweeps are usually associated with the galleys of the Mediterranean, or the galleases of the Spanish Armada in the sixteenth century. For various reasons sweeps were introduced to the English Navy during the latter part of the seventeenth century. One vessel of this period was the 46-gun Fourth Rate, *Tiger*, built at Deptford in 1681. I would imagine that due to her size (two complete gundecks), sweeps were used primarily for manoeuvering. One reason for their re-introduction was the number of successful attacks made on British ships by the swift galleys used by the Barbary corsairs. The corsairs would take advantage of the relatively weak defences at the head and stern of a

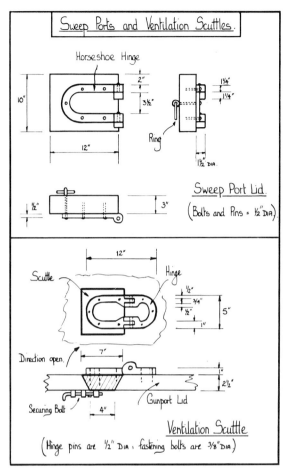

Fig 7/8

vessel, where there was very little armament. A galley would carry her armament at her head and stern, facing fore or aft, and therefore she manoeuvered ahead or astern of a vessel and proceeded to rake the unfortunate vessel.

To combat this problem, the galley frigate was introduced, the first being the *Charles Galley* of 1676. This vessel carried the majority of her armament on the upper deck, and a few guns on the deck below. The remainder of the lower deck was pierced with 19 sweep ports on each side. The concept of a vessel both propelled by oar and sail proved relatively successful, and the design was used until the nineteenth century.

By 1712 a similar type of vessel with 32 guns had been introduced. These Fifth Rates carried twenty 6-pounders on their upperdeck (or main) and eight 9-pounders on their lower deck. The remaining space upon the lower deck was used for 18 sweeps each side. In 1719 a class of 20-gun Sixth Rates was introduced, based on the Fifth Rates. Although these were very similar, their armament was on the upper deck only. A single ballast port and 18 sweep ports, were pierced on the lower deck. One such vessel was the *Blandford* of 1719, a model of which is on display at the Science Museum, London. Between 1719 and 1727, twenty-one of these vessels were built, thereby proving their adaptability. Other vessels were built to similar designs in later years. These included the *Dolphin*, a 20-gun sloop built in 1731 and a class of 24-gun ships built after 1741 which mounted some guns on the lower or berthing deck.

In 1750 the idea of having a few guns on the berthing deck was dispensed with by lowering the gundeck to give more cover for those manning the guns. Therefore the berthing deck became too low so the sweep ports were moved to the upper level and placed between the gunports. This was to remain the general fashion until the disappearance of sweeps in the nineteenth century.

Over the next fifty years the number of ships carrying sweeps decreased. However, the potential of vessels that could be swiftly manoeuvred was shortly to be realised again upon the outbreak of the Napoleonic Wars. One of the most successful designs was that of the gun brig which carried either 16 or 18 guns. These guns were either of the normal carriage type or carronades. These vessels, often referred to as the 'Colombine' class proved so useful, that between the years 1803 and 1846 some sixty such craft were built. In 1826, after their initial introduction, they were improved by Symonds. The larger of these vessels were very often rigged as barque rigged sloops; the smaller vessels remained purely brigs.

A smaller type of gun vessel was also introduced in 1801, which carried ten carronades on the upper deck and two guns below the raised forecastle, both of which faced directly ahead. These two types of vessel appear to be the last in the navy to have employed sweeps and it would seem very probable that those of the 'Columbine' class that were built towards the year 1846 would not have been fitted out for sweeps.

The construction of sweep ports was relatively simple, for unlike the gunport lids, a second layer of vertical planking was not required, the sweep cover being made up from the same sized plank used for the ship's side. These ports were approximately 9 to 12in wide and 7 to 10in deep, varying according to the diameter of the sweep. The covers were always hinged at the fore side so that they did not hinder the performance of the sweeps, the hinges being fashioned in the form of a horseshoe. Only one ring was fitted, this being on the inside of the cover to which the lanyard used for closing it was attached (see Fig 7/8).

THE VENTILATION SCUTTLES

One of the contributing factors to the ill health of eighteenth-century seamen was dampness, caused by insufficient ventilation on the lower decks. It was on this deck that the majority of the ship's company lived, slept and ate. The atmosphere was generally dim and life was cramped for months at a time. What ventilation there was normally came through the gratings between each deck. This could not be improved by the casual opening of the gunports, for fear of flooding in heavy seas. The problem was alleviated somewhat by the introduction, in about 1778, of small scuttles, similar to those already employed for sweeps. They were first fitted at every other gunport lid throughout the lower decks. Their

success influenced the Navy Board, so that authorisation was given in 1789 for ventilation scuttles of this nature to be fitted at every gunport lid. The manner of their construction is clearly shown in Fig 7/8. These scuttles gave an opening of about 7in², and not only gave adequate ventilation but also considerable light to the deck. Further improvements were made to the scuttles, for in 1809 thick glass illuminators superseded the original wooden doors. Within 15 years glass illuminators were also fitted in the ship's side, angled down to give extra light to the berthing decks of single decked ships. This can be seen on board the frigates *Unicorn* and *Foudroyant*, and the original type can be seen on the *Victory*.

THE ENTRY PORTS

An entry port at the ship's side was fitted only to vessels with three decks. This included those of 80-guns, built in the earlier part of the eighteenth century. These entrances were equal in width to the gunports of the respective deck, and from 4ft 6in to 4ft 9in high. They were used between 1660 and 1810, though some ships retained this feature after this date. Their function was to give access to the ship without having to scale the entire height of the hull from the waterline. Prior to the Restoration in 1660, it appears that only one entry port was fitted, to the port side of a vessel providing a small landing stage or sponson at deck level. Entry was at the middle deck only. Two entry ports were fitted for the first time (one on each side of the ship) in 1671. It is believed that this was done on the 100-gun ship *Royal James* built by Sir Anthony Deane. The actual position for the entry ports of vessels of this period can be determined from contemporary models at Greenwich, of a 90-gun ship of 1675, and a 60-gun ship of the following year. The former vessel had the entry placed between the eighth and ninth gunports on the middle deck, the latter between the sixth and seventh.

The style of ornamentation surrounding the entrance was a close-fitting, shallow-arched canopy supported by caryatids. A small grating supported by carved brackets acted as the landing stage. Often this was integral to the end of the main channel. By 1690, the canopy became more decorative, with carvings of dogs, lions or fish. It was also during this year that vessels were authorised to have entry ports fitted on both sides of the hull.

The decorative work forming the architrave around the entry became simpler, due to the restrictions on carved work imposed by the Navy Board in 1703. The canopies became more pronounced in their curvature, and the supporting pillars less ornate. Mouldings were employed on both the canopy and the pillars in preference to carved work. It was also during this period that two modifications were made that altered the overall style of the entry ports. The first was the raising of the main channel to the level of the upper gundeck. As a result, the landing stage or sponson had to be constructed separately. A second entry port was introduced on some vessels at the level of the upper deck. This was fitted on one or both sides of the ship. An example of this can be seen on a model of a 96-gun ship of about 1703 at the National Maritime Museum. The

Entry Ports

Arch with carved
Pillar supporters.
(Prince. 1670)

Double Crossed Arch Form. c 1756

NB - Turned Pillars were often used as an
alternative design 20 years earlier.

Single Arch Form.

This form became popular towards
the end of the 18th Century.
Note the use of Bracket Supporters
instead of Pillars - this aspect was
due to the reduction of the Tumblehome.

Fig 7/9

entry port is on the middle gundeck at the fore end of the main channel. A second entry is fitted on the upper gundeck adjacent to the third from aft gunport. The fitting of balustrading around the sponson was also introduced during the first half of the eighteenth century. Designers next considered that it would be preferable to use one of the existing gunports as a point of entry, instead of having it placed between the ports. This was done because the hull was considerably weakened by having three piercings close to each other. In practice this made good sense but it did reduce the firepower of a broadside.

The Gangways

Prior to and during the Restoration access to the forecastle, quarterdeck and poop was by way of a relatively short ladderway ascending to a gangway fitted on each side of the deck in question. This gangway was only about 6 to 8ft long, and between 2ft 6in and 3ft wide, stepped below the level of the adjacent deck. Elaborately carved balustrading adorned the ladderway and gangway, matching that of the breast rail of the deck to which they

were attached. Both the gangway and the ladderway were supported by small cabins constructed below. The height of the ladderway from the gangway varied, according to which deck it was fitted to, and was between 3 and 5ft. This type of gangway was constructed on most large ships until 1703, when those at the forecastle and poop were abolished, the curved ladder being retained. The gangways at the break of the quarterdeck remained for another eleven years, though in most cases they were not of sufficient length to reach the point of entry to the vessel. During the reign of Queen Anne the ladders were adapted, and were known as 'bell' ladders, because their width increased in a gentle curve towards their lower end. In the early years of George I, all ladders became straight and parallel.

Until 1744 access to the forecastle and quarterdeck was by ladders to and from the upper deck. This was found to be a great disadvantage, especially during action, for the time taken to relay orders from one part of the ship to another was prolonged, due to the fact that the messenger was impeded by recoiling guns and busy gun crews. To alleviate this, narrow gangboards were fitted as a temporary measure between the two decks concerned, on both sides of the ship. These boards were about 1ft 6in wide, and supported by small timber knees or iron brackets. For a number of years after their introduction, these gangways were set below the levels of the quarterdeck and forecastle, due to their position relative to the upper edge of the gunwale. Over the next 20 years the width of the gangways increased to 2ft 6in or 3ft in breadth, and in most vessels they became permanent. This precipitated another alteration to ship design, finally leading to the closing of the waist. This was the fitting of a number of temporary skid beams, placed athwartships between the gangways. The function of these was to provide stowage for the ship's boats and spare spars clear of the guns on the upper deck. The iron brackets that supported the gangways were redesigned with a crutch to receive and house the ends of the skid beams (see Fig 8/6). These were introduced about 1768.

The next change was made in 1782 when the Navy Board ordered that the gangways at the waist be raised level with the deck of the forecastle and quarterdeck. This order also stipulated that the gangways were to be made permanent on all classes of vessels, although this had been done occasionally during the last decade. To enable this, the gunwales had to be raised to the level required.

After 1790 the width of the gangways was increased further, to about 5ft. However, this was not done by adding planking on the inboard side, but on the outboard side. This was achieved by reducing the degree of tumblehome, a proposal that had been made by Mr Snodgrass, a Surveyor for the East India Company. His idea was that by reducing the tumblehome, the waist could be increased in width, thus giving wider gangways, to allow more room for the crew to operate certain parts of the rigging without hindrance. Over the next 20 years gangways were progressively increased in width, by reducing the open space at the centre of the deck. By 1813 each gangway was approximately one-third of the ship's width at the waist. This increase continued until 1832 when Sir William

Symonds, the new Surveyor of the Navy, authorised the complete closing of the waist. The deck was now completely planked except for a narrow line of gratings along the centreline. The forecastle and quarterdeck still retained their names, even though there was no apparent division. The idea of the closure may well have come from a new class of 60-gun frigates that was introduced in 1813–14. These vessels, *Leander*, *Newcastle* and *Java*, had a second tier of guns mounted along the entire length of the forecastle, quarterdeck and waist, the waist having been planked in to accommodate them.

THE CENTRAL GANGWAY AT THE QUARTERDECK

In most vessels built in the second half of the seventeenth century the quarterdeck terminated 8 to 10ft aft of the mainmast. Difficulties occurred in the operation of the rigging (downhaulers, lifts, jeers, and other halliards etc) at this point. To overcome these problems, modifications were made by extending a platform to the mast from the fore edge of the quarterdeck. This was a relatively simple affair and was adapted from existing fittings in the vicinity. This was achieved by utilising the upper cross beam of the main topsail bitts, or by increasing the height of the bitt pins and spanning their heads with a beam. The upper beam of the bitts was generally called the gallows. Once this was done, the beam was used to support the fore ends of the fore and aft bearers, or carlings, which extended from the foremost beam of the quarterdeck. The platform bearer was probably made from pitch pine, about 4in by 3½in in cross-section, the after end being tenoned into the foremost beam of the quarterdeck, the fore end bolted down upon the gallows.

The decking built on the bearers was usually a series of gratings. These were nailed in position, those in the vicinity of the mast being fashioned to fit its periphery. The first sign of this form of construction was on the 50-gun ships of about 1701. Over the next 15 years alterations were made, by extending the planking of the quarterdeck to the foremost extremity of the gangway. Another alteration was the fitting of a fore and aft breast rail along one side of the gangway. Provision was made for access from the quarterdeck, by making a break in the breast rail that ran athwartships along its edge. The central gangway remained in use in most ships until 1759 when it was decided to extend the length of the quarterdeck to terminate a little forward of the mainmast.

The Catheads

Catheads are the heavily built brackets (or davits) from which the ship's anchors were suspended when not in use. Two were fitted on all vessels except cutters, one projecting from each side of the ship on the forecastle. To ensure that these timbers could bear the weight of an anchor, their scantlings were large. In most cases oak was used. Catheads were usually set with their angles in two planes. When viewed from directly ahead, they inclined upwards towards their extremities at between 15 and 20 degrees. In their plan view, they inclined forward at approximately 45 degrees to the centreline. They were about 90 degrees to the plane of the lower head rail. Between 1648 and the introduction of the round bow, these angles varied very little. During the earlier years catheads were usually fitted at the level of the upper gundeck, except on single-decked ships, but by 1656 they were raised to the level of the forecastle.

The outboard ends of the cathead were fitted with two or three vertical slots. These were fitted with sheaves through which the tackle for the catblock was received. An end cap of wood, which was usually richly carved, was secured at the extremity of the cathead. This not only provided decoration, but also prevented damp entering the end grain of the timber. A lion's head was the most common motif, hence the name cathead. Other designs were adopted during the eighteenth century.

The inboard end of the cathead was called the cat-tail. Its design varied, depending on the manner in which the cathead was fastened to the ship. The overall design of the cathead varied according to the period and to whether the ship was constructed with a built up round bow, or a square beakhead bulkhead. The design carved did not always conform to a set pattern, compatible with the form of construction used for the ship's head.

There were four methods for securing the cat-tail to the ship's structure: vertical, transverse, diagonal and longitudinal. The diagonal method can be sub-divided into three categories: straight, overlaid and underlaid. Before describing these methods some idea of the cathead's size must be given. I have not been able to calculate its dimensions in relation to another part of the ship, but have provided estimated sizes taken from a number of draughts. These scantlings appear to be general for the period. Most vessels had their catheads square in cross-section, although there were some exceptions where the breadth was about two-thirds of the width. The following table gives approximate dimensions of square section catheads: Ship, rate (size in inches) – First (20); Second (18); Third (17); Fourth (16); Fifth (14); Sixth (12); cutters etc (9–10).

METHODS OF SECURING THE CATHEADS
Vertical

For this method the timber had to be specially selected for its shape and grain strength. The cat-tail itself was fayed and bolted to the inboard side of the bulwark at the forecastle. Its position was such that it coincided with one of the ship's timbers. The bolts were driven from within, passing through both the inner and outer planking and the timber itself, and then firmly clenched (see Fig 7/10). This method was generally used on small craft, such as sloops, brigs, schooners and some cutters. These vessels only carried relatively light anchors, and therefore strength was not so important. I assume that in all cases the cathead was not only placed at a ship's timber, but also where a deck beam was present, as this would increase the transverse strength of the frames to which the

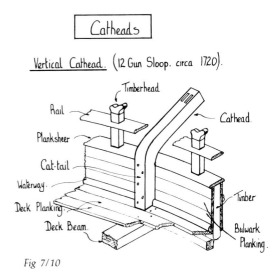

Catheads

Vertical Cathead. (12 Gun Sloop. circa 1720).

Fig 7/10

cathead was fitted. Catheads fastened in this manner can be seen on a model of a 12-gun sloop of 1720 and on an 18-gun schooner of 1850, at the National Maritime Museum.

Transverse

This method was used on most vessels built with a square beakhead bulkhead. To accommodate the cat-tails, the foremost beam of the forecastle was fashioned to greater scantlings, and was called the catbeam. The timber for this cathead was specially chosen compass oak. Finding such pieces of timber must have proved very difficult. The length of the inboard portion of the cat-tail was generally made to the following specifications;

Length of the cat-tail = (length of the catbeam/2) + Y + Z

where Y = width of the ship's timber at the height of the cathead;
Z = width of the ship's external planking at that height

Here it can be seen that the length was independent of the part of the cathead that projected from the ship's side. The underside of the cat-tail was fayed and bolted down upon the catbeam, in such a manner that the heels of each cathead butted together at the centre of the beam (see Fig 7/11). Generally a plank was bolted down over the butt joints, to prevent water seepage to the ends of the timbers. An alternative method was to taper the cat-tail towards its heel. This was done to the after face. Once both catheads were bolted to the beam, a 'fish' plank was fayed and bolted across both cat-tail after faces. This was also bolted down upon the catbeam, thus locking the whole structure in two planes (see Fig 7/11). As usual a suitable plank was bolted across the upper surfaces of the cat-tails, to prevent water seeping into the joints.

A second method was to have the cat-tails shorter. The formula for the determination of their length is given as follows:

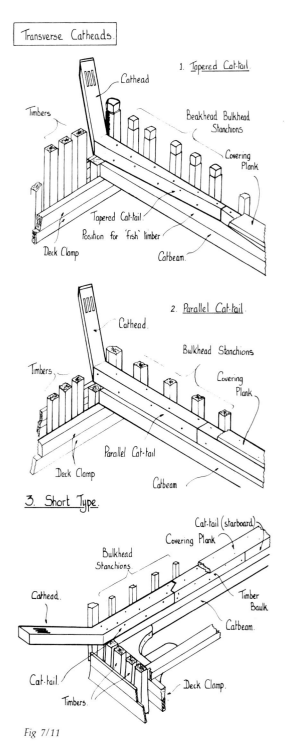

Transverse Catheads.

1. Tapered Cat-tail.

2. Parallel Cat-tail.

3. Short Type.

Fig 7/11

Length of the cat-tail = (length of the catbeam/3) + Y + Z

The values of Y and Z are the same as in the previous formula.

This method was only used when suitable timber for the cathead could not be acquired. The remaining space between the heels of each cat-tail was fitted out with a baulk of timber, a suitable plank being worked across the structure on completion (see Fig 7/11(3)).

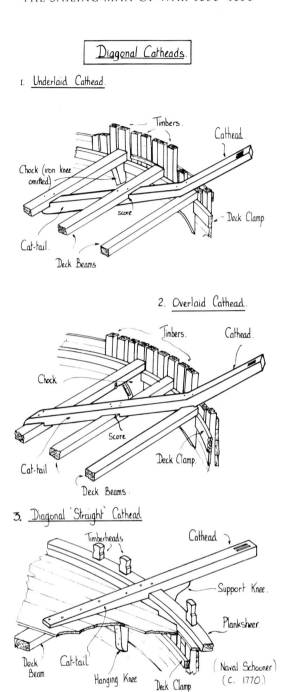

Fig 7/12

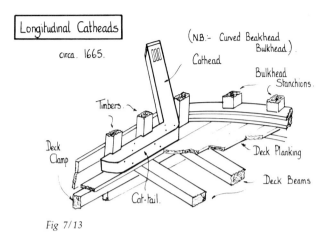

Fig 7/13

These methods were generally employed from about 1665 until the introduction of the round bow. As the round bow was introduced to sloops around 1732, the diagonal fashion became the most commonly used. As the round bow became adopted by larger ships, so the fashion of the cathead altered. Examples of the transverse cathead are non-existent. Both the *Unicorn* and the *Foudroyant* have a round bow while the *Victory* (which has a square beakhead bulkhead) has been restored incorrectly at this point, because of the impracticality of reconstruction, and scarcity of timber.

Diagonal

This style can be divided into three categories: straight, underlaid and overlaid. Each was employed irrespective of whether the ship was built with a beakhead bulkhead or with a round bow.

Underlaid   This type of cathead was more common on vessels with the built-up round bow such as the frigates and sloops of the second half of the eighteenth century. It was also found on ships of larger rating that were built during the earlier years of the nineteenth century, following the initial introduction of the round bow in 1803. As with most cathead designs a specific piece of timber was used because of the complexity of the shape required.

The length of the cat-tail was approximately equal to the portion that protruded beyond the hull. In some cases it was a little longer; this depended on the relative position of the deck beams of the forecastle. Where the cat-tail passed below the beams (hence the term 'underlaid'), its upper surface was scored to a depth of $1\frac{1}{2}$ to 3in. This allowed the cat-tail to be let up to the underside of the beams. Two bolts were driven through at each beam position, and firmly clenched. The cathead itself passed directly through the ship's side, or passed up through the deck planking (see Fig 7/12(1)).

Two examples of this form can be seen today, on the *Foudroyant* and the *Unicorn*. The latter example shows how the depth of the cat-tail was increased in its scantling, and given a rounded heel in the vicinity of the beam (see Fig 7/12). This may have been common practice during the second quarter of the nineteenth century, to ensure strength at the point of fixture. Other draughts show that extra carlings were often placed near the heel of the cat-tail, for example, the 20-gun *Brilliant* of 1842, a 22-gun frigate of 1805, and the 90-gun *Albion* of 1842. The comparatively short length of the cat-tail in relation to the cathead can be attributed to the loading stresses conveyed throughout the adjacent beams.

Overlaid   There are similarities between this method and the 'underlaid' style. The difference was that the cat-tail was scored on

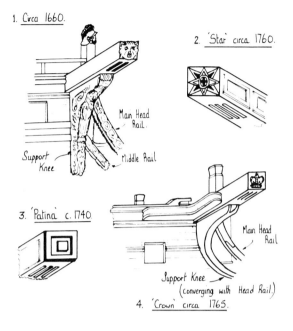

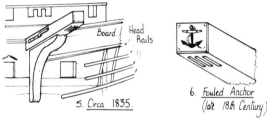

Fig 7/14

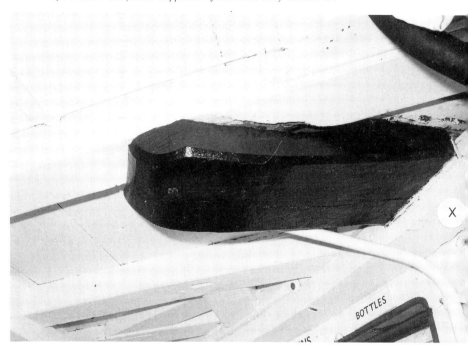

Foudroyant. Heel of the starboard cathead. This cathead is of the diagonal underlaid type, generally used on ships fitted with a round bow. The heel is bolted to the underside of the beam and further supported by the beam shelf marked 'x'.

and bolted down through to the deck beams, the bolts being clenched below (see Fig 7/12).

This form was occasionally employed on the larger men-of-war before 1660, when the upward angle of the part which protruded was less pronounced. This form was abolished on the larger ships, due to its apparent weakness at the point where it was fastened. It was therefore only used on small ships, where anchor weights were less, and the loading stresses caused little trouble.

Longitudinal

This form of securing the cathead to the structure is rare, and applies mainly to a few vessels built prior to 1685. The cat-tail in this case was set longitudinally, projecting aft. The outboard face was bolted to the ship's timbers. The length of the cat-tail varied from one to one and a half times the part of the cathead which projected beyond the hull (see Fig 7/13).

This method was soon superseded by the more practical diagonal or transverse forms. The cat-tail fitted in its longitudinal position impeded the working of the guns forward on the upper gundeck. Also the weight borne by the cathead was only distributed over a small area, causing excessive loading to the ship's timbers and a torque effect to the cathead itself. This may have been practical when they were fitted on the level of the upper gundeck, but loading problems arose when raised to the level of the forecastle. With the introduction of the transverse style, the catbeam was introduced for fixing the cat-tail.

its lower surface, and let down upon the beams. Two bolts were driven through vertically, where a joint was formed at a beam, and clenched on the underside (see Fig 7/12(2)). The only problem with this was that the cathead often interfered with the lay of the deck planking upon the forecastle. This was overcome by the careful use of margin planks, worked around the point of entry to the deck. The overlaid pattern was generally used on vessels with the round bow (for instance the 120-gun *Neptune* of 1833), but was also probably employed prior to the full introduction of the catbeam in the last quarter of the seventeenth century. It was used as an alternative between 1660 and 1680.

Straight This was mainly used on small craft such as yachts, schooners, bomb ketches and some brigs. Most of these vessels had short forecastles, with very low or nonexistent bulwarks. In their plan view, the catheads appear parallel throughout their length, while in side elevation the lower face of the cat-tail tapered towards its heel. The cat-tail itself was not an integral part of the hull, as in all of the other styles. It was positioned on the forecastle deck planking

THE SHEAVES AND SHEAVE HOLES

The purpose of the cathead was to support the anchors and assist in hoisting them to the housed position. This of course could not be achieved without the incorporation of pulley sheaves. The position and size of these sheaves, in relation to the cathead, was important, in order to ensure that the structure was in no way weakened by their presence. In general, catheads were fashioned to receive either two or three sheaves. The number depended entirely on the form of catblock employed to raise the anchor. If the catblock was of the single purchase type, then the cathead would have two sheaves. If the catblock was of the twofold purchase type, then three sheaves were fitted. The size of the sheave and the hole (or slot) in which it was fitted can be calculated from the cathead's width and breadth.

The Sheaves

These were generally made from lignum vitae, and later iron. They were held in position by an axial pin, set horizontally through the cathead. This pin was usually made from either muntz or iron, one single pin passing through all of the sheaves. The approximate sizes of the sheaves can be calculated in the following manner. (There are two formulae for the axial pin because muntz was considerably weaker than iron, therefore it had to be thicker.)

$$\textit{Sheave diameter} = \textit{breadth of the cathead} \times {}^{25}\!/_{32}$$

$$\textit{Sheave width} = \textit{diameter of the sheave}/6$$

$$\textit{Diameter of muntz axial pin} = \textit{diameter of the sheave}/8$$

$$\textit{Diameter of iron axial pin} = \textit{diameter of the sheave}/6$$

The Sheave Hole (or Slot)

Having determined the dimensions of the sheaves, the size of the slots into which they were received can be calculated. These slots were cut vertically through the cathead, and made to a sufficient length to prevent the catfalls from fouling. This was done by accommodating the sheaves at a position a little off-centre of the slot length towards the inboard end. The dimensions of the slots were all equal, and can be calculated in the following manner:

$$\textit{Length of the slot} = \textit{diameter of the sheave} \times 2$$

$$\textit{Width of the slot} = \textit{width of the sheave} + {}^{1}\!/_{4}\textit{in (for clearance)}$$

The distance of the end of the slot from the cathead's extremity (excluding the end cap) was about equal to the cathead's breadth.

It was previously stated that the sheaves were off-set, to ensure that the catfalls did not foul the sheave slots. It is therefore necessary to calculate the position of the pin. This measurement is taken from the outboard end of the slot, and can be determined as follows.

$$\textit{Relative position of pin (laterally)} = \textit{length of slot} \times {}^{3}\!/_{5}$$

The vertical position of the pin was such that the sheaves were level with the upper surface of the cathead. The measurement, taken vertically from the upper surface, was thus equal to the sheave's radius. The sheave was therefore off-set vertically and laterally.

THE CATHEAD SUPPORTER (OR KNEE)

The cathead was supported by a large knee, which was bolted to the ship's side. The purpose of this knee was to distribute the weight exerted at the extremity of the cathead. The dimensions of this knee can be determined in the following manner.

$$\textit{Length of supporting arm} = \textit{projected length of cathead} \times {}^{17}\!/_{32}$$

$$\textit{Siding of knee} = \textit{width of cathead} \times {}^{9}\!/_{16}$$

The siding of the knee usually diminished towards the heel of the vertical arm, and in most cases it faired in, converging with one of the head rails. Prior to 1670, the cathead knee was fashioned as a single component, with its heel set vertical. The aftermost ends of the head rails were then faired in to butt against the fore face of the vertical arm. This can be seen on a number of models at the National Maritime Museum at Greenwich, for instance the 58-gun ship of around 1665, the 32-gun ship of around 1660, and the *St Michael* of 1669. After 1670 most draughts show the heel of the knee faired round to join with the head rails. Variations of this practice occur. Some draughts show the heel converging with the lower head rail, while others show the heel joined to the middle head rail (draught of a Fourth Rate by Keltridge around 1684).

Although there does not appear to have been a standard practice, most vessels built prior to 1715 had the heel converging with the middle head rail. After this, most ships had the heel of the knee joined to the lower head rail. There are a number of exceptions to the rule which probably occurred because of the designer's need to produce fair lines on the ship's head.

With the introduction of the round bow to all classes of ships in the earlier years of the nineteenth century, the shape of the knee altered. Like a number of other fittings, it reverted back to an old form. Head rails were made with less curvature, and their after ends were once again butted to the fore face of the knee. Thus the knee became a separate component once again, for instance *Unicorn* of 1824, at Dundee. This form was first used about 1810 and by 1820 became general practice. The *Nelson*, which was launched in 1814, was one of the earliest ships built with this style. Here the middle head rail was butted to the fore side of the knee. A second knee was fitted in the horizontal plane, to the after side of the cathead, giving additional support. The lengths of the arms were equal to the arm of the supporting knee. They appear to have been used on the larger vessels, between 1735 and 1807.

The Quarter Galleries

Quarter galleries were first introduced during the reign of Elizabeth I, and were used either for latrines, or as an area for officers to exercise. By the end of the Tudor period, they had become partially enclosed, with panelled sides, and arched stanchions terminating at the ship's sides. Over the top of these stanchions, awnings were fastened to give some degree of protection from the elements. During the first decade of the seventeenth century a more permanent canopy was adopted, and additional screens were fitted close to the access door cut in the ship's side. By 1630 the whole structure was fully closed in, with panels and windows, all of which became the focus for decoration and carved work. The original canopy was superseded by a series of half domes which surmounted the whole of the assembly. The lower part of the structure was supported by oak brackets, or by a large piece of timber commonly known as a lower finishing. In either method of construction, these items were firmly bolted to the ship's side. In most cases the lower finishing was richly carved, to disguise its true function.

Quarter galleries of the Commonwealth period were generally five-sided on the outboard face, with the centre portion projecting a little beyond the confines of the rest of the structure. This design resembles the modern day bay window. Each individual face of the gallery was divided into panels, surrounded with carved pillars and mouldings, and often painted with symbols. The top of the gallery was made up of three domes, the centre one being of greater size than the other two.

With the restoration of the monarchy in 1660, the overall design of the quarter galleries underwent some alterations, which gave the structure more graceful lines. This was done by bringing the fore end closer to the side of the ship, and making the after end conform with the rake and contour of the stern. The three domes were abandoned in favour of a single dome, that surmounted the entire gallery. The top of this dome was generally finished with a carved crown or badge, or, in the case of the *Prince* of 1670, the plumes of the Prince of Wales. Another introduction at this time was a second gallery, level with the upper gundeck. This is believed to have been first adopted on the 90-gun *St Michael* in 1669. This quickly spread to other larger ships of the fleet, and by the turn of the eighteenth century tiered galleries had become normal. Quarter figures were also introduced at this period, extending from the lower gallery to the taffrail. The painting of panels along the side of the galleries, and other carved work was soon abolished. This was due to the Navy Board Order of 1703, which stipulated the reduction of carved and gilt work. This was followed by the fitting of small carved pillars and simple mouldings, which were to remain a common feature of quarter galleries for the remainder of the eighteenth century. One other aspect of the close of the seventeenth century was that in some cases the upper gallery was left partially open, but these galleries were very narrow, and in some cases only two feet wide (for example in the 100-gun *Britannia* of 1700).

Over the next 50 years a number of small changes were made in the relationship between the quarter galleries and the stern gallery.

Foudroyant. Port quarter gallery undergoing restoration. The lower portion of the quarter post and the underside of the quarter rail can be seen. Note the mortices cut in the latter for the heads of the stiffeners. The 'head' is original, the flushing pipe is on the left, and the cistern is set above the upper stool.

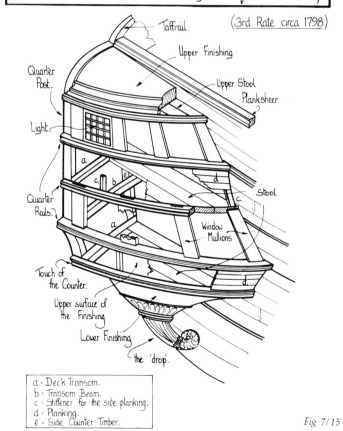

The Construction of the Quarter Gallery on a Square Sterned Ship.

(3rd Rate circa 1798)

Taffrail.
Upper Finishing
Quarter Post.
Upper Stool
Planksheer
Light.
Quarter Rails.
Stool
Window Mullions
Touch of the Counter.
Upper surface of the Finishing
Lower Finishing
the 'drop'.

a = Deck Transom.
b = Transom Beam.
c = Stiffener for the side planking.
d = Planking.
e = Side Counter Timber.

Fig 7/15

Foudroyant. Port quarter gallery. This photograph was taken looking upwards and forwards at the quarter rail. Mortices for the side planking stiffeners can be clearly identified.

Some designs show that the stern gallery was extended around the quarters, while in other cases the quarter galleries terminated at the line of the stern. The disposition of the quarter pieces also affected the overall design, and formed an archway over the point where the open gallery met with the open stern walk (about 1740). After 1760 the quarter galleries remained 'closed in', and very few alterations were made, except to the projecting galleries of the circular stern introduced by Seppings in 1817. Although this was but a brief interlude from the normal fashion, the basic construction remained fairly similar.

CONSTRUCTION

The principal components of the framework of the quarter gallery were as follows: the lower finishing, the stools, the quarter post, the quarter rails, the upper finishing and the window frames (or mullions).

The first item to be fitted was the lower stool. This consisted of a number of planks about 3 to 4in thick, fayed and bolted together, forming a platform. Before being fastened to the ship they were sawn to shape, conforming to the plan of the gallery. The inner face was chamfered to the angle required for its round up or camber. When being bolted to the ship's side it was laid with the sheer and camber of the deck. Once the stool was fitted, it was supported by a baulk of timber known as the lower finishing. This was made from a single piece of oak. This timber was bolted to the ship's side directly beneath the stool, to which it was further secured with iron dumps or spikes driven from above. Both the inboard and upper surfaces of the lower finishing had to be fashioned to conform to the ship's side angle and the camber of the stool. This assembly formed the foundation for the whole structure of the quarter galleries.

The next timber was the quarter post, which acted as the vertical strengthening member. There is little information as to how this timber was shaped. It appears from inspection of the *Victory* that it may well have been made from one piece of oak in the same manner as the stern counter timbers. Alternatively, it may have been made from two pieces scarphed together, the lower portion being shaped to the curvature of the upper counter timbers. Once it was manufactured, it was set up upon the after outboard corner of the stool, and firmly bolted in position. It was further supported throughout its height by the various moulded rails that were worked across the after faces of the stern counter timbers. The whole assembly was fastened together with iron dumps or spikes. The quarter post was usually of considerable size, its siding varying from 8 to 12in, its width varying between two-thirds and three-quarters of the siding. The remaining stools, which also served as either a deck or deckhead to each gallery were then fitted and bolted to the side of the ship in the same manner as the lower stool. Bolts were then driven through the quarter post, into the stools, thus giving greater rigidity to the structure.

At the top of the quarter post the upper finishing was fitted, in the same manner as the lower finishing. Similarly, it was fashioned in this period's style of decoration. The quarter rails were employed to stiffen the whole structure longitudinally. These were fitted between the quarter post and the ship's side, at the fore end of the gallery. The fore end was sniped at a suitable angle to meet the ship's side planking, both ends being fastened with spikes or bolts. Like the quarter post, these timbers were of considerable dimension, about 12in wide and 8in deep. Its depth was approximately two-thirds of its width. The outboard face of this timber was heavily moulded, while its inboard face was slotted to receive the heels of the window frames. The number of quarter rails depended on the number of decks the vessel had. One was fitted at the level of the window sills in each gallery, which was approximately 18in above the deck level to the upper edge of the sill.

Quarter rails of lesser scantling were also fitted a little below the level of the stools, and fastened in the same manner as those previously mentioned. Similarly, they were moulded on their

Egmont. The port quarter of a model showing galleries, taffrail, mizzen channel and its chains. The sheer and drift rails and the secondary steering arrangements are also evident.

outboard side and slotted on the internal face for the heads of the window frames. Finally, the space between the sills and the stools was planked in with oak, 4 to 6in broad and 1½ to 2in thick, each plank being secured with spikes. All that remained was the fastening of the window frames or mullions between the two sizes of quarter rails. These, too, were secured with spikes. Their width varied from 5 to 7in and they were about 2in thick (see Fig 7/15).

The differences in the construction of seventeenth-century quarter galleries apply mainly to the fore and aft members, and the planking. When five-sided galleries were constructed, the equivalent of the quarter rails were made in short individual lengths. Likewise, the planking or panelling was of short lengths worked between the vertical stanchions. This construction also required stanchions fitted between the sill and the stools at the point of

Unicorn. *The captain's day cabin showing the entrances to the three galleries and the relative positions of the gunports on the Seppings circular stern. The gallery to starboard was originally fitted out as a shower room, that to port served as the captain's personal heads, while the centre gallery was used purely for leisure and observation.*

change in angle of the sides. The domes which surmounted the structure appear to be of a plank and frame construction. How they were actually made is unknown, but two methods could have been employed. If the construction consisted of a frame, it would have been very impractical to build, as the frames would have been made from solid pieces of timber. Contemporary models at the National Maritime Museum suggest the frame method was used. The use of solid timbers would have imposed a great deal of strain upon the after frame timbers of the hull. On the other hand, the same effect would have been produced by the large carved quarter figures introduced a few years later. This weight problem was one of the reasons why quarter pieces were to be restricted, and eventually abolished, in the next century. A more practical explanation would be that the domes of the larger vessels were of frame and plank construction, while on smaller ships solid baulks of timbers, shaped as required, were employed.

The galleries of the circular stern extended completely around the stern in individual sponsons. The draught of the *Melampus* built at Pembroke Yard, gives the following information regarding the

Unicorn. *Profile of the circular stern showing the 'sponsoned' galleries, a modification introduced by Robert Seppings in 1817.*

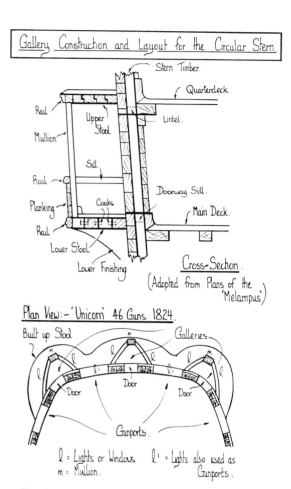

Gallery Construction and Layout for the Circular Stern

Stern Timber.
Quarterdeck
Rail
Upper Stool
Lintel.
Mullion
Rail
Sill.
Doorway Sill.
Planking
Coaks
Main Deck.
Rail
Lower Stool
Lower Finishing
Cross-Section.
(Adapted from Plans of the 'Melampus')

Plan View:- 'Unicorn' 46 Guns 1824.
Built up Stool
Galleries
Door
Door
Door
Gunports.
l = Lights or Windows   l¹ = Lights also used as
m = Mullion.   Gunports.

Fig 7/16

construction. As in all cases, the stools were bolted to the ship. The lower stool was 8in deep, and the upper stool 6in deep, each extending a maximum of 3ft 7in beyond the external planking. Each stool appears to have been made up from a number of timbers, each bolted together and 'coaked' with oak coaks, 3in long and 3in diameter. The lower stool was further supported by a baulk of timber, in the same manner as that of the lower finishing. Two rails were wrought around the after end, one 3½in thick and another 2in. The frames forming the windows were 3½in thick and about 13in wide, worked vertically between the upper and lower stools. The timber finishings below the lower stool were bolted to the ship's structure, and its curious shape was probably made with adzes, so that it faired into the hull with room for the rudder. For details, refer to Fig 7/16.

BADGES

Smaller vessels such as sloops were not built with quarter galleries, but with a quarter light (or window) cut through the ship's side. As in most cases this was a focal point for ornamentation. The construction was relatively simple, and consisted of mouldings and carved pillars bolted to the surrounding structure. The top of the light was adorned with such items as a crown or badge or occasionally scrollwork. Badges were generally restricted to vessels of under 250 tons including brigs. By the eighteenth century, badges had become very plain, with mouldings and a flat pillar on each side.

Victory. *The manger on the lower gundeck, with its rabbetted stanchion fitted at the ship's side. Note the beam arms and the beam scarphs at the deckhead. The open grating provided ventilation to the orlop, and this opening could be used for fire-fighting purposes. All the shoring is temporary.*

CHAPTER 8

Minor Fittings

The Figurehead

The ship's head had been adorned with a carved figure since before the time of the Vikings. By 1650 the figurehead was a firmly established feature and had become a major focus of ornamentation. Many figureheads have survived, and can be seen in numerous museums, naval establishments and even in churchyards. One can see from the many existing examples that they varied considerably in size and style.

The figureheads of the Cromwellian Navy were either in the classical style, or took the form of some kind of beast, such as a unicorn. The *Naseby* had a figurehead of Cromwell on horseback, trampling over his enemies. This remarkable carving was removed from the vessel after her return to England from Holland with the exiled king, Charles II. The entire figurehead was burned in front of the jubilant Royalist crowds, including Samuel Pepys.

After the restoration of the monarchy, the standard pattern of figureheads on naval ships was the crowned 'lyon', except on First Rates, which were privileged in having individual figures. Most First Rates were named after a royal personage, and had an equestrian figurehead. There were of course variations, for example the *St Michael* of 1669 which had the figure of Jupiter riding in a chariot. After 1670 the figureheads of the larger ships became far more complex, with additional figures. The *Lion* of 1670 had a lion with cupids set to each side of it, and the *Coronation* of 1685 had a cupid mounted on the back of an 'enraged' lion. When William III ascended to the throne, the 'double' equestrian figure became popular for larger ships, while the crowned lion was retained on vessels of 80 guns and less. All figureheads of this period were either varnished or gilded.

The restrictions on carving and gilt work introduced in 1703 eliminated the large expensive double figureheads, and there was a general reversion to the crowned lion. The 'double' figure was occasionally employed on prestige First Rates, until the end of the eighteenth century. Two examples are the 100-gun *Royal George* of 1756, and the *Victory* of 1765. The latter had a very ornate figure which was removed during her refit in 1803, and replaced with a more modest affair that can still be seen today, though even this figurehead had two figures.

The lion figure was standard until restrictions were moderated in 1727, when the Navy Board gave authorisation that all ships could carry individual figureheads, suited to the ship's name. This privilege was not at first taken advantage of, and many ships retained the lion figure until as late as 1760. It was also during that year that the practice of having figures gilded was superseded by having them painted with bright colours. This was more practical because paint gave a better protective cover from the elements, and also proved less costly. This was quite important, for the painting of a vessel was generally at the captain's own expense. This practice first appeared about 1737, when restrictions were imposed on gilt work.

From 1760 very few alterations were made to figureheads, until 1796, when the Navy Board decided to abolish full figures, and replace them with either half figures, busts or scrolls. This was done to save money because of the rising cost of the war with France. Figureheads of this nature were standard for a further sixty years.

Stern Lanterns

Lanterns were first fitted on the sterns of naval ships at the end of the sixteenth century. They were common until the end of the eighteenth century; by 1815 they had disappeared. Stern lanterns were probably introduced to differentiate flagships within their squadron. The potential of these lamps as a navigational aid was

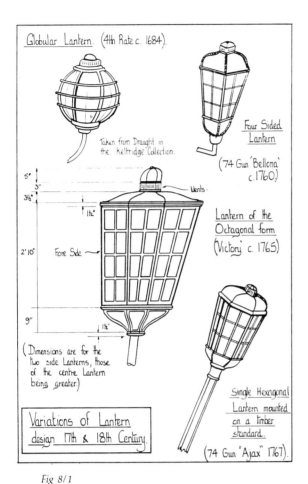

Fig 8/1

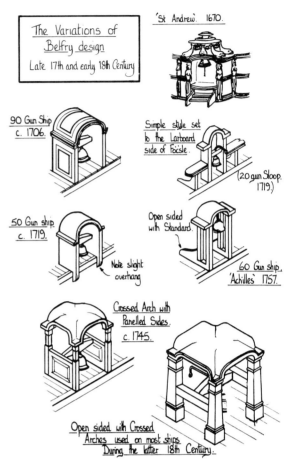

Fig 8/2

soon appreciated. Subsequently they were fitted to most large vessels.

Three lanterns, the centre one of the greatest dimension, appears to have been the general rule during the latter half of the seventeenth century (though it was not unknown for there only to be one or two). Single lamps were not introduced until the second decade of the eighteenth century. An early example is shown on the model of an 80-gun ship built to the Establishment of 1719, at the Science Museum in London. This type of lantern was also found on smaller ships such as the 32-gun frigate of 1761, the *Lowestoft*. Later ships also had single lamps, such as the 120-gun *Nelson* of 1814. This can clearly be seen on the excellent drawings produced by the draughtsman John Pringle, who was attached to Woolwich Dockyard. Irrespective of class or size of vessel, the number of lanterns fitted varied according to the individual tastes of the builder.

Between 1650 and 1690 lanterns were usually globular, with a diameter of about 3ft 6in to 4ft. After this, the octagonal form was introduced, and was to remain common until the use of lanterns declined. Design details varied from one ship to another. Illustrations from original draughts and models are reproduced in Fig 8/1. The style of the support brackets also varied from a single

arm to a triple arm, again this reflected the taste of the individual designer. In a number of cases, the fore face was closed in and formed the entry door for lighting the lamp. This proves that the lanterns were for aiding navigation, when the vessels in a squadron were sailing in line ahead during the night or in inclement weather. They were usually made from iron and sometimes brass. Gilt work and paint often disguise the fact that iron was used. Originally lanterns were illuminated by large candles, but by the turn of the eighteenth century oil was used, either sperm whale oil or colza. The latter is produced from crushing rape seeds.

Lanterns of similar size were occasionally fitted in other positions. The *Victory* has what is known as an admiral's lantern, fitted to the after side of the main top. This must have been a great fire hazard among the canvas and rigging. Another unusual fixture can be seen on the model of the 20-gun *Dolphin* of 1731, at the Transport Museum in Glasgow. This has lanterns set up on stanchions on each side of the forecastle. This model may not be entirely accurate as a similar model in the National Maritime Museum has no lamps. The glazing was probably originally made from mica, commonly known as Muscovy glass, which was also used for the stern windows. This was superseded by normal glass in the early eighteenth century.

The Belfry

Originally the belfry was fitted on the quarterdeck of British ships, but by 1665 it had, for practical reasons, been moved to the break of the forecastle. This alteration had occurred in most foreign ships earlier. Some British ships did, however, have this modification before 1665. A model of a 50-gun ship of 1653 at the National Maritime Museum, has a belfry on the forecastle. By 1670, larger vessels had very ornate belfries. The bell itself was placed within an elaborate enclosure, built as an integral part of the forecastle bulkhead. Access was at an open after side, by a short flight of steps. The sides of the compartment were panelled, and subdivided with carved false pillars, and heavy mouldings. The canopy was furnished with an ornate dome, similar in appearance to the domes fitted to the quarter galleries. This feature can be seen on the model of the *Prince* in the Science Museum.

The belfry on smaller ships of the period was less elaborate, and consisted of a single arched canopy supported by carved pillars, usually in the form of nude nymphs. The canopy itself was either plain or adorned with figures or beasts. Such features can be seen on the model of the 48-gun *Mordaunt* of 1681.

With the general reduction in carved work in 1703, the enclosed belfry finally disappeared and was replaced by a simplified version of that used on smaller ships. The canopy was made with a more pronounced arch, supported by panelled sides, the whole construction being rather heavy in appearance. The normal position for the belfry was directly amidships at the break of the forecastle though some vessels had alternative arrangements. One such class was that of the 20-gun sloops built between 1719 and 1727. These had the belfry fitted to the port side of the forecastle, allowance being made for the galley flue on the opposite side because the forecastle was too short to allow the two fittings to be placed fore and aft of each other. This layout also applied to 20-gun sloops, built around 1741. After this, there is a short period when most had a canopy supported by pillars only and some belfries retained the panels in the lower half only.

The next alteration was made to the canopy, which on the larger vessels became fashioned in the form of crossed arches. Also the height of the arches was diminished, and they became flatter in appearance. Most of the smaller vessels retained the single arch in the new style, and often the foremost pillars were braced with short standards. Both the *Centurion* and the 64-gun ship *Achilles* had this feature.

The finest example of the crossed arch style of belfry is on board the *Victory*. Here the headstock for the bell is supported by two fore and aft beams set between the pillars (see Fig 8/2). One exception to the rule during the latter part of the seventeenth century was the belfry fitted on the *Boyne* where there were half-panels and standards. From this evidence it appears wrong to assume that there were specific designs for belfries throughout the period. The style was influenced by the taste of the builder.

Very few changes were made after 1760, except that the overall size diminished slightly. The only reference to standardisation of belfries was made in 1815. The Navy Board authorised the size of the bell for all ships of Third Rate and above. It was to be made to a diameter of 1ft 6½in, and 15in high. Finally, with the general closing of the waist in 1832, the belfry, ironically, was once again placed aft. I have not given any measurements because of the many permutations in design, which are illustrated in Fig 8/2.

Hatchways and Scuttles

Throughout each deck there were hatchways and scuttles, varying in size according to their specific functions. The largest was the main hatch, which was fitted a little afore the mainmast. This opening was present at each deck level, and was used to convey stores to the hold. A little aft of the break of the forecastle was the second largest hatch, the fore hatch. This served a similar function to the main hatch.

A hatchway was built from two fore and aft members known as

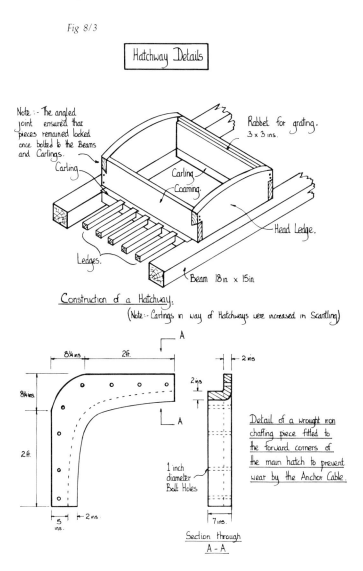

Fig 8/3

Hatchway Details

Note :- The angled joint ensured that pieces remained locked once bolted to the Beams and Carlings.

Rabbet for grating. 3 x 3 ins.

Carling

Carling

Coaming

Head Ledge.

Ledges.

Beam 18in x 15in

Construction of a Hatchway.
(Note:- Carlings in way of Hatchways were increased in Scantling)

8¼ ins   2 ft.

8¼ ins

2 ft.

1 inch diameter Bolt Holes

5 ins.   2 ins.

A

A

2 ins

2 ins

7 ins.

Detail of a wrought iron chaffing piece fitted to the forward corners of the main hatch to prevent wear by the Anchor Cable.

Section through A - A

coamings and two transverse timbers called head ledges. These timbers were usually made from oak, and were all 6 to 10in thick. The depth varied according to the period, and the deck on which they were fitted. The nearer the hatch was to the waterline, the greater the depth of the timbers. This ensured that the ship remained dry. However, earlier vessels had rather low coamings, thus water was able to enter. This was uncomfortable for the crew and a hazard to the stores kept below. This problem was finally solved by a Navy Board order of 1795, which stipulated that coamings were to be built well clear of the deck, approximately 15 to 18in above deck level. The main hatch was set with its after edge against the beam afore the mainmast. Its width was approximately one-sixth of the ship's moulded beam, while its fore and aft length was between one-quarter and one-third greater than its width.

Below each coaming an additional carling of larger scantling was added to give support, the head ledges being set upon the beams themselves. The coamings and head ledges were fitted together with a halving joint, which in some cases was angled to prevent the two pieces from unlocking. The timbers were bolted to their respective beams and carlings and to each other, with dumps or spikes. Suitably sized battens, about 3in square section, were worked on the internal faces of the hatch to support the grating or other covering. In later years it was common to give the top surfaces of the head ledges a convex face, the grating or covering being manufactured to conform to this shape. The construction of the fore hatch was similar to that of the main hatchway, except in its dimensions. Generally it was square, or it was wider than its length, as was the after hatch. The dimensions below give the overall length and width, including the thickness of the coamings and head ledges.

The hatch to the fish room was generally about 4ft 6in fore and aft and approximately 5ft wide. Smaller hatches and scuttles were dispersed throughout the remaining decks, for the passing of cartridges, magazine light rooms, magazine entry, and various storerooms on the orlop and in the hold. Scuttles were usually square and large enough only for a man to pass through. Most scuttles fitted on men-of-war were about 2ft square or 2ft 6in by 2ft. Solid covers were usually used to reduce the problem of damp, and risk of fire.

Scuppers

The function of the scuppers was to channel water from the free surface areas of the decks, or to discharge the water from the bilge pumps overboard. They are rarely shown on draughts or contemporary models, and information on dimensions and disposition is sparse until adequate documentation becomes available for the years towards the end of the eighteenth century. The number employed and their nominal bore sizes are clearly given in the list of dimensions and scantlings in the *Shipbuilder's Repository* of 1789.

In general the number disposed along each deck varied from six

Dimensions of the Main Hatchway about 1675

Rate of ship	Fore and aft		Breadth		Battens square
	ft	in	ft	in	in
First	8	6	6	10	3½
Second	8	4	6	8	3½
Third	8	2	6	6	3
Fourth	8		6		3
Fifth	7	6	5	9	3
Sixth	6	6	5	6	2½

Hatchway Dimensions (Based on Dimensions Specified for Naval Vessels around 1780)

No of guns	Length		Breadth		Afore the mainmast centre	
	ft	in	ft	in	ft	in
Main Hatch						
100	8	10	6	10	5	8
90	8	10	6	9	5	8
74	8	4	6	6	6	2
64	8		6		5	2
44	7	3	5	10	3	6
38	7	6	5	8	4	5
36	6	8	5	6	4	
32	6	8	5		3	4
28	6	4	5		3	4
24	6		4	10	3	4
Sloop	5	6	4	6	3	3
Cutter	5	7	4	8	—	
Fore Hatch						
100	5	5	5	2	32	
90	4	6	5		28	3
74	4	4	4	10	32	2
64	4	8	4	8	25	3
44	4	8	4	8	23	8
38	5		4	8	27	3
36	4	5	4	6	26	
32	4	8	4	5	23	9
28	4	6	4	4	22	
24	4	3	4	4	20	
Sloop	4		4		10	
Cutter	4	2	4		—	
After Hatch abaft the Mizzen Mast						
100	4	8	5	2	12	7
90	4	7	5		11	4
74	4	6	4	10	12	4
64	4	8	4	8	10	3
44	4	8	4	8	10	
38	4	8	4	8	9	
36	4	8	3	10	8	2
32	4	8	3	8	7	10
28	4		3	6	7	8
24	3	10	3	4	7	6
Sloop	3	9	3	4	9	
Cutter	2	4	4		7	6

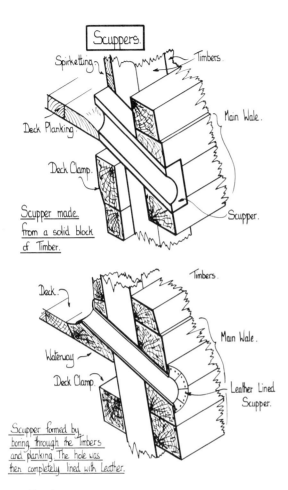

Scuppers.

Scupper made from a solid block of Timber.

Scupper formed by boring through the timbers and planking. The hole was then completely lined with Leather.

Fig 8/4

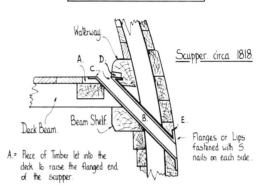

Methods of Fitting Scuppers.

Scupper circa 1818.

A. = Piece of Timber let into the deck to raise the flanged end of the scupper.

B. = Lead Scupper with a 4½ inch diameter bore.

C. = Lips or Flanges to prevent leakage, therefore designed to 'work' with the Ship.

D. = Piece of Wood worked into the Waterway on the 'flap' of the Scupper, this was always Caulked.

E. = Flanges are sealed with a jointing compound of Flannel dipped in Tar.

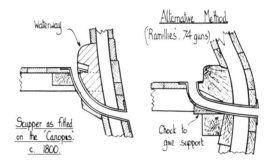

Scupper as fitted on the 'Canopus'. c. 1800.

Alternative Method ('Ramillies', 74 guns)

Chock to give support

Fig 8/5

to eight, depending on the ship's length. The bore diameter also varied from 2 to 6in according to the height of the deck above the waterline. Those used for the bilge pump discharges were usually greater in diameter, and either equal in size or a little smaller than the bore of the pump dale. In all cases the scuppers were fitted with an incline downwards of approximately 25 degrees, to ensure the exit of water and to prevent a backflow from without.

During the latter part of the seventeenth century and the earlier years of the eighteenth century, two methods of construction were used. Firstly, a simple lead pipe was passed through the ship's side and carefully caulked for watertightness. The second type was made in the form of a suitably sized 'fitted' wooden block, generally made from elm, which was bored through as required and lined with leather. In either case the external end was furnished with a leather flap or 'sock' to prevent water intrusion. The lead pipe form was generally used in preference to the wooden block type (see Fig 8/4 and 8/5.) The following figures are taken from the 1789 edition of the *Shipbuilder's Repository*.

Number and Diameter of Lead Pipes

No of guns	Number fitted	Diameter in inches
Lower Gundeck – each side		
100	8	5½
90	9	5¼
74	6	5
64	6	4
44	6	4

Upper Deck – each side (lower deck of single decked ships and middle deck of First Rates)		
100	8	3½
90	8	3½
74	8	3¼
64	7	3
44	7	3
38	6	3
36	6	2¾
32	6	2¾
28	5	2¾
24	5	2¾
Sloops	5	2½
Cutters	4	2¼

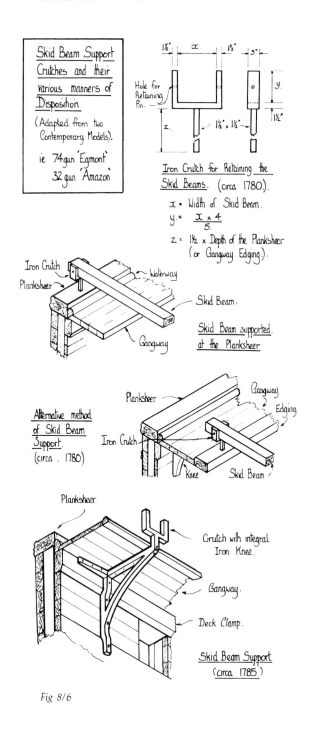

Skid Beam Support Crutches and their various manners of Disposition

(Adapted from two Contemporary Models).

ie 74 gun 'Egmont'
32 gun 'Amazon'

Iron Crutch for Retaining the Skid Beams. (circa 1780).

x = Width of Skid Beam.
$y = \dfrac{x \times 4}{5}$.
z = 1½ × Depth of the Planksheer (or Gangway Edging).

Iron Crutch
Planksheer
Waterway
Skid Beam.
Gangway

Skid Beam supported at the Planksheer

Alternative method of Skid Beam Support.
(circa . 1780)

Planksheer
Gangway
Edging
Iron Crutch
Knee
Skid Beam

Planksheer
Crutch with integral Iron Knee.
Gangway.
Deck Clamp.

Skid Beam Support
(circa 1785.)

Fig 8/6

The Skid Beams

Prior to the introduction of the gangways on each side of the ship's waist, the manner in which the boats were stowed was somewhat basic. A number of spare booms and spars were laid longitudinally between the quarterdeck and the forecastle. These booms formed a natural 'cradle' in which the boats rested. By 1765, temporary gangways had become a permanent fixture, supported by a series of timber hanging knees which gave the whole structure rigidity. This enabled lightweight beams of fir to be laid transversely between the gangways, upon which the boats were now stowed, aided by chocks.

At first these skid beams were only temporarily fitted, and could be removed when required. This was done by having the ends of the beams set into iron crutches, which were dispersed along the planksheer (see Fig 8/6). There are a number of contemporary models at the National Maritime Museum which illustrate this. These include a 32-gun frigate of the 'Amazon' class, of 1793. Alternatively a simple slotted plank was set longitudinally along each gangway, but this method is very rare. The next alteration was introduced in 1778, when the gangways were raised to the level of the quarterdeck and forecastle. Improvements in their support were also made, and iron brackets often replaced the timber hanging knees. A crutch was integral to the bracket's design. This form can be seen on a number of contemporary models, including the 98-gun *Boyne* at the National Maritime Museum, an illustration of this type appears in Fig 8/6. It can be assumed that from about 1790, most large vessels were fitted out in this manner, to support the ends of the skid beams. At this time, very few frigates were fitted with skid beams.

One of the major problems in ship design was the hogging effect caused by the extra topweight at each end of the vessel. It was soon realised by the more radical shipbuilders that by fitting the skid beams on a permanent basis, additional stiffening could be given to the hull. These beams were therefore built integral to the hull, in the same way as those employed on the forecastle and quarterdeck. By 1800 this was general practice on most ships from Fourth Rate upwards. The permanent fitting of skid beams on frigates took place during the American War of 1812–14. British ship designers found that the American frigates, built with beams at the waist, were considerably stiffer in their hull. Thus permanent beams became universally fitted throughout the Fleet. There are of course some exceptions to the rule, for instance the 'Banterer' class frigates, built at the time of Trafalgar. The introduction of 'fixed' beams at the waist was later to lead to the closing of the waist, forming a continuous upper deck fore and aft.

Dimensions for the temporary skid beams are very variable; their width was usually about two-thirds of that of the adjacent fixed beams. Their depth was about two-thirds of their width. When these beams became fixed, their dimensions corresponded with those of the quarterdeck beams.

The Hammock Stowage

The original function of the hammock stowages was twofold. Firstly, they acted as a wind break, in much the same manner as canvas dodgers on modern racing yachts. Secondly, by having the crew's hammocks stowed in a form of barricade, protection was given from musket fire and flying splinters during action.

HAMMOCK CRANES

These first appeared around 1710, and were mainly fitted on smaller ships such as frigates and sloops, their use being limited to the quarterdeck and forecastle. The stanchions, made from wrought iron, took the form of U-shaped brackets, with a single spike at the base, set down into the planksheer. These cranes were then covered with a tarred canvas screen. An example of this form can be seen on the model of a 60-gun ship built to the Establishment of 1719, in the Science Museum in South Kensington.

Over the next 30 years the employment of hammock cranes became fashionable, and they were used extensively on upper decks, including the poop decks of the larger vessels. Finally, in 1746 the Navy Board recognised the advantages of this practice, and submitted a letter of authorisation to the Admiralty on 26 September, stating that they were to be fitted on all ships. Within ten years this arrangement had become universal throughout the Fleet.

By 1770 the design had altered, becoming more square in shape with an additional tie bar set between the heads of each upright. This type can be seen on board the *Victory*. This form is illustrated in Fig 8/7 (2 and 3). Another alteration was the introduction of netting suspended between the inner and outer stanchions. This proved more practical. The netting used had 4 to 6in² holes. Canvas covers were still used, but it was found that during hot weather the tar stained the hammocks. This was eliminated by a Navy Board order of 1780, that the covering cloths were to be painted either white or yellow.

HAMMOCK TROUGHS (OR BOXES)

Towards the end of the eighteenth century it was decided to follow the French practice of having the bulwarks built up solid. This gave far better protection during close action. This became a general feature on naval vessels by 1810, though the rail along the waist, with its hammock nettings, was retained. This still proved to be a vulnerable point, and improvements were made to overcome this problem. The new design of hammock stowage took the form of a box or a trough, which was open at the top, to allow hammocks to be deposited. These were covered with a canvas cloth to prevent dampness. At first this structure was relatively light and generally made from fir, but by 1820 other designs, which incorporated iron stanchions or stiffeners were used. It was quickly realised that a similar structure could be adopted to fit the quarterdeck and forecastle bulwarks; these were shallower due to their position. The various designs illustrated in Fig 8/8, are based on contemporary models. By 1840 hammock troughs were standardised, although there were a few exceptions. One such was the *Unicorn*. Here access to the hammocks was gained by panelled doors fitted to the inboard side (see Fig 8/8).

Fig 8/7

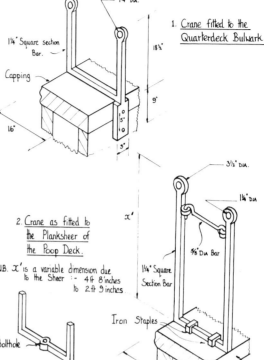

Hammock Cranes fitted on the *Victory*

1. Crane fitted to the Quarterdeck Bulwark.

2. Crane as fitted to the Planksheer of the Poop Deck.

NB. x is a variable dimension due to the Sheer :- 4ft 8 inches to 2ft 9 inches

3. Alternative method of securing.

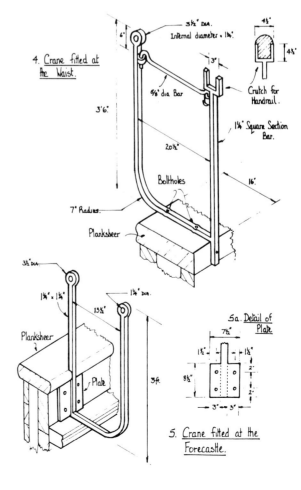

4. Crane fitted at the Waist.

5a. Detail of Plate

5. Crane fitted at the Forecastle.

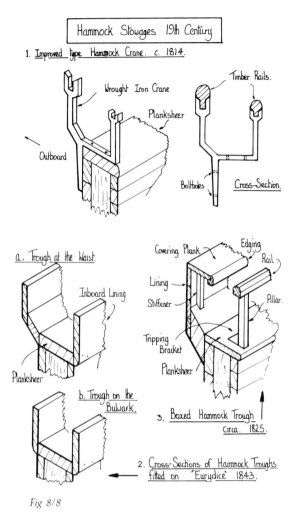

Fig 8/8

The Fish Davits

This type of davit was employed solely for raising the anchors from the vertical position when suspended from the cathead, to their horizontal stowed position. The latter was commonly referred to as being 'fished', for the anchor was hooked at its flukes and hauled up to its required place on the ship's side. Between 1650 and 1733 the fish davit was fashioned in the form of a long, square-sectioned beam, made to a length equal to that of the ship's breadth. This timber was portable, with a large block fitted at each end for raising the anchor. When stowed, the extremities were supported by specially designed 'pads' fitted to the upper edge of the forecastle bulwark. The additional fittings were called fish davit cleats (these are discussed later in this section).

When the anchor needed to be fished, one end was extended out beyond the confines of the vessel, the inboard end being secured to eyebolts fitted in the deck, which prevented movement and took the weight. To move the davit, two items were used. Firstly, there was a hand rope that extended along the fore and after faces. Secondly, two eyebolts were fitted on the upper face. These were used for the topping lift, which took the weight when moving the

davit, while the hand ropes were employed for manipulation and adjustment. Each eyebolt was set approximately one-quarter of the davit's overall length, from one end. The extremities were fashioned in a similar manner to the timberhead, to allow a strop for the fish block to be secured. The overall dimensions of this form of davit can be determined as follows:

Length of davit = extreme breadth of vessel

Square section dimension at centre of
$$length = length \times \frac{1}{2} \ (inches)$$

Width and depth of extreme ends = dimension at centre × ⅘

From 1733 onwards, the use of the single heavy beam davit was superseded by a new shorter type, that was fitted to each side of the ship. This had two advantages: firstly, the forecastle could be kept clear of obstacles. Secondly, the shorter version was far easier to manipulate, and could be stowed away when not in use. The lower end was fashioned to fit the angle between the ship's side and the

Fig 8/9

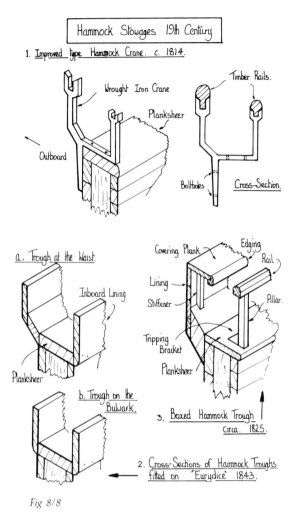

channel, an iron or timber shoe being placed at the heel to prevent it slipping. In cross-section it was both square and octagonal.

$$Overall\ length = extreme\ breadth\ of\ vessel \times {}^{3}/_{10}$$

$$Width = 1in\ per\ foot\ of\ overall\ length$$

$$Length\ of\ square\ portion = length \times {}^{3}/_{14}$$

$$Length\ of\ octagonal\ portion = length \times {}^{11}/_{14}$$

Three eyebolts were fitted, each being secured one-ninth of the overall length of the davit, from the uppermost end. Two of these served for the guy ropes set on the fore and after faces. The remaining eyebolt was used for the topping lift, which was fitted on the top face. The head was fashioned with a necking to allow the strop for the fish block to be fitted. Details of this are given in Fig 8/9. This type of davit remained in general service until about 1840, when a number of small modifications were made.

From 1840 the davit was set up on either the fore channel or the billboard. The only difference was that the cross-section remained octagonal throughout its entirety, and the eyebolts for the guys were omitted. The guys were usually spliced around the necked head. The heel was generally reinforced with an iron band about 3in wide and ¾in thick. The heel was set into a specially fashioned step or 'shoe', which was made from wood and iron. The shoe was set up at the required angle for the davit. (For details see Fig 8/9.)

According to Darcy Lever's *Young Sea Officer's Sheet Anchor*, some small vessels did not carry the standard fish davit, but had a short boom run out over the bulwark, with its heel set on the forecastle. The outer end was fitted with a snatch sheave, through which passed a pendant on which the fish block or fish hook was suspended. Even smaller vessels, such as cutters, did not have any form of fish davit. Here the fish hook was secured to runners, and the relevant tackle which was run up to the masthead. When the fish davit was not in use it was retained in a special housing or cleat. These were mounted either at the top of the ship's side, or in later years on the fore channel. The design of these fittings varied enormously (see Fig 8/10). The cleats were bolted as necessary, according to the design.

The Boat Davits

Prior to 1790, the ship's boats were raised and lowered from the ship by tackle suspended from the main and fore yardarms. This procedure was both impractical and tedious, and a form of crane, commonly called a davit, was introduced. When davits were first used, they were fitted in the vicinity of the mizzen channel on each side of the ship. By 1800, davits were also fitted to the transom above the stern lights of smaller vessels, and within a few years this practice spread throughout all rates. The difference between these

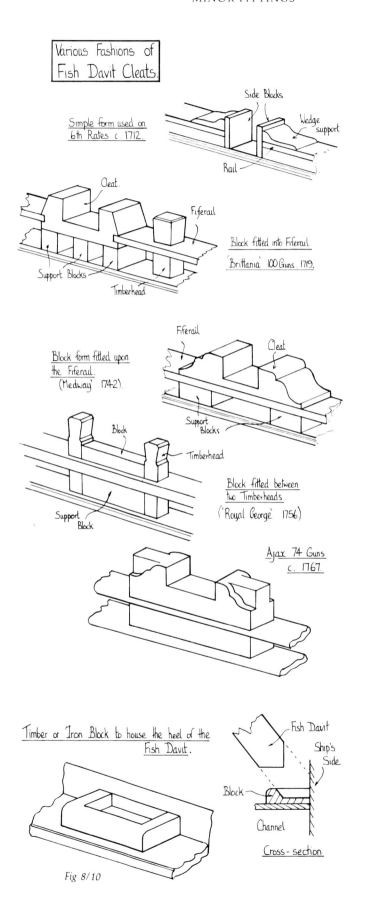

Various Fashions of Fish Davit Cleats.

Simple form used on 6th Rates c 1712.

Block fitted into Fiferail 'Britannia' 100 Guns 1719.

Block form fitted upon the Fiferail. ('Medway' 1742).

Block fitted between two Timberheads ('Royal George' 1756)

Ajax 74 Guns c. 1767

Timber or Iron Block to house the heel of the Fish Davit.

Cross-section

Fig 8/10

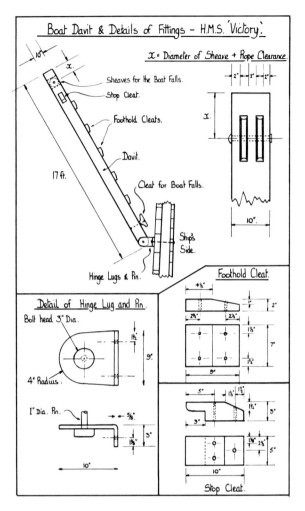

Fig 8/11

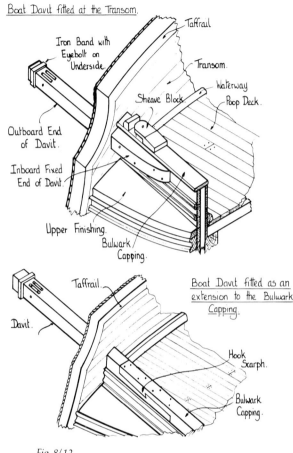

Fig 8/12

and the davits fitted at the ship's side was that they were fixed in position, and could not be raised or lowered.

Each individual davit consisted of a baulk of square-sectioned pitch pine, the length being sufficient to allow the boats to be lowered clear of the ship's side. This dimension was therefore governed by the degree of tumblehome on the vessel. The davits on the *Victory* were 17ft long, 10in wide and deep and 19ft apart fore and aft. At the outboard extremities, provision was made for two sheaves for the boat falls, the sheaves being made to a diameter equal to the width of the davit. The precise position for the axial pin for these sheaves was such that the sheave slots were set at half the diameter of the sheave plus the clearance for the rope from the outboard end. The inboard end was a semi-circular shape, to allow for radial movement, and was secured to the ship's side with two lugs and a pin (see Fig 8/11).

The upper surface of the davit had foothold cleats, to enable men to lie out to the end to carry out maintenance or embark the boat. Stop cleats were also fitted on each side at the outer end to retain the jackstay. Each pair of davits shared a common jackstay, which in turn was secured to a topping lift. This lift was passed up to a single

purchase block suspended on a pendant secured to the mizzen mast below the top. The loose end was then passed down to a circular fife rail at the base of the mast. An eyebolt was secured to the deck in the vicinity of the mast, to which was attached a snatch block, which was employed when it was required to raise or lower the davits.

The davits that were fitted to the transom were secured to the hull by one of two methods. Either they were made as a continuation of the bulwark capping, or passed through the transom at the outboard side of the ship's side planking, at a level directly below the bulwark capping, and bolted through the ship's side. To ensure that the davits remained rigid, they were made to a length that gave sufficient fastening. The additional length given to the inboard side was approximately three-quarters of that projecting beyond the boundary of the transom. Those fitted on the *Victory* protrude for a distance of 8ft, with a length inboard of 6ft, thereby giving an overall measurement of 14ft. The outer face of the timber was usually faired off towards the fore end, giving a more pleasing appearance (see Fig 8/12). In both types of davit a cleat was fitted at the inboard end, to which the falls were secured.

By 1810 a number of small modifications were made to improve the performance. Firstly, the stop cleats were replaced by eyebolts, and secondly a support crutch was added where the davit was fitted above the mizzen channel. This relieved the strain on the topping lifts. In this case the scantlings of the davit were made smaller, therefore, instead of having the timber cut 10in square, it could be 8in square. The davit was retained in its housed position by means of a forelock bolt, passing through the arms of the crutch. This form of davit was introduced by Sir Robert Seppings.

An experiment was carried out on the *Dryad* in 1811, whereby the topping lift was passed to an iron stanchion bolted to the inboard side of the bulwark. I assume that this was aimed at altering the direction of the lift, to prevent it fouling with other parts of the rigging. The positions of fittings are clearly given in the accompanying illustrations.

The Latrines or Heads

The latrines were situated far forward, within the head of the ship, hence the modern term heads. Heads were also fitted at other points throughout a ship, for use by the officers; these were usually confined to the quarter galleries. Between 1650 and 1850 various forms can be found, though they all relate more or less to the basic design. Each type can be seen on the many models displayed at the National Maritime Museum and other museums. In some cases details are omitted from models, especially vessels built in the third quarter of the seventeenth century. By 1780 an early form of water closet was fitted. By 1830, measures had been taken to give more privacy to those using them.

As there were so many variations only the more general ones will be discussed. The design depended mainly on the joiners who carried out the fitting, thus specific details are never included in the draughts. Sanitation facilities are often mentioned within the building contracts, even as far back as 1694 (see contract for the Sixth Rate *Biddeford* in Appendix 1b).

THE HEADS FOR THE SHIP'S COMPANY

These were usually situated on the small 'prow' deck, forward of the beakhead bulkhead, or the bulwark of the bow on vessels with a round bow. These took the form of a box structure, open to the sea on their underside, and furnished with a circular hole of suitable diameter on their top face. The number fitted generally corresponded to the size of the ship's complement. However, this was not always so, for vessels of the late seventeenth and early eighteenth centuries often had two fitted. These were always found at each outboard end of the beakhead bulkhead, adjacent to the head rail, which at least gave the user some protection from the elements. Where more than two were required, additional 'seats of ease' were fitted on each side of the bowsprit, upon the gratings forming the prow deck. These were generally in the form of single components,

Unicorn. Heads which served as the crew's latrines were commonly known as the 'seats of ease'. The prow deck is made up of a series of gratings set over light beams. To the right is the planked inside of the ship's head rail which is very similar to the old form of beak found on Elizabethan ships.

Fig 8/13

but towards the end of the eighteenth century these boxes were built to accommodate two and in some cases three persons. In a like fashion, those fitted at the corners of the beakhead bulkhead were in some cases tiered, as shown in the illustration of 74-gun ship *Warrior* of 1781, which can be seen in the Science Museum. The use of these 'multi' latrines must have been quite a social event during calm weather. When in harbour, canvas discharge trunkings were often fitted, but it is unlikely that these were used at sea, as they would be washed away. As an alternative, lightly built wooden trunkings were employed to ensure that the waste was passed clear of the ship. Some of the seats of ease used between 1650 and 1850 are shown in Fig 8/13.

THE HEADS FOR THE OFFICERS

These were generally fitted within the quarter galleries, and until about 1800 were not much more sophisticated than those used by the crew, just a little more private. It is widely believed that these were first fitted at the fore end of the lower gallery. Evidence supporting this can be obtained from a sketch made by Van De Velde the Elder of the *Constant Reformation* as she appeared in 1648. Here one can see a small roundhouse built separately at the fore end of the lower gallery. A similar form is illustrated in *Olde Time Ships* by J R Stevens. This roundhouse, however, is fitted on the after end of the main channel.

By 1780 a simple form of water closet had been introduced. This was not adopted by all vessels at first, but indicates that some improvements in sanitation were being made. The water was obtained from a cistern fitted under the poop deck, or in one of the quarter galleries above. This was also used as an early form of shower unit, in which the officers could wash. It was first used as such during the 1780s, but did not become a regular feature until the second quarter of the nineteenth century. The *Unicorn* was fitted with this arrangement in one of the circular galleries at her stern.

PISSDALES

There is evidence that these were incorporated on men-of-war between 1680 and 1760. However, it is very likely that they were in existence well before then. They were fitted to the inboard side of the bulwarks that surrounded the upper deck, either a little forward or aft of the waist. They were made in the form of a semi-circular bowl of a suitable radius, from either lead, copper or occasionally wood. When made from metal, they were supported by three curved legs bolted at their feet to the deck. The flat side of the bowl was fastened to the bulwark with suitable bolts. A small drainage pipe passed to the ship's side from the base of the bowl. This, too, was made from lead or copper. These fittings appear to have fallen into disuse after 1760 though it could be that they were omitted from models. A similar feature was incorporated on vessels built in the second quarter of the nineteenth century, but this was more

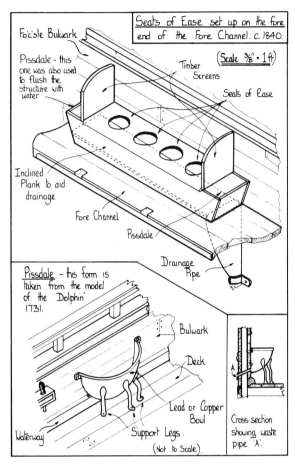

Fig 8/14

complex, and a step towards better sanitation. This later form was integral to the construction of the ship, with a long seat-of-ease, fitted at the fore end of the fore channel. This type had a flushing system, passing buckets of water into a sluice duct and some degree of privacy was attained by having vertical screens fitted at each end. Both forms are illustrated in Fig 8/14.

OTHER DESIGNS

There were many variations in the design of heads, so I will only give a few examples of the more common ones on 10-gun sloops built between 1741 and 1766. Here the head was made in the form of an inverted dome fitted to the outboard side of the forecastle at each side of the vessel. At the top, within the confines of the dome, a seat of ease was constructed, the waste being discharged through a hole at the base of the dome (see Fig 8/13(2)). There is a model of one in the Science Museum.

By the 1840s many improvements had been carried out, especially in respect to privacy. At last latrines were constructed within the ship, instead of some precarious position at the ship's head. These were built in a similar manner to those inside the roundhouses at the old beakhead bulkhead. I have made a careful illustration of this type from draughts of the *Vanguard* of 1841, which shows the panelled bulkheads on three of the sides adjacent to the ship's side under the forecastle (see Fig 8/13(5)).

The Ringbolts and Eyebolts fitted for the Gun Tackle

Each gun required a number of ringbolts and eyebolts for fastening the gun tackle and breeching ropes to the ship's side. These iron fittings were secured in one of two ways. The common fashion was to have them driven home in the same manner as a normal bolt. In this case the outboard end was clenched with a rove to the outer surface of the timbers beneath the external planking. An alternative practice, which was more commonly employed during the later years, was the use of 'barbed' or 'ragged' bolts. These, once driven home, were held in place by the rugged surface in contact with the wood. When fitted, this type did not require any roves, and once in place were very difficult to withdraw without tearing away the surrounding timber.

The dimensions of the bolts, eyes and rings were determined by the size of gun which was to be secured. Obviously the heavier the

gun the greater the thickness of the bolt. The table adjacent gives the size of bolt in relation to the various weights of gun in service. By using this table the modelmaker may fit ringbolts and eyebolts suitable to the vessel's armament, though few 74-gun ships carried 24-pounders on their lower gundeck, and not all frigates were armed with 18-pounders, so this table is purely a guide. The figures are based on the *Shipbuilder's Repository* of 1789. For modelling purposes the sizes given are accurate enough for all vessels built between 1650 and 1850.

Each gun required five fixed ringbolts and eyebolts. One of each was fitted on each side of the gunport, and one ringbolt was driven into the deck behind the gun. The latter was usually fastened into the binding strake, a heavier band of deck planking that was worked along the line of the hatches etc near the centreline. Often another pair of eyebolts was driven into the ship's side above the gunport. These were smaller, and used for securing the gun muzzle when the gun was not in use while in passage at sea.

Ringbolt and Eyebolt Sizes

Gun size	Ringbolts		Eyebolts	
	Bolt diameter	Ring internal diameter	Bolt diameter	Eye internal diameter
	in	in	in	in
42 pdr —	1½	6	1¼	2¾
32 pdr (long)	1½	5¾	1¼	2¾
32 pdr (short)	1½	5¾	1¼	2⅝
24 pdr (long)	1¼	5½	1⅛	2⅝
24 pdr (short)	1¼	5¼	1⅛	2½
18 pdr (long)	1¼	5	1⅛	2⅜
18 pdr (short)	1¼	4⅞	1⅛	2⅜
12 pdr (long)	1⅛	4¾	1	2¼
12 pdr (short)	1⅛	4½	1	2
9 pdr —	1	4¼	¾	2
6 pdr —	1	4	¾	2
3 pdr —	1	3¾	¾	1¾

Shot Garlands

The function of the shot garlands was to house the ready-use stock of round shot. Garlands were usually made from a plank of oak of suitable length, fashioned with hollows or bowls in which the shot sat. The width and depth of the plank was governed by the size of the shot, therefore it can be assumed that its width was generally twice that of the diameter of the shot and its depth no less than three-quarters of the shot diameter. The hollows had to be sufficiently deep to ensure that the ball would not roll out when the ship was heeling in heavy seas. The depth was a little greater than half the ball's diameter.

Usually each garland was situated around hatches and other features along the centreline of the deck. They were also fitted to the ship's side and to the bulwarks of the forecastle and the quarterdeck, but this practice was elminated by the end of the eighteenth century. Their abolition was ordered by the Navy Board in 1780. This ensured that most of the weight borne by the vessel was as close to the centreline as possible.

Egmont. *The disposition of the main jeer and topsail sheet bitts and the chain pump cisterns. Afore the bitts is the main hatch. Note the beam arms and the beams made from three pieces of timber and the fenders fitted to the ship's side.*

CHAPTER 9

The Fittings Associated with the Rigging

Topsail Sheet and Jeer Bitts

The bitts discussed in this chapter are not to be confused with those used for the anchor cables, known as the riding bitts, although their construction was very similar. The style of construction altered very little, the only major change being in about 1660, when the cross beam was introduced, for securing rigging, and later for holding belaying pegs. The modelmaker should be aware that prior to 1660 the bitts consisted of vertical posts fitted with or without a belaying bar. There are a few exceptions to the rule, for example where the two vertical timbers curve inwards towards each other at their heels, and form one single heel (Fig 9/1).

The construction of the more common types consisted of two vertical timbers of oak set a specific distance apart in the athwartships direction, their heels fastened to the deck beams with clench bolts. In some cases the upright timbers were long enough to be secured to the beams directly below, and in other cases long enough to be secured at two deck levels. Over the years it became necessary to fashion the vertical timbers to receive sheaves for the running rigging. These were set in the vertical plane in a fore and aft direction, the number varying according to the size and rig of the vessel. It was usual to have the heads of the upright timbers fashioned in the 'timberhead' form, though during the seventeenth century 'knight's heads' were also common.

The cross beams were fitted approximately 18in down from the head of the vertical timber, or bitt pin as it was often called. They were fastened with clench bolts, the bitt pin being given a slight score to receive the cross beam. This score was varied between a depth of 1½ and 2½in. The depth was determined from the size of the bitt pins, and was approximately one-seventh the thickness of the bitt pin. The ends of the cross beam were fashioned in various ways, either with the end squared off with a slight bearding on the corners or in the timberhead style. In some cases part of the ends

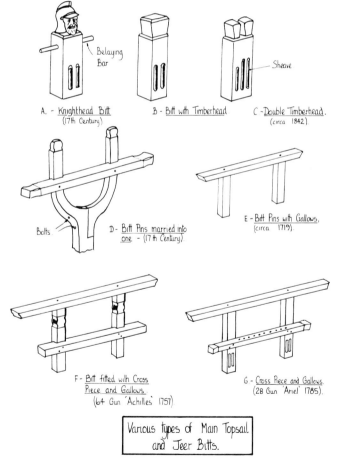

A. - Knighthead Bitt (17th Century)

B - Bitt with Timberhead

C - Double Timberhead. (circa 1842).

D - Bitt Pins married into one - (17th Century).

Bolts

E - Bitt Pins with Gallows, (circa 1719).

F - Bitt fitted with Cross Piece and Gallows. (64 Gun 'Achilles' 1757)

G. - Cross Piece and Gallows. (28 Gun 'Ariel' 1785).

Belaying Bar

Sheave

Various types of Main Topsail and Jeer Bitts.

Fig 9/1

219

were cylindrical. When provision was made for belaying pins, holes were bored vertically along the centre of the cross beam and only at a distance that spanned the two bitt pins. Although only one cross beam was fitted, one can see from many models of ships built prior to the lengthening of the quarterdeck that the main topsail bitts were greater in height, and were fitted with an additional cross beam. This was usually of a greater length than the others, and was often called the 'gallows'. This beam acted as stowage for spare spars, and it was usually fashioned to accommodate them (see Fig 9/1). I have wondered if this gallows beam played some part in the increase of the quarterdeck. On some models one can see that gratings were extended from the quarterdeck to the upper edge of the gallows and later, gangboards were fitted instead. This gave easier access to the rigging connected with the mainmast. This central gangway to the mainmast generally appeared on ships of 50 guns and upward from about 1701. On the model of the 28-gun frigate *Ariel* of 1785, in the Science Museum, the quarterdeck is still set aft of the mainmast, and the bitts were fitted with a gallows. Other fine examples of double cross beams can be seen on the model of the *Victory* of 1737 in the Maritime Museum at Greenwich, and the 64-gun ship *Achilles* in the Science Museum.

Returning to discuss the single-beamed bitts, on some ships during the first quarter of the eighteenth century, the single cross beam capped the bitt pins instead of being fitted at a given distance below the heads. There were, of course, numerous exceptions and variations from ship to ship throughout the period. The more common types used are illustrated in Fig 9/1.

The mizzen topsail bitts, however, did not pass through to the deck beams below. Therefore additional support was given by a standard fitted to either the fore or after face of the bitt pin, always on the side away from the mast. There does not seem to be any hard and fast rule as to whether the mizzen bitts should be forward or aft of the mast. The draught of a 74-gun ship in Rees' *Naval Architecture* shows the bitts fitted to the fore side of the mast, whereas the *Victory* at Portsmouth has them fitted aft of the mast which appears to have been more common. There are some cases where two sets of bitts are fitted. This can be seen on the well-known frame model of the *Bellona*, a 74-gun ship of 1760. There is also a model in the Maritime Museum of a 74-gun ship of the 1790s, which also has two sets of bitts fitted. In all cases the foremast had a set of jeer and a set of topsail bitts.

The tables on the facing page give the dimensions for the main and foremast jeer and topsail bitts. These are taken from 'The Principal Dimensions and Scantlings' from the 1789 edition of the *Shipbuilder's Repository*.

Kevels, Staghorns, Cavel Blocks and Cleats

Various timber and iron fittings were required for securing the running rigging. These were positioned at various points around the area of the open decks of the forecastle, quarterdeck, and poop. I

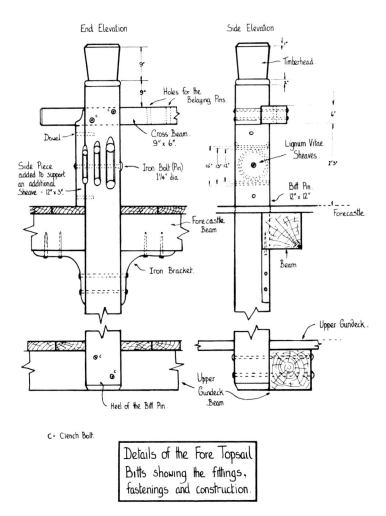

Details of the Fore Topsail Bitts showing the fittings, fastenings and construction.

Fig 9/2

have not been able to include dimensions as these fittings were not generally included in the ship's draughts, and were probably added by those completing the furniture of a vessel. This work was done by experience and not to any rule. I have shown rough scantlings on illustrations where possible.

KEVELS

These acted as belaying points for rigging, such as sheets and braces. They consisted of two timberheads secured to a baulk of wood. Because there were two pieces of timber, the rope in question could be attached in a figure of eight, to ensure security. According to Sutherland in *Shipbuilding Unveiled* 1717, kevels are 'Pieces of oak shaped like timberheads and fitted into mortices cut through other pieces of timber which are fastened to the ship's side'.

Until about 1775, these two timbers were usually married at their lower ends and thus formed a U shape as shown in Fig 9/3. After this date, we see a tendency to omit the lower parts of the timbers, and the whole structure takes the form of 'staghorns'. In some

The Main Jeer and Topsail Bitts

Component	*No of guns* 100 *ft*	*in*	74 *ft*	*in*	44 *ft*	*in*	36 *ft*	*in*	28 *ft*	*in*	Sloop *ft*	*in*
Square bitts	1	2	1	1		10½		11		9½		8
Cross pieces to the bitts –deep		8		7½		6½		6		5		4¾
–broad		10		9¾		9		8		7		6½
Scored to the bitt pins		2		1¾		1½		1½		1½		1½
The cross piece for the gallows –sided		11		10		9		8½		8		6¼
–deep	1	4½	1	3¾	1	2¾	1	2½	1	1		10
–long	12		12		11		10	6	9	6	8	10
The upper side above the deck		7	6	11	6	8	6	6	6	4	6	2

The Fore Jeer and Topsail Bitts

Component	*No of guns* 100 *ft*	*in*	74 *ft*	*in*	44 *ft*	*in*	36 *ft*	*in*	28 *ft*	*in*	Sloop *ft*	*in*
Bitts to be square	1	1½	1			9½		9½		8		7½
Their heads above the deck	4	6	3	10	3	6	3	4	3	1	3	
The cross pieces –deep		8		7		5½		5		4¼		4½
–broad		9½		9		7½		7½		6½		6
Scored to the bitts		1⅝		1½		1¼		1¼		1		1

seventeenth-century building contracts, kevels are often referred to as 'kevills'. (See Appendix 1b for *Biddeford*'s contract).

STAGHORNS

A number of these were fitted throughout the vessel for fastening the sheets and braces to. They generally superseded the older form of kevels. Those originally fitted to the *Victory* consisted of a single baulk of timber of between 5 and 7ft long and 9in deep and wide. The actual parts forming the staghorns were about 9in wide, 4½in thick and 15in long, with a further 6in set into the baulk and bolted. Each staghorn was set at an angle of 60 degrees. The dimensions for the staghorns fitted to smaller vessels would be a little smaller (see Fig 9/3).

The Main Bitts

The dimensions of the main bitts, taken from Steel's *Naval Architecture*, are below.

Table 1

No of Guns	100 *ft*	*in*	90 *ft*	*in*	80 *ft*	*in*	74 *ft*	*in*	64 *ft*	*in*	50 *ft*	*in*	44 *ft*	*in*
A	1	2	1	1½	1	1	1	1	1	0	1	0	1	0
B	2	9	2	9	2	8	2	8	2	8	2	8	2	8
C		1¾		1¾		1½		1½		1½		1½		1¼
D		1⅛		1⅛		1⅛		1⅛		1		1		⅞
E		4		4		3½		3½		3		3		3
F	1	0	1	0		11		11		10		10		10
G		10½		10¼		10		10		9½		9½		9
H		9		9		8½		8½		8		8		7½
J	2	0	2	0	1	10	1	10	1	10	1	10	1	10
K		2		2		2		1½		1½		1½		1½
L	2	2	2	2	2	0	2	0	1	10	1	10	1	7
M		1		1		⅞		⅞		⅞		⅞		⅞
N		11		10½		10		10		9½		9½		9
P	1	5	1	4	1	4	1	4	1	3	1	3	1	3
Q	13	0	12	9	12	6	12	6	12	0	12	0	11	6
R	7	0	7	0	7	0	7	0	6	10	6	9	6	9

Table 2

No of Guns	38 *ft*	*in*	36 *ft*	*in*	32 *ft*	*in*	28 *ft*	*in*	24 *ft*	*in*	Sloop *ft*	*in*	Cutter *ft*	*in*
A	1	0	1	0		11		10½		10½		9		8
B	2	8	2	8	2	7	2	6	2	6	2	6	1	9
C		1¼		1¼		1¼		1¼		1¼		1¼		1
D		⅓		⅞		⅞		¾		¾		¾		¾
E		3		3		3		2¾		2¾		2½		2
F		10		10		10		9½		9½		8¾		7
G		9		8½		8½		8		7		6		6¼
H		7½		7¼		7		6¾		6½		5½		4½
J	1	10	1	10	1	10	1	10	1	10	1	10	1	7
K		1½		1½		1½		1½		1½		1½		1¾
L	1	7	1	5	1	5	1	4	1	4	1	3	1	3
M		⅞		⅞		⅞		⅞		⅞		¾		¾
N		9		9		8½		8½		8½		8		6
P	1	3	1	2¾	1	2½	1	2	1	1	1	0		9
Q	11	0	10	9	10	9	10	6	10	6	9	6	8	2
R	6	8	6	8	6	6	6	6	6	5	5	6	5	0

Key to the tables
A = The cross section of the bitt pins.
B = The height that the bitt pin is set above the deck.
C = Depth of the scoring upon the pin for the cross piece.
D = The diameter of the bolts to fasten the heels of the pins.
E = Cheeks – thickness of cheek blocks.
F = Diameter of the sheaves.
G = Breadth of the cross piece.
J = Depth of the cross piece.
K = Height of the cross piece above the deck.
L = Depth of the scoring to fit the cross piece to the bitt pins.
M = Diameter of the two bolts to fasten the cross piece to the pins.
N = The siding of the gallows piece.
P = Depth of the gallows.
Q = Length of the gallows.
R = Height of the gallows above the deck.

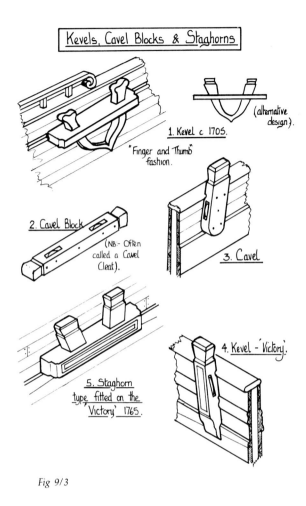

Fig 9/3

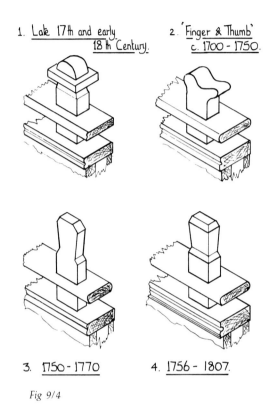

Fig 9/4

CAVEL BLOCKS

These were either single- or double-sheaved. The former type was generally fitted in the upright position at the bulwark. The latter form was fitted in various positions, ranging from the bulwarks to the fore edge of the quarterdeck, and was always set horizontally. On the single block type, the head was generally fashioned in the timberhead style, with a single sheave set in a slot below. In some cases this slot was angled away from the ship's side, to allow a better run for the rope in question (see Fig 9/3).

The double sheaved type generally had the two ends fashioned in timberhead style, and the sheaves were set parallel to the timber, and adjacent to each other (see Fig 9/3). In both types the timber was usually between 9 and 12in in square section, and between 3ft 6in and 2ft 6in long.

CLEATS

These were fitted in many positions throughout the vessel, and varied in size from as much as 2ft, down to 6in. They were usually made from oak, elm or iron. By the beginning of the nineteenth

century, many fittings were made from cast or wrought iron. The staghorns in the waist of the *Victory* are of the iron type, and were probably installed during her refit in 1802–03, or perhaps later. Once the use of iron fittings had become common, the styles and sizes became numerous.

FASTENING

The kevels, staghorns, cavel blocks and cleats were secured with iron bolts, trennals, and in some cases copper or muntz bolts. Some builders used 'rag bolts' to ensure that the fittings would not work loose. These were such that the surface of the shaft of the bolt was 'barbed', thus, once driven home, the ragged edges would dig into the timber when trying to work out.

The Timberheads

For a number of years it was the common practice for the builder to allow some of the heads of the toptimbers to protrude above the limit of the bulwarks. The reasons for this were twofold. Firstly, the timberheads supported the fife rail, and secondly they formed rigid securing points for ropes. It was a simple matter to have the heads

stanchions of that bulkhead. The rectangular type was generally made to a breadth of half its width, the tapered section being approximately 12in high (see Fig 9/4 and 9/5). After 1703 it is very rare to find timberheads for the use of belaying at the quarterdeck and poop bulwarks. The exception was two large fairleads found near the break of the quarterdeck during the last two decades of the eighteenth century. From the late 1790s, all the bulwarks were built

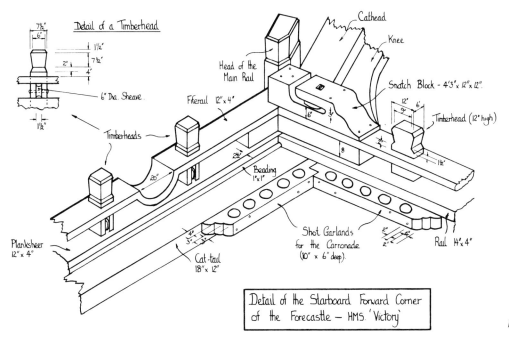

Detail of the Starboard Forward Corner of the Forecastle — HMS 'Victory'

Fig 9/5

fashioned with a tenon to fit into the fife rail. Where the timberheads were used as belaying points, they were made in a manner that ensured that the rope fastened to it remained secure. The patterns used for this altered considerably throughout the period in which the timberheads were common. Fashioned timberheads first appear about 1670, when they seem to have been employed at intervals along the bulwarks of the quarterdeck and the poop. This style is clearly illustrated in Fig 9/4. Their use upon the bulwark of the forecastle is not apparent at this period.

The design altered around 1685–90, when it became more robust, with a form of domed head as shown in Fig 9/4(1). It was at about this time that timberheads became more widely used, and appeared in the vicinity of the forecastle.

By 1703 a more practical fashion emerged, known as the 'finger and thumb' style. This is shown in Fig 9/4(2). Here the rope could be more easily turned on or off, due to the rounded features. This type of timberhead remained common until the middle of the eighteenth century. After 1750 the style became more severe, and far more practical. The head of the timber was made with an inverted taper, bearded off towards the 'post', and on the top surface. The cross-section was either rectangular or square, depending on where it was fitted. The latter form was usually found across the upper edge of the beakhead bulkhead, and was fashioned from the heads of the

solid and squared off where they terminated. With this the use of timberheads declined, with only a few made in the form of fairleads, built within the limits of the bulwarks themselves.

The Boomkins

Their function was to extend the lead of the fore course tack, and to ensure that the foresail clew could be braced fully. They were first introduced around 1710, but may have been used twenty years earlier on some ships. They superseded the dead block, which was basically a fairlead made in the form of a square block of timber, with a hole at its centre through which the tack passed to a belaying point on the prow deck. The block was fitted between the head rails and was usually ornate, in the form of a head with the rope passing through the mouth.

Fir was used for making boomkins, though I often wonder if an alternative material was used in earlier years for those with sharp angles. This subject is dealt with in the section on ship construction, because it is a fixed item, unlike the masts and yards.

The boomkin, or bumkin as it was often called, consisted of a spar that projected downwards and forwards over the main head rail.

The heel of the spar either butted against the knightheads or was bolted to them. The latter practice was generally used from the end of the eighteenth century onwards. The outboard end was fashioned with a neck for the strop of a single purchase block, through which the tack passed, which then led to a belaying point by the knighthead. Although boomkins generally appear around 1710, it was another decade before deadblocks finally disappeared from use. Throughout the next 140 years, the style of the boomkin changed as follows.

BOOMKIN STYLES

1710 – 1730

At first boomkins were usually made in square section, with the outboard end angled sharply downward beyond the rail. They were relatively short, and extended 6 to 8ft. Their width was approximately 1in per foot of their overall length, and remained a constant width throughout their length.

1730 – 1780

Very little alteration was made to the boomkin during this period. The overall length was extended, and the angle was diminished. The inboard end was now octagonal in cross-section, the outer part being round. It was also tapered towards the extremity, and thus was approximately three quarters of its initial diameter at the end.

1780 – 1805

The overall appearance changed little, except that the boomkin remained straight throughout its length, and in some cases was of completely round section.

1805

The inboard end was now generally bolted to the knighthead, and was often made in half round-section, the outer end retaining the usual round form. An additional fitting consisting of an iron band with integral eyes, for the boomkin shrouds was fitted; there were usually three shrouds.

1825

By this date the spar had regained its square section, its depth about 1in greater than its width. An additional eye for the securing of a slip was incorporated.

CHAPTER 10

Hull Protection

Hull Deterioration

The major problem with ships built from timber was their deterioration due to rot, and attack from sea-worm. The number of vessels that suffered from rot was quite considerable. The 64-gun *Ardent* was launched in 1764, and her original cost for building was £23,000. Within seven years her hull had deteriorated to such an extent that the estimated cost for repairs was £17,000. There were many reasons why so many vessels fell into a state of unseaworthiness. One of the main factors was the use of unseasoned, or green, timber. Timber had so many uses during the eighteenth century, besides that of naval construction, that it is impossible to blame one industry for the general depletion of timber supplies. Throughout the eighteenth century, England spent quite a number of years at war, which made constant demands on the naval construction programme. This, with normal domestic requirements, meant that the forests were rapidly disappearing. The shortages led to malpractices in construction, the major one being that ships were often built without leaving the frame unplanked long enough to 'weather and settle'. It became common for ships to be planked up over green timbers, due to the urgency of the naval situation. This resulted in many vessels beginning to rot before they were even launched.

The second reason for rot was bad design and building techniques. It was discovered that decay could be retarded to some degree by allowing adequate air to pass the timbers of the ship, thus keeping them relatively dry. By the second half of the eighteenth century, a system for ventilating the timbers became normal practice. This was done by incorporating ventilation spaces between selected strakes of internal planking, and by boring vertical holes through the spacing blocks that were set between the frames.

Thirdly, timber supplies were often unobtainable because of the industrial dictatorship imposed by the leading suppliers. Private

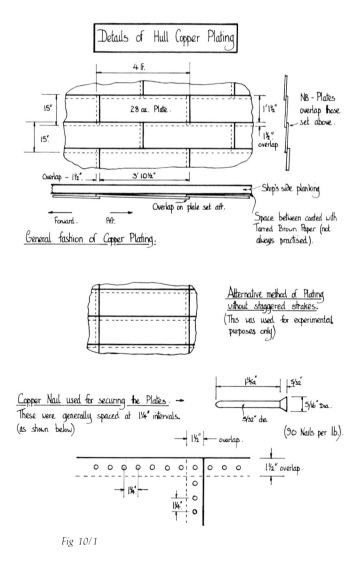

Fig 10/1

timber merchants often sold inferior wood to the dockyards, at prices which made them massive profits at the government's expense. All the timber was inspected by the supplier's own inspectors. In 1801, when Lord St Vincent became the First Lord of the Admiralty, he decided to check the suppliers' deliveries by having the timber examined by his own inspectors. The immediate reaction by leading suppliers was to withhold all timber until the Admiralty ceased the employment of these inspectors. The embargo proved fatal to the general maintenance of the Fleet, especially when hostilities with France broke out again in 1803. Repairs were carried out as well as possible, even if green timber had to be used.

Because of shortages in the early part of the nineteenth century, supplies were supplemented by various woods imported from America, Australia, New Zealand, India and Africa. The design of warships was also altered, enabling smaller pieces of timber to be used, which not only economised on timber but increased strength. The type of large heavy timbers previously used were reproduced in fabricated form, giving smaller, stronger timbers. This practice also reduced wastage.

METHODS OF PROTECTION

The other problem was due to sea-worm, or 'teredo navalis'. This worm would bore its way through all the timbers below the waterline, and if unchecked would leave a hull honeycombed, causing the total collapse of the timbers. This worm tended to live in tropical waters, and vessels in these stations were more prone to this problem. Since the Tudor period many methods had been invented and employed to combat the problem of sea-worm, including various solutions containing a poison which was payed to the hull and boarded over with thin planks.

One method involved paying the hull with a composition of tallow, horsehair and sulphur. The tallow was primarily used to bind the other two substances together, and adhere them to the hull. Horsehair was employed because it was believed to choke the worms as they attempted to devour the timber. The sulphur acted as poison to kill off the worm. An alternative method consisted of lining the hull with felt, which was presumed to act in the same manner as the horsehair. Both methods were completed by sheathing the hull in boards.

Both of these methods had two disadvantages: the additional weight of the boarding reduced the speed of the vessel, and if an inspection of the hull was required, the long tedious job of removing the boarding had to be carried out. It is difficult to assess whether the compositions actually deterred the worm, for many ships still suffered from the problem.

Lead Sheathing

It was in 1674 that some attempt was made to alleviate the problem. Trials were carried out on some vessels which had their hulls sheathed in lead. The project failed due to the galvanic action between the lead and the iron nails used to fasten it to the hull planking. The speed of the vessels was also reduced by the weight of the lead. Therefore the original and tried practice was reverted to. Only vessels selected for service on foreign stations such as the West Indies had the bottom of their hulls sheathed with deal boards. Vessels serving in cooler climates were only protected by being payed with the usual compounds. No further attempts were made at improving hull protection until the mid eighteenth century. The use of copper plating was proposed as early as 1708 but because of its impracticality due to corrosion by electrolysis, and cost, the idea was turned down.

Careening

Stricter rules were introduced governing the frequency at which ships were to be careened, in the Cruisers and Convoys Act of 1708. This stated that vessels should be careened at least three times each year. Careening is the term given to the removal of weed and marine crustaceans that build up on the ship's bottom, by scraping and burning. This was done by beaching the vessel after the removal of guns, topmasts and other heavy equipment. The ship was heeled over on one side at a time to allow the work to progress. In 1737 a new compound was invented by Lee, the Master Caulker at Portsmouth Dockyard. The compound consisted of a mixture of pitch, tallow and sulphur. These not only deterred the worm, but could be easily ignited for breaming (burning off marine growths and weed). The compound was adopted after completing trials comparing it with the other options.

Copper Sheathing

When Anson returned from his voyage of circumnavigation in 1744, his ship the *Centurion* was found to be riddled with sea-worm. In 1761, Anson proposed that further experiments should be carried out with copper sheathing, fastened this time with copper nails. It was also decided that only non-ferrous metals should be used for the bolts used for the hull below the waterline.

This time the results were successful but the practice was not carried out universally, due to the expense. In further trials the *Marlborough* was sheathed with lead and the *Aurora* and *Stag* with copper, but these proved disastrous, so the concept of sheathing was shelved until the latter 1770s. Then it was decided that copper sheathing was the only method that would meet the requirements of the Fleet, and became general practice in 1782. It was found that the copper not only stopped sea-worm, but also reduced the build-up of marine growth on the hull, leaving the ship's bottom far cleaner. This reduced the frequency with which the hull had to be careened, and made the ships faster sailers.

Each sheet of copper plating used on naval vessels was generally 4ft long and 1ft 3in wide. The size was probably governed by the limitations imposed by the manufacturing techniques of the period. The individual weight of each plate varied according to the relative position at which it was fitted. The most commonly used plate weighed 28oz per square foot, giving a total weight of 8¾lb. Heavier plating was used in areas of the hull where excessive wear or errosion occurred. The most common areas were at the bow, the waterline, and around the vicinity of the rudder. The heaviest plate was about 6·4lb per square foot giving a total weight of 32lb.

The overall weight which copper plating added to a ship's tonnage was considerable, a 74-gun ship required approximately 3300 plates, weighing in total just under 13 tons. In addition were the nails for securing the plates, which were usually 1½in long and ¼in diameter.

The plates were fastened so that they overlapped each other by 1½in on both the upper and after edges. Usually 16 nails were used to hold each plate in place. For full details of the method used on naval ships see Fig 10/1.

In 1779 the Navy Board ordered that all frigates were to be sheathed with copper and although this authorisation was not extended to all naval ships until 1782 quite a number of vessels in this category did have plating fitted. Verification of this can be found in Captain C Orde-Browne's article which was printed in the 1891 edition of *The Engineer*. This states that the *Victory* was coppered in 1779. From this it can be seen that larger ships were plated as convenient, according to their relevent refit programmes. The use of copper plating to deter both rot and worm continued until the last years of the fighting sail. During the earlier years of its use problems still arose with the electrolytic action between the copper and the iron nails and bolts used on the hull. This was primarily overcome by lining the hull with paper before fitting each plate. The final solution was achieved by having all fastenings below the waterline made from copper or bronze which although not as strong as iron did prove satisfactory.

Hull Fastening

FISH PLATES

These were used to fasten the stempost, sternpost and the inner sternpost to the keel. Prior to the general introduction of copper sheathing in about 1780 these fittings were made from wrought iron plate, approximately 1¼in thick. Copper sheathing was introduced because of the problems caused by the electrolysis of the iron plates and copper bolts which fastened them. The plates fitted at the heel of the sternpost and the inner post were made in the form of two opposed trapeziums, the narrow neck being set in line with the upper edge of the keel. The timber in the vicinity of the plate

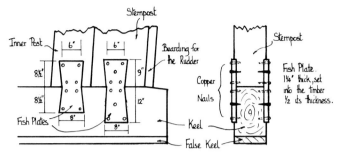

Fig.1 Detail of the Fish Plates fitted at the Sternpost and Inner Post.

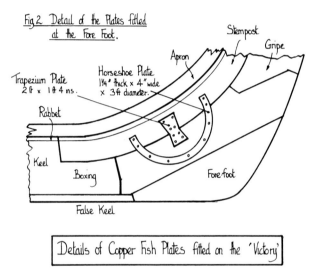

Fig 2 Detail of the Plates fitted at the Fore Foot.

Details of Copper Fish Plates fitted on the 'Victory'

Fig 10/2

was recessed, and the plate was set into the wood for a depth of half its thickness. Thus a 1in thick plate would be set down for ½in. Each plate was fastened with copper clench bolts, passing from one plate to the other. The number of bolts varied according to the size of the plate, generally between six and ten bolts were used.

The plates fitted at the stempost did not secure the stempost to the keel, but fastened the forefoot to the stempost. This plate was very different, and was in the form of the horseshoe. It would have measured up to 3ft from heel to toe. Like those at the sternpost, they were bolted together, the bolts passing through the timber, and clenched. Usually five to nine bolts were used, depending on the size of the plate.

In some cases an additional plate was used at the forefoot similar to that employed aft, and was set inside the horseshoe plate. There is a fine example of this on the *Victory* at Portsmouth.

Appendices

Dimensions and scantlings from the contract specification for the construction of four vessels in 1673

Source: PRO Adm 160/3071(2008)

Note. All text in quotation marks is direct quote from the contract. These ships were intended for construction at Waterford in Ireland, but when Spragge was killed at the Battle of the Texel, the contract lapsed. However, the scantlings may have been used for the *Oxford* of 1674 which had similar dimensions.

'This Indenture made this Eighteenth day of May in ye yeare of our Lord 1673, in [   ] of an Order from his Royall Highness, James, Duke of Yorke, Lord High Admiral of England, and dated the Sixth day of January 1672 – Betweene the Pinciple Officers and Commisioners of his Majestys Navy, for and on the behalf of his Majesty of the one part and Sir Edward Spragge and Nicholas Armorer ... of their own proper cost and charges well and workmanlike Erect and Build off the Stocks for the use of the King, foure good and substantiall new ships or ffriggots of good and well seasoned tymber and planck of fresh Oake and Elme and that each of the said ships or ffriggots shall containe in length by the Kiele [keel] One hundred and nine feet. Each in Breath from outside to outside of the planck thirty three feet, each Depth in Hold from the Top of the Cieling to the uper edge of the Gundeck Beames – fifteen feet, breadth at the Transome Twenty one foot foure inches, Rake forward of the Stem ffourteene feet at the Harpin, Rake aft five feet to the maine Transome. The Kiele to have five foot scarphs – tabled in the Kiele and to be well bolted with six bolts of an inch Auger. To have a firme substantiall Stem of fffifteene inches thwart ships and sixteene inches fore and aft with a sufficient false Stem of Eight inches thick and two feet foure inches broad with scarph Foure feet and six inches long, Six bolts in each scarph ...'

Keel	Siding 15in, depth 15in (at the midships position)
Sternpost	2ft deep with another post (the inner post) within it, fashioned to the lower transoms with a long-armed knee 6ft long. Each arm was to be bolted with 'inch and a quarter auger fastening the same together.'
Space of timber and room	2ft 2in
Floor timbers	15in deep upon the keel, 11in 'in and out' at the rungheads and sided 13in fore and aft.
Naval timber	'to fill the Roomes being at least twelve inches fore and aft and to have at least a Six feet six inch scarph.'

The timbers upwards at the gundeck were to be 9in in and out, and sided fore and aft 10in, and given scarphs 6ft long, with the room filled with timber.

Keelson	This was to be in three pieces, with a siding of 18in and a depth of 14in 'to be well bolted with inch and a quarter Auger through every other Tymber and to bolt every other ffloore Tymber through the Kiele and through the Stem.'
Toptimbers	'to be in proportion unto the ffloores'.
Thickstuff	'to put Six strakes of Sleepers in Hold on each side of the Rungheads'. Four strakes to be 6in thick the other two strakes 7in thick. All six strakes were wrought 15in broad.
Middlebands	Two strakes each side, 6in thick and 15in broad.

Deck clamps	'Two strakes on each side fore and aft under the Beames of the Gundeck of seaven inches thick and sixteene inches broad – each to be Hooked one into the other to prevent working.'
Footwaling	'all the rest of the footwaling in Hold to be good Foure inch planck.'
Riders	There were to be four sets of riders placed in the hold, 'three of them to be placed before the Mast [mainmast] and the other abaft.' These were each 18in broad and 16in deep. The floor rider and futtock riders were to be 12in square and each fastened with seven $1\frac{1}{4}$in diameter bolts and the vertical scarphs 7ft long.
Orlop beams	Six in number, 'and to make platforms upon them for the strengthening of the ship and stowing Cable thereon'. These beams to be 13in broad and 14in deep. Each supported with two lodging knees and two standards, and further supported with a rider head 13ft long and 2ft deep at the beam. [It can be assumed that the head of the rider would be increased in its scantling to form a knee or more specifically a chock similar to those used at the end of the eighteenth century.] 'at the Beame tayled into the beams and to be well bolted with Eight bolts of inch and half a quarter [$1\frac{1}{8}$in] Auger'.
Knees	'one knee fore and aft at each of every Beame.' These were lodging knees.
Mast step	'To have a Rider or Saddle for the Mainmast of sufficient bigness'.

Pillars These were to be fitted in the hold under the beams of the gundeck and the orlop at the centreline. Each was 7in square.

Gundeck beams Breadth 14in, depth 13in 'fitted under each Port of the Gundeck and one Beame betweene each Port of the Gundeck'. This rule applied except in way of the main hatch, where the space was 7ft.

Knees Four knees fitted to each of the gundeck beams, siding 9in. Two of the knees placed 'fore and aft hooked into the Beames [lodging knees] and two up and down [hanging knees]. Each knee was to be fastened with five bolts 1⅛in diameter.

Carlings Two tiers of carlings were to be wrought fore and aft on the gundeck, each 9in wide and 6in deep.

Ledges These were to be worked between the carlings and set 8in apart. Each was 6in wide and 5in deep.

Waterways 7in thick and 14in wide.

Gundeck planking 3in thick oak plank.

Note. Both the waterways and the gundeck planking were fastened to the beams etc in the following manner – 'treenayled and spiked with two spikes in each Beame and two treenayles in each Ledge'.

Scuppers Eight lead scuppers were fitted to each side of the gundeck.

Hatches 'To make as many Hatches in the Hatchways as shal be convenient of two inch plank with the Hatchway abaft the Mast for the storing of provisions and Hatchway to the fforward Roomes and for the Boatswains and Gunners Storerooms and powder roomes to be built of ordinary Deales of such bigness.'

Manger 'To make a Manger on the same deck and to have two, foure inch Scuuppers in it of Lead'.

Hawse holes 'to put in foure Hause [hawse] Pieces two feet six inches broad each, and to cut out foure Hause holes in them'.

Riding bitts 'to place two paires of Carrick Bitts'. The after pair to be 17in broad and 16in thick. The fore pair to be 14in broad and 13in thick, this set being fitted with crosspieces and supported with knees (standards).

Standards Six to be fitted on each side of the gundeck, and bolted with three 1⅛in diameter bolts in each arm.

Breast hooks Four fitted in the hold each being 14in deep and 14ft long. These were fastened with seven bolts each 1⅛in diameter.

Spirketting The spirketting of the gundeck was to be wrought in two strakes and made from oak 5in thick.

Gunports 11 fitted each side of the gundeck, plus an additional two aft, each made to the following dimensions: height 2ft 8in, width 2ft 2in with instructions to 'hang them with hooks and hinges and to fitt and drive all Ringbolts, Eybolts and Staples'.

Partners For the main and foremast were 10in thick.

Pillar 'for the Main Capstan to be Ironbound for the end of the spindle to stand in'.

Deck planking Oak plank 4in thick.

'To raise the Hatches over the Deck and bolt the Planckes into the Beames and to have round Pillars under the Beames, foure inch planck for the pillar to rest upon with Staircases up into the Quarter deck …'

Breast hooks Two fitted between the decks, each 14ft long and 14in deep and secured in the same manner as those previously mentioned.

Transoms 'as many Transomes abaft below the plancks' each set 12in apart, one fitted at the head of the sternpost for the helm port. Each one secured with a knee to be bolted with 1in diameter bolts.

Upper deck gunports 2ft 4in high and 2ft 6in wide. Two were also to be fitted under the forecastle 1ft 10in high and 2ft wide and instructions were given 'to Garnish them with Carved work fore and aft'.

Rising (deck clamps) These to be fitted under the beams of the upper deck, made from oak 4in thick and 16in deep.

Quickwork The sides above the spirketting were planked up with 3in plank.

Upper deck beams Width 11in, depth 8in, set 6ft apart except at the gunroom where they were placed 2ft apart, and all were given a 'round up' of 9in 'betweene and under every Port'.

Deck height From plank to plank amidships 6ft 7in.

Knees Four to each beam, each with a siding of 6in. These to be fastened with two bolts into the beam and three bolts into the ship's side. The diameter of the bolts ¾in.

Carlings Two tiers of carlings with 'sufficient Ledges'.

Deck planking Deal 2½in thick.

Waterway Oak 4in thick.

Spirketting Oak 3in thick, wrought up to the sills of the gunports.

'to have Combings [Coamings], Headledges with grateing [gratings] Hatchways before and abaft the Mast [mainmast] and the Grateing forward for the vent of Smoake of the Ordnance, to fitt Topsail Sheet Bitts with Catts, Davit, clasp of Iron, Partners for the main and Jeere Capstans and partners for all the Masts.'

Scuppers Nine in total, fitted to each side of the upper deck.

Capstan 'To make a main and Jeere Capstan with Capstan barrs and iron pawles.'

'To make a large Quarter Deck and fforecastle with two sound bulkheads in each side of the fforecastle and Quarterdeck abaft for Cabbins and in the Midships of the Bulkhead to place a Cookroome for Rosting and Boyling and to set all the Bulkheads upon six inch plank eight inches broad and to be well fayed to the Deck and laid with Tarr and Hair.'

Bulkhead ports Two fitted in the forecastle bulkhead, and two fitted in the bulkhead of the steerage.

The beams of the forecastle and the steerage 'to be kneed [because of the anchors], Dovetayled and bolted to the Rising.'

The rising Set under the beams of the forecastle and the steerage, 6in thick.

Gun ports   'to cut out eleaven ports on the Uperdeck betweene each port of the Gundeck of bigness afore mentioned and two ports right aft and to make and hang portsills with hooks and hinges.'

Transoms   'under the windowes in the Cabbin and one under the ports', each of which was kneed at each end and bolted with 5in bolts.

Roundhouses   'as large a Roundhouse as the worke with conveniency will give leave with a Bulkhead and Doore to the same'.

Platforms in the hold to have bulkheads and partitions for the powder room, gunner's storeroom, 'Sayleroome', boatswain's storerooms and cabins for the officers and carpenters, the steward's room, the 'ffishroome' and the captain's provisions and bread room.

Each of these compartments were to be 'sheathed with lead or lym [lime] plate [   ] thorow [thorough] dryed with Charcoal (the leading, lyming or plateing which Breadroome is to be at his makers Charge).'

Note. It is unclear as to exactly what process the above passage refers. Presumably it applies to some form of paying the bulkheads with a protective coating, and whitewashing (lime) to brighten the areas. The 'leading' referred to must have been a protection against sparks within the magazines.

The External Planking:

Bottom planking   From the 'kiele to the Chain wayles', to be of 3in oak with the exception of six strakes of planking which were wrought as follows: two strakes below the wale, two between the wales and two above the same wales.

Wales   Oak, 13in broad and 7in thick.

Wales for the chain plates   Two strakes each 5in thick and 9in broad.

Ship's side planking   One strake of oak, 3in thick and 10in broad, wrought between the two strakes of the wales for the chain plates. The remainder of the side to be planked up with 2in oak, and the quarter with 2in deals.

The ship's head   'a firme and substantiall Knee and Cheeks, trible [triple] rayles [head rails] with trayleboard [trailboard] Beast [figurehead] and Brackets'.

Stern   'open Gallery with a house of Officers in it with Carved works and Brackets, windowes and Casement into the Cabbin'. The decoration at the stern consists of the King's arms, cherubs, 'pillersters and Terms'.

Other Details

'To have a paire of Chesstrees'.

'Mizon Chainwales wel bolted and Chainbolts and Chain Plates sufficient for number and size fixed compleat.'

'To have a Rank Gripe wel bolted with Dovetayles and a stirrup on the Skegg well bolted'.

Rudder   (or rother) hung with six pairs of gudgeons and pintles.

Gunwale   Wrought fore and aft as required.

'To find and sett a compleat Suite of Masts and Yards fitt and suitable for such a ship or ffriggot with Capps and Crosstrees, fflagg, Ensigne and Jackstaffs'.

'and compleat finishing the said ships likewise to doe and perform all Joyners works within and without board, finding Deales, Locks, Iron barrs, hinges for Storeroomes' etc, and 'leaden Scuppers'.

'to find, doe and perform all Glaziers worke of Muscovia glass and to find and hang all Casements and Scuttles for Cabbin windowes and to find all painters worke and Guilding both within and without board.'

Dimensions and scantlings from the contract with Nicholas Barrett for the building of the Sixth Rate *Biddeford*, launched in 1695. The contract is dated 11 May 1694.

Source: PRO Adm 106/3071

Note. All text in quotation marks is direct quote from the contract

Keel — To be made from elm in no more than three lengths, 10in square at midships. Scarph length, no less than 3ft 8in and to be tabled, lined with tar and hair, and bolted with five bolts of ¾in diameter.

False keel — Made from elm 3in thick. The space between the keel and false keel layered with tar and hair. Fastening with both trennals and spikes.

Stempost — To be made from oak. Width athwartships at the keel, 10in. Fore and aft siding 11in. Each scarph to be no less than 3ft 2in long. Scarphs to be fastened with five bolts ¾in diameter.

False stem — Width athwartships 16in. Fore and aft siding 4½in. Scarph lengths 12in, each giving shift to those of the stempost. The timbers to be secured in the same manner as those of the stempost.

Sternpost — Square at the head 11in. Fore and aft siding at the heel 2ft 4in.

Rising wood — Two, of sufficient scantling, running fore and aft.

Sternson knee — Vertical arm length 5ft 6in. Fore and aft arm length 7ft minimum. Bolted to both the rising wood and the sternpost every 24in. Bolt size ⅞in. This to be assisted by additional rising wood which is to be set against the knee for the strength of the half timbers which are themselves let into the rising wood and fastened.

Main transom — 9in thick.

Deck transom — 8in thick.

Remaining transoms — 7in thick.

Timber and room (room and space) — 1ft 10in.

Floor timbers — Fore and aft siding amidships 9in, depth upon the keel 10in. Those fitted afore and abaft having a fore and aft siding of 8½in, the depth at the keel 10in.

Lower futtocks — Fore and aft siding amidships 9in, those fitted afore and abaft siding 8½in. All scarphs 1ft 6in minimum length.

Second futtocks — Fore and aft siding at their heels 8in, fore and aft siding at their heads 7in. Thickness at the height of the breadth 4½in.

Toptimbers — Fore and aft siding at their heels 7½in, fore and aft siding at their heads 6½in. Thickness at the height of the gunwale 2in.

Hawse pieces — Two each side, with a width of 20in.

Keelson — To be made of no more than three pieces. Depth 11in, siding 11½in. Scored down upon the timbers for a depth of 1½in. Scarph lengths 3ft 9in. Bolted through to the keel at every other timber with bolts of ⅞in diameter. Each scarph is given a shaft to those of the keel scarphs.

Limberboards — Breadth 12in, thickness 2in. One set each side of the keelson.

Footwaling — Five strakes set on each side at the rungheads. Thickness of first three strakes 3in, the remaining two strakes 2in. Width of each strake 13in. Each strake to be wrought narrower towards the fore and after ends. Four of the strakes to lie on the line of chocking at the floorheads and heels of the upper futtocks. The fifth strake is laid adjacent to the limberboards and is 3in thick.

Middle plank (or band) — Two strakes on each side each 2½in thick and 14in broad.

Deck clamp — Two strakes, one 4in thick the other 3in thick, both 14in broad.
These strakes are tabled together and scarphed with a 'flemish hook and butt'. Scarph lengths 3ft 2in.

Ceiling — Oak plank 1½in thick.

False beams and carlings to be fitted as required to support the platforms, cable tiers and storerooms.

Floor riders — Three. Fore and aft siding 12in. Depth at the keelson 8½in. Depth at the rungheads 8in. Length 13ft. Fastened with five bolts in each arm, ⅞in diameter.

Breast hooks 9in deep and disposed as follows: one under the hawse pieces, one at the deck and two in the hold. There was also to be one for the foremast step, having arms 5ft long, and secured with four bolts ⅞in diameter to each arm.

Standard This was to be fitted upon the after end of the keelson and bolted to the sternpost.

Crutches Two to be fitted in the bread room. Siding 8in. Length of the arms 5ft. Fastened with eight bolts ⅞in diameter.

Transom One to be fayed to the cant frames. Breadth 8½in. Length of
knees the fore and aft arm 7ft 6in at the main transom. Remaining knees all sided 7½in. Bolted at intervals of 20in.

Ladders fitted where necessary and suitable deals employed for the platforms, cabins for the officers, and storerooms (built as required in the hold). The bulkheads to be sealed with plaster of lime and the seams filled with hair. The bread room to be lined with dry seasoned deal. The well, including the shot lockers, to be planked up with oak boards 1½in thick.

Main deck Width 9in, depth 7in. These beams are disposed as follows:
beams one under and one between the gunports, except those 'in wake of the Main Hatchway which lye Six feet abroad'. Each beam to be 'dovetailed into the Clamps and single Kneed' with one hanging knee, 'except those Beames by the Masts and at the Bitts, these being double kneed at each end'.

Hanging Siding 5½in. Vertical arm length 5ft 6in. Athwartships arm 3ft
knees 6in. Fastened with six bolts ¾in diameter.

Pillars 'To place under each Beam in the Hold and on the Keelson, One pillar of Four and Half inches square in section'.

Carlings Two tiers worked between the beams, each timber being 7in wide and 6in deep.

Ledges Made 3½in wide and 3in deep, each set 9in apart.

Waterways 4in thick and 14in broad.

Deck 'Dry Seasoned English Oak Plank'. Thickness 2in. Four strakes
planking to be laid, set off from the waterway each side of the ship and one strake on each side of the coamings 'where the ironwork is drove'. The remainder of the deck is lined with 'good seasoned Beech' 2in thick.

Bitt pins Made from oak 13in in cross-section, the heels of each stepped in the hold. The beams in wake to be scored for a depth of 1½in to receive the bitt pins. Each bitt pin to be fastened to the beams with two bolts ⅞in diameter.

Cross pieces 13in square and scored for a depth of 1½in, to sit against the
for the bitts bitt pins. To be retained by means of iron hooks and eyes.

Standards for 'To fix a pair of Standards upon substantial Carlins fitted
the bitts between the Beames in wake'. Fore and aft arm length 5ft. Scored on their underside for a depth of 1in to sit down upon the beams. Fastened with five bolts in each standard, each ⅞in diameter.

Mainmast To have provision to move fore and aft. 6in thick.
partners

Foremast 4in thick, with the hole cut as necessary.
partners

Capstan 4in thick with the hole cut as necessary.
partners

False partners 3in thick and fitted below the beams to prevent the capstan
for the from rising.
capstan

'to make Hatches and Scuttles as convenient, fitted with Coamings and Head Ledges' each 3½in in height above deck level. The main hatchway is to be made in 'as many parts as possible using Prussian Deal'.
'Rails and Bannisters to be fitted at the Officers Hatchway to the Cabbins'.

Manger Plank thickness 3in. To be built with 'sufficient compass around the Hawses'.

Scuppers Four to be fitted within the confines of the manger, each being made to a diameter of 3in and manufactured from 'Cast Lead of eight pound to the foot square'.
Remaining Scuppers 'and as many Scuppers of 3 inches in diameter along the deck as necessary'.

Spirketting English oak plank worked up to the lower sills of the ports. Thickness 3in.

Waist Oak planking 4in thick and 6in broad. Scored for a depth of
stringer 1in at intervals to allow it to sit well against the timbers of the ship.

Gunports Eleven on each side. Width 2ft 4in, height 2ft.

Quickwork 'berthed up between the Ports with Prussian Deale'.

Clamp or rising of the quarterdeck Oak 2½in thick and 14in broad.

'and the Rising into the Great Cabbin on which the Beames shall be dovetailed and bolted'. This to be made from elm, 6in thick on the upper side and 2½in thick at the bottom edge and 10in broad. The timber is secured with bolts ¾in diameter set every 16in and 'well clenched within board'.

Short 'for handling the sayles'. This to have a lightly constructed
forecastle bulkhead with 'no Cabbins', and fitted to 'shelter the Firehearth'. The beams to be supported with hanging knees each sided 4in, the vertical arm being 3ft long and fastened with four bolts ⅝in in diameter.

Firehearth 'Build within the Bulkhead [forecastle bulkhead] one Firehearth for a Double Kettle, lining up the sides with durable white plaster and cant the same with good Oak … and fixing it with Oak planking fitt in every respect for the Bricklayers Work, brickwork to be bonded with Iron to prevent bricks shaking loose'. [Some words in the original are barely legible, so the above may not be entirely accurate.]

Topsail, sheet and jeer bitts fitted at each mast. Ladders, gratings, gangways, rings and 'kevills' (kevels) furnished as necessary.

Lower wales Made from oak plank 5½in thick and 9¼in broad. When wrought they have a strake of English oar worked between them and one strake worked below. Each of these two strakes are 12in wide and 2½in thick.

Single strake Oak plank worked over the outside of the rungheads. This is 2½in thick.

Bottom planking Oak planking 2in thick.

Chain bolt wale   Depth 7in, width 3½in.

'To bring on a Wale on each side drifting with the Blackstrake'. This strake to be 4in thick and 5in deep. One strake of oak, 2in thick is wrought fore and aft below the chain bolt wale. The rest of the side is to be berthed up with Prussian deal.

Channels   Main and fore channels made from 3in plank of suitable length and breadth. The mizzen channel made from 2½in plank. All of the channels to be fastened with bolts of ⅝in diameter.

Sweep ports   'Cut and Fix Oar Scuttles below the Ports as convenient'.

Head   'Build a Fair Head with a frame and a substantial Knee, and Cheeks, Rails, Trailboard and Brackets and to furnish the same with Gratings and Seats of Easement for the Saylors and with mortices in the Knee for the Gammoning also Washboards under the Cheeks'.

'To have a complete pair of Gallows and to furnish up the same and the Stern abaft with Lights and Handsome Carved Workes to the Gunwhale Rail'.

'Fife Rail to be fitted and a Breast Rail at the fore part of the Quarter Deck'.

'To make and Hang a substantial Rother to run up thro' the Quarter Deck'.

Lights   'Fitted out Sash fashion', and glazed with 'Stone Ground Glass', each made 12in by 10in.

Caulking   From the contract it can be seen that the quantities of oakum varied according to the size of the seam to be caulked. Seams of 2in were to be filled with two double threads of oakum and one of hair (possibly horse hair), while 3in seams were to be payed with four double threads of oakum and one of hair.

The underwater body of the vessel was to be coated in the following manner: 'grave the ship underwater with White Stuff, butt if this cannot be had then Black and Tallow upon it for three or four strakes underwater and the side upward to be payed with Rosin and Tallow'.

Dimensions and scantlings from the contract for the Third Rate *Devonshire*, launched in 1692. The contract is dated 12 March 1691.

Source: PRO Adm 106/3071

Keel	Siding 15½in, depth 16½in. Made from elm in no less than four pieces, each scarph being 4ft 6in long.
False keel	Elm, 4in thick.
Stempost	Fore and aft siding 16in, width 17in, scarph length 4ft.
False stem	Fore and aft siding 9in, width 2ft 6in and the scarphs 1ft.
Sternpost	Fore and aft at the foot 2ft 6in. Square at the head 16in.
False post	Siding fore and aft 16in, width 2ft 2in.
Room and space	2ft 3in.
Keelson	Siding 16in, width 18in. To be made in five pieces with the scarph length 3ft, fastened with bolts 1⅜in diameter.
Limber strakes	Fitted each side of the keelson, worked up to the rungheads, each strake being 15in broad but varying in thickness as follows: first strake 4in; next three strakes 8in; next two strakes 7in; last two strakes 5in.
Middlebands	Siding 7in thick and 15in broad.
Riders	Five bands of floor and futtock riders.
Floor riders	fore and aft siding 18in, thickness 12in, and 15in deep at the rungheads.
Futtock riders	fore and aft siding 15in, depth 15in. Each of these timbers to be fastened with seven bolts of 1¾in diameter.
Orlop beams	11 to be fitted, each 16in wide and 15in deep (six fitted afore the mainmast and five abaft).
Orlop hanging knees and lodging knees	Siding 7in, short arm length 3ft, each secured with six bolts of 1⅜in diameter.
Platforms	Deal planking.
Saddles for the mast (steps)	Mainmast: fore and aft 2ft 7in. Depth sufficient for being set on the keelson.
	Foremast: fore and aft 2ft 4in. Depth as required. Each secured with eight bolts 1¼in diameter.
Pillars	Fitted upon the keelson 8in in square section.
Cross pillars	Five pairs, bolted at their heads to the gundeck beams and feet at the heads of the floor riders.
Well	Boarded up with 3in oak plank.
Wing transom	14in deep. Remaining transoms 12in deep.
Gundeck clamps	Thickness 8¼in, breadth 17in. Each length joined to each other with a Flemish hook and butt scarph.
Gundeck beams	Width 16¼in, depth 15in. One fitted under and one between each gunport.
Hanging and lodging knees	Siding 10in, arms 3ft long (minimum). Fastened with bolts 1¼in diameter.
Gundeck carlings	Width 10in, depth 9in. Five tiers each side of the deck.
Ledges	Width 6in, depth 5in, each set 9in apart.
Waterways	Thickness 6in, depth 4in.
Gundeck planking	English oak plank 4in thick. These boards to be secured to the beams with spikes, and with trennals to the carlings and ledges.
Hawse pieces	Two each side of the stem, each being 2ft 3in broad.
Carrick bitts	Fore set 18in², after set 16in². Heels passed down to the ceiling of the hold and bolted. Timbers to be fastened at each point where they are adjacent to the beams.
Cross pieces for the bitts	Each made to a square section equal to their respective bitt pins. They were also to be scored on their after faces to butt against the pins. Fastening with iron hooks and eyes.
Standards for the bitts	Secured with five bolts 1¼in diameter.
Capstan partners	14in wide and 12in deep. Supported by pillars set on a false partner below.
Main hatch	8ft wide. Coamings 3in English oak set with a rise of 2in above deck level.

Gunports 14 cut each side of the ship; each being 2ft 8in high and 2ft 5in wide. Two chase ports, and four cut through the stern, of similar dimensions.

Upper gundeck beams Width 13in, depth 11in, each set 5ft apart.

Carlings Two tiers each side of the deck, some being 12in² and others at 8in².

Waterways Thickness 5in, breadth 14in.

Deck planking English oak plank and deal 3in thick.

Partners Main and foremasts 7in thick. Mizzen mast 5in thick. All are secured with 1in diameter bolts.

Bittacle [binnacle] Fitted by the mizzen mast.

Jeer capstan 24in diameter. Drumhead and bars made from English elm.

Spirketting 4in thick, plus one strake 5in thick and 10in deep worked up to the gunport sills.

Scuppers Nine each side, 3in diameter. Made of lead of 9lbs to the square foot.

Standards Three pairs each, sided 9in, with arms 4ft long, secured with five bolts, 1in diameter. Each pair to be disposed at the forecastle bulkhead, after bulkhead and the bulkhead of the great cabin.

Gunwale 4in thick and 8in broad.

Quickwork Oak or Prussian deal 3in thick.

Transom Depth 6in, width 9in. Secured by stiffening knees at each end.

Bulkhead stanchions (forecastle) 4in² covered with boards of Prussian deal 2in thick. The boards to be rabbeted together.

Knees Sided 6in, and secured with four bolts ⅞in diameter.

Cook room 4in oak plank to support the brickwork of the hearth and chimney. 'Line the same with place for the Bricklayer and to lead the seams of the deck with sheet Lead lined with Tar and Hair under the Brickwork of the same'.

Forecastle ports Three on each side, plus two chase ports.

Forecastle carlings 14in wide, 5in deep.

Forecastle beams 8½in wide, 6½in deep, set 5ft apart.

Half deck Eight gunports, each 2ft 4in wide and 2ft deep.

Beams 9in wide, 7in deep, each set 20in apart.

Hanging knees Sided 6in, with arms 4ft 6in long. Fastened with five bolts ⅞in diameter.

Deck planking English oak 2in thick, laid under the guns and at the bulkheads and roundhouse. The remaining deck to be wrought with deal.

Waterways 4in thick oak plank.

Spirketting 3in thick with one stronger of oak, 5in thick and 8in in breadth.

Scuppers Three, 2in diameter, made from lead, fitted each side of the vessel.

Stern timbers Fore and aft siding 10in, width 7in.

Transom under the lights Width 12in, depth 7in. One also worked for the Lower sills. Each stiffened with an iron knee at its extremity.

Side planking 2in thick deal.

Roundhouse on the half deck Two gunports cut each side plus four cabins for trumpeters fitted by the taffrail.

Roundhouse beams Width 7in, depth 5in, each set 16in apart.

Stringer Elm, 3in thick and 10in broad.

Knees Fastened with bolts of ¾in diameter.

External planking From the keel to a height of 8ft: elm or beech, 4in thick. Upward from this point to the channel wale: English oak, 4in thick. Six strakes of English oak, 6in thick and 14in broad, tapering to 4in thick at the fore and after ends. These strakes to be wrought above and below the wales.

Lower wales Laid in two strakes, each of oak 4in thick and 9½in broad.

Channel wales Two strakes 6in thick and 7in broad.

Strakes between the channel wales Oak 4in thick and 4½in wide.

Strakes between the channel wales and the gunwale Oak 3in thick and Prussian deal 2in thick, worked at the quarters.

Main and fore channels 9in deep.

Glass for the lights 12in deep, 4in wide.

The quantities of timber used in ship construction

Source: quoted in *The Royal George* by Brigadier A F Johnson

---

The *Blenheim*, 90 guns
Building commenced 1 January 1756
Launched 5 July 1761

Dimensions:

Length of keel for tonnage	142ft 7in
Length of the gundeck	176ft 1in
Extreme beam	49ft 1in
Tons burthen	1827 tons
Length of the sternpost	29ft 8in
Rake of the after side of the main post at the wing transom	1ft 6in
False keel, thick	5½in

Timber used in construction	Loads	Feet
Straight oak	957	29
Compass oak	1605	17
Elm	64	26
Fir	281	30
Knees, square	102	3
Knees, raking	94	4
Thick stuff 10in	64	23
Thick stuff 9½in	0	40
Thick stuff 9in	74	38
Thick stuff 8½in	1	10
Thick stuff 8in	53	12
Thick stuff 7½in	32	20
Thick stuff 7in	71	35
Thick stuff 6½in	5	20
Thick stuff 6in	90	36
Thick stuff 5½in	8	30
Thick stuff 5in	65	35
English oak plank 4in	130	44
English oak plank 3in	71	40
English oak plank 2½in	5	26
Total number of loads	3773	18ft³

Therefore total of timber used was 188,668ft³

Note   1 Load = 50ft³

The *Royal George*, 100 guns
Building commenced 8 January 1746
Launched 18 February 1756

Dimensions:

Length of keel for tonnage	143ft 5½in
Length of the gundeck	178ft
Extreme beam	51ft 9½in
Tons burthen	2046. 80/94 tons
Depth in the hold	21ft 6in

Timber used in construction	Loads	Feet
Straight oak	2309	6
Compass oak	2306	40
Elm	125	10
Fir	214	8
Knees, square	170	8
Knees, raking	149	33
English oak plank 4in thick	135	8
English oak plank 3in thick	94	9
English oak plank 2½in thick	17	33
English oak plank 2in thick	15	4
Dantzic oak plank 4in thick	174	14
Dantzic oak plank 3in thick	42	13
Elm plank 4in thick	4	39
Elm plank 3in thick	2	0
Total number of loads	5760	25ft³

Therefore the total of timber used was 288,025ft³

Note 50ft³ = timber merchant's measure for a load, whereas builder's measurement = 40ft³ per load

APPENDIX 3

Navy Board Order on painting ships dated 18 July 1715

Source: PRO Adm 198/2507

'You are to use good husbandry in painters works and not to refresh oftener to the weather than once a year or two and the inboard works that are from the weather. Only upon Rebuilding and Great Repairs or after a long foreign voyage when a ship hath not been painted in the usual colour yellow and ground black and that both inside and out be of plain colour only except such part of the Head, Stern and Galleries as are usually friezed and that both ships boats be painted only as the painters contract directs and not otherwise, though even at private change.'

APPENDIX 4a

The 1719 Establishment List

Source: Adm 170/429
National Maritime Museum, Greenwich.

Hon Sirs,

In obedience to the Rt. Honble: the Navy Board Warrt. of the 5th of June last, we have maturely Considered, with what Dimensions and Scantlings the Ships of the Royll Navy may more properly be built, So as to prove good Sailers as well as Ships of Force; and having Drawn out the Same at Large in a Book and sent an abstract thereof to the Board; we herewith Send the same at Large to your Hons. and are humbly of Opinion that the Complying with the whole (when it may be done) will be of advantage to the Service not only in making the said Ships Stronger and Lighter; but also cause them to be Built Cheaper and be better Sea Boats, all which is most humbly Submitted to your Better Judgement by

Hon Sirs

Your most obediant Servants

Rich. Stacey. Benj. Rosewell. Jnᵒ Naish Jnᵒ Haynes. Will. Rosewell

Deptford. 11th Novr. 1719.
To the Honble Jacob Acworth Esqr.
Surveyr. of his Majty Navy.

Note. The layout, punctuation, and spelling have, in some places, been modified by the author to make the Establishment List clearer.

		Ship, Number of Guns								
		100	*90*	*80*	*70*	*60*	*50*	*40*	*30*	*20*
Length: by the keel for Tunnage		140ft 7in	132ft 5in	128ft 2in	123ft 2in	117ft 7in	109ft 8in	101ft 8in	93ft 0in	87ft 9in
On the Gundeck from the Rabbet of the Stem to the Rabbet of the Post		174ft	164ft	158ft	151ft	144ft	134ft	124ft	114ft	106ft
Breadth: Extreme		50ft	47ft 2in	44ft 6in	41ft 6in	39ft	36ft	33ft 2in	30ft 6in	28ft 4in
At the afterpart of the Main Wing Transom from out to outside of the Plank		28ft 10in	27ft 2in	25ft 7in	23ft 10in	22ft 4in	20ft 8in	19ft	17ft 4in	16ft 2in
At the Toptimber Line from out to out	Afore	32ft 2½in	30ft 4in	28ft 8in	26ft 9in	23ft 5¼in	19ft 8in	18ft 1½in	16ft 11in	–
	Midships	35ft	33ft	31ft 2in	31ft 1½in	29ft 3in	27ft 4in	25ft 2in	23ft 6in	22ft 10in
	Abaft	20ft 6in	19ft 3½in	18ft 2in	17ft 8in	17ft	15ft 11in	14ft 10in	13ft 8in	13ft
Of the Stern at the Fiferaile abaft		18ft 5in	17ft 10in	17ft 3in	16ft 4in	15ft 8in	14ft 11in	13ft 11in	12ft 11in	12ft 9in
Height: Of the Cutting down in the Midships (Dead Flat) above the Keel		1ft 7½in	1ft 6½in	1ft 5½in	1ft 5in	1ft 5in	1ft 4½in	1ft 4in	1ft 3½in	1ft 3in
Of the Toptimber Line or upper Edge of the	Afore	47ft 7½in	45ft 8in	43ft 6in	35ft 3in	33ft 11½in	31ft 7½in	30ft 2in	26ft 9in	23ft 4in
Wast raile above the Bottom of the false keel	Midships	42ft 4¾in	42ft 3½in	40ft 8¾in	32ft 11½in	31ft 6¼in	29ft 7½in	27ft 10½in	25ft 0¾in	24ft 4¾in
	Abaft	55ft 6½in	52ft 4in	50ft 6in	41ft 9in	39ft 11½in	36ft 11½in	34ft 5in	30ft 9in	26ft 6in
Rising of the Midships Flat		5in	5in	5in	5in	6in	7in	8in	9in	10in
Depth in Hold taken from the Strake next the Limberboards		20ft	18ft 10in	18ft 2in	17ft 4in	16ft 5in	15ft 2in	14ft	12ft	9ft 2in
Strake next the Limberboards	Thick	8in	7¾in	7in	7in	6in	6in	6in	5in	5in
	Broad, if to be had	1ft 3in	1ft 3in	1ft 2½in	1ft 2½in	1ft 2in	1ft 2in	1ft 1in	1ft 1in	1ft 0in
Burthen in Tunns		1869⁴²/₉₄	1566⁸⁴/₉₄	1350	1128²⁹/₉₄	951²²/₉₄	755⁴⁹/₉₄	594⁵⁵/₉₄	462⁴⁹/₉₄	374⁴⁴/₉₄
Draught of Water	Afore	21ft 6in	20ft 2in	19ft 0in	17ft 7in	16ft 6in	15ft 3in	13ft 10in	12ft 3in	11ft 4in
	Abaft	22ft 10in	21ft 6in	20ft 4in	18ft 11in	17ft 10in	16ft 5in	14ft 10in	13ft 5in	12ft 4in
Orlop										
Beams to Round Two Inches in all Ships										
Height from the Upper Edge of the Beam to the Gundeck Plank	At the Middle of the Beam	6ft 6in	6ft 3in	6ft 1in	5ft 11in	5ft 9in	5ft 7in	5ft 6in	5ft 4in	–
Platform										
Abaft height between Plank and Plank		6ft 8in	6ft 7in	6ft 5in	6ft 4in	6ft 3in	6ft 1in	6ft 0in	5ft 11in	–
Afore height between Plank and Plank		6ft 6in	6ft 3in	6ft 1in	5ft 11in	5ft 9in	5ft 7in	5ft 6in	5ft 4in	–
Gundeck										
Beams to Round		5in	4¾in	4½in	4¼in	4in	3¾in	3½in	3¼in	3in
Plank, Thick		4in	4in	3½in	3½in	3in	3in	2½in	2in	2in
Height: To the upper Edge of the Middle or Upper Deck Beams at the middle of the Beam – (Afore, Abaft and Midships)		7ft 2in	7ft 0in	6ft 11in	6ft 11in	6ft 10in	6ft 7½in	6ft 6in	6ft 0in	5ft 9in
To the Port Cills		2ft 4in	2ft 4in	2ft 4in	2ft 3in	2ft 3in	2ft 2in	1ft 11in	1ft 9in	2ft 4in
of the Ports from the Water in the Midships		4ft 5½in	4ft 5½in	4ft 8½in	5ft 0in	5ft 0in	4ft 11in	4ft 10in	3ft 10in	7ft 6in U.Dk Ports 2ft 7in Oar Ports
Ports:	Deep	2ft 9in	2ft 8in	2ft 8in	2ft 8in	2ft 8in	2ft 7in	2ft 6in	2ft 4in	–
	Fore and Aft	3ft 5in	3ft 5in	3ft 5in	3ft 3in	3ft 3in	2ft 11in	2ft 9in	2ft 6in	–
Hanging of the Deck		2ft 1in	1ft 11in	1ft 10in	1ft 9in	1ft 8in	1ft 7in	1ft 5½in	1ft 4in	1ft 3in
Higher Abaft than Afore		8in	8in	8in	8in	8in	6in	4in	4in	0in
Beams to Round		7in	6¾in	6½in	–	–	–	–	–	–
Middle Gundeck										
Plank, Thick		3in	3in	3in	–	–	–	–	–	–
Height: To the Upper Edge of the Upper Deck Beams at the Middle of the Beam	Afore	7ft 1in	6ft 10in	6ft 8in	–	–	–	–	–	–
	Midships	7ft 3in	7ft 0in	6ft 9in	–	–	–	–	–	–
	Abaft	7ft 3in	7ft 0in	6ft 9in	–	–	–	–	–	–
To the Port Cills		2ft 2in	2ft 2in	1ft 11in	–	–	–	–	–	–
Ports:	Deep	2ft 9in	2ft 8in	2ft 8in	–	–	–	–	–	–
	Fore and Aft	3ft 3in	3ft 1in	2ft 11in	–	–	–	–	–	–

		Ship, Number of Guns								
		100	90	80	70	60	50	40	30	20
Upper Gundeck										
Beams to Round		8in	7¾in	7½in	7¼in	7in	6¾in	6½in	6¼in	6in
Plank, Thick		3in	3in	3in	3in	2½in	2½in	2½in	2in	2in
Height: To the Upper Edge of the Quarter { Afore		7ft 6in	6ft 10in	6ft 8in	6ft 8in	6ft 6½in	6ft 6in	6ft 5½in	6ft 5in	6ft 5in
Deck Beams at the Middle of the Beam { Abaft		7ft 9in	7ft 1in	6ft 11in	6ft 11in	6ft 9in	6ft 8in	6ft 7in	6ft 7in	6ft 6in
Of the Waste		5ft 8in	5ft 4in	4ft 10in	5ft 3in	5ft 0in	4ft 8in	4ft 2in	4ft 2in	3 10in
To the Port Cills		1ft 10in	1ft 9in	1ft 7in	1ft 10in	1ft 8in	1ft 8in	1ft 6in	1ft 6in	1ft 6in
To the Upper Edge of the Forecastle Beams { Afore		6ft8in	6ft 6in	5ft 10in	6ft 4in	6ft 1in	5ft 9in	5ft 4in	5ft 2in	4ft 8in
at the Middle of the Beam { Abaft		6ft 8in	6ft 6in	5ft 10in	6ft 4in	6ft 1in	5ft 9in	5ft 4in	5ft 2in	4ft 8in
Ports: Deep		2ft 8in	2ft 7in	2ft 7in	2ft 7in	2ft 6in	2ft 4in	2ft 2in	2ft 2in	2ft 0in
Fore and Aft		3ft 0in	2ft 9in	2ft 9in	2ft 9in	2ft 6in	2ft 5in	2ft 4in	2ft 4in	2ft 4in
Forecastle										
Beams to Round		7in	6¾in	6½in	6¼in	6in	5¾in	5½in	5¼in	5in
Plank, Thick		2in	2in	2in	2in	2in	2in	2in	2in	2in
Long: From the Foreside of the Stanchions		36ft 3in	31ft 7in	10ft 4in	31ft 6in	26ft 6in	26ft 6in	21ft 9in	20ft 0in	7ft 3in
Quarter Deck										
Beams to Round		8in	7½in	7¼in	7in	6¾in	6½in	6¼in	6in	6in
Plank, Thick		2½in	2½in	2½in	2½in	2in	2in	2in	2in	2in
Height: To the Upper Edge of the Round { Afore		6ft 8in	6ft 6in	6ft 2in	6ft 5in	6ft 5in	5ft 5in	4ft 8in	–	–
House Beams at the Middle of the Beam { Abaft		6ft 10in	6ft 8in	6ft 4in	6ft 7in	6ft 7in	5ft 7in	4ft 10in	–	–
To the Port Cills		1ft 7in	1ft 7in	1ft 6in	1ft 6in	1ft 6in	1ft 6in	–	1ft 6in	–
Ports, Deep		2ft 6in	2ft 6in	2ft 5in	2ft 4in	2ft 3in	2ft 2in	–	2ft 0in	–
Fore and Aft		2ft 9in	2ft 8in	2ft 7in	2ft 6in	2ft 5in	2ft 4in	–	2ft 2in	–
Long: Taken in the Midships from the after part of the Stern Timbers		79ft 0in	76ft 3in	66ft 3in	68ft 6in	62ft 0in	56ft 6in	45ft 3in	43ft 0in	16ft 9in
Roundhouse										
Beams to Round		9in	8½in	8½in	8½in	8½in	8in	8in	–	–
Plank, Thick		2in	2in	2in	2in	2in	2in	2in	–	–
Height: To the Upper Edge of the Topgallant Round House { Afore		5ft 10in								
Beams at the Middle of the Beam { Abaft		6ft 0in								
Long: Taken in the Midships from the after part of the Stern Timbers		45ft 0in	42ft 7in	16ft 2in	34ft 3in	32 0in	10 6in	8ft 6in	–	–
Topgallant Round House										
Beams to Round		1ft	–	–	–	–	–	–	–	–
Long: taken at the Midships from the after part of the Stern Timbers		10ft 6in	–	–	–	–	–	–	–	–
Length, from the Foreside of the Tafferaile at the height of the Fiferail to the Foreside of the Figure of the Head at a line parallel to the keel		210ft 2in	197ft 6in	188ft 10in	176ft 3in	167 0in	155 9in	143 2in	132 0in	121 11in
The Rounding of the Stern Aft at the Wing Transom		1ft 0in	11in	10¼in	9½in	8¾in	8in	7¼in	6½in	6in
at the Lower Counter Raile		1ft 2in	1ft 1in	1ft 0¼in	11½in	10¾in	10in	9¼in	8½in	8in
Gundeck, Perpendicular Height above the Upper Edge { Afore		24ft 4½in	22ft 11¼in	22ft 0½in	21ft 0½in	19ft 11in	18ft 7½in	17ft 4in	15ft 0½in	12ft 3in
of the Keel to the Upper Edge of the { Abaft		25ft 0½in	23ft 7¼in	22ft 8½in	21ft 8½in	20ft 7in	19ft 1½in	17ft 8in	15ft 4½in	12ft 3in
Plank at the Middle of the Deck										
The Back of the False Post to Rake 2½ inches in a Foot, and the Upright of the Stern Three Inches										
Stem to Rake Forward above the Gundeck to the Top of it, One inch in a Foot										
Height of the After Side of the Wing Transom above the Upper Edge of the Keel at the Post		27ft 5in	25ft 11¾in	25ft 1in	24ft 0in	22ft 10½in	21ft 4in	19ft 7½in	17ft 2in	15ft 6¼in
Lower Height of the Breadth above the Upper edge of the Keel in the Midships		18ft 9in	17ft 8in	16ft 8½in	15ft 6in	14ft 8in	13ft 7¾in	12ft 5½in	11ft 4in	10ft 5in
Upper Height of the Breadth above the Upper Edge of the Keel in the Midships		21ft 9in	20ft 5in	19ft 2½in	17ft 9in	16ft 8in	15ft 4¾in	13ft 11½in	12ft 7in	11ft 5in
From the Upper Edge of the Keel to the Lower Edge of the Counter Raile at the Middle Line		31ft 11in	30ft 4in	29ft 5in	28ft 2in	27ft 0in	25ft 5in	23ft 10½in	21ft 1½in	18ft 6in
From the Aft side of the Wing Transom to the After part of the Counter at the Middle Line		5ft 9in	5ft 8in	5ft 7in	5ft 4in	4ft 9in	4 6in	4ft 3in	4ft 0in	3ft 4in
The Second Counter … Ditto …		7ft 5in	7ft 3in	7ft 1in	6ft 10in	6ft 2in	5ft10in	5ft 6in	5ft 2in	–
From the Upper Edge of the Keel to the Lower Edge of the Raile under the Wardroom Lights in 3 Deck Ships and under the Great Cabbin Lights in 2 Deck Ships		35ft 1in	33ft 6in	32ft 6in	31ft 7in	30ft 4½in	28ft 9in	27ft 2½in	24ft 5½in	–

	Ship, Number of Guns								
	100	*90*	*80*	*70*	*60*	*50*	*40*	*30*	*20*
Parts of the Frame									
Keel: Main of Elm of Beach, No of Pieces not to Exceed, (if can be procurred)	6	6	5	5	5	5	4	4	4
Square in the Midships	1ft 7in	1ft 6in	1ft 5in	1ft 4in	1ft 3in	1ft 2¼in	1ft 1½in	1ft 0½in	1ft 0in
Scarphs, (Laid with Tarr and Hair Thrice their Breadth)	4ft 8in	4ft 6in	4ft 4in	4ft 2in	4ft 0in	3ft 10in	3ft 8in	3ft 6in	3ft 4in
Number and Size of Bolts in Each	8 × 1¼in	8 × 1¼in	8 × 1¼in	8 × 1¼in	8 × 1⅛in	6 × 1in	6 × 1in	6 × ⅞in	6 × ⅞in
Sided Afore	1ft 5in	1ft 4in	1ft 3in	1ft 2in	1ft 1in	1ft 0¾in	1ft 0in	11in	10½in
Sided at the Rabbet of the Post	1ft 0½in	1ft 0in	11½in	11in	10½in	9½in	9in	8½in	7½in
False, Thick	5in	5in	4½in	4in	4in	4in	3½in	3in	3in
Number of Pieces (False Keel)	The Same or One More than the Keel								
Stem, Main, Breadth of the Head athwartships	2ft 5in	2ft 3in	2ft 1in	1ft 11in	1ft 9in	1ft 7in	1ft 5in	1ft 3½in	1ft 2in
Below the Hance	The Bigness of the Keel Amidships								
Fore and Aft at the Head	1ft 9in	1ft 7½in	1ft 6in	1ft 5in	1ft 4in	1ft 3in	1ft 2in	1ft 1in	1ft 0in
At the Fore Foot	The Same as the Keel								
Scarphs Long, not less than	4ft 0in	3ft 10in	3ft 8in	3ft 6in	3ft 4in	3ft 3in	3ft 2in	3ft 1in	3ft 0in
Number and Size of Bolts in each, & to Lodge thro' the False Stem	6 × 1⅛in	6 × 1⅛in	6 × 1⅛in	6 × 1⅛in	6 × 1⅛in	6 × 1in	6 × 1in	6 × 1⅞in	6 × 1⅞in
False Stem: Thick (to overlaunch the Scarphs of the Stem above and below)	1ft 0in	11½in	11in	10½in	9½in	9in	8in	7in	6in
Broad (if can be had)	2ft 5½in	2ft 4in	2ft 2in	2ft 1in	1ft 11in	1ft 10in	1ft 8in	1ft 7in	1ft 6in
Scarphs Long	1ft 2in	1ft 2in	1ft 0in	1ft 0in	1ft 0in	1ft 0in	1ft 0in	1ft 0in	1ft 0in
Post [Stern] Main: Square at the Upper End, the Top end to be wrought upwards if to be had	2ft 0in	1ft 11in	1ft 10in	1ft 9in	1ft 8in	1ft 6in	1ft 4in	1ft 2in	1ft 0in
Fore and Aft on the Keel, After False Post included	2ft 9in	2ft 8in	2ft 7in	2ft 6in	2ft 5in	2ft 4in	2ft 2in	2ft 1in	2ft 0in
Abaft the Rabbet at the Wing Transom	11in	10in	9in	8in	7½in	7in	6½in	6in	6½in
False [Post]: the back of it abaft the Rabbitt on the Keel	2ft 1in	2ft 0in	1ft 11in	1ft 10in	1ft 9in	1ft 8in	1ft 7in	1ft 6in	1ft 5in
The Inner [Post]: Fore and Aft (The Top end upwards)	1ft 4in	1ft 3in	1ft 2in	1ft 1in	1ft 0in	11in	10in	9in	8in
Fore and Aft on the Keel (if can be had)	1ft 8in	1ft 7in	1ft 6in	1ft 5in	1ft 4in	1ft 3in	1ft 1in	11in	9in
Transoms, Wing: Sided	1ft 3in	1ft 2in	1ft 1½in	1ft 1in	1ft 0½in	1ft 0in	11½in	11in	10½in
Moulded at the Ends	1ft 8in	1ft 7in	1ft 6in	1ft 5in	1ft 4in	1ft 2in	1ft 2in	1ft 1in	1ft 0in
Deck transoms: To lye close to the Gundeck for the Plank of the said Deck to bolt into the same									
Sided	1ft 2in	1ft 1in	1ft 0¼in	1ft 0in	11½in	11in	10in	9in	8½in
Moulded: As broad as conveniently maybe for the Better fastening the Plank of the Deck									
Transoms: Between the Wing and Deck, so thick as to leave 2 or 2½ Inches on each side for Air between the Wing Transom and Gundeck Plank									
Under the Deck Transom, (1st, 2nd and Lower) Sided, not less than	1ft 1in	1ft 0in	11½in	11in	10½in	10in	9in	8in	7½in
Half to lye clear of the Whole Transoms for Air, at least 3 inches									
Rising Wood: A sufficient number of Pieces Afore and Abaft.									
Abaft (if a Short Piece of Keel), to overlaunch the Scarph at least 6 feet, if a Long piece of Keel to drop short of the Scarph 8 feet									
Depth in the Midships on the Keel	10in	9½in	8½in	8in	8in	8in	8in	7½in	7in
Breadth, in the Midships 3 Inches on each side more than the Keel (if can be had)									
Knee: against the Post, upon the Lower piece of Deadwood, Length of the up & down Arm	7ft 0in	6ft 8in	6ft 0in	5ft 6in	5ft 0in	5ft 0in	4ft 6in	4ft 0in	4ft 0in
Fore and Aft Arme (if can be had)	9ft 0in	8ft 6in	8ft 0in	7ft 6in	7ft 0in	6ft 6in	6ft 0in	5ft 6in	5ft 0in
Distance (in Inches) that the Bolts are set	22in	22in	22in	22in	22in	22in	22in	22in	22in
Diameter of the Bolts employed	1½in	1½in	1⅜in	1⅜in	1¼in	1¼in	1¼in	1⅛in	1in
Bolted through the Keel and Post, and upon the said Knee to bring on the rest of the Rising Wood fastend in the same manner									
Hawse Pieces: Number on each side, Two, and a Piece between, or Four as can conveniently be had									
If in Two, each piece to be Broad	2ft 8in	2ft 7in	2ft 6in	2ft 5in	2ft 4in	2ft 3in	2ft 2in	2ft 1in	2ft 0in
Holes (Hawse) in Diameter	1ft 4in	1ft 3in	1ft 2in	1ft 1½in	1ft 1in	1ft 0in	11in	10in	9in

	Ship, Number of Guns								
	100	90	80	70	60	50	40	30	20
Timbers: Room and Space	2ft 7in	2ft 7in	2ft 7in	2ft 7in	2ft 7in	2ft 7in	2ft 6in	2ft 5in	2ft 5in
Floor and Foothook in the Bearing of the Ship to Fill up the Rooms and Space, especially for large Ships (if conveniently be had)									
Next the Flats Sided	1ft 2in	1ft 2in	1ft 1½in	1ft 1¼in	1ft 1in	1ft 0in	11in	10in	9in
Afore and Abaft, in the wake of the Half Timbers, 2 Inches less than in the Midships from 100 to 60 Guns, 50 Gun Ships 1½in, and the 40 Gun Ships and Downwards, 1½ Inches less									
At the Wrongheads Midships wrought in and out	1ft 2in	1ft 1½in	1ft 0¾in	1ft 0in	11in	10in	9in	8in	7in
Afore and Abaft in and out	1ft 1in	1ft 0½in	11¾in	11in	10in	9in	8in	7in	6in
Every other bolted through the Keel by bolts of diameter	1½in	1½in	1⅜in	1⅜in	1¼in	1¼in	1¼in	1⅛in	1in
Heads to lye above the Bearing of the Floor Midships	1ft 8in	1ft 6in	1ft 4in	1ft 4in	1ft 4in	1ft 4in	1ft 4in	1ft 4in	1ft 4in
Foothooks: Lower sided in the Midships next the Flats a small distance Afore and Abaft the Bearing of the Ship	1ft 2in	1ft 2in	1ft 1½in	1ft 1¼in	1ft 1in	1ft 0in	11in	10in	9in
Afore and Abaft	1ft 0in	1ft 0in	11½in	11¼in	11in	10½in	10in	9in	8in
Heels, to Scarph below the Floorheads at least	8ft 0in	7ft 9in	7ft 6in	7ft 2in	6ft 10in	6ft 6in	6ft 2in	5ft 10in	5ft 6in
In and Out at the Heads in the Midships	11½in	11in	10½in	10in	9in	8in	7in	6in	5½in
Scarphs, upwards, Long	7ft 9in	7ft 5in	7ft 0in	6ft 10in	6ft 9in	6ft 4in	7ft 6in	6ft 4½in	5ft 4in
Afore and Abaft, not less than	6ft 6in	6ft 3in	6ft 0in	6ft 0in	6ft 0in	6ft 0in	6ft 0in	5ft 6in	5ft 0in
Second: Sided in the Midships	1ft 1½in	1ft 1½in	1ft 1in	1ft 0¾in	1ft 0½in	11½in	10½in	9½in	8½in
Afore and Abaft	11½in	11½in	11in	10¾in	10½in	10in	9½in	8½in	7½in
Scarphs Long in the Midships	7ft 9in	7ft 5in	7ft 0in	6ft 10in	6ft 9in	6ft 4in	7ft 6in	6ft 4½in	5ft 4in
Afore and Abaft, not less than	6ft 6in	6ft 3in	6ft 0in	6ft 0in	6ft 0in	6ft 0in	6ft 0in	5ft 6in	5ft 0in
Third: Sided in the Midships	1ft 1in	1ft 1in	1ft 0½in	1ft 0¼in	1ft 0in	11in	–	–	–
Afore and Abaft	11½in	11½in	11in	10¾in	10½in	9½in	–	–	–
Scarphs, Long in the Midships	7ft 9in	7ft 5in	7ft 0in	6ft 10in	6ft 9in	6ft 4in	–	–	–
Afore and Abaft, not less than	6ft 6in	6ft 3in	6ft 0in	6ft 0in	6ft 0in	6ft 0in	–	–	–
Upper: Sided in the Midships (at their Heads, One Inch less)	1ft 1in	1ft 1in	1ft 0½in	1ft 0¼in	1ft 0in	11in	10in	9in	8in
Afore and abaft (at their Heads, One Inch less)	11½in	11½in	11in	10¾in	10½in	10in	9½in	8½in	7½in
At the Gundeck, in and out at the Midships	11in	10½in	10in	9½in	8½in	7½in	6½in	5½in	5in
Timbers: Scarph Long, Upper (In the Midships) to reach the Upper Deck Clamps of 2 deck Ships and the Middle Deck Clamps of 3 decked Ships, and on Wake of the Channels to run up as high as the Deck (if can be had)									
Lower, in the Midships	7ft 9in	7ft 5in	7ft 0in	6ft 10in	6ft 9in	6ft 4in	7ft 6in	6ft 4½in	5ft 4in
Upper (Afore and Abaft) To reach the Upper or Middle Deck Clamps									
Lower, Afore and abaft	6ft 6in	6ft 3in	6ft 0in	6ft 0in	6ft 0in	6ft 0in	6ft 0in	5ft 6in	5ft 0in
Top Timber Sided at the Heels and the Upper Futtock Heads	1ft 1in	1ft 1in	1ft 0½in	1ft 0¼in	1ft 0in	11in	10in	9in	8in
Heads	9½in	9½in	9in	9in	8½in	8in	7½in	7in	6in
Timber: Top, in and out at the Gunnell or top of the Side	5in	4¾	4in	4in	3¾in	3¼in	2¾in	2½in	2¼in
In 50 Gun Ships, at the Side of the Gundeck Ports to make Top Timbers and Upper Foothooks in one, and in all other Ships in the Wake of the Channells, some on each side if can be had									

In Hold

	100	90	80	70	60	50	40	30	20
Keelson Square	1ft 7in	1ft 6in	1ft 5in	1ft 4½in	1ft 3½in	1ft 2½in	1ft 1½in	1ft 0½in	11½in
Number of Pieces, if can be had	6	6	5	5	5	5	4	4	4
Length of the Scarphs to reach Three Floor Timbers, and to be bolted with Bolts of the same Size of the Floor Timbers and Two small Bolts in the Ends of the Scarphs									
Standard upon or under the Keelson Abaft, the up and down Arme to but under the Lower Transom if can be had									
The other Arme long	9ft 0in	8ft 9in	8ft 6in	8ft 3in	8ft 0in	7ft 9in	7ft 6in	7ft 3in	7ft 0in
Sided at least	1ft 1in	1ft 1in	1ft 0½in	1ft 0½in	1ft 0in	11½in	11in	10½in	10in
Limber Boards { Thick	3in	3in	3in	3in	3in	2½in	2½in	2½in	2in
{ Broad	1ft 2in	1ft 2in	1ft 2in	1ft 2in	1ft 2in	1ft 2in	1ft 2in	1ft 2in	1ft 0in

		Ship, Number of Guns								
		100	*90*	*80*	*70*	*60*	*50*	*40*	*30*	*20*
Strake next the Limber Boards, the Second,	Thick	6in	5in	–	–	–	–	–	–	–
	Broad	1ft 3in	1ft 3in	(if can be had)		–	–	–	–	–
Thick Stuff at the Floorheads	Thick	9in	9in	8in	8in	7in	6in	6in	5in	5in
Middle Strake;	Broad, if can be had	1ft 4in	1ft 3½in	1ft 3in	1ft 3in	1ft 3in	1ft 3in	1ft 2in	1ft 1½in	1ft 1½in
Number & Thickness of the Strakes;	Above the Middle Strake	1 of 9in	1 of 9in	1 of 8in	1 of 8in	1 of 7in	1 of 6in	–	–	–
		1 of 9in	1 of 7½in	1 of 6in		1 of 5in	1 of 4in	1 of 5in	1 of 5in	1 of 3in
	Below the Middle Strake	1 of 9in	1 of 9in	1 of 8in	1 of 8in	1 of 7in	1 of 6in	–	–	–
		1 of 8in	1 of 7½in	1 of 6in	1 of 5in	1 of 5in	1 of 4in	1 of 5in	1 of 6in	1 of 3in
No more than 3 Strakes Afore and Abaft: for those Ships of 3 Decks to be but 4 Inches, the 70, 60, and 50 Gun Ships, 3 Inches, the 40 and 30 Gun Ships, 2 Strakes of 3 Inches, and the 20 Gun Ships, One Strake of 2½ Inches										
Thick Stuff at the Lower Foothook Heads One Strake, Above the Middle Strake, Thick		7½in	6½in	5½in	5in	4½in	4in	4in	3in	2½in
Middle Strake	Thick	8½in	7½in	6½in	6½	6in	5in	5in	4in	3½in
	Broad if can be had	1ft 3in	1ft 2½in	1ft 2in	1ft 2in	1ft 2in	1ft 2in	1ft 1½in	1ft 1in	1ft 0in
One Strake, Below, the Middle Strake, Thick		7½in	6½in	5½in	5in	4½in	4in	4in	3in	2½
Footwaling The rest thick in the Midships		4in	4in	4in	4in	3in	3in	3in	2½in	2½in
Afore and Abaft		3in	3in	3in	3in	2½in	2in	2in	2in	1¾in
Orlope Clamps Upper Strake, Thick		8in	7½in	7in	7in	6in	5½in	5in	4in	–
Lower Strake, Thick		7in	6½in	6in	6in	5½in	4½in	4in	3in	–
Beams To Butt against the Timbers, and where there are Lodging Knees to fay them to the Timbers										
Number Afore the Mainmast		(One under every other Gundeck beam, except				3in	2in	2in	2in	–
Number Abaft the Mainmast		in the Main Hatchway & Mainmast room,				3in	3in	2in	2in	–
		one under each)								
Sided		1ft 4in	1ft 3½in	1ft 2½in	1ft 2in	1ft 1in	11in	10in	9in	–
Moulded		1ft 4in	1ft 3½in	1ft 2½in	1ft 2in	1ft 1in	11in	10in	9in	–
Knees, Lodging: the Shortest Arme not less than		4ft 9in	4ft 6in	4ft 3in	4ft 0in	3ft 9in	3ft 6in	3ft 4in	3ft 4in	–
Sided		10in	9½in	9in	8½in	8in	7½in	7in	6in	–
Number and Size of Bolts in each		7 × 1⅜in	7 × 1¼in	7 × 1¼in	7 × 1⅛in	7 × 1⅛in	6 × 1⅛in	6 × 1in	6 × ⅞in	–
To lye below the Upper Edge of the Beame		3in	3in	2½in	2¼in	2in	1¾in	1½in	1½in	–
Plank or Board, Thick		1½in	1½in	1½in	1½in	1¼in	1¼in	1in	1in	–
Thick Stuff, on the Ends of the Beams, Thick		7in	6½in	6in	6in	5in	4in	3½	3	–
Broad		Proper for leaving Sufficient opening under the Gundeck Clamps								
Standard Knees (Where there are no Futtock Riders) Sided The Size and Number of Bolts in Each		The same as the Other Knees								
Carlings and Ledges, The same as the Gundeck										
Transom Knees, The Wing, Sided		1ft 2in	1ft 1½in	1ft 1in	1ft 0in	11in	10½in	9½in	8½in	7in
The Fore and Aft Arme to be Scored into the Transoms, 1½ inches, and to Scarph with Hook and Butt, at the Fore end on the Spirketting, a Sufficient Length										
Fore and Aft Arme, long, (if can be had)		20ft 0in	19ft 0in	18ft 0in	16ft 0in	14ft 0in	13ft 0in	12ft 6in	11ft 0in	10ft 0in
Shortest Arme, long, (if can be had)		10ft 0in	9ft 6in	9ft 0in	8ft 6in	8ft 0in	7ft 6in	7ft 0in	6ft 6in	6ft 0in
Distance set between the Bolts		24in	24in	24in	24in	24in	24in	24in	24in	24in
Size of the Bolts		1⅜in	1¼in	1¼in	1¼in	1⅛in	1⅛in	1in	⅞in	¾in
Transom Knees										
Deck, Side and Bolted the same Size as the Gundeck Knees, their Number of Bolts increasing according to their lengths										
Length of the Longest Arme		10ft 0in	9ft 9in	9ft 0in	8ft 6in	8ft 0in	7ft 6in	7ft 0in	6ft 6in	6ft 0in
Distance and Size of Bolts the Same as the Wing Transom Knees										
Below the Gundeck, Sided 2 Inches less than the Transom										
Longest Arm, Long		10ft 0in	9ft 9in	9ft 0in	8ft 6in	8ft 0in	7ft 6in	7ft 0in	6ft 6in	6ft 0in
Distance and Size of Bolts, the same as the Wing Transom Knees										

	Ship, Number of Guns								
	100	*90*	*80*	*70*	*60*	*50*	*40*	*30*	*20*
Riders									
Floor, number	5	4	3	2	2	–	–	–	–
Length	29ft 0in	27ft 6in	26ft 0in	24ft 6in	23ft 0in	–	–	–	–
Sided	1ft 7in	1ft 6in	1ft 5in	1ft 4in	1ft 3in	–	–	–	–
Deep on the Keelson	1ft 2in	1ft 1in	1ft 0in	1ft 0in	1ft 0in	–	–	–	–
Deep at the Floor Head	1ft 4in	1ft 3½in	1ft 3in	1ft 2in	1ft 1in	–	–	–	–
Number of Bolts and Size in each	12 × 1½in	12 × 1½in	10 × 1⅜in	10 × 1¼in	10 × 1⅛in	–	–	–	–
Lower Foothook: Number on each Side	8	7	6	5	5	3	3	2	–
To have pieces Scarphed & Hooked on the Heels of them Cross the Keelson where there are no Floor Riders									
Scarphed each way Upwards, (if can be had), from the Floor Head	To the Lower Edge of the Orlope Beams								
Scarphed each way Downwards, (if can be had), from the Floor Heads	7ft 9in	7ft 6in	7ft 4in	7ft 2in	7ft 0in	6ft 9in	6ft 6in	6ft 3in	–
Sided	1ft 5in	1ft 4¼in	1ft 4in	1ft 4in	1ft 3in	1ft 3in	1ft 2in	1ft 1in	–
Moulded at the Floor Head	1ft 4in	1ft 3½in	1ft 3in	1ft 2in	1ft 1in	1ft 0in	11in	10in	–
Number and Size of Bolts in each	9 × 1½in	9 × 1½in	9 × 1⅜in	8 × 1⅜in	8 × 1¼in	8 × 1¼in	8 × 1¼in	8 × 1⅛in	–
Upper Foothook: Number on each Side	8	7	6	5	–	–	–	–	–
Length, Downward, if can be had	To the Heads of the Floor Riders								
Length Upwards	To the Gundeck Lodging Knees								
Sided	1ft 3in	1ft 2½in	1ft 2in	1ft 2in	–	–	–	–	–
Moulded at the Upper End	1ft 1in	1ft 0in	11in	10in	–	–	–	–	–
To be Bolted to the Orlope Beams with 2 Bolts of the same Size as the Orlope Knees									
Number and Size of Bolts through the Side	8 × 1⅜in	8 × 1¼in	8 × 1¼in	8 × 1¼in	–	–	–	–	–
Crotches									
Number	2	2	2	2	1	1	1	1	1
Lengths of each Arm (if can be had)	9ft 0in	8ft 6in	8ft 0in	7ft 6in	7ft 0in	6ft 6in	6ft 0in	5ft 6in	5ft 0in
Sided	1ft 2in	1ft 2in	1ft 1in	1ft 1in	1ft 0in	11in	10in	9in	8in
Number and Size of Bolts in each	8 × 1⅜in	8 × 1¼in	8 × 1¼in	6 × 1¼in	6 × 1⅛in	6 × 1in	6 × 1in	6 × 1⅞in	6 × 0¾in
Steps									
Main, Sided	To the Diameter of the Mainmast in the Partners								
Deep on the Keelson	1ft 7in	1ft 6in	1ft 5in	1ft 4in	1ft 3in	1ft 3in	1ft 2in	1ft 1in	1ft 0in
Fore, Sided	To the Diameter of the Foremast in the Partners								
On the Keelson	a Sufficient Depth								
Length, if can be had	15ft 0in	14ft 0in	13ft 0in	12ft 0in	11ft 0in	10ft 0in	9ft 0in	8ft 0in	7ft 0in
Number and Size of Bolts	8 × 1½in	8 × 1½in	8 × 1⅜in	8 × 1⅜in	8 × 1¼in	8 × 1¼in	8 × 1¼in	8 × 1⅛in	8 × 1in
Mizen, Sided	The Diameter of the Mizen Mast in the Partners								
Deep on the Keelson	a Sufficient Depth								
Number and Size of Bolts	8 × 1⅜in	8 × 1¼in	8 × 1¼in	6 × 1¼in	6 × 1⅛in	6 × 1in	6 × 1in	6 × ⅞in	6 × ¾in
Main Capstan, Broad	2ft 0in	1ft 10in	1ft 9in	1ft 8in	1ft 7in	1ft 6in	1ft 5in	1ft 4in	1ft 3in
Deep	1ft 4in	1ft 3in	1ft 2½in	1ft 2in	1ft 2in	1ft 1in	1ft 1in	1ft 0in	1ft 0in
Breasthooks: under the Deckhook, Lower	1ft 3in	1ft 2½in	1ft 2in	1ft 2in	1ft 1in	1ft 0in	11in	10in	9in
Second	1ft 3in	1ft 2½in	1ft 2in	1ft 2in	1ft 1in	1ft 0in	11in	10in	–
Third	1ft 3in	1ft 2½in	1ft 2in	1ft 2in	1ft 1in	1ft 0in	11in	–	–
Fourth	1ft 3in	1ft 2½in	1ft 2in	1ft 2in	–	–	–	–	–
Length, (if can be had)	17ft 0in	16ft 6in	16ft 0in	15ft 6in	15ft 0in	14ft 6in	14ft 0in	13ft 0in	12ft 0in
Number and Size of Bolts	13 × 1½in	13 × 1½in	13 × 1⅜in	11 × 1⅜in	11 × 1¼in	9 × 1¼in	9 × 1¼in	9 × 1⅛in	9 × 1in
Pillars: Upright, under the Beams, Square	9in	8½in	8in	8in	7½in	7in	6½in	6in	5in
To be placed under the Middle of each Beam and in the Quarters on the Scarphs of the Riders where there is no Pointers									
Pointers: Square	1ft 0in	11in	10in	9in	8½in	–	–	–	–
Number of Pairs to meet under the Gundeck Beams, and to be Scored 1½ Inches into the Orlope Beames	5	4	3	2	2	–	–	–	–
To be Bolted to the Gundeck Beams with up and down Bolts, and to the Orlope Beams, Fore and aft, each Pointer to have Bolts in each	2 × 1¼in	2 × 1⅛in	2 × 1⅛in	2 × 1⅛in	2 × 1in	–	–	–	–

	Ship, Number of Guns								
	100	*90*	*80*	*70*	*60*	*50*	*40*	*30*	*20*
Well: Fore and Aft	9ft 8in	9ft 4in	9ft 0in	7ft 8in	7ft 4in	7ft 0in	6ft 8in	6ft 4in	6ft 0in
Thwartships	10ft 1in	9ft 11in	9ft 0in	7ft 7in	7ft 3in	6ft 10in	6ft 5in	6ft 1in	5ft 8in
Plank under the Orlope, Thick	3in	3in	3in	3in	3in	3in	2½in	2in	2in
Shot Lockers: Number, (one abaft and one afore the Well)	2	2	2	2	2	2	1	1	1
Fore and Aft in the Clear	2ft 6in	2ft 6in	2ft 4in	2ft 4in	2ft 2in	2ft 1in	2ft 0in	1ft 11in	1ft 10in
Plank, Thick	3in	3in	3in	3in	3in	3in	2in	2in	2in
At the After Bitts	1	1	1	–	–	–	–	–	–
Bulkhead: Length, from the Inside of the Rabbet to the Stem, on the Gundeck to the After Bulkhead of the Magazine	35ft 6in	34ft 6in	33ft 6in	32ft 6in	31ft 6in	29ft 6in	26ft 6in	23ft 0in	18ft 6in
Length, from the Inside of the Rabbet of the Post, on the Gundeck to the Foreside of the Bulkhead of the Breadroom	32ft 0in	30ft 6in	29ft 0in	27ft 6in	25ft 6in	23ft 6in	21ft 6in	19ft 6in	–
Length, from the Bulkhead of the Breadroom to the Forepart of the Bulkhead of the Captains Storeroom and Pursers Sloproom	21ft 0in	20ft 6in	19ft 6in	18ft 6in	18ft 0in	17ft 6in	16ft 6in	15ft 6in	–
The Fishroom Bulkhead to be Abaft the Bulkhead of the Captains Storeroom and the Pursers Storeroom				Five Feet: To each Ship					

The Gundeck

		100	*90*	*80*	*70*	*60*	*50*	*40*	*30*	*20*
Clamps: Upper Strake,	Thick	9in	8½in	8¼in	8in	7in	–	–	–	–
	Broad	1ft 3in	1ft 3in	1ft 2½in	1ft 2in	1ft 2in	–	–	–	–
Second Strake, (To be tabled 2 Inches into each other)	Thick	8in	7½in	7¼in	7in	6in	–	–	–	–
	Broad	1ft 1in	1ft 0in	1ft 0in	1ft 0in	1ft 0in	–	–	–	–
Lower Strake,	Thick	7in	6½in	6¼in	6in	5in	–	–	–	–
	Broad	1ft 0in	1ft 0in	1ft 0in	1ft 0in	11in	–	–	–	–
If in Two Strakes										
Upper Strake	Thick	–	–	–	–	–	6in	5½in	5in	4in
	Broad	1ft 5½in	1ft 5in	1ft 5in	1ft 4½in	1ft 4in	1ft 3in	1ft 2in	1ft 2in	1ft 2in
Lower Strake	Thick	–	–	–	–	–	5in	4½in	4in	3in
	Broad	1ft 4½in	1ft 4in	1ft 4in	1ft 3½in	1ft 3in	1ft 2in	1ft 1in	1ft 1in	1ft 1in
Length of the Scarphs		3ft 8in	3ft 7in	3ft 6in	3ft 5in	3ft 4in	3ft 3in	3ft 2in	3ft 1in	3ft 0in
Openings under them		10in	10in	10in	9½in	9in	8in	8in	8in	8in
Breasthooks: and Hook under the Hawses		1ft 3in	1ft 2½in	1ft 2in	1ft 1½in	1ft 1in	1ft 0in	11in	10in	9in
Length		17ft 0in	16ft 6in	16ft 0in	15ft 6in	15ft 0in	14ft 6in	14ft 0in	13ft 0in	12ft 0in
Number and Size of Bolts		13 × 1⅜in	13 × 1¼in	13 × 1¼in	11 × 1¼in	11 × 1⅛in	9 × 1⅛in	9 × 1in	9 × ⅞in	9 × ¾in
Under the Gundeck to have a large Chock and to be left as much as possible fore and aft, for the better Coaking and Fastening the Planks of the Gundeck to the Same										
Beams: Sided, (In the Midships and One Inch less each way Afore and Abaft)		1ft 6in	1ft 5in	1ft 4in	1ft 3in	1ft 2in	1ft 1in	1ft 0in	10in	8in
Moulded (In the Midships and One Inch less each way Afore and Abaft)		1ft 5in	1ft 4in	1ft 3in	1ft 2in	1ft 1in	1ft 0in	11in	9in	7in
One to be placed, under, and one between each Port where it Conveniently may be done, except in wake of the Hatchways and Masts, and there to have Double armd Beams, that one part may be proper for a Standard and the other to come under the Ports, to be double kneed at each End with One Hanging and One Lodging Knee										
Knees: Sided, Lodging, those in wake of the Main and Fore Mast and Main Hatch to be Half an Inch Bigger		10½in	10in	9½in	9in	8½in	8in	7½in	6½in	5½in
Sided, Hanging, As above stated for those Knees concerned		11in	10½in	10in	9½in	9in	8½in	8in	7in	6in
Knees: Hanging Knee, Long (if to be had)		6ft 6in	6ft 4in	6ft 2in	5ft 9in	5ft 6in	5ft 3in	5ft 0in	4ft 9in	4ft 6in
Lodging Arm, to the Beam, Long		5ft 0in	4ft 10in	4ft 6in	4ft 3in	4ft 0in	3ft 9in	3ft 6in	3ft 3in	3ft 0in
Number and Size of Bolt in each Hanging Knee		7 × 1⅜in	7 × 1¼in	7 × 1¼in	7 × 1¼in	6 × 1⅛in	6 × 1⅛in	6 × 1in	6 × ⅞in	6 × ¾in
To have 4 Bolts in the Lower Arm of the Hanging Knees especially in the Wake of the Masts, and Hatchways, and where the Knees can be got of Sufficient Length										

	Ship, Number of Guns								
	100	90	80	70	60	50	40	30	20
Carlings: Number of Tire [Tier] on each side	3	3	2	2	2	2	2	2	2
Three Carlings in the wake of the Main and Fore Hatches & Mainmast									
Broad	11in	10in	9in	8½in	8in	7½in	7in	6in	5½in
Deep	9½in	9in	8½in	8in	7½in	7in	6in	5in	4½in
Ledges: To lye asunder, not less than 9 Inches, nor more than 12 Inches									
Broad	6in	5½in	5½in	5in	5in	4½in	4in	3½in	3in
Deep	5in	5in	5in	5in	4½in	4½in	3½in	3in	2½in
Bitts: Number of Pair	2	2	2	2	2	2	2	2	1½
The Foremost to be Abaft the Rabbet of the Stem	29ft 10in	26ft 2in	25ft 10in	26ft 0in	21ft 3in	20ft 6in	16ft 2in	15ft 0in	26ft 0in
The Aftermost to be Abaft the Foreside of the Foremost	11ft 8in	11ft 2in	10ft 4in	10ft 6in	10ft 1in	10ft 6in	9ft 9in	9ft 4in	—
Distance between them Thwartships Foremost	4ft 0in	3ft 10in	3ft 8in	3ft 5in	3ft 2in	2ft 11in	2ft 8in	2ft 6in	—
Aftermost	4ft 10in	4ft 7in	4ft 4in	4ft 0in	3ft 8in	3ft 5in	3ft 2in	3ft 0in	—
Aftermost, Square	1ft 11in	1ft 10in	1ft 8in	1ft 6in	1ft 5in	1ft 4in	1ft 3in	1ft 2in	1ft 1in
Foremost, Square	1ft 10in	1ft 9in	1ft 7½in	1ft 6in	1ft 4½in	1ft 3in	1ft 1½in	1ft 0in	11in
Crosspieces									
Foremost Deep	1ft 7in	1ft 6in	1ft 5in	1ft 4in	1ft 3in	1ft 2in	1ft 1in	1ft 0in	11in
Fore and aft	1ft 8in	1ft 7in	1ft 6½in	1ft 5½in	1ft 4½in	1ft 3½in	1ft 3in	1ft 2½in	1ft 2in
Aftermost Deep	1ft 10in	1ft 9½in	1ft 9in	1ft 8½in	1ft 8in	1ft 7in	1ft 6in	1ft 5in	1ft 4in
Fore and aft	1ft 9in	1ft 8½in	1ft 8in	1ft 7½in	1ft 7in	1ft 6in	1ft 5in	1ft 4in	1ft 3in
Lower Edge above the Deck Foremost	1ft 7in	1ft 6in	1ft 5in	1ft 4in	1ft 3in	1ft 2in	1ft 1in	1ft 0in	11in
Aftermost	1ft 8in	1ft 7in	1ft 6½in	1ft 5½in	1ft 4½in	1ft 3½in	1ft 3in	1ft 2½in	1ft 2in
Scored in, Deep	3in	3in	3in	3in	2½in	2in	2in	2in	2in
Elme backs of	6in	6in	6in	6in	6in	5½in	5in	4½in	4in
Standard Knees: Sided	1ft 1in	1ft 0½in	1ft 0in	11½in	11in	10½in	10in	9½in	9in
To be Sufficiently Deep to make the Carling if to be Had. The Arm upon the Deck to be as long as the Bitt Pins are asunder or if to be had, and the Forepart to be Flush with the Deck									
Number and Size of Bolts in Each	4 × 1⅜in	4 × 1¼in	4 × 1¼in	4 × 1¼in	4 × 1¼in	4 × 1⅛in	4 × 1⅛in	4 × 1⅛in	4 × 1in
Waterway: Thick in the Chine	One Inch Thicker than the Plank on the Deck								
Plank: On the Flat to be English in the wake of the Standards. Two Strakes next the Coamings to be One Inch Thicker than the rest of the Deck and to be let down an Inch on the Beams, to be bolted with Two Small Bolts in each beam and One Treenaile in each Ledge, the Size of the Bolts to be 5/8 of an Inch in the Great Ships and 1/2 an Inch in all under 70 Guns and to be One Inch longer than Twice the Thickness of the Plank. All the rest to be bolted … with One Bolt in each Beam and One Treenaile in each Ledge									
Partners: For the Mast, Main, to be Carlings, Broad	1ft 5in	1ft 4½in	1ft 4in	1ft 3½in	1ft 3in	1ft 2in	1ft 1in	1ft 0in	11in
Deep	1ft 6in	1ft 5½in	1ft 5in	1ft 4½in	1ft 4in	1ft 3in	1ft 2in	1ft 1in	1ft 0in
Fore, Thick	7in	7in	7in	6½in	6in	5½in	5in	4½in	4in
Mizen, Thick	No Thicker than the Deck								
Bowsprit, Thick	10in	10in	9in	8in	7in	6½in	6in	5½in	5in
Main Capstan, Thick	7in	7in	7in	6½in	6½in	6in	5½in	5in	5
False, for the Main Capstan, under the Beams, Thick	4in	4in	4in	4in	3in	3in	3in	3in	2½in
Step: For the Main Jeer Capstan (To be no higher above the Deck than 4 Inches, where it can be done) Thick	1ft 4in	1ft 3½in	1ft 2in	1ft 1½in	1ft 1in	1ft 0½in	1ft 0in	1ft 0in	1ft 0in
Triple Jeer Capstan (To be no higher above the Deck than 4 Inches, where it can be done) Thick	1ft 0in	11½in	11½in	—	—	—	—	—	—

	Ship, Number of Guns								
	100	90	80	70	60	50	40	30	20
Hatches: Main Fore and Aft	8ft 10in	8ft 7in	8ft 4in	8ft 0in	7ft 8in	7ft 4in	7ft 0in	6ft 8in	5ft 0in
Thwartships	6ft 10in	6ft 7in	6ft 4in	6ft 0in	5ft 8in	5ft 4in	5ft 0in	4ft 8in	4ft 2in
									3ft 1in
									Upper
Fore: Fore and Aft	4ft 8in	4ft 8in	4ft 8in	4ft 8in	4ft 8in	4ft 8in	4ft 8in	4ft 8in	–
Thwartships	4ft 10in	4ft 10in	4ft 8in	4ft 7in	3ft 8in	3ft 7in	3ft 7in	3ft 2in	–
Next Abaft the Mainmast, Fore and Aft	4ft 8in	4ft 8in	4ft 8in	4ft 8in	4ft 8in	4ft 8in	4ft 8in	4ft 8in	–
Thwartships	4ft 10in	4ft 10in	4ft 8in	3ft 9in	3ft 7in	3ft 3in	3ft 3in	3ft 2in	–
Over the Fishroom: Fore and Aft	4ft 8in	4ft 8in	4ft 8in	4ft 8in	4ft 8in	4ft 8in	4ft 8in	4ft 8in	–
Thwartships	4ft 10in	4ft 10in	4ft 8in	3ft 9in	3ft 7in	3ft 3in	3ft 3in	3ft 2in	–
To the Steward Room Fore and Aft	3ft 4in	3ft 3in	3ft 2in	3ft 1in	3ft 0in	2ft 10in	–	–	–
Thwartships	4ft 0in	3ft 11in	3ft 10in	3ft 9in	3ft 8in	3ft 7in	–	–	–
Plank for the Hatches: One and half Inches to each									
Height above the Deck: Two Inches each									
Scuppers: Lead Number on each Side	4	4	4	4	4	4	3	–	–
Diameter in the Clear	4in	4in	4in	4in	4in	4in	4in	–	–
Manger: Plank, Thick	4in	4in	4in	4in	4in	4in	3in	3in	3in
Scuppers, Number each Side	2	2	2	2	2	2	2	2	2
Diameter in the Clear	5in	5in	5in	5in	5in	5in	4½in	4in	4in
Pump Dale Scupper: Diameter in the Clear	6in	6in	6in	6in	6in	6in	6in	6in	6in
Spirketting: Number of Strakes on each Side to be Bolted in the next Timber to									
each Butt one Bolt	3 or 2	3 or 2	3 or 2	3 or 2	3 or 2	3 or 2	2	2	2
Thickness in the Midships, Lower Edge	8in	7½in	7in	6in	5in	4½in	4in	3½in	3in
Upper Edge	6½in	6in	5½in	4½in	4in	3½in	3in	2½in	2½in
Plank: Between the Spirketting and the Upper or Middle Deck Clamps, Thick	4in	3½in	3in	3in	3in	2½in	2½in	2in	2in
Ports: in the Counter, Number	4	4	2	2	2	2	2	2	2
Oar, Number	–	–	–	–	–	–	30	24 or 8	36
Depth	–	–	–	–	–	–	8½in	8½in	8in
Fore and Aft	–	–	–	–	–	–	8in	8in	7½in
Standards: Number on each Side, the Foremost pair to be of Iron	5	5	4	3	2	–	–	–	–
Sided	1ft 1in	1ft 0½in	1ft 0in	1ft 0in	11in	–	–	–	–
The Up and Down Arms so long as to take hold of the Middle or Upper Deck Clamp, (if it can be had) and a Bolt to be placed as near the Upper end as conveniently may be									
Shortest Arm, Long, if can be had	4ft 6in	4ft 4½in	4ft 3in	4ft 1½in	4ft 0in	–	–	–	–
Number and Size of Bolts	7 × 1⅜in	7 × 1¼in	7 × 1¼in	7 × 1¼in	7 × 1¼in	–	–	–	–
Standards of Iron: No dimensions stated here									
Capstan: Main Diameter at the Partners	2ft 1in	2ft 0in	1ft 11in	1ft 10in	1ft 9in	1ft 8in	1ft 7in	1ft 5in	–
Diameter of the Lower part including the whelps Not Stated									
Bars, Number	12	12	12	12	12	12	10	10	–
Length, (of the Bars)	14ft 0in	13ft 6in	13ft 0in	12ft 6in	12ft 0in	11ft 0in	10ft 6in	9ft 6in	–
Number of Iron Pawls, Four to each where they can be fitted, Two of which to fall upon the Heads or Trundleheads and to answer the Pawls on the Deck									
Pillars: Turnd Square	8in	7½in	7¼in	7in	6½in	6in	5½in	5in	4½in
Tiller: Square in the Biggest place	1ft 1in	1ft 0in	11in	10½in	10in	9½in	9in	8½in	8in
Sweep to be Flush with the Beam, Thickness	3in	3in	3in	2½in	2½in	2½in	2½in	2¼in	2in
Sweep, Broad	1ft 0in	11in	10in	9in	8in	7½in	7in	6½in	6½in
Transom, Deep	1ft 0in	11in	10in	9½in	9in	8½in	8in	7½in	7in
Transom Knees, Deep	10in	9½in	9in	8½in	8in	7½in	7in	6½in	6in
Transom Knees, Armes, Fore and Aft (long, if can be had)	11ft 6in	11ft 0in	10ft 6in	10ft 0in	9ft 6in	9ft 0in	8ft 6in	8ft 0in	7ft 6in
Transom Knees, Armes, Thwartships (long, if can be had)	6ft 0in	6ft 0in	5ft 8in	5ft 4in	5ft 0in	4ft 8in	4ft 4in	4ft 0in	3ft 8in

	Ship, Number of Guns								
	100	90	80	70	60	50	40	30	20
Bolts: Ring and Eye for each Port, Number and Size	6 × 1⅜in	6 × 1¼in	6 × 1¼in	6 × 1¼in	4 × 1¼in	4 × 1⅛in	4 × 1⅛in	4 × 1in	–
Diameter of the Rings in the clear	5½in	5½in	5¼in	5in	5in	4⅝in	4⅝in	4½in	–
The Iron of the Ring to be Something less than the Bolts									
Rings on the Flat of for the Gun Size, the Diameter of Rings Sufficient to hook the Tacles [Tackles]	1⅛in	1⅛in	1⅛in	1in	1in	⅞in	⅞in	¾in	–
Stopper, Size	1¾in	1⅝in	1⅝in	1½in	1½in	1⅜in	1⅜in	1¼in	1¼in
Stopper, Diameter of the Ring in the Clear	7½in	7¼in	6½in	6in	5½in	5¼in	5in	4¾in	4½in
Eyes, over the Ports for Lashing the Guns, Size	1¼in	1⅛in	1⅛in	1⅛in	1⅛in	1in	1in	⅞in	–
Diameter of the Eyes in the Clear	2½in	2½in	2⅜in	2⅜in	2¼in	2¼in	2in	2in	–
Ring, Eye and Stopper to be let so well in as only to let the Rings have play. Ring and Eye and all others that go through the side are to be Forelockd, the Ring to be let into the Side and a Short Thick Forelock hole, and short thick Point to the Bolt									
Cisterns, for the Pumps, Plank of the Bottom, Thick	4in	4in	4in	4in	4in	3½in	3½in	3in	3in
Plank of the Ends, Thick	5in	5in	5in	5in	5in	4½in	4½in	4in	4in
Plank of the Side, Thick	3in	3in	3in	3in	3in	3in	3in	2½in	2½in
Fore and Aft (from out to out)	2ft 0in	2ft 0in	2ft 0in	2ft 0in	1ft 11½in	1ft 11in	1ft 10in	1ft 9in	1ft 8in
Deep	2ft 8in	2ft 8in	2ft 8in	2ft 7in	2ft 7in	2ft 7in	2ft 6in	2ft 6in	2ft 0in
Height above the Planking of the Deck	1ft 0in	1ft 0in	1ft 0in	1ft 0in	1ft 0in	1ft 0in	1ft 0in	1ft 0in	1ft 6in
Centers of the Masts: The Fore-mast, One-Tenth of the Length of the Gundeck abaft the Rabbet of the Stem, and to stand upright									
The Mainmast, One Twenty-second of the Deck abaft the Middle of the Deck (its Bag or Convex part always aft), and to make One Inch in the Yard									
Mizenmast: Four Twenty-thirds of the Length of the Deck before the Rabbet of the Post and to Rake Five Eighths of an Inch to the Foot									
Knee: Fore and aft against the Apron of the Stem to reach the next Beam afore the Foremast, Sided	1ft 2in	1ft 1in	1ft 0in	and bolted as the Gundeck Knees					
Knee: against the Stern Post to reach Four Beams if can be had, with a Long Carling prickd up under the Beams to reach the Beam next the Mizenmast and give a sufficient Scarph to the Knee, and both Knee and Carling to Bolt through each Beam with Bolts of the same Size as the Gundeck Knees, and be Sided	1ft 2in	1ft 1in	1ft 0in	–	–	–	–	–	–

Middle Deck

	100	90	80	70	60	50	40	30	20
Clamps: To be wrought Anchorstock Fashion with Hooks and Coaks, Number of Strakes each side	1	1	1	–	–	–	–	–	–
Thick at the Upper Edge	7in	6½in	6in	–	–	–	–	–	–
Thick at the Lower Edge	6in	5½in	5in	–	–	–	–	–	–
Depth	As much as can be allowed								
Beams: Sided	1ft 3in	1ft 2in	1ft 1in	–	–	–	–	–	–
Moulded	1ft 1in	1ft 0in	11in	–	–	–	–	–	–
To lye under and One between each Port where they may conveniently be placed and as near as possible over the Gundeck Beams, to have a long Carling under the Furnaces, to Take hold of the Beam next the Foremast and that next the foreside of the After Bitts, the Carling to be deep	1ft 3½in	3ft ½in	1ft 1½in	–	–	–	–	–	–
Carling, Broad	11½in	10½in	9½in	–	–	–	–	–	–
Knees: Hanging, Sided at each end	9½in	9in	8in	–	–	–	–	–	–
Lodging, Sided at each end	9in	8½in	8in	–	–	–	–	–	–
The up and down Arm to reach the Spirketting									
Shortest Arm long, (if can be had)	4ft 0in	3ft 9in	3ft 6in	–	–	–	–	–	–
Number and Size of Bolts	6 × 1⅛in	6 × 1⅛in	6 × 1in	–	–	–	–	–	–
The Two upper Bolts of the Hanging Knees to be placed as high as Conveniently can be done and the like for the Hanging Knees of all other Decks for the better keeping the [Britch] of the Knee to the side									

	Ship, Number of Guns								
	100	90	80	70	60	50	40	30	20
Transom: Deck, Deep	13in	10in	9in	–	–	–	–	–	–
Knees, at each end Sided	9½in	9in	8in	–	–	–	–	–	–
Armes, Fore and Aft, Long	As long as Conveniently wrought and had								
Shortest, Long	4ft 6in	4ft 3in	4ft 0in	–	–	–	–	–	–
at the Lower port cills, deep (to be Kneed at each end)	8in	7½in	7in	–	–	–	–	–	–
Breasthook: Sided	1ft 3in	1ft 2in	1ft 1in	–	–	–	–	–	–
Long, (if can be had)	17ft 0in	16ft 6in	16ft 0in	–	–	–	–	–	–
Number and Size of bolts	13 × 1¼in	13 × 1¼in	13 × 1¼in	–	–	–	–	–	–
Carlings: Number of Tire [tiers] on each Side	3	3	3	–	–	–	–	–	–
Broad,	10in	9in	8in	–	–	–	–	–	–
Deep,	8in	7in	6in	–	–	–	–	–	–
Ledges, Broad	4¾in	4½in	4½	–	–	–	–	–	–
Deep	4¼in	4in	3½in	–	–	–	–	–	–
To lye asunder: from 9 to 12 Inches									
Carlings: Short with Long Coamings of Oak upon them prickd down on the Beams, 1 Inch									
Coamings to lye above the Deck	2in	2in	2in	–	–	–	–	–	–
Coamings Broad with the Rabbet	1ft 0in	11½in	11in	–	–	–	–	–	–
Waterways: Thick in the chine	To be One thicker than the Flat of the Deck								
Partners: for the Masts, The Main to be Carlings, Broad	1ft 5in	1ft 4½in	1ft 4in	–	–	–	–	–	–
Deep	1ft 6in	1ft 5½in	1ft 5in	–	–	–	–	–	–
Foremast	6½in	6½in	6½in	–	–	–	–	–	–
Mizenmast and whipstaff	4in	4in	4in	–	–	–	–	–	–
Jeer Capstan	6in	6in	6in	–	–	–	–	–	–
Tripple Jeer Capstan	5in	5in	5in	–	–	–	–	–	–
Bolted with Bolts of	¾in	¾in	⅝in	–	–	–	–	–	–
Capstan: Main Jeer Diameter in the Partners	2ft 1in	2ft 0in	1ft 11in	–	–	–	–	–	–
Including the whelps									
Length of the Barrs	14ft 0in	13ft 6in	13ft 0in	–	–	–	–	–	–
Number of Barrs	12	12	12	–	–	–	–	–	–
Number of Iron Pawls, Four to each where they can be fitted, Two of which to fall upon the Heads or Trundleheads and to answer the Pawls on the Deck									
Where there is Six Whelps, each Bolt to be drove through and clenched, and if Five Whelps to be bolted with Small Bolts and Clenched on the Barrel									
Flat: to be laid with English Plank in Wake of the Standards and from the Cookroom forward in the Middle of the Deck	3in	3in	3in	–	–	–	–	–	–
Two Strakes next the Coamings to be Coaked and Bolted down to the Hook and Transom, to have two bolts in each Beam and to be pricked down, on the Beams One Inch. The rest to be laid with Prutia Deal	4in	4in	4in	–	–	–	–	–	–
Spirketting: Number of Strakes on each Side	2 or 3	2 or 3	2 or 3	–	–	–	–	–	–
Lower Edge	6½in	6in	5in	–	–	–	–	–	–
Thickness in the Midships, Upper edge	5½in	5in	4in	–	–	–	–	–	–
Plank: or Deal between the Spirketting and Upper Deck Clamp, thick	3in	2½in	2in	–	–	–	–	–	–
Scuppers: Lead, Number on each side	6	6	6	–	–	–	–	–	–
Diameter in the Clear	3in	3in	3in	–	–	–	–	–	–
Standards: All of Iron, Number of pair	7	6	5	–	–	–	–	–	–
The up and down Arme to reach the Upper Edge of the Upper Deck Clamp as near the upper end as conveniently may be									
Shortest Arme, Long	5ft 6in	5ft 3in	5ft 0in	–	–	–	–	–	–
Standards: all of Iron, Number and Sizes of Bolts in each	7 × 1⅛in	7 × 1⅛in	7 × 1in	–	–	–	–	–	–

	Ship, Number of Guns								
	100	90	80	70	60	50	40	30	20
Pillars: Turnd, The Square	7in	6½in	6in	–	–	–	–	–	–
Bolts: Ring and Eye for the Ports, Number and Size	4 × 1¼in	4 × 1¼in	4 × 1¼in	–	–	–	–	–	–
Diameter of the Rings in the Clear	5in	4¾in	4¼in	–	–	–	–	–	–
On the Flat of the Deck for the Guns, Size	1in	1in	1in	–	–	–	–	–	–
Eye over the Ports for lashing the Guns, Size	1⅛in	1⅛in	1⅛in	–	–	–	–	–	–
Diameter of the Eye in the Clear	2⅜in	2⅜in	2¼in	–	–	–	–	–	–

Upper Gundeck

	100	90	80	70	60	50	40	30	20
Clamps: To be wrought Anchor Stock fashion with Hook and Butt									
Thick at the Upper Edge	6in	5½in	5in	5in	5in	4in	4in	3½in	3in
Thick at the Lower Edge	5in	4½in	4in	4in	4in	3½in	3½in	3in	2½in
Beams: Sided	1ft 1in	1ft 0½in	11in	1ft 1in	1ft 0in	10½in	9½in	9in	8½in
Moulded	11in	10½in	8in	11in	10in	8½in	7½in	7in	6½in
To lye One under and One Between each Port, where they can be Conveniently be placed and as near as possible over the Beams of the Middle or Gundeck and under the Great Cabbin the Distance of the others. To have a Long Carling under the Furnaces, to take hold of the Beam abaft the Foremast and that next the Foreside of the After Bitts, The									
Carling to be Deep	–	–	–	1ft 0½in	11½in	10½in	9in	8in	–
Broad	–	–	–	9in	8½in	8in	7in	6in	–
Knees: Knees Double at each end, Hanging and Lodging, Sided	8½in	8in	7in	7½in	7in	6½in	6in	5½in	5in
The up and down Arme to reach the Spirketting									
The Shortest Arme, Long, if can be had	3ft 6in	3ft 5in	3ft 4in	3ft 3in	3ft 2in	3ft 1in	3ft 0in	2ft 11in	2ft 10in
Number and Size of Bolts in each	6 × 1in	6 × 1in	6 × ⅞in	6 × ⅞in	6 × ⅞in	6 × ⅞in	6 × ¾in	5 × ¾in	5 × ⅝in
Carlings: Broad	9in	8in	7½in	8in	7½in	7in	6¾in	6½in	6in
Deep	7in	6in	5½in	6in	5½in	5in	4¾in	4½in	4½in
Number of Tire (Tier) on each side except in wake of the Hatchways and Mainmast and there Three on Ships of 100, 90, 80 and 70 Guns	2	2	2	2	2	2	2	2	2
Short, with Long Coamings of Oak on them, pricked down One Inch into the Beams									
Coamings to lye above the Deck	2½in	2½in	2½in	2½in	2½in	2½in	2½in	2½in	3in
Coamings Broad with the Rabbet	1ft 0in	11½in	11in	11in	10½in	10in	9½in	9in	8½in
Ledges: Broad	4½in	4in	4in	4in	3¾in	3½in	3½in	3¼in	3¼in
Deep	4in	3½in	3½in	3½in	3½in	3¼in	3¼in	3in	3in
to lye Asunder: from 9 to 12 Inches									
Waterway: Thick in the Chine					One Inch more than the Flat of the Deck				
Partners: For the Foremast, Thick	6in	6in	6in	6in	6in	5½in	5½in	5in	5in
For the Jeer and Tripple Jeer Capstan, Thick	5in	5in	5in	6in	6in	6in	5½in	5in	–
For the Mizenmast and Whipstaff, Thick	4½in	4½in	4½in	4½in	4in	4in	4in	3½in	3½in
Flat: Three Strakes next the Waterways and all the Forepart of the Deck to be Oake; Thick	2½in	2½in	2½in	2½in	2½in	2½in	2½in	2in	2in
Two Strakes of Oake next the Coamings to give Scarph to each other and be prickd down One Inch into the Beams, Tayld and hookd into the Transom and Deckhook, and bolted to the Beams, Breasthook and Transome, The rest to be of Prutia Deal									
Capstans: Triple Jeer, Diameter in the Partners, (excluding the Whelps)	1ft 7in	1ft 6in	1ft 5in	–	–	–	–	–	–
Barrs, Long	9ft 0in	9ft 0in	9ft 0in	–	–	–	–	–	–
Barrs, Number of,	10	10	10	–	–	–	–	–	–
Number of Iron Palls	1	1	1	–	–	–	–	–	–

	Ship, Number of Guns								
	100	*90*	*80*	*70*	*60*	*50*	*40*	*30*	*20*
Main Jeer, Diameter in the Partners	–	–	–	1ft 10in	1ft 9in	1ft 8in	1ft 7in	1ft 5in	–
Barrs, Long	–	–	–	12ft 0in	11ft 6in	10ft 6in	10ft 0in	9ft 0in	–
Barrs, Number of,	–	–	–	12	12	12	10	10	–
Number of Iron Palls, Four to each, Two of which to fall on the Trundleheads and to answer the Palls on the Deck									
Spirketting: Number of Strakes on each Side, Two to each (vessel)									
Thickness at the Lower Edge	4in	4in	4in	4in	4in	3in	3in	3in	2½in
Thickness at the Upper Edge	3½in	3½in	3½in	3½in	3½in	2½in	2½in	2½in	2in
Scuppers: Lead, on each Side, Number	6in	6in	6in	6in	6in	6in	6in	6in	6in
Diameter in the Clear	3in	3in	3in	3in	3in	3½in	3½in	4½in	4½in
Standards of Iron, No of Pairs	4	4	3	4	3	2	2	2	1
The up and down Arme to reach the Upper Edge of and Bolt thro' The Forecastle and Quarter Deck Clamps									
The Shortest Arm, Long	3ft 6in	3ft 5in	3ft 4in	3ft 3in	3ft 2in	3ft 1in	3ft 0in	2ft 11in	2ft 10in
Number and Size of Bolts in each	6 × 1in	6 × 1in	6 × ⅞in	6 × ⅞in	6 × ⅞in	6 × ¾in	6 × ¾in	5 × ¾in	5 × ⅝in
String: In the Wast, Thick In and Out	4½in	4in	3in	4in	4in	3in	String & Planksheer in One		
Collar Beam: Square	–	–	–	10in	9½in	9in	8½in	8in	–
Transom at the Lower Port Cills, Deep, (Kneed at each end)	–	–	–	6½in	6in	5½in	5¼in	5in	4½in
Bitts: Main Topsaile Sheat and Jeer, Square	1ft 1in	1ft 0½in	11½in	10½in	9½in	8¾in	8in	7½in	7in
Jeer, High above the Deck	3ft 10in	3ft 9in	3ft 8in	3ft 7in	3ft 6in	3ft 5in	3ft 4in	3ft 3in	3ft 2in
Bitts: Sheat and Jeer, Crosspieces, Fore and Aft	11in	10½in	10in	9½in	9in	8½in	7½in	7in	6in
Deep	9½in	9in	8½in	8in	7½in	7in	6in	5½in	5in
Crosspieces, Scored into the Bitts	2in	2in	2in	2in	2in	2in	2in	1½in	1½in
The Crosspiece of the Gallows, Sided	11½in	11in	10½in	9½in	8½in	7¾in	7in	6½in	–
Deep	1ft 6in	1ft 5in	1ft 4in	1ft 3in	1ft 2in	1ft 1in	1ft 0in	11in	–
Long	13ft 8in	13ft 0in	12ft 4in	11ft 8in	11ft 0in	10ft 4in	9ft 8in	9ft 0in	–
Upper edge of it above the Deck	7ft 6in	7ft 0in	6ft 9in	6ft 11in	6ft 8in	6ft 6in	6ft 4in	6ft 2in	–
Scored in	2in	2in	2in	2in	2in	2in	2in	1½in	–
Bolts, Ring and Eye for the Ports, Number and Size of each	4 × 1⅛in	4 × 1⅛in	4 × 1in	4 × 1in	4 × 1in	4 × ⅞in	4 × ⅞in	4 × ⅞in	4 × ¾in
Diameter of the Rings in the Clear	4½in	4¼in	4⅓in	4½in	4⅓in	4¼in	4⅓in	4in	4in
On the Flat of the Deck for the Guns	1in	1in	1in	1in	⅞in	⅞in	¾in	¾in	¾in
Eye for Lashing the Blocks on each side the Mainmast and Foremast, Size	1⅛in	1⅛in	1in	1in	1in	⅞in	⅞in	⅞in	¾in
Eyes, For the Toptackles, Diameter	1¾in	1¾in	1½in	1½in	1⅝in	1⅝in	1⅝in	1¼in	1¼in
All Carlings and Ledges afore and abaft where they are Shorter to be made Lesser than in the Midships									

Quarter Deck

	100	*90*	*80*	*70*	*60*	*50*	*40*	*30*	*20*
Clamps: Upper, Edge Thick	4½in	4in	4in	4in	4in	3in	3in	3in	3in
Lower, Edge Thick	3in	3in	3in	3in	2½in	2in	2in	2in	2in
String: of Oake in the Great Cabbin, Upper, Thick	6in	6in	5½in	5½in	5¼in	5in	4in	4in	2¾in
Lower, Thick	3½in	3½in	3in	3in	2¾in	2½in	2in	2in	2in
Broad, if can be had	1ft 4in	1ft 3½in	1ft 3in	1ft 2½in	1ft 2in	1ft 1½in	1ft 1in	1ft 0½in	1ft 0in
Beams: To have a Small Strap of Iron round the Timber to every 2nd and 3rd Beam in Wake of the Cabbin; Sided	9½in	9½in	8in	9in	8in	6½in	6in	6in	5½in
Moulded	7½in	7in	6in	7in	6in	5½in	5in	5in	4½in
To lye Asunder, from 2 feet and 4 inches and 2 feet 2 inches where they can be conveniently placed									
In the Great Cabbin to be Bolted into the Strings at their Ends with Bolts of, Diameter	¾in	¾in	¾in	¾in	¾in	⅝in	⅝in	⅝in	⅝in
Knees: Hanging, Sided	6½in	6in	5½in	5½in	5in	4½in	4¼in	4in	–
The up and down Arme to reach the Spirketting Shortest Arme, Long	3ft 0in	2ft 11in	2ft 10in	2ft 9in	2ft 8in	2ft 7in	2ft 6in	2ft 5in	–
Number and Size of Bolts in each	5 × ⅞in	5 × ⅞in	5 × ¾in	5 × ¾in	5 × ¾in	5 × ⅝in	5 × ⅝in	5 × ⅝in	–

	Ship, Number of Guns								
	100	*90*	*80*	*70*	*60*	*50*	*40*	*30*	*20*
Waterways: In the Chine:- One Inch Thicker than the Plank of the Deck									
Gratings: Broad in the Clear	3ft 8in	3ft 6in	3ft 4in	3ft 2in	3ft 0in	2ft 10in	2ft 8in	2ft 6in	–
Spirketting: Lower, edge Thick	3½in	3in	3in	3in	3in	2½in	2in	2in	2in
Upper, edge Thick	3in	2½in	2½in	2½in	2½in	2in	2in	2in	2in
Quickwork: Birthed up with Deale of	2in	2in	2in	2in	2in	1½in	1½in	1½in	1½in
Bolts, Ring and Eye, Number and Size for each Port	4 × 1in	4 × 1in	4 × ⅞in	4 × ⅞in	4 × ⅞in	4 × ⅞in	–	4 × ¾in	–
Diameter of the Rings in the Clear	4in	4in	3¾in	3¾in	3½in	3½in	–	3½in	–

Forecastle

	100	90	80	70	60	50	40	30	20
Clamps: Thick	4½in	4in	4in	4in	4in	3in	3in	3in	2½in
Broad	1ft 3in	1ft 3in	1ft 3in	1ft 3in	1ft 3in	1ft 2in	1ft 2in	1ft 2in	–
Beams: Sided	9½in	9in	7½in	8½in	7½in	6½in	6in	6in	4in
Moulded	7½in	7in	6in	7in	6in	5½in	5in	5in	3in
Assunder	2ft 0in	2ft 0in	2ft 0in	2ft 0in	2ft 0in	2ft 0in	2ft 0in	2ft 0in	2ft 0in
At the Bulkhead and Furnaces and Fireplace, to be Double Kneed and all the other, Single Kneed									
Knees: Hanging, Sided	6½in	6in	5in	5½in	5in	4½in	4¼in	4in	–
Up and down to reach the Spirketting									
Shortest Arm, Long	3ft 0in	2ft 11in	2ft 10in	2ft 9in	2ft 8in	2ft 7in	2ft 6in	2ft 5in	–
Number and Size of Bolts in each	5 × ¾in	5 × ¾in	5 × ¾in	5 × ¾in	5 × ¾in	5 × ⅝in	5 × ⅝in	5 × ⅝in	–
Waterways: Thick in the Chine: One Inch thicker than the Deck									
Beam: at the Forepart of the Forecastle to fasten the Cathead, Broad or double	2ft 6in	2ft 5in	2ft 4in	2ft 3in	2ft 2in	2ft 0in	1ft 10in	1ft 9in	1ft 2in
Deep (under the Rabbet of the Deck)	7½in	7in	7in	7in	6in	5½in	5in	5in	5in
Stanchions: of the Beakhead, Square, to be Stepd well in with a Double Step in the Collar Beam and scored into the stanchions at the Forecastle Beam no more than Half … that to be shoulderd into the Beam	6in	6in	6in	5½in	5½in	5½in	4½in	4½in	–
Catheads: Fore and Aft	1ft 7in	1ft 6in	1ft 5in	1ft 3in	1ft 2in	1ft 0½in	11in	10in	9in
Up and Down	1ft 6in	1ft 4in	1ft 4in	1ft 3in	1ft 2in	1ft 0½in	11in	10in	9in
Bitts: Fore Topsaile Sheat, Square to meet in the Middle									
Jeer Topsaile Sheat, Square to meet in the Middle	11½in	11in	10½in	9½in	8½in	7¾in	7in	6½in	6in
High above the Deck	3ft 10in	3ft 9in	3ft 8in	3ft 7in	3ft 6in	3ft 5in	3ft 4in	3ft 3in	3ft 2in
Crosspieces, Fore and Aft	10in	9½in	9in	8½in	8in	7½in	7in	6½in	6in
Crosspieces, Deep	8½in	8in	7½in	7in	7in	6½in	6in	5½in	5in
Crosspieces, Scored into the Bitts	One and a Half Inches to each Ship								
Bolts, Spanshackle (the Corners of the Shackle to be Round) The size of the Bolt	1⅞in	1¾in	1¾in	1½in	1⅝in	1⅝in	1⅝in	1¼in	1¼in
Eye for the Main Topmast Stay	1¼in	1¼in	1¼in	1⅛in	1⅛in	1⅛in	1in	1in	⅞in

Roundhouse

	100	90	80	70	60	50	40	30	20
String: Thick	4in	4in	3in	4in	4in	3in	2in	–	–
Broad	1ft 1in	1ft 0½in	1ft 0in	11½in	11in	10½in	10in	–	–
Beams: To have a Small Strap of Iron round the Timber bolted to every other Beam									
Sided	7in	7in	6in	6½in	6¼in	4½in	4in	–	–
Moulded	5½in	5½in	4½in	5in	5in	3½in	3in	–	–
Assunder	2in	2in	2in	2in	2in	2in	2in	–	–
Bolted into the String at each End with Bolts of	⅝in	⅝in	⅝in	⅝in	⅝in	½in	½in	–	–
Knees: at the Bulkhead, Hanging, Sided	5½in	5in	4in	4½in	4in	4in	3½in	–	–
The up and dowm Arme to reach the Spirketting									
Shortest Arme, Long	2ft 6in	2ft 5in	2ft 3in	2ft 4in	2ft 3in	2ft 3in	2ft 3in	–	–
Number and Size of Bolts	5 × ⅝in	5 × ⅝in	5 × ⅝in	5 × ⅝in	5 × ⅝in	5 × ⅝in	5 × ⅝in	–	–
Waterways: Thick in the Chine; One Inch thicker than the Plank of the Deck									
Gunnell: to the Tafferell, Deep	–	6in	5½in	5in	4½in	4in	4in	3½in	3in

	Ship, Number of Guns								
	100	*90*	*80*	*70*	*60*	*50*	*40*	*30*	*20*

Topgallant Roundhouse

	100	90	80	70	60	50	40	30	20
String: Thick	3in	–	–	–	–	–	–	–	–
Broad	1ft 0in	–	–	–	–	–	–	–	–
Beams: To have a Small Strap of Iron round the Timber bolted to every other Beam									
Sided	6in	–	–	–	–	–	–	–	–
Moulded	4½in	–	–	–	–	–	–	–	–
Assunder	2ft 0in	–	–	–	–	–	–	–	–
Bolted into the String at each End with Bolts of	3⅝in	–	–	–	–	–	–	–	–
Waterway: Thick in the Chine	3in	–	–	–	–	–	–	–	–
Flat: Thick	2in	–	–	–	–	–	–	–	–
Gunnell: To the Tafferell, Thick	6in	–	–	–	–	–	–	–	–

Note No Holes to be bored into the Toptimbers when first put up except one for the [ ] nor any Treenail hole in Wake of the Ring and Eye Bolts for Ports Chain Bolts or any other Bolts that may sufficiently fasten the work without Treenails.

All Thick Stuff and Plank of 10 Inches Broad and under to be only Cross boared. Cabbins and all other Joyners work to be framd and Pannelld with Deale where it may conveniently be done. The Port Cills upon each Deck to Cant out half an Inch from a Levell.

Without Board

	100	90	80	70	60	50	40	30	20
Wales: and the Stuff between to be of an Equal Thickness; To be worked withe Hook and Butt									
Deep from the Upper to the Lower Edge	5ft 2in	4ft 10in	4ft 6in	4ft 2in	3ft 10in	3ft 6in	3ft 2in	2ft 10in	2ft 6in
Thick	10in	9in	8¼in	7½in	7in	5½in	5in	5in	4in
One Strake above them Thick	8in	7in	6½in	6in	5½in	4in	4in	4in	3in
Strakes: below the Wales, Number (This refers to the Diminishing Strakes)	7	6	5	5	4	2	2	1	1
Thickness of the Upper Edge of the Upper Strake	8in	7in	6½in	6in	5½in	4in	4in	4in	3in
Thickness of the Lower Edge of the Lower Strake	4in	4in	4in	4in	4in	3in	3in	3in	2½in
The Rest of the Plank under the Thickstuff to be wrought full of these thicknesses at the Floorhead	4in	4in	4in	4in	4in	3in	3in	3in	2½in
Wales: Channell, Broad from the Upper to the Lower Edge	2ft 9in	2ft 8in	2ft 6½in	2ft 5in	2ft 4in	2ft 2½in	2ft 1½in	2ft 0in	–
Wrought all of a Thickness to	5½in	5½in	5¼in	5in	4in	4in	3½in	3½in	–
The Strake above and below them Thick	4in	4in	4in	4in	3in	3in	2½in	–	–
Sheer; in Two Strakes, Broad	2ft 3in	2ft 2in	2ft 1in	–	–	–	–	–	–
Thick	4in	4in	4in	–	–	–	–	–	–
The Strake above and below them, Thick	3in	3in	3in	–	–	–	–	–	–
Deal: in the Wast, at the Top of the Side, Thick	2½in	2½in	2in	2in	2in	2in	2in	2in	2in
Channells: Main; (if the ports will admit). Length	38ft 0in	35ft 6in	33ft 0in	30ft 6in	28ft 0in	25ft 6in	23ft 0in	20ft 0in	17ft 0in
Breadth at the Foremost End. (But however sufficient to Carry the Shrouds clear of the Gunnell and Fiferails)	2ft 10in	2ft 9in	2ft 8in	2ft 6in	2ft 4in	2ft 2in	1ft 11in	1ft 9in	1ft 7in
Thickness at the Inner Edges	6in	6in	5¾in	5½in	5½in	5in	4½in	4in	4in
Thickness at the Outer Edges	4½in	4½in	4¼in	4in	4in	3½in	3in	2¾in	2¾in
Number and Size of Bolts for Fastening	10 × 1⅛in	10 × 1⅛in	9 × 1in	9 × 1in	8 × 1in	7 × ⅞in	7 × ⅞in	6 × ¾in	6 × ¾in
Fore; Length (if the Ports will admit)	31ft 0in	29ft 0in	27ft 0in	25ft 0in	23ft 0in	21ft 0in	19ft 0in	17ft 0in	15ft 0in
Breadth at the After end, (but however sufficient to Carry the Shrouds clear of the Gunnell)	2ft 8in	2ft 6in	2ft 4in	2ft 2in	2ft 0in	1ft 10in	1ft 8in	1ft 6in	1ft 4in
Thickness of the Inner Edge	6in	6in	5¾in	5½in	5½in	5in	4½in	4in	4in
Thickness of the Outer Edge	4½in	4½in	4¼in	4in	4in	3½in	3in	2¾in	2¾in
Number and Size of Bolts for Fastening	9 × 1⅛in	9 × 1⅛in	8 × 1in	8 × 1in	7 × 1in	6 × ⅞in	6 × ⅞in	5 × ¾in	5 × ¾in

	Ship, Number of Guns								
	100	*90*	*80*	*70*	*60*	*50*	*40*	*30*	*20*
Mizen; Length	17ft 6in	16ft 0in	14ft 6in	13ft 6in	12ft 6in	11ft 6in	10ft 6in	9ft 0in	7ft 0in
Breadth (but however sufficient to Carry the Shrouds clear of the Gunnell and Fiferails)	2ft 1in	1ft 11½in	1ft 10in	1ft 8½in	1ft 7in	1ft 5½in	1ft 4in	1ft 2½in	1ft 1in
Thickness of the Inner Edge	5in	5in	4¾in	4½in	4in	3½in	3in	2¾in	2½in
Thickness of the Outer Edge	3½in	3½in	3¼in	3in	3in	2½in	2in	2in	1¾in
Channells: Mizen; Number and Size of Bolts for Fastening	5 × ⅞in	5 × ⅞in	5 × ⅞in	5 × ⅞in	4 × ⅞in	4 × ¾in	3 × ¾in	3 × ¾in	3 × ¾in
Chain Plates: Main and Fore, Broad	4in	4in	3⅓in	3¾in	3½in	3¼in	3in	2¾in	2½in
Thick in the Middle	1½in	1½in	1½in	1⅜in	1⅜in	1¼in	1⅛in	1in	⅞in
Thick at the Edges	1in	1in	⅞in	⅞in	⅞in	¾in	⅝in	½in	½in
Size of the Bolts	2¼in	2⅛in	2in	1⅞in	1¾in	1⅝in	1½in	1⅜in	1¼in
Mizen: Broad	3¼in	3¼in	3⅛in	3in	2¾in	2½in	2¼in	2in	1¾in
Thick in the Middle	1¼in	1⅛in	1⅛in	1in	1in	⅞in	¾in	⅝in	⅝in
Thick at the Edges	¾in	¾in	¾in	⅝in	⅝in	½in	½in	⅜in	⅜in
Size of the Bolts	1⅝in	1½in	1½in	1⅜in	1⅜in	1¼in	1¼in	1⅛in	1⅛in
Plates: Ring and Backstay; for the Fore and Main Chains to have the same Breadth and Thickness and the same Size Bolts in the Mizen Chain Plates									
Bindings: For the Deadeyes for the Main Channell, Size	1¾in	1⅝in	1½in	1½in	1⅜in	1¼in	1¼in	1⅛in	1⅛in
Fore Channell, Size	1¾in	1⅝in	1½in	1½in	1⅜in	1¼in	1¼in	1⅛in	1⅛in
Mizen Channell, Size	1¼in	1¼in	1⅛in	1⅛in	1in	⅞in	⅞in	¾in	¾in
Deadeyes: for the Main Channell. Number of. (including a spare one)	11	10	10	9	9	8	8	7	6
Size, Diameter	1ft 5in	1ft 4½in	1ft 3½in	1ft 2½in	1ft 1½in	1ft 0½in	1ft 0in	11½in	11in
Fore Channell. Number of (including a spare one)	10	9	9	8	8	7	7	6	5
Size, Diameter	1ft 4in	1ft 3½in	1ft 2½in	1ft 1½in	1ft 0½in	11½in	11in	10½in	10in
For the Main and Fore Channell to be in Thickness, ¾ of an Inch more than Half the Diameters									
Mizen Channell. Number of	7	6	5	5	5	4	4	4	3
Size, Diameter	11in	10½in	10in	10in	10in	9in	8in	8in	7in
To be in Thickness ½ an Inch more than Half the Diameter									
Deadeyes:									
For the Main Topmast Backstays, Number of (each side)	3	3	3	3	3	3	3	3	2
Size	11in	10in	10in	10in	9in	8in	7in	7in	7in
Main Topgallant Backstays, Number of (each side)	1	1	1	1	1	1	1	1	1
Size	8in	7in	6in	6in	6in	6in	5in	5in	5in
Fore Topmast Backstays, Number of (each side)	3	3	3	3	3	3	2	2	2
Size	10in	9in	9in	9in	8in	7in	6in	6in	6in
Fore Topgallant Backstays, Number of (each side)	1	1	1	1	1	1	1	1	1
Size	8in	7in	6in	6in	6in	6in	5in	5in	5in
Mizen Topmast Backstays, Number of (each side)	1	1	1	1	1	1	1	1	1
Size	8in	7in	6in	6in	6in	5in	5in	5in	5in
Rother Head: Thwartships (if can conveniently be had)	2ft 4in	2ft 3in	2ft 2in	2ft 0in	1ft 10in	1ft 7½in	1ft 5in	1ft 3in	1ft 1in
Fore and Aft (if can conveniently be had)	2ft 6in	2ft 5in	2ft 4in	2ft 2in	2ft 0in	1ft 9½in	1ft 7in	1ft 5in	1ft 3in
At the Lower end Fore and Aft, One Eighth Part of the Ships Extreme Breadth from the Hundred to the Eighty Gun Ships, One Ninth to the Seventy Gun Ships and One Tenth for the Lesser Classes.	6ft 3in	5ft 10in	5ft 6in	4ft 7¼in	3ft 10¾in	3ft 7¼in	3ft 3¼in	3ft 1in	2ft 10in
Braces and Pintles, Number of pairs	7	7	7	6	6	6	5	5	5
Upper, afore the Rabbet of the Post, Long	4ft 3in	4ft 0in	3ft 9in	3ft 6in	3ft 3in	3ft 0in	2ft 10in	2ft 8in	2ft 6in
Lower, afore the Back of the Post, Long	7ft 0in	6ft 6in	6ft 0in	5ft 6in	5ft 0in	4ft 9in	4ft 6in	4ft 3in	4ft 0in
To be hung Flemish Fashion and secured with Chocks above the Water to prevent its unhanging									
Pintles, Diameter	3¼in	3¼in	3⅛in	3in	2⅞in	2⅝in	2⅜in	2⅛in	2in
Length of the Upper Pintles	1ft 3in	1ft 2¼in	1ft 1½in	1ft 0¾in	1ft 0in	11¼in	10½in	9¾in	9in
Length of the Lower Pintles only to be	1ft 5in	1ft 4¼in	1ft 3½in	1ft 2¾in	1ft 2in	1ft 1¼in	1ft 0½in	11¾in	11in
Braces and Straps for Pintles, Broad	5in	4¾in	4½in	4¼in	4in	3¾in	3½in	3¼in	3in
Thick in the Shoulder at the Return	2⅛in	2in	1⅞in	1¾in	1⅝in	1½in	1⅜in	1¼in	1⅛in
To have an Iron Strap on the Back and at each corner an Eye well Clenched on the side of the Strap of Sufficient Bigness to receive an Ovall Ring.									

	Ship, Number of Guns								
	100	*90*	*80*	*70*	*60*	*50*	*40*	*30*	*20*
Head: The Knee to be as Thick as the Stem									
Size of the Two Upper Bolts in the Knee	2¼in	2¼in	2⅛in	2in	1⅞in	1¾in	1⅝in	1½in	1⅜in
Size of the Two Upper Bolts in the Stem	2in	2in	1⅞in	1¾in	1⅝in	1½in	1⅜in	1¼in	1¼in
Cheeks; Lower, Sided (if can conveniently be had)	1ft 2in	1ft 1in	1ft 0in	11in	10in	9in	8½in	7½in	7in
Upper, Sided (if can conveniently be had)	1ft 1in	1ft 0in	11in	10in	9in	8in	7½in	6½in	6in
Length of the Arm next the Side (if can be had). The Bolts the same size as the Gundeck Knees	13ft 6in	12ft 6in	11ft 6in	10ft 6in	9ft 6in	9ft 0in	8ft 6in	7ft 6in	6ft 6in
Timbers, Sided from	8¼–5¼in	8–5in	7½–4½in	7–4¼in	6½–4in	5¾–3¾in	5–3½in	4½–3¼in	4–3in
Length from the Foreside of the Stem to the Foreside of the Knee of the Head	16ft 6in	15ft 6in	13ft 6in	11ft 6in	10ft 6in	9ft 6in	8ft 6in	7ft 6in	7ft 0in
Length to the Beakhead Bulkhead	9ft 0in	8ft 6in	8ft 0in	7ft 0in	6ft 6in	6ft 0in	5ft 6in	5ft 0in	–
Standard, in the Head, Sided (Bolted, as the Gundeck Knees)	1ft 0in	11½in	11in	10½in	10in	9in	8½in	8in	7½in
Upper Rails, at the after end, Fore and aft	1ft 2in	1ft 1in	1ft 0½in	11½in	10½in	9½in	9in	8in	7in
Thwartships	10¼in	9¾in	9½in	8¾in	8in	7¼in	6¾in	6in	5¼in
Chestrees: Sided at the Gunnell	–	–	–	7in	6½in	6in	5½in	5in	4½in
Fenders: Sided at the Gunnell	4in	4in	4in	3in	3in	3in	3in	2½in	2½in
Fenders: Against the Hatchways, Assunder	1ft 4in	1ft 4in	1ft 4in	1ft 4in	1ft 4in	1ft 4in	1ft 4in	1ft 4in	1ft 4in
Linings: of the Anchors, Thick	3in	3in	3in	2½in	2½in	2½in	2in	2in	2in
Rails: on the Side, the Sheer, Broad	10½in	10in	9¼in	8½in	8in	7½in	7in	6½in	6in
Thick	4in	3¾in	3½in	3¼in	3in	3in	2¾in	2½in	2¼in
Wast, Broad	8½in	8½in	7½in	7in	6½in	6in	6in	5½in	5½in
Thick	4¼in	4in	3¾in	3¾in	3¾in	3½in	–	–	–
After Drift, Broad	7½in	7in	6½in	6in	5½in	5in	4¾in	4½in	4in
Thick	3¾in	3½in	3¼in	3in	3in	2¾in	2¾in	2½in	2½in
Fife, Broad	1ft 0½in	1ft 0in	11in	11in	10in	9½in	9in	8½in	8in
Thick	3¾in	3¾in	3½in	3½in	3in	3in	3in	2¾in	2½in
Plankshere: in the Wast; Thick	3in	3in	2½in	3in	2½in	2½in	–	–	–
Drifts; Thick	2in	2in	2in	2in	2in	2in	2in	2in	2in
To be Struck with an Astricall within and without and the Square to overhang the Plank or Deal Half an Inch within and without Board									
Shankpainter Chain: Long	20ft 6in	19ft 0in	17ft 6in	16ft 0in	15ft 0in	14ft 0in	13ft 0in	12ft 0in	10ft 6in
Size of the Links	1 1/16in	1in	15/16in	15/16in	⅞in	⅞in	13/16in	13/16in	¾in
Port Hinges: Gundeck, Broad	3⅞in	3⅞in	3¾in	3¾in	3½in	3⅜in	3¼in	3⅛in	–
Thick	1⅛in	1⅛in	1in	1in	⅞in	¾in	¾in	⅝in	–
Middle Deck, Broad	3½in	3⅜in	3¼in						
Thick	⅞in	⅞in	¾in						
Hooks: Gundeck, Size to be Clenched	1⅛in	1⅛in	1⅛in	1in	1in	1in	⅞in	⅞in	–
Middle Deck, Size to be Clenched	1in	1in	1in						
Gundeck									
Shackles; to Clench on the Hinges, Number and Size	2 × ⅞in	2 × ⅞in	2 × ⅞in	2 × ⅞in	2 × ¾in	2 × ¾in	2 × ⅝in	2 × ⅝in	–
Rings, Diameter in the Clear	4in	4in	3¾in	3⅝in	3½in	3¼in	3in	2¾in	–
Rings with eyes for the Port ropes to goe thro' the Hinges and Clench with inside. Number and Size	2 × ¾in	2 × ¾in	2 × ¾in	2 × ¾in	2⅝in	1 × ⅝in	1 × ⅝in	1 × ½in	–
Diameter of the Rings in the Clear	2½in	2½in	2⅜in	2¼in	2¼in	2⅛in	2in	1⅞in	–
Middle Deck									
Shackles, Number and Size	1 × ⅝in	1 × ⅝in	1 × ⅝in	–	–	–	–	–	–
Diameter of the Rings in the clear	3½in	3⅜in	3¼in	–	–	–	–	–	–
Rings with eyes for the Port ropes to goe thro' the Hinges, Number and Size	2 × ⅝in	2 × ⅝in	2 × ⅝in	–	–	–	–	–	–
Diameter of the Rings in the Clear	2¼in	2¼in	2¼in	–	–	–	–	–	–
Bolts: for the Butt ends under water where they are Necessary to be placed in the Timbers next the Butt end and to be Clenched within side, Size	1in	1in	1in	⅞in	⅞in	¾in	¾in	¾in	¾in

	Ship, Number of Guns								
	100	*90*	*80*	*70*	*60*	*50*	*40*	*30*	*20*
Eyes: for the Standing part of the Main and Fore Sheats, Size	1⅝in	1⅝in	1½in	1½in	1⅜in	1⅜in	1¼in	1¼in	1⅛in
for the Mizen Seat, Main Brace, Main and Fore Topsaile Halyards, Bowsprit									
Shrouds and in wake of the Chain Plates, Sizes	1⅝in	1⅝in	1¼in	1¼in	1⅜in	1⅜in	1in	1in	1in
For the Mizen Topsaile Hallyards and Mizen Truss, Size	1⅛in	1⅛in	1⅛in	1in	1in	1in	⅞in	¾in	¾in
Swivle: For the Longboat, Size	1⅜in	1⅜in	1¼in	1¼in	1⅛in	1⅛in	1in	1in	1in
Diameter of the Ring in the Clear	4½in	4½in	4¼in	4in	3¾in	3½in	3¼in	3in	2¾in
Lining of the Hawse: between the Holes, Thick	9in	8½in	8in	7½in	7in	6½in	6in	5½in	5in
Bolt holes to be bored through, Size	1in	1in	1in	1in	⅞in	¾in	¾in	⅝in	⅝in

To Determine the Burthen in Tunns

First instead of Measuring from the back of the Main Post to the Perpendicular, or Square from the Keel at the fore part of the Stem at the Top thereof or from a Square or Perpendicular from the Keel at the Forepart of the Stem at the Upper Edge of the Lower harpin, as hath been usefull both which Extreams are liable to many uncertaintys and maybe Considerably Varied by Encreasing or lessening the Main or false Post without the Rabbet abaft or by raising or Lowering the Harpin forward, the Raking the Upper part of the Stem more or less, or adding or diminishing to the Scantlings of the Same before the Rabbet of the Stem, none of which are essentiall for Determining the Tunnage.

Therefore instead thereof, Erect a Square or Perpendicular from a line Ranging Straight with the Lower part of the Rabbet of the Keel to the after part of the Plank (or Rabbet) at the Upper Edge of the Wing Transome, and also another Square or Perpendicular from the Forepart of the Plank (or Rabbet) of the Stem at ⅚ parts of the height of the Wing Transom, then measure the Length between the perpendicular Lines and add these to $\frac{1}{24}$ of the Extream Breadth for the Scantlings

of the Stem before, and the Post abaft the Plank (without regarding whether there be a False Post or no) from which Sum subtract $\frac{6}{25}$ of the Height of the Wing Transom (for the Rake abaft) and ⅗ of the Main Breadth (for the Rake forward), the Residue is to be accounted the Length of the Keel for Tunnage which multiplyed by the Extream Breadth, and the Product by the half Breadth, and the Sum divided by 94 gives the Burthen in Tunns. This for Square Sterned Ships:-

But for Round Sterned Vessells (or were there is no Wing Transome) Set off ⅗ of the Extream Breadth from the Lower part of the Rabbet of the Keel on the Aft part of the Rabbet of the Post, for the Supposed height of the Wing Transom from whence the Perpendicular is to be let fall as before from the Wing Transom and the other forward, let fall from the Forepart of the Rabbet of the Stem at ⅚ parts of that Height and then take the Distance of those two Perpendiculars and Work from them as before directed in Square Sternd Ships.

NB. The Extream Breadth is to be taken from the outside to outside of the Plank or thick stuff either above or below the Wales, where the Ship shall be Broadest, always deducting the Doubling or Sheathing from the said Breadth.

Dimension and weight of iron standards on the gundeck, middle deck, upper deck and quarterdeck of Royal Naval ships

Source: Adm 170/429
National Maritime Museum, Greenwich

	Ship, Number of Guns															
	100		90		80		70		60		50		44		24	
	ft	in	ft	in	ft	in	ft	in	ft	in	ft	in	ft	in	ft	in
Gundeck																
Length of the Arm to the Side	6	7	6	7	6	9	6	2	6	0½	6	2	6	2	5	3
Length of the Shortest Arm	5	0	4	10	4	7	4	4	4	1	4	0	3	9	3	6
Thick in the Throat	–	11	–	10½	–	10	–	9½	–	9	–	8½	–	8	–	7
Thick, Next to it	–	6	–	5½	–	5¼	–	5	–	4¾	–	4½	–	4	–	3½
Thick, at the Ends	–	3	–	2½	–	2¼	–	2	–	1⅞	–	1¾	–	1⅝	–	1½
Breadth of the Iron	–	7	–	6½	–	6¼	–	6	–	5¾	–	5½	–	5	–	4½
Middle Deck																
Length of the Arm to the Side	7	3	6	10	6	6	–		–		–		–		–	
Length of the Shortest Arm	5	0	4	10	4	8	–		–		–		–		–	
Thick in the Throat	–	10	–	9½	–	9	–		–		–		–		–	
Next to it	–	5½	–	5¼	–	5	–		–		–		–		–	
at the Ends	–	3	–	2½	–	2¼	–		–		–		–		–	
Breadth of the Iron	–	6½	–	6	–	5¾	–		–		–		–		–	
Upper Deck																
Length of the Arm to the Side	5	8	4	10	4	10	5	2½	5	3	4	11	4	4	3	8
Length of the Shortest Arm	4	0	3	10	3	8	3	6	3	5	3	4	3	2	3	0
Thick in the Throat	–	9½	–	9¼	–	9	–	9	–	8¾	–	8½	–	8¼	–	7
Thick, Next to it	–	4½	–	4¼	–	4¼	–	4	–	4	–	3⅞	–	3⅝	–	3
Thick, at the Ends	–	2	–	2	–	2	–	2	–	1¾	–	1⅝	–	1½	–	1¼
Breadth of the Iron	–	6	–	5¾	–	5½	–	5¼	–	5	–	4¾	–	4½	–	4
Quarter Deck																
Length of the Arm to the Side																
To Reach Lower Side of the Lodging																
knee or Planksheer above it																
Length of the Shortest Arm	3	6	3	4	–		3	2	3	2	–		–		–	
Thick at the Throat	–	7	–	6½	–		–	6	–	6	–		–		–	
Thick, Next to it	–	3½	–	3½	–		–	3	–	3	–		–		–	
Thick, at the Ends	–	1½	–	1¼	–		–	1¼	–	1¼	–		–		–	
Breadth of the Iron	–	4	–	3¾	–		–	3½	–	3¼	–		–		–	

	Number and Size of Bolts	no in	no in	no in	no in	no in	no in	no in	no in
Gundeck	Arm to the Side	4 × 1½	4 × 1⅜	4 × 1⅜	4 × 1¼	4 × 1¼	4 × 1⅛	4 × 1⅛	4 × 1
	Arm to the Beam	4 × 1½	4 × 1⅜	4 × 1⅜	4 × 1¼	4 × 1¼	4 × 1⅛	4 × 1⅛	4 × 1
Middle Deck	Arm to the Side	4 × 1¼	4 × 1¼	4 × 1⅛	4 × 1⅛	–	–	–	–
	Arm to the Beam	4 × 1¼	4 × 1¼	4 × 1⅛	4 × 1⅛	–	–	–	–
Upper Deck	Arm to the Side	4 × 1⅛	4 × 1⅛	3 × 1	4 × 1⅛	4 × 1	4 × 1	3 × 0⅞	3 × 0¾
	Arm to the Beam	4 × 1⅛	4 × 1⅛	3 × 1	4 × 1⅛	4 × 1	4 × 1	3 × 0⅞	3 × 0¾
Quarter Deck	Arm to the Side	3 × 0⅞	3 × 0⅞	–	3 × 0¾	3 × 0¾	–	–	–
	Arm to the Beam	3 × 0⅞	3 × 0⅞	–	3 × 0¾	3 × 0¾	–	–	–

The weight of standards had been settled about the time that *Torbay* and *Nottingham* were building. Both vessels were rebuilds of vessels of the 1706 Establishment. The 80-gun *Torbay* was launched on 23 May 1719 and the 60-gun *Nottingham* on 5 October 1719.

Guns			cwt	qtr	lbs
100	Iron Standard fitted on	Gundeck	6	0	0
		Middle Deck	4	3	0
		Upper Deck	3	2	0
		Quarter Deck	2	2	0
90	Iron Standard fitted on	Gundeck	5	2	0
		Middle Deck	4	2	0
		Upper Deck	3	1	0
		Quarter Deck	2	1	0
80	Iron Standard fitted on	Gundeck	5	0	0
		Middle Deck	4	1	0
		Upper Deck	3	0	0
		Quarter Deck	2	0	0
70	Iron Standard fitted on	Gundeck	4	2	0
		Upper Deck	3	0	0
		Quarter Deck	1	3	0
60	Iron Standard fitted on	Gundeck	4	0	0
		Upper Deck	2	3	0
		Quarter Deck	1	3	0
50	Iron Standard fitted on	Gundeck	3	3	0
		Upper Deck	2	3	0
		Quarter Deck	–	–	–
44	Iron Standard fitted on	Gundeck	–	–	–
		Upper Deck	–	–	–
24	Iron Standard fitted on	Lower Deck	–	–	–
		Gundeck	–	–	–

Guns			cwt	qtr	lbs
	Torbay's Standards				
	Weighed	Gundeck	4	2	0
	Nottingham's Standards				
	Weighed	Gundeck	3	1	0
		Upper Deck	2	3	0

'The Length of the Arm to the Side is to the Lower side of the Lodging Knee above it on the Upper edge of the String on the Wast on to the Plankshire. The Heel of the Standard has as much of it Cast off as to allow the passage of Water, equal to the Scuppers on Each Deck, the Size is meant of the Auger for Bolting the Standards, the Breadth of the Iron is the same in the Middle as the ends, the Thickness next to the Throat is meant where the Size of the Throat castes with each Arm.'

APPENDIX 4c

The 1745 Establishment List

Source: Adm 170/430
National Maritime Museum, Greenwich

Deptford Yard, 5th August 1745

R[t] Hono[ble].

    Pursuent to your Directions of the 8th past, for our preparing and delivering the Principal Scantlings and etc: proper for a Ship of each Class in the Royal Navy, according to the Dimensions resolved on by your honours the 5th and 8th of that Month; The following are in our Opinion proper for Ships to be Built of the said Dimensions, which is humbly submitted by.

                                    R[t] Hono[ble]:
                                      Your most Obedient Servants,

                                      Allan, Lock, Ward, Holland.

To the R[t] Hono[ble] Sir John Norris and the List
of Gentlemen appointed to fix on an Establishment
for Building his Majestys Ships.

Note. The layout, punctuation, and spelling have, in some places, been modified by the author to make the Establishment List clearer.

	Ship, Number of Guns							
	100	*90*	*80*	*70*	*60*	*50*	*44*	*24*

Principal Dimensions

	100	90	80	70	60	50	44	24
Length: by the Keel for Tunnage	144ft 6½in	138ft 4in	134ft 10¾	131ft 4in	123ft 0½in	117ft 8½in	100ft 10in	93ft 4in
On the Gundeck from the Rabbet of the Stem to the Rabbet of the Post	178ft 0in	170ft 2in	165ft 0in	160ft 0in	150ft 0in	144ft 0in	133ft 0in	113ft 0in
Breadth: Extream	51ft 0in	48ft 6in	47ft 0in	45ft 0in	42ft 0in	41ft 0in	37ft 6in	32ft 0in
at the After part of the Main or Wing Transom from outside to outside of the Plank;	33ft 0in	31ft 5in	30ft 5in	27ft 6in	26ft 0in	25ft 0in	22ft 9in	18ft 4in
at the Toptimber Line from outside to outside of the Plank — Afore	33ft 0in	31ft 6in	30ft 6in	27ft 6in	26ft 0in	25ft 0in	22 11in	19ft 0in
Midships	36ft 6in	34ft 9in	33ft 6in	33ft 9in	32ft 0in	30ft 9in	28ft 11in	26ft 0in
Abaft	23ft 6in	22ft 4in	21ft 8in	21ft 0in	20ft 0in	19ft 2in	17ft 6in	14ft 9in
of the Stern at the Fife Raile abaft, from the outside to the outside of the Plank				[No measurement Stated]				
Height: of the Cutting Down of the Midships above the Keel	1ft 8in	1ft 7½in	1ft 6½in	1ft 6in	1ft 5½in	1ft 5in	1ft 4½in	1ft 5in
of the Toptimber Line, or Upper Edge of the Wast Raile above the Upper Edge of the Main Keele — Afore	47ft 0in	45ft 4¾in	44ft 6in	36ft 7in	34ft 1in	33ft 5in	30ft 9in	25ft 4in
Midships	43ft 7in	42ft 4in	40in 11in	34ft 0in	32ft 4in	31ft 0in	28ft 11in	23ft 1in
Abaft	53ft 0in	52ft 4in	50ft 2in	42ft 8in	43ft 0in	37ft 9in	34ft 4in	20ft 3in
Rising: of the Midships Flatt	4in	4in	4in	5½in	6in	6½in	8in	9in
Depth: in the Hold taken from the Strake next the Limber Boards	21ft 6in	20ft 6in	20ft 0in	19ft 4in	18ft 6in	17ft 8in	16ft 0in	11ft 0in
Strake: next the Limberboards, Thick	8in	8in	7½in	7½in	6½in	6in	6in	5½in
Broad, if can be had	1ft 3in	1ft 3in	1ft 2½in	1ft 2½in	1ft 2in	1ft 2in	1ft 1in	1ft 0in
Burthen in Tunns:	2000	1730	1585⁵⁄₉₄	1414⁵⁶⁄₉₄	1191	1052⁴⁷⁄₉₄	814⁵⁴⁄₉₄	508³²⁄₉₄
Draught: of water. Afore	22ft 3in	21ft 1in	20ft 4in	19ft 4in	18ft 3in	17ft 3in	16ft 0in	12ft 11in
Abaft	23ft 5in	22ft 3in	21ft 6in	20ft 6in	19ft 5in	18ft 4in	17ft 2in	14ft 1in
Orlope: Beams to Round				Two Inches in All Classes of Ships				
Height from the Upper Edge of the Beam to the Gundeck Plank at the Middle of the Beam;	7ft 2in	7ft 1in	7ft 0in	6ft 10in	6ft 9in	6ft 8½in	6ft 7½in	–
Platform: Height between the Plank and Plank, Afore and Abaft	7ft 2in	7ft 1in	7ft 0in	6ft 10in	6ft 9in	6ft 8½in	6ft 7½in	–
Gundeck: Beams to Round	5½in	5¼in	5in	4¾in	4½in	4¼in	4in	3½in
Plank, Thick	4in	4in	4in	4in	4in	3½in	3in	2½in
Gundeck: Height from the Plank to the Upper Edge of the Middle or Upper Deck Beams, at the Middle of the Beams — Afore Midships Abaft	7ft 2in	7ft 0in	7ft 0in	7ft 0in	6ft 10½in	6ft 9in	6ft 8in	6ft 7in
to the Port Cills	2ft 4in	2ft 4in	2ft 4in	2ft 4in	2ft 3in	2ft 3in	2ft 1in	1ft 11in
of the Ports from the water in the Midships	5ft 3in	5ft 3in	5ft 4in	5ft 9in	5ft 11in	5ft 11in	5ft 2in	–
Ports; Deep	2ft 9in	2ft 8in	2ft 8in	2ft 2in	2ft 8in	2ft 7in	2ft 6in	2ft 2in
Fore and Aft	3ft 5in	3ft 5in	3ft 5in	3ft 5in	3ft 4in	3ft 3in	2ft 11in	2ft 6in
Hanging of the Deck in the middle Line	2ft 1½in	2ft 0in	1ft 11in	1ft 10in	1ft 9in	1ft 8in	1ft 7in	1ft 4in
Higher Abaft than afore from the Keel	8in	8in	8in	8in	8in	7in	6in	4in
Middle Deck:								
Beams to Round	7½in	7¼in	7in	–	–	–	–	–
Plank, Thick	3in	3in	3in	–	–	–	–	–
Height from the Plank; to the Upper Edge of the Upper Deck Beams at the Middle of the Beam — Afore Midships Abaft	7ft 1in	7ft 0in	6ft 10in	–	–	–	–	–
to the Port Cills	2ft 3in	2ft 2in	1ft 11in	–	–	–	–	–
Ports; Deep	2ft 9in	2ft 8in	2ft 8in	–	–	–	–	–
Fore and Aft	3ft 3in	3ft 1in	2ft 11in	–	–	–	–	–

				Ship, Number of Guns				
	100	90	80	70	60	50	44	24
Upper Deck:								
Beams to Round	8½in	8¼in	8in	7¾in	7½in	7¼in	7in	6½in
Plank, Thick	3in	3in	3in	3in	3in	3in	2½in	2½in
to the upper Edge of the Quarter Deck Beams at the middle of the Beams { Afore	7ft 0in	6ft 10in	6ft 8in	6ft 8in	6ft 7in	6ft 7in	6ft 6in	6ft 5in
{ Abaft	7ft 4in	7ft 1in	6ft 11in	6ft 11in	6ft 9in	6ft 8½in	6ft 7½in	6ft 7in
Height from the Plank; to the Upper Edge of the Forecastle Beams at the Middle of the Beams { Afore { Abaft	6ft 8in	6ft 6in	6ft 0in	6ft 4in	6ft 2in	5ft 10in	5ft 5in	5ft 3in
of the Wast	5ft 8in	5ft 7in	5ft 0in	5ft 10in	5ft 3in	5ft 0in	4ft 8in	4ft 4in
to the Port Cills	1ft 10in	1ft 10in	1ft 8in	1ft 11in	1ft 9in	1ft 9in	1ft 8in	1ft 8in
Ports. Deep	2ft 8in	2ft 7in	2ft 7in	2ft 8in	2ft 7in	2ft 7in	2ft 4in	2ft 4in
Broad, Afore and Abaft	3ft 0in	2ft 9in	2ft 9in	2ft 10in	2ft 8in	2ft 8in	2ft 5in	2ft 5in
Forecastle:								
Beams to Round	7½in	7in	7in	6½in	6½in	6¼in	6in	5½in
Plank, Thick	2½in	2½in	2½in	2½in	2½in	2½in	2in	2in
Long, from the foreside of the Stantions of the Beakhead	38ft 0in	36ft 0in	36ft 0in	33ft 0in	28ft 0in	27ft 0in	25ft 6in	18ft 6in
Quarter Deck:								
Beams to Round	9in	8¾in	8½in	8in	7½in	7¼in	7in	6¾in
Plank, Thick	3in	3in	3in	3in	3in	2½in	2½in	2in
Height from the Plank, To the upper Edge of the Roundhouse Beams at the middle of the Beams; { Afore	6ft 6in	6ft 6in	6ft 3in	6ft 6in	6ft 6in	5ft 8in	–	–
{ Abaft	6ft 9in	6ft 9in	6ft 6in	6ft 8in	6ft 8in	5ft 10in	–	–
To the Port Cills	1ft 7in	1ft 7in	1ft 6in	1ft 8in	1ft 6in	1ft 6in	1ft 6in	1ft 4in
Ports; Deep	2ft 6in	2ft 6in	2ft 5in	2ft 5in	2ft 4in	2ft 4in	2ft 3in	–
Fore and Aft	2ft 9in	2ft 8in	2ft 7in	2ft 8in	2ft 6in	2ft 5in	2ft 4in	–
Long, Taken in the Midships from the afterpart of the Stern Timbers	To go as far Foreward as the Main Jeers in the Midships							
Roundhouse:								
Beams to Round	10in	10in	10in	9in	9in	8½in	–	–
Plank, Thick	2½in	2½in	2½in	2½in	2½in	2½in	–	–
Height from the Plank; To the Upper edge of the Topgallant Roundhouse Beams at the Middle of the Beams { Afore { Abaft	No Topgallant Roundhouse to be Allowed							
Long, taken in the Midships from the afterpart of the Stern Timbers	47ft 0in	45ft 0in	16ft 0in	36ft 0in	33ft 0in	15ft 0in	–	–
Topgallant Roundhouse: Not Applicable at this Period				Not Applicable				
Length: from the Foreside of the Taffarell at the Height of the Fiferaile to the Foreside of the Figure of the Head by a Line Parallel to the Keel	212ft 9in	203ft 0in	196ft 0in	186ft 0in	175ft 0in	167ft 0in	154ft 0in	131ft 0in
From the Foreside of the Stem to the Forepart of the Knee of the Head	17ft 6in	16ft 6in	14ft 6in	12ft 1in	11ft 6in	11ft 0in	10ft 0in	8ft 0in
From the Foreside of the Stem to the Beakhead Bulkhead	9ft 0in	8ft 6in	8ft 0in	7ft 0in	6ft 6in	6ft 2in	5ft 6in	4ft 8in
From the After side of the Wing Transom to the afterpart of the Counter at the Middle Line	6ft 8in	6ft 6in	6ft 2in	5ft 11in	5ft 6in	5ft 3in	5ft 0in	4ft 0in
From the After side of the Wing Transom to the afterpart of the Second Counter at the Middle Line	8ft 4in	8ft 1in	7ft 8in	7ft 5in	6ft 11in	6ft 7in	6ft 3in	5ft 2in
Height: of the Gundeck by a Perpendicular from the upper edge of the Keel, to the Upperside of the Plank at the Middle of the Deck { Afore	26ft 0in	24ft 9in	24ft 6in	23ft 3in	22ft 3in	21ft 3in	19ft 5½in	14ft 2in
{ Abaft	26ft 8in	25ft 5in	24ft 8in	23ft 11in	22ft 11in	21ft 11in	19ft 11½in	14ft 6in
of the Afterside of the Wing Transom above the upper Edge of the Keel at the Post	29ft 0in	27ft 9in	27ft 0in	26ft 3in	25ft 2in	24ft 1in	22ft 0in	16ft 4in
From the Upper Edge of the Keel, to the Lower Edge of the Counter Raile at the Middle Line	33ft 4in	32ft 8in	31ft 9in	30ft 4in	29ft 4in	28ft 0in	26ft 0in	20ft 4in
From the Upper Edge of the Keel, to the Lower Edge of the Raile under the Wardroom Lights, in 3 Deck Ships and under the Great Cabbin Lights in 2 Deck Ships	36ft 6in	35ft 4in	34ft 5in	33ft 6in	32ft 5in	31ft 4in	29ft 3in	23ft 4in

	100	90	80	70	60	50	44	24
Ship, Number of Guns								
Height of the Breadth above the Upper Edge of the Keel in the Midships;								
Lower	18ft 0in	18ft 0in	17ft 6in	16ft 3in	15ft 7in	14ft 11in	13ft 5in	11ft 4in
Upper	22ft 9in	21ft 9in	21ft 0in	20ft 4in	19ft 4in	18ft 0in	16ft 6in	13ft 8in
Rounding of the Stern Aft, at the Lower Counter Raile	1ft 2in	1ft 1in	1ft 0½in	1ft 0in	11in	10in	9½in	8½in
The Back of the Falsepost to Rake 2½ Inches in a Foot, and the upright of the Stern, Three Inches. The Stem to Rake forward above the Gundeck to the Top of it, Two Inches in a Foot.								
Room and Space: of the Timbers	2ft 7in	2ft 6in	2ft 6in	2ft 5in	2ft 5in	2ft 5in	2ft 4in	2ft 2in
The Floor and Futtock Timbers in the Bearing of the Ship to Fill up the Rooms and Spaces, Especially for the Large Ships (if can Conveniently be got)								
Floor Timbers: Next the Flats, Sided	1ft 3in	1ft 2½in	1ft 2in	1ft 2in	1ft 1½in	1ft 1in	1ft 0½in	11½in
Afore and Abaft in Wake of the Half Timbers	1ft 2in	1ft 1½in	1ft 1in	1ft 1in	1ft 0½in	1ft 0in	11½in	10½in
at the Wrongheads, midships, wrought in and out	1ft 2½in	1ft 2¼in	1ft 2in	1ft 1½in	1ft 1in	1ft 0in	11in	9in
at the Wrongheads, Afore and abaft, in and out	1ft 1½in	1ft 1¼in	1ft 1in	1ft 0½in	1ft 0in	11in	10in	8in
Lower Futtocks: Sided, in the Midships next the Flatts a small Distance afore and abaft the Bearing of the Ship	1ft 3in	1ft 2½in	1ft 2in	1ft 2in	1ft 1½in	1ft 1in	1ft 0½in	11½in
Sided, Afore and Abaft	1ft 2in	1ft 1½in	1ft 1in	1ft 1in	1ft 0½in	1ft 0in	11½in	10½in
In and Out at the Heads of the Midships	1ft 1¾in	1ft 1½in	1ft 1⅜in	1ft 1in	1ft 0½in	11½in	10½in	8¼in
Second Futtocks: Sided in the Midships	1ft 2in	1ft 2in	1ft 2in	1ft 1½in	1ft 0¾in	1ft 0½in	11¾in	11in
Afore and Abaft	1ft 1in	1ft 1in	1ft 1in	1ft 0½in	11¾in	11½in	10¾in	10in
Third Futtocks: Sided in the Midships	1ft 1½in	1ft 1½in	1ft 1½in	1ft 1in	1ft 0½in	1ft 0in	–	–
Afore and Abaft	1ft 1in	1ft 1in	1ft 1in	1ft 1in	1ft 0in	11½in	–	–
Upper Futtocks: Sided in the Midships								
Afore and Abaft	1ft 1½in	1ft 1½in	1ft 1½in	1ft 1in	1ft 0½in	1ft 0in	11in	10in
At the Gundeck in and out at the Midships	1ft 0½in	1ft 0½in	1ft 0in	11½in	10¾in	10in	9in	7½in
Toptimbers: Sided, at the Heels and at the Upper Futtock Heads	1ft 1½in	1ft 1½in	1ft 1½in	1ft 1in	1ft 0½in	1ft 0in	11in	10in
Sided at the Heads	1ft 1½in	1ft 1½in	1ft 1½in	1ft 1in	1ft 0½in	1ft 0in	11in	10in
In and Out at the Top of the Side	5½in	5¼in	5in	5in	4¾in	4½in	4¼in	4in
Orlope Beams: Sided	1ft 5in	1ft 4in	1ft 3½in	1ft 3in	1ft 2in	1ft 1½in	1ft 0½in	–
Moulded	1ft 5in	1ft 4in	1ft 3½in	1ft 3in	1ft 2in	1ft 1½in	1ft 0½in	–
Gundeck Beams: Sided. In the Midships and One Inch less each way Afore and Abaft)	1ft 6in	1ft 5½in	1ft 4¾in	1ft 4½in	1ft 3½in	1ft 2¾in	1ft 1¾in	10in
Moulded	1ft 6in	1ft 5½in	1ft 4¾in	1ft 4½in	1ft 3in	1ft 2¼in	1ft 1½in	9in
Middle Deck Beams: Sided	1ft 3½in	1ft 2¾in	1ft 2½in					
Moulded	1ft 1½in	1ft 1in	1ft 0½in					
Upper Deck Beams: Sided	1ft 1½in	1ft 1in	1ft 0in	1ft 2in	1ft 1in	1ft 0½in	10½in	10in
Moulded	11¼in	11in	10½in	1ft 0in	11in	10¼in	9¼in	8½in
Quarter Deck Beams: Sided	10in	10in	9in	9½in	9in	8in	6½in	6in
Moulded	8¼in	7¾in	7in	8in	7in	6½in	5½in	5in
Forecastle Beams: Sided	10in	10in	9in	9½in	9in	8in	6½in	6in
Moulded	8¼in	7¾in	7in	8in	7in	6½in	5½in	5in
Beam: at the Forepart of the Forecastle to fasten the Cathead; Sided	2ft 6in	2ft 5in	2ft 4in	2ft 3in	2ft 2in	2ft 1in	1ft 10in	1ft 6in
Moulded	8¼in	7¾in	7in	8in	7in	6½in	5½in	5in
Roundhouse Beams: Sided	7½in	7½in	6½in	7in	6¾in	4¾in	–	–
Moulded	5½in	5½in	4½in	5½in	5in	3¾in	–	–
Topgallant Round House Beams: Not Applicable	No Measurements Stated for this Period							
Rother: Fore and Aft at the Lower End with a small back if occasion and to have always a piece of 4 Inch plank at the bottom to preserve it from Worm	6ft 8in	6ft 4in	6ft 1in	5ft 7½in	5ft 3½in	5ft 1½in	4ft 8in	4ft 0in

Bibliography

ANDERSON, R C *The Rigging of Ships in the Days of the Spritsail Topmast*, London, 1926, reprinted 1984.

Seventeenth Century Rigging, Hemel Hempstead, 1955.

ARCHIBALD, E H H *The Wooden Fighting Ship in the Royal Navy*, London, 1968.

BATHE, B W *Ship Models, Sailing Ships from 1700 AD*, Science Museum Publication, London, 1964.

BUGLER, A R, *HMS Victory: Building, Restoration and Repair*, HMSO, 1967.

BROWN, CAPTAIN C OORDE, 'HMS Victory, the History and Construction', *The Engineer*, London, 1891.

CHARNOCK, J *A History of Marine Architecture*, 3 vols, 1800–02.

CLOWES, G S L *Sailing Ships, their History and Development*, 2 vols, Science Museum Publication, London, 1930–32.

DEANE, SIR ANTHONY *Doctrine of Naval Architecture, 1670*, ed B Lavery, London, 1979.

Establishment Book, 1719.

Establishment Book, 1745.

FALCONER, WILLIAM *The Universal Dictionary of the Marine*, 1769, reprinted 1970.

FINCHAM, JOHN *A History of Naval Architecture*, 1851, reprinted 1979.

An Introductory Outline of the Practice of Shipbuilding, 1821.

GILL, G S *The Old Wooden Walls, Their Construction and Equipment*, London, 1930.

HOLLAND, A J *Ships of British Oak*, Newton Abbott, 1971.

HOUGH, RICHARD *Fighting Ships*, London, 1969.

HOWARD, FRANK *Sailing Ships of War 1400–1860*, London, 1979.

JOHNSON, BRIGADIER A F *The Royal George*, London, 1971.

LANSTRÖM, B *The Ship*, London, 1961.

LAUGHTON, L C CARR *Old Ship Figureheads and Sterns*, London, 1927.

LAVERY, B *The Ship of the Line*, vol 1, London, 1983.

The Ship of the Line, vol 2, London, 1984.

LEES, J *The Masting and Rigging of English Ships of War 1625–1860*, London, 1979.

LEVER, DARCY *The Young Officer's Sheet Anchor*, 2nd edition, London, 1819, reprinted 1827.

LONGRIDGE, C NEPEAN *The Anatomy of Nelson's Ships*, London, 1955, 1961 and 1970.

MCDERMOTT, A C 'The Lighting of Poop Lanterns', *The Mariner's Mirror*, vol 41, 1955.

MURRAY, MUNGO *A Treatise on Shipbuilding and Navigation*, 1765.

Naval Administration, 1715–1750, ed D A Baugh, Navy Records Society, vol 120, 1977.

PEAKE, JAMES *The Rudiments of Naval Architecture*, London, 1884.

REES, ABRAHAM *The Cyclopaedia, 1819–20*, reprinted as *Naval Architecture*, Newton Abbott, 1970.

SALISBURY, W, and ANDERSON, R C *A Treatise on Shipbuilding and a Treatise on Rigging* (written about 1620–25), Society for Nautical Research, 1958.

Shipbuilder's Repository, 1789.

Ships and Shipbuilding in Nelson's Time (facsimiles of drawings and articles from *Encyclopaedia Britannia, 1797*), Arcturus Press, 1983.

STALKAARTT, MARMADUKE *Naval Architecture, 1781.*

STEEL, DAVID *Elements and Practice of Naval Architecture, 1804.*

STEVENS, J R *Old Time Ships and Their Embellishment*, Toronto, 1949.

SUTHERLAND, WILLIAM, *England's Glory or Shipbuilding Unveiled, 1717.*

The Shipbuilder's Assistant, 1711.

The Timber Problem of the Royal Navy – 1652–1862, Society for Nautical Research.

Index

Note. References to ships in photographs are given in *italics*.